TASTING BEER

AN INSIDER'S GUIDE TO THE WORLD'S GREATEST DRINK
2nd Edition

RANDY MOSHER

Storey Publishing

This book is dedicated to my father.

Not much of a beer man himself,
he patiently taught me from a very early age
how to figure out the way everything in
the world works.

The mission of Storey Publishing is to serve our customers by
publishing practical information that encourages
personal independence in harmony with the environment.

Edited by Margaret Sutherland and Sarah Guare
Art direction by Alethea Morrison
Book design by Dan O. Williams and Alethea Morrison
Text production by Jennifer Jepson Smith
Indexed by Christine R. Lindemer, Boston Road
  Communications

Cover photography by © Jonathan Levin, front (author);
  © Lara Ferroni, front (bottom right); Mars Vilaubi, front
  (bottom left) and back
Cover and interior historical photographs, illustrations, and
  ephemera courtesy of the author, except antique hops
  illustration © 2000 Visual Language®, front (top left),
  spine, 7, and throughout
Interior photography credits on page 357
Infographics by Randy Mosher, except page 212 by
  Dan Williams

The information in this book is true and complete to
the best of our knowledge. All recommendations are made
without guarantee on the part of the author or Storey
Publishing. The author and publisher disclaim any liability
in connection with the use of this information.

Storey books are available at special discounts when purchased in bulk for premiums and sales promotions as well as
for fund-raising or educational use. Special editions or book
excerpts can also be created to specification. For details, please
call 800-827-8673, or send an email to sales@storey.com.

Storey Publishing
210 MASS MoCA Way
North Adams, MA 01247
storey.com

Printed in China through World Print Ltd.
10 9 8 7 6 5

LIBRARY OF CONGRESS CATALOGING-IN-PUBLICATION DATA
Names: Mosher, Randy author.
Title: Tasting beer : an insider's guide to the world's greatest
  drink /
  Randy Mosher.
Description: 2nd edition. | North Adams, MA : Storey
  Publishing, [2017] |
  Includes bibliographical references and index.
Identifiers: LCCN 2016051465 (print) | LCCN 2016052284
  (ebook) | ISBN
  9781612127774 (pbk. : alk. paper) | ISBN 9781612127811
  (hardcover : alk. paper) | ISBN 9781612127781 (Ebook)
Subjects: LCSH: Beer tasting. | Beer—History. |
  Brewing—History.
Classification: LCC TP577 .M68 2017 (print) | LCC TP577
  (ebook) | DDC
  641.2/3—dc23
LC record available at https://lccn.loc.gov/2016051465

CONTENTS

ACKNOWLEDGMENTS

A book like this could only happen in a community such as the one that swirls around great beer in North America. Its creators and sustainers are far too numerous to mention. You know who you are.

As far as specifics, thanks to Lyn Kruger and Keith Lemcke of the Siebel Institute for plenty of technical information and for allowing me to hone my skills and story on their students. Thanks go out to my technical editor Stan Heironymous; my wife, Nancy, for copyediting and keeping me in the active tense; and to a number of other people who reviewed part or all of the book: Ed Bronson, Steve Hamburg, and Tom Schmidlin. A huge thank-you to Cicerone's Pat Fahey, who questioned everything in this second edition, which was incredibly helpful. Thanks to Dick Cantwell, Ken Grossman, Jim Koch, Marty Jones, Mark Linsner, Andy Musser, and Charlie Papazian for various tidbits. Thanks also to the other members (besides Ray Daniels and Pat Fahey) of our Beer and Food Working Group: Lindsay Barr, Chef Adam Dulye, Nicole Garneau, PhD, and Julia Herz. Special thanks to Jonathan Levin for the portrait photo.

Thanks to Ray Daniels for his insights, friendship, and keeping me honest. I also wish to thank my partners and collaborators at my two breweries close to home, 5 Rabbit Cerveceria and Forbidden Root Botanic Beer, for making me a part of their journey.

Others who helped get the book off the ground include Sam Calagione and my agent, Clare Pelino, along with the many, many fine folks at Storey Publishing, especially Sarah Guare.

It couldn't have happened without the warm and supportive community of brewers, beer professionals, and enthusiasts all over the world. Cheers to all.

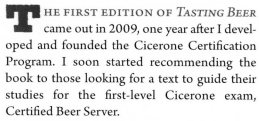

FOREWORD
TO THE SECOND EDITION

THE FIRST EDITION OF *TASTING BEER* came out in 2009, one year after I developed and founded the Cicerone Certification Program. I soon started recommending the book to those looking for a text to guide their studies for the first-level Cicerone exam, Certified Beer Server.

Over the years, the connection between Cicerone and *Tasting Beer* has continued, so much so that some people think Randy and I coordinated to create a text that would serve the program's needs. This is not the case. Rather, it is a happy coincidence that our paths through beer led us to create complementary offerings at about the same time. Cicerone challenges beer professionals to learn about their beverage and its culture. Randy's *Tasting Beer* addresses the questions posed by every student of beer and in the process provides an excellent text to aid in the journey.

This second edition of *Tasting Beer* expands coverage of some key topics that relate to the Cicerone journey beyond the first level, such as draft systems. In addition, I find that the integrated understanding of beer this edition presents would serve those studying for just about any level of Cicerone program exam. Any candidate who has not read *Tasting Beer* for a few years would be well advised to read this new edition. The connections and insights it offers will help you organize and integrate all of the details you learn from a variety of sources into a more cogent and nuanced understanding of beer.

But *Tasting Beer* goes much further than just knowledge. Its organization and presentation telegraph the decades that Randy has spent *thinking* about beer. The broad spectrum of his thoughtful studies has led him to understand answers to questions that those with a more focused view have never thought to ask. As a result, he possesses — and presents — an uncommon understanding of the full universe of beer.

And here's the best part: Given the depth of his exploration and the sheer volume of knowledge he presents, you might expect this text to be weighty and ponderous. Such is not the case. Indeed, Randy writes with a precise but conversational voice. The resulting text could not be easier to read. And his long professional experience in presenting information graphically comes to the fore in a variety of illustrations that illuminate the subject in ways that words alone could never do.

The true magic of Randy's work comes in his insights, in his seasoned understanding of how the many facts about beer connect in complex and varied ways to create this living, breathing thing that we capture with the simple word "beer." Whether you literally wish to learn more about tasting or simply hope to garner a basic understanding of beer, *Tasting Beer* will satisfy your thirst in a readable and memorable way.

— Ray Daniels
Founder and Director of the
Cicerone Certification Program

FOREWORD
TO THE FIRST EDITION

WHEN I MET RANDY MOSHER he was coming at me with a hammer in his hand and a maniacal smile on his face. We were at Chicago's Real Ale Festival in 1998 and he was helping prepare casks of unfiltered, unpasteurized, naturally carbonated real ale for serving. His enthusiasm was infectious — as lively as the beers contained in those casks. I have gotten to know Randy better in the last 5 years as we have served together on the board of directors of the Brewers Association. He earned his seat at the table representing the American Homebrewers Association, but in time it became apparent that his perspective, knowledge, and passion encompassed the whole world of beer lovers and makers: enthusiasts, amateurs, pros, and beyond. Randy is a true beer evangelist. In this book, and in all aspects of his beer-soaked life, he is saving souls one pint at a time.

Tasting Beer tackles the experience of choosing and imbibing beer with just enough technical and scientific information to explain the events but not so much that the beer novice feels overwhelmed. Randy doesn't preach his personal preferences here. He celebrates the fact that our individual palates are as unique as snowflakes. *Tasting Beer* is like a collection of many fine books bound together. Beer history, the science of brewing, the disciplines of tasting and evaluation, the wide array of beer styles, pairings of food and beer, beer terminology — it's all in here. This book is like an imperial pint full of knowledge, and Randy's cup runneth over. I am hopeful that *Tasting Beer* will find a home with professionals in addition to beer enthusiasts. I can think of no better single tool for brewers, bartenders, connoisseurs, chefs, salespeople, and everyone else in the beer trade for enhancing their beer IQ.

Despite the fact that beer's history is as ancient as wine's and that there are more styles and flavors of beer than wine, beer is still considered a less complex beverage by too many foodies and connoisseurs. Randy helps to dispel this myth in *Tasting Beer*. Much of the beer sold throughout the world is some slight variation on the light lager style, but Randy points out that centuries before the *Reinheitsgebot*, beers were being brewed with diverse ingredients such as honey, bog myrtle, cranberries, and coriander. Craft breweries today have reinvigorated this ancient tradition, using spices, herbs, sugars, fruits, and more. Randy gives equal time to each of the diverse, exciting beers that drinkers are trading up to, from the exotic eccentrics to the popular classic styles.

As international beer culture evolves, the brewers of these exciting craft beers are achieving growth and recognition disproportionate to that of the industrial, conglomerate light beer producers. After reading this book it is easy to see why. Beer culture is tremendously diverse, distinguished, and nuanced. As Randy writes, "Like any art, beer needs a proper context to be truly compelling." *Tasting Beer* gives us this context in spades. Drink up as you read up on the world's most storied and beloved adult beverage. Cheers.

— Sam Calagione
Owner of Dogfish Head Craft Brewery and the author of *Brewing Up a Business*

PREFACE

AS YOU READ THESE WORDS, consider the beer-filled glass in your hand. Look closely. Study the rich color and slight viscosity of the liquid. Observe the way the light plays on the shimmering highlights. Watch the bubbles as they form and rise lazily through the beer, adding to the creamy foam on top, hushed and peaceful as a snowfall.

Lift the glass to your lips, but first, pause to inhale and ponder the aroma. Draw in the bready, caramelly, or roasty foundation of malt; the brisk green counterpoint of hops; and perhaps the swirling cupboard of spices and fruit, earth and wood. These scents can fire off neurons in the forgotten happy corners of your memory, as powerful an experience as any art form.

Finally, have a taste. The beer floods in, cool and crisp or warm and rich. Observe the first blush of flavor and the tart tingle of carbonation. As the beer warms in your mouth, it releases a new round of flavors and sensations: malty sweetness, bright herbal hops, a touch of toast, all building to a bittersweet crescendo. It's not one single taste; it's an ever-evolving cinematic experience unspooling as you drink. A soft exhalation presents the nose with a new layer of beery perfume. These pleasures have been savored for millennia.

If you can read the meaning in these sensations, the whole history of brewing opens up and the long process reveals itself in the beer, from golden barley fields to steam-filled brewhouse to the tireless working of the first domesticated microbe — yeast.

The grand finale comes as a long-fading aftertaste, with lingering wisps of resin, toast, or honey, concluding perhaps with a gentle, warming alcohol sensation in your throat. The empty glass, now spent, is clad in an immodest slip of lace. . . .

Don't even consider starting this book without a beer in your hand.

WELCOME TO BEER

I WISH THE BEER EXPERIENCE WERE always this ecstatic, and when it's good it really can be. Truth be told, we don't always give our beer the attention it deserves, and we are the poorer for it. Like any aspect of a consciously lived life, enjoying beer to the fullest takes education, experience, and a proper frame of mind.

That isn't to say that learning to understand and appreciate beer is hard work. It is among the most enjoyable things you can do. But to get the most out of beer, you have to put a little effort into it. This book lays out the experience of beer in all its glory, in a logical and systematic way. Beer may be humble, but it is not simple.

Beer is brewed nearly everywhere that grain grows except, ironically, in its own homeland of the Middle East. It spans the full range of the sacred and the profane, a participant with equal gusto in ancient religious mysteries and raucous frat-house revelries. Whether it's essential nutrition and a safe source of water or an unobtainable luxury, there is a beer to satisfy every need or whim. It may be harvested with sickles, brewed in baskets, and drunk through reeds, or conjured up with a simple push of a button in automated space-age breweries. It can be a faceless, industrial commodity or an artistic creation as treasured

and transfixing as the finest wine. Light, dark, strong, weak, fizzy, flat, canned, bottled, or draft, beer has fluidly adapted to serve every role it has been asked to play, and it has done so with extraordinary grace. Beer is *the* universal beverage.

Yet despite this impressive résumé, it is surprising how little most people know about it. Even the most basic concepts are fuzzy: "What is beer?" "What is it made from?" "Why is dark beer dark?" If we remain uninformed, we can be trapped in our own limited beer world, not knowing what delights we're missing, such as which beer might be perfect with a barbecue sandwich, or when it's okay to send back a bad beer. It takes a little information to open up the extraordinary universe of beer.

Beer is a complicated subject, more difficult to grasp than wine in terms of what is actually in the glass. It can be brewed from dozens of ingredients, processed in hundreds of different ways. The brewer constructs a recipe to yield a product to suit his or her vision. Every brew requires choice after choice, each of which you can taste in the glass if you understand the process. The many dozens of styles are not fixed beacons but shifting shoals that change with the tide of generations, each with its own past, present, and future. Finally, bad information abounds — a *lot* of bad information.

The oyle of malt and juyce of sprightly nectar
Have made my muse more valiant than Hector.
— Richard Brathwaite, *Barnabae Itinerarium*, 1638

The Depth and Breadth of Beer

In a concise and visual way, this book aims to introduce you to the wide world of beer and to give you the tools to understand and, more importantly, enjoy it.

Beer has a history that predates civilization, and in its own way, beer has shaped us as much as we have shaped it. Our complex relationship with beer is the key to understanding its many roles in society, and this in turn helps make sense of the cornucopia of colors, strengths, and flavors that form the family of beer.

Beer is democratic. It does not depend on the finest real estate or limited geographical designations. The many choices made by the maltster and brewer create aromas, flavors, textures, and colors, transforming a few simple commodities into exquisite works of art. Anyone with skill, passion, and creativity can learn to make great beer. For a taster, each glance, each telltale whiff and studied sip of a beer can be like peering into the soul of the man or woman who brewed it. This dependence on a human rather than a heavenly touch is one of beer's great delights.

Sack makes men from words
Fall to drawing of swords,
And quarreling endeth their quaffing:
Whilst Dagger ale barrels
Bear off many quarrels,
And often turn chiding to laughing.

— from *In Praise of Ale*, 1888, a collection of old English beer poetry, author unknown

As a passionate fan of beer, you may be called upon to introduce others to its charms. As with anything else, presentation is half the game. It's not cheating. A great beer poured into a perfect glass at just the right temperature, in the best possible setting, should always be the goal. Anything less cheats the brewer and drinker alike.

By the end of the book, and with a lot of practice on your own, you'll be on your way to understanding all the many things that come together to form the wonderfulness of a well-brewed — and thoroughly enjoyed — beer.

The Community of Beer

Gemütlichkeit is a German word meaning "coziness," and it is most often used to describe the warm and cheery atmosphere of the log- and taxidermy-decorated bars in such places as Wisconsin. It's a great word, for it has a broader and more important connotation that I like to think of as "cousin-ness." I'm referring to a sense of easy community, where people in a certain space have decided to put aside differences and suspicions and consciously work at being convivial. The Czechs, Dutch, Russians, and Danes have similar concepts in their languages, but English has to borrow the German term.

There is definitely something about beer. Look at the mirth just bursting out of those Bruegel paintings as Flemish peasants drink beer and dance despite their rough and challenging lives. Civilization and civility thrive where there is a pot of beer. Beer brings people together on common ground and has been doing so for thousands of years.

Peasant Dance **by Pieter Bruegel the Elder, 1568**
For millennia, beer has been an indispensable glue holding the fabric of society together.
Here, sixteenth-century peasants live it up.

The business of beer has a good deal of the same camaraderie. In an era when market competitors in most businesses loathe each other like Cold War rivals, such antipathy is hard to find in brewing. Marketing people may go at it hammer and tongs, but brewers are pals. Maybe it's just the satisfaction of being a member of the small club of people who absolutely, positively know that what they do for a living makes a lot of people happy.

Beer Today

Times grow ever more interesting for good beer. While classic styles remain meaningful, the action is with creative brewers hell-bent on pushing the art forward and making a name for themselves, encouraged by their fans' neverending search for the next big thing. Everywhere, brewers are looking for ways to make the beers their own, incorporating local ingredients and cultural attitudes into the final product, often in thrilling ways. There are breweries specializing in wild and wood-aged and spontaneous beers, culinary botanic and foraged beers, farm-brewed beers, ethnocentric beers, cask beers, session beers, lost historic beers, and more.

Despite many examples of sublime subtlety, most craft beers are bold, even brash — an antidote to so much that is bland and faceless out there. The great brewing traditions of Britain, Germany, and Belgium may be brewed with reverential attention to authenticity or viewed as just loose starting points.

There is an arms race going on. From the use of massive blasts of hops to the "imperializing" of every imaginable style, craft brewers are piling on the flavor. At the top are supergravity beers currently weighing in at as much as 27 percent alcohol, right up there with port and close to the level of spirits. Some, like the Samuel Adams Utopias, sell for upwards of $200, stratospheric for the beer world but still a bargain by the heady standards of the exotic

Sam Adams Utopias in Repose
Barrels are another antiquated technology making a comeback for flavor reasons.

spirits world. At the same time, there has never been more interest in "sessionable" beers that pack plenty of flavor into their modest gravity.

In England, real ale, once the national drink, has become a specialty beer, and there is an alarming shift away from drinking in pubs, driven by cost, driving restrictions, and other factors. The fantastic, classic Belgian beers we love represent just 15 percent of their home market. Germany rightly loves its beers, but given the sameness of many of them, the place is ripe for consolidation. The same could be said of the Czech Republic. But in all those hallowed beer capitals, a new generation of brewers is breaking with stifling tradition, trying to make their local beers meaningful, fresh, and exciting again — and sometimes breaking the mold altogether.

Increasingly the past inspires the future. Many obscure styles are being reanimated into living, breathing things. Just look at the explosion of tangy, salty gose and other North German "outlaw" beers in the United States and elsewhere. Shoveled onto the scrap heap by the bulldozer of modernity in the early twentieth century, these and other antiquated styles are finding favor with brewers and drinkers thirsty for their appealing blend of authenticity and creativity.

Whatever the historical reality of "farmhouse" beers, the notion is irresistibly charming today in our industrialized world. As a result, brewers are happily translating that idea into characterful, drinkable beers, often brewed with rustic touches such as oak and wild microorganisms that bring a lot of depth into these otherwise simple creations.

Hops, which only recently threatened to subsume everything else into a sea of green bitterness, are now stepping back into their rightful place as *one* of the ways to make a delicious

Sitka Spruce Tips
Hops may be the main seasoning now, but beer remains a botanical product.
Spruce tips like these are still used in Alaska, echoing pioneer brews.

and characterful beer. However, hops remain so popular that IPA has radiated into a whole cascade (pun intended) of variations: white, red, black, rye, Belgian, brett, and session, as well as India pale lagers.

At the same time, many craft brewers are looking to move beyond hops, seeking to brew something meaningful using local food and drink traditions, as well as indigenous plants. From Alaska to Australia, there is huge interest in creating beers that incorporate local ingredients, such as Sitka spruce tips, roasted wattleseed, imburana wood, prickly pear fruit, dulce de leche, red rice, chestnuts, figs, bog myrtle, cupuaçu, wormwood, and elderflower. It's a thrilling adventure.

Fruit beer has finally gotten serious. A few brewers are creating beers with a fruity impact more along the lines of a fine wine. Sugar, too, is out of the closet, and brewers are using such exotic types as piloncillo, rapadura, and Belgian brewer's caramel to lighten the body

and enhance the drinkability of stronger beers. Wheat, rye, buckwheat, and other unusual adjunct beers abound. Pumpkin ales are popular around Halloween, and chile beers pop up from time to time, as do the ancient techniques of stone beer and smoked malt. Bourbon barrels have found their way into breweries, yielding vanilla and toasted coconut notes to strong beers after a few months of aging.

The late — and sorely missed — beer writer Michael Jackson was fond of shocking audiences in 1990s Europe by saying that the United States was the best place on the planet to drink beer. He was right. And there continues to be more styles, more choices, and more beers bursting with flavor and personality in the United States than anywhere else. It wasn't always so. By the mid-1970s, there were pitifully few American beers worth drinking. The lack of a living beer tradition worth preserving left us free to build a new beer culture from scratch. A new generation of American brewers took to the task with passion and imagination. Within a few short decades, their efforts have put craft beer at the forefront of desirability, share of mind, and flat-out coolness, if not in total market share.

The success of their tasty, characterful craft beers inspired the rest of the world, and today it's a fully international movement. Frank Zappa once famously said, "You can't be a real country unless you have a beer and an airline." Today, "craft brewery", or even "IPA" might be a better measure. They're everywhere, and more are on their way. Craft brewing is a business, of course, but it's much more than that. It's a *movement* with artistic, social, and political dimensions. Given the obstacles — in distribution, raw materials, profitability, equipment, taxation, and competition — the sense of mission helps brewers endure in the face of such steep odds.

There are more battles to come. Having failed to come up with much innovation on their own, multinational brewers are gobbling up many of the more successful craft brewers as a way to get closer to their hip, young consumers and authentic brand stories. This is not a problem in itself, but already there are moves to solidify their portfolios and lock out independent brands from their powerful distribution networks, a very troubling development for small brewers that should be equally alarming to enthusiasts as well. In the past, most of these acquired brands have failed to materialize into the powerhouses they expected. Compared to the 1990s, big brewers have learned to not try to reinvent their craft acquisitions in their own image, but time will tell if they can resist the urge to tamper and whether they will get where they wanted to go with them.

Despite the potential storm clouds, it's a very good time for beer. Craft brewers everywhere remain passionate about their calling to make delicious and creative beer, stay close to their fans, and sustain the kind of businesses of which we all can be proud. I'll definitely drink to that.

Beer really is the world's best beverage. It may be quenching or nourishing, cooling or warming, simple or worthy of deep meditation. It is a drink of a thousand aromas, a rainbow of color, and a range of character as diverse as the people who brew and enjoy it. It has ten thousand years of history, with gods, goddesses, heroes, and songs to celebrate its glories. It brings us together. Beer makes us happy.

In *Tasting Beer* it is my hope to help guide you to a better understanding of the many things that make beer and our relationship with it so magical. With effort and information, you can gain the power to peer knowingly into its amber depths, approach it with keener senses, and find within the meaning of beer.

Come, fill me a glass, fill it high,
A bumper, a bumper I'll have:
He's a fool that will flinch, I'll not bate an inch,
Though I drink myself into my grave.
Come, my lads, move the glass, drink about,
We'll drink the whole universe dry,
We'll set foot and drink it all out,
If once we grow sober we die.

— Mr. Philips, "Bachanalian Song," from *In Praise of Ale*, 1888

CHAPTER 1

THE STORY OF BEER

Beer is the great family of starch-based alcoholic beverages produced without distillation. Today in the industrialized world, beer is usually brewed from barley malt, with other grains such as rice, corn, wheat, or oats thrown in for reasons of cost, texture, or tradition, and seasoned with hops. This is but a small subset of all possible beers. In the vast span of history, and in the diverse cultures of preindustrial societies, many other variations are found. Every imaginable starchy vegetable product has been used, even manioc and millet.

THE STARCH IN GRAIN is not readily fermentable by brewer's yeast, so some chemical process must be used to break down the starches into fermentable sugars. For Andean *chicha*, women chew maize, and enzymes in their saliva do the trick. In sake (yes, it's beer, not wine), *Aspergillis* fungus is used to provide the necessary enzymes. Fortunately, grains such as barley and wheat already contain enzymes capable of doing the job, when given the opportunity.

We know beer as a delicious treat; these days it is not essential for survival. But in the days of poor sanitation — just a century or two ago — beer was one of the few cheap, safe sources of potable water. Beer can also contain a lot of protein and carbohydrates, depending on how it is brewed, and this has earned it the nickname "liquid bread." Beer also contains alcohol, long prized for its ability to ease social tensions and create a sense of well-being, despite the risks to those who overindulge.

Beer can be brewed to suit many different tastes, and for a host of different purposes. It is typical to see, in most cultural contexts, a range of beers from weak to strong filling different roles in the day, the season, or the society.

Those who study the birth of civilizations and beer note that the two happened at just about the same time. Barley was one of the earliest cultivated grains, and the fact that it emerged in domesticated form with just the right characteristics for brewing tells us a lot. Leaving the nomadic life behind for a pot of gruel is one thing, but toss in beer, and it's a hard deal to turn down.

It is my belief that squeezing people into cities generates a certain amount of itchy friction, but this can be eased by a social lubricant like beer, served up in that other beloved institution, the tavern, which appeared on the scene not long after beer.

Beer, in many times and places, was not a casual consumer choice, but something much more meaningful. The ancient Middle Eastern peoples had gods and goddesses dedicated to the stuff, and they wove the creation of beer into their own epic tales. In the Sumerian Epic of Gilgamesh, it is a sip of beer that makes the wild man civilized. In Egyptian legend, it saved the world. Through the millennia, beer has been accorded the highest possible status in culture after culture. We owe it to beer to understand it, to nurture it, to respect it. Like all human art forms, it survives only at our pleasure. We get out of it what we put into it.

Millet Beer, Bobo-Dioulasso, Burkina Faso
Brewing is a global tradition, almost as widespread as humanity itself.

A Little Beer History

The history of beer is a wide and deeply fascinating subject and deserves a great deal more attention than I'm going to be able to give it in this short chapter. All I can hope to do here is lay out the broad strokes so that the rest of the pieces, especially with regard to styles, will fit into the framework I'm providing.

AGRICULTURE'S START

The story begins around 22,000 BCE, as the last Ice Age ended and changing climates made the part of the Middle East now known as Kurdistan more habitable. As people settled the area, they made use of wild-harvested plants, including grasses, as a good source of nutrition and more. Chemical evidence from a place called Göbekli Tepe indicates that people may have been brewing beer from wild grasses as early as 15,000 BCE. By saving the best seeds and replanting year after year, they bred these grasses into barley and wheat, and as they did, turned themselves into farmers. And brewers.

Their domesticated grasses had large, starch-swollen seeds well suited to the foods and drinks they produced. Their wheat had plenty of the sticky protein called gluten that gives structure to leavened bread, and the grains threshed free of their gritty husks, another vital characteristic for good bread. Their barley had less gluten than wheat, and many varieties threshed with the husk intact — two qualities that are very helpful in brewing. The full story is fairly complicated, but even in that early era, the fundamentals were there for barley beer and wheaten bread.

Kurdistan
The hills of this Middle Eastern region are thought to be the birthplace of many domesticated grasses.

The Earliest Beer?
Vessels and residues suggest that brewing was underway as early as 15,000 BCE in the vicinity of the temple complex at Göbekli Tepe, Turkey.

It is unclear how mashing — the enzyme conversion of starch to sugar — was discovered. It is postulated that the essential step of malting (sprouting the grain, then drying it, which also activates the starch-degrading enzymes) was originally done to preserve the grain and to add to its nutritive value. And in a day when the gruel du jour must have been monotonous in the extreme, it may have livened things up quite a bit when somebody discovered that if you mix malt with hot water, a few minutes later you get a nutritious broth that is quite sweet — it actually tastes a lot like Grape-Nuts.

Staking their fate on the cultivation of those tiny grass seeds was a bold step for these ancient people. Animal herding was well suited to a nomadic lifestyle, as people followed the herds season to season in search of pasturage. Grain is not particularly portable, so throwing your lot in with agriculture meant the loss of a certain kind of wind-in-the-hair freedom. Personally, I find this loss much more acceptable when the trade-off is beer, as compared to bread or gruel. Those more scholarly than I make the claim that beer is one thing that allowed people to come together in unnaturally

Recent evidence has pointed to a similarly early date for beer brewing in central China, first with rice, and then contemporaneously with the rise of civilizations in the Near East, with barley and sorghum as well.

"Hymn to Ninkasi" (excerpt)
Ninkasi, you are the one who spreads
the cooked mash on large reed mats,
Coolness overcomes.
You are the one who holds with both hands
the great sweet wort,
Brewing [it] with honey and wine
— Translated by Miguel Civil

crowded settings such as cities. It's certainly true today that beer helps to take the edge off and makes cities much more livable. I'm not pointing any fingers, but look at the places where beer is absolutely forbidden. It's easy to see the contrast.

It appears that wine and beer developed at about the same time and place. Even in that early day, wine was a much more luxurious product, by and large reserved for royalty and other upper-crusty types, while *everyone* drank beer. The Greeks, and the Romans after them, propagated this notion of wine's superiority that has come down in a direct line ever since. Consider this the next time you are banging your head in frustration over the automatic sense of class and status accorded to wine relative to beer. I do believe we have the power to change this to some degree, but it is important to know what we are up against.

BEER IN ANCIENT CIVILIZATIONS

The Sumerians were the first great civilization of the ancient Middle East. They were very fond of beer. Their word for beer, *kaš*, literally means "what the mouth desires," and this gives us a good idea of how central beer was to their culture. By 3000 BCE, the art of beer was well established, as evidenced by an expansive vocabulary of ingredients, brewing vessels, and beer types. Malt kilns made red, brown, and black beers possible, and there were fresh and aged, strong and weak, and even a diet beer, the name for which, *eb-la*, literally meant "lessens the waist." Yeast was known as the motive power of beer, but its nature would remain a mystery for another 5,000 years.

In that day, women were the brewers as well as the retailers of beer, as they were in Europe throughout the Middle Ages. It's not surprising

Sumerian Cuneiform Tablet
This ancient Mesopotamian tablet records the allocation of beer. Writing may have been invented to track the inventory and movement of grain and other agricultural products.

that the Sumerian deity of beer, Ninkasi, was a female and a daughter of Ninhursag, the Mother Goddess. There is a detailed poem, the "Hymn to Ninkasi," which describes the brewing of beer.

Barley was malted, kilned, and ground. It was then either formed into conical cakes and baked or used as is. Baking the cakes would have added some caramelization and presumably begun the enzymatic conversion of starch to sugar. The cakes would then have been a kind of "instant mash," and adding them to hot water would have been an easy and portable way to get brewing started. The beer was often drunk out of a communal vessel through long straws typically made of reeds. High-status individuals had straws made of more precious materials.

Brewers in Egypt c. 2325 BCE
Beer, along with bread and onions, was the
lifeblood of ancient Egypt.

THE BABYLONIANS, PHOENICIANS, Akkadians, Hittites, and other ancient Middle Eastern people were also beer lovers. The Bible does mention wine frequently, and something called *shekar*, which is usually translated as "strong drink." Scholars seem to have come around to the view that this could refer to beer, but it may also refer to any alcohol other than grape wine, including beer fortified with dates, figs, or honey, or wines made from them.

But just across the desert in Egypt, we see beer on a grand scale. Breweries were associated with temples there and were similar in size to the brewpubs of today. Egyptian beer was called *hekt* or *hqt*, and because of its near-industrial scale, brewing was in the domain of men. Beer was such a vital staple of Egyptian life that a model brewery was seen as essential to ensure a happy afterlife. Beer, along with bread and onions, is credited with fueling vast construction projects such as the pyramids. As in Mesopotamia, the beer was often brewed from specially prepared cakes of malted barley. Much of it was bottled in tall clay jars with special clay seals.

There is a tale from Egyptian mythology that shows the value that culture placed on beer. Sekhmet, the lion-headed woman, was a goddess of destruction, blood, and periodic renewal. Her father, Ra, the big-daddy god of ancient Egypt, felt that humanity was backsliding and was not worshipping him in the manner to which he was accustomed. So he sent Sekhmet out to teach the people a lesson. Things got out of hand with a lot of hacking and smacking and drinking of blood. If she were to continue, humanity would be destroyed. So someone had the bright idea to

May you have "bread that doesn't crumble, and beer that doesn't go sour."
— Ebers Papyrus, 1552 BCE

give her 80,000 jars of red beer to drink as an alternate to all that blood. And just to play it safe, they laced the beer with mandrake root, a powerful sedative. She drank it, went to sleep, and humankind was saved. Who wouldn't think kindly of beer after a close call like that?

Vestiges of this ancient beer tradition still survive in Egypt and the Sudan to the south, in the form of a primitive folk brew called *bouza*. Indigenous brewers there still make cakes of malted barley to brew this chunky and nutritious beer.

T HE GREEKS BELIEVED WINE to be the drink of civilized people; for them the defining characteristic of barbarism was beer drinking. Their disdain for beer, however, didn't stop them from stealing the very hip god of beer, Sabazius (later Attis), from the beer-drinking Lydians and Phrygians to the north, stripping him of his dignity, dolling him up with a crown of leaves, renaming him Dionysus, and enthroning him as their very own god of wine.

Evidence of the Phrygians' fondness for beer comes to us by way of their famous ruler, King Midas. Archaeologists in the 1950s dug down through an ancient mound in Gordion, Turkey, into a heavy timber structure; once inside, they found a burial site, determined to be that of Midas himself, holding the remains of a funerary feast. The objects were recovered and put on display, and scrapings from the cauldrons and drinking vessels were stored away for future analysis. Their time came a few years later, when a professor from the University of Pennsylvania named Patrick McGovern happened upon them. He was using molecular archaeology to research the early history of wine. Using sophisticated analytical methods such as gas chromatography, McGovern was

Ancient Persian Drinking Boot, c. 200–100 BCE
Surely they must have known about this vessel's tendency to splash when the beer in the toe gushes forth. Was the boot a drinking game then as it is today?

looking for individual molecules of substances that would offer clues to the nature of ancient foods or drinks. What he and his team found, in addition to a lamb and lentil stew, was a drink containing barley, grapes, and honey.

To announce the results a party was held, for which Sam Calagione of Dogfish Head Craft Brewery was asked to make the beer. This evolved into a regular product, Midas Touch. It is impossible to say how much this modern brew resembles the ancient one, but it is delicious and gives us a tantalizing glimpse into the lives of these ancient beer-loving people.

Seasonings of Ancient Northern Beers
Juniper, honey, cranberries, and an herb called meadowsweet were used in beers
thousands of years ago and still find brewing uses today.

T HE ROMANS, just like the Greeks, whose culture they absorbed, never did warm up to beer. This points out a key fact of beer geography: there is a line south of which grapes grow well and wine becomes the dominant drink. North of this line, ancient Romans encountered enthusiastic beer drinkers at the fringes of their empire.

Beverages made from grain mixed with honey or fruit occurred throughout ancient northern Europe. Honey is a willing, if scarce, source of fermentable sugar, and grapes harbor yeast. The dull, waxy haze you see on the surface of grapes is actually brewer's yeast in its natural habitat. This was known in ancient times, and it appears that grapes or raisins were sometimes added for the purpose of kickstarting fermentation in beer.

Other ingredients found their way into beer and other drinks as well. Images of poppy pods

Yeast in the Wild
The waxy haze on the skin of grapes and many
other fruits is actually brewer's yeast.

suggest that opium was involved in Dionysian rituals. Further afield, the Scythians (in present-day Ukraine) seem to have been enamored of hemp. Greek writers of the time report saunalike tents with heated rocks inside, upon which they threw hemp, which, Herodotus notes, gave off a "vapor unsurpassed by any vapor-bath one could find in Greece. The Scythians enjoy this so much that they howl with pleasure."

Chemical analysis of scrapings from Bronze Age burials has turned up barley, honey, cranberries, and two herbs: meadowsweet and bog myrtle (*Filipendula ulmaria* and *Myrica gale*). At this time, the widespread adoption of hops was still far in the future. The *Kalevala*, the national epic story of the Finns and Hungarians, has a delightful account of the creation of beer, which took a great deal longer to explain than the creation of the earth. Osmotar, the Brewster, aided by the "magic maiden" Kalevatar, is desperately seeking fermentation of the beer she's just brewed. They try pinecones and bear spit before resorting to honey, which works like a charm: "upward in the tub of birch-wood/ Foaming higher, higher, higher."

There is also a strong and very old tradition of incorporating juniper in these northern brews, which continues to this day in the unhopped Finnish farmhouse ale called *sahti*, a delicious and unassumingly strong brew made from malt and rye, in which juniper is added to the water as well as the mash, the branches are used as a filtering bed, and the wood is made into drinking vessels.

The Legend of Pictish Heather Ale
The story goes that the last of the Picts went to his death rather than reveal the "secret" of heather ale (whatever it may have been) to the invading Celts.

A LITTLE SOUTH, in the British Isles, beers seasoned with heather were being brewed by the Picts, the original inhabitants who built Stonehenge before the Celts displaced them. There is a delightfully romantic tale (described in Robert Louis Stevenson's poem "Heather Ale") about the last of the Picts, who allows his son to be flung over a cliff rather than reveal the "secret" of heather ale to the advancing Celts. As it's difficult to find any spot in northern Scotland without heather in sight, it's not hard to fathom what the secret was. But it's still a great story.

The beer-drinking barbarians left the world with many gifts, not the least of which was the wooden barrel. It's a technological achievement of amazing durability, maintaining the same form and construction since its first creation around 0 CE. Barrels were largely phased out of everyday use for beer by the middle of the twentieth century and have now returned for special purposes. For spirits and wine, nothing else serves quite as well.

BEER IN THE MIDDLE AGES

In the Middle Ages, beer and brewing settled into the familiar premodern pattern. Women called alewives brewed beer on a domestic scale, and its sale offered a reliable source of income for widows or others in need of honest cash. There were also institutional breweries, either monastic or owned by landed gentry as well as some commercial, or "common" breweries. These become more widespread as time went on.

Prior to 1000 CE, almost all beer in Europe was brewed without hops, seasoned with a pricey mixture called "gruit," sold by the holder of the local *Gruitrecht*, or "gruit right," which was the usual coterie of bigwigs: church, state, or in between. The purchase of gruit was mandatory for brewers, serving as an early form of taxation. A testament to the importance of gruit still stands in Bruges, Belgium, in the form of an opulent building, now serving as a medieval folklife museum.

The composition of gruit was a big secret, and its spices were mixed with ground grain to further confound would-be counterfeiters. Bog myrtle, a.k.a. sweet gale, is one herb always mentioned. It's a pretty nicely flavored

The Gruitrecht headquarters (now the Gruuthusemuseum) in Bruges, Built in the 1500s
This stately building stands as a reminder of the enormous power of gruit in medieval times.

herb — kind of resiny and piney — not far from hops. Yarrow (*Achillea millefolium*) is another, although it has a rough bitterness that's not pleasing to modern tastes. A third, *Ledum palustre*, which sometimes goes by the name of "wild rosemary," seems to have been held in lower regard than bog myrtle. It has a menthol, resiny bitterness, and historically there are suggestions of mind-altering properties, although this appears not to be the case. It does have some toxicity and is a pretty effective bug repellent. This witches' brew was supplemented by whatever culinary seasonings were available: juniper, caraway, aniseed, and possibly more exotic spices such as cinnamon, nutmeg, and ginger. I've tasted a number of homebrewed gruits, and I can report that either tastes have changed since then or we're missing some important part of the formula.

Hopped Beer

Chemical evidence of hops in beer dates to its first appearance in 550 BCE in Pombia, near Lake Maggiore in northern Italy, but this may have been a false start. It would take another 1,500 years or so before hops began their takeover of European beer.

The first hopped beers appear before the year 1000 CE in the northern German Hansa trading league city of Bremen. Many of the early adopters of hops were "free" cities beyond the reach of the church, and as such were not obligated to use gruit. At that time, brewers of gruit beer were known as "red" beer brewers, making brown or amber-colored beers. Those using hops brewed "white" beer, which usually included a fair amount of wheat in the grist along with the barley. The guilds for each were totally separate, and towns were often known for one or the other. The brewers of Bremen

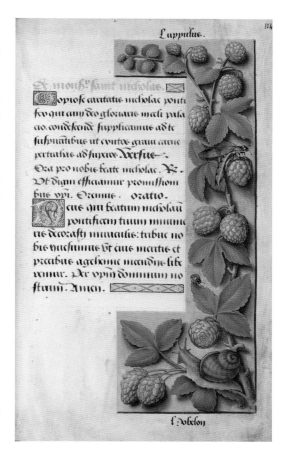

Hops on a Manuscript, c. 1500
Hops may have been a relatively new fashion at the time it was immortalized in this prayer book.

and Hamburg shipped an awful lot of beer to Amsterdam, which was just getting going at the time and was thirsty for the great, refreshing taste of imported beer. It took about a hundred years for the local brewers to figure out that they could brew this hopped white beer in Amsterdam, and they soon began exporting to Flanders, repeating the cycle. Hopped beer eventually washed ashore in England with a flood of Flemish immigrants and was pretty well established by the year 1500.

Hopped beer was a success not only because it tastes great, but because hops have preservative properties that retard certain beer-spoiling bacteria. This allowed table-strength beer to remain drinkable for a few months rather than a few weeks. Despite some grumblings about the despicable foreignness of it, hopped beer was accepted into England without too much fuss, and by about 1600 all English beer and ale had hops in some quantity.

As northern Europe flourished, hopped beer became the norm. Parts south, such as Italy and Spain, had little or no beer culture. Italy was rightly satisfied with its wonderful wines, and the antialcohol Muslims weren't kicked out of Spain until 1614. The brewing action was in the German states, Flanders, the Netherlands, and England, and that remains the case 500 years later, although craft beer culture has sprung to life in Italy, Spain, and elsewhere. The northern beer cultures are the sources for all the classic styles I'll be covering in detail later in the book.

The Rise of Porter

The changes that would culminate in the Industrial Revolution began in England in the mid-seventeenth century. Many large public works projects to open canals and improve harbors would affect brewing, as they improved access to raw materials and opened distant markets. Farmers were being forced off the land through the restriction of their access to what had previously been common areas of cultivation and grazing. Many of them found new lives in the cities.

Simultaneously, London encountered a patch of tough times: the civil war of 1642 and the subsequent turbulence of Oliver Cromwell's leadership from 1653 to 1658, plague in 1665, and a devastating fire in 1666. The latter actually proved to be a stimulus to new growth and development; peasants and gentry alike flooded into the city to make their fortunes. And there's one thing we all know about hard work: it makes us very thirsty.

About that time, a type of inexpensive brown malt from Hertfordshire was becoming available in London, and it was adopted as the standard malt there. As always, beers were brewed at different strengths, and the stronger sorts were aged until they acquired a particular sourish tang. Such aged beer was called "stale," and not in the negative sense, as it sold for a higher price than fresh, or "running," beer. Bar patrons were fond of ordering blends of two, three, or even five separate beers, which must have kept the bar hands busy. The oft-told story goes that porter was invented in October 1722 by Ralph Harwood in his Bell Brewery in Shoreditch to replace these blends, particularly one called "three threads." There's no evidence any of this is true; the story didn't appear until 1810 in the book *Picture of London*, nearly a century after the supposed events of 1722.

Whatever the reason for its genesis, the new hoppy brown beer was a huge craze, and by the 1720s it had acquired the porter name. Because of the large amount of capital needed to hold beer for an extended period while maturing, moneyed people began buying stocks of the new beer and aging it for a year or more, setting the stage for the enormous enterprises that porter breweries would soon become.

Aided by new technologies such as steam, instrumentation, and cast iron, scale increased to dizzying levels, giving rise to the largest breweries the world had ever known. By 1796, Whitbread alone was brewing 202,000 thirty-six-gallon barrels a year; combined, London porter breweries brewed 1,200,000 barrels in 1810. At that time it took more money to finance a brewery than any other business except a bank. This new industrial scale was important, because it increased pressure on brewers to find efficiencies that had been insignificant in a more artisanal setting. In a competitive market, businesses live and die by these efficiencies, but as breweries strive to get the most for the least, the customer doesn't always benefit. The brewing texts of the time are full of wistful quotes telling us how much better the beer was in the good old days. Some of this is simply nostalgia, of course, but if you look at the recipes, changes over time are rarely made with the aim of making the beer taste better.

While the particulars of the rise of pale ale are fascinating enough (and will be discussed in chapter 9), they were very much a continuation of the industrialization of beer begun by porter. Both porter and pale ale were hugely influential well beyond the borders of Britain. England was the superpower of the day, and its cultural trends were closely watched and occasionally adopted. Even in tradition-bound Germany, there was an interest in porter, and the globe-drenching success of pale ale was one of the things that pushed the town fathers of Plzeň to create their famous golden lager. But we're getting ahead of ourselves.

Westminster Ale and Porter Brewery on Horseferry Road, London, c. 1840
Porter was big business in Victorian London, brewed on an enormous scale.

TECHNOLOGICAL CHANGES IN BREWING, 1700–1900

Steam Power

Although useful steam engines for mining were developed about 1700, it was not until the improvements of James Watt and others that they became practical for the brewing industry. The first steam engine installed in a brewery was in 1784 in London. Steam replaced manual, water, and horse power for many tasks and made brewing on a large industrial scale possible.

Brewery Steam Engine, Czech Republic
Steam powered just about everything that moved in early industrial breweries.

The Thermometer

Although the technology had been around for some time, it was Gabriel Fahrenheit who created the first mercury thermometer and standardized scale in 1714. The Celsius scale was devised in 1742. James Baverstock was the first brewer to seriously investigate the use of a thermometer, but he had to hide his efforts from his conservative family, who opposed "new-fangled ideas." Michael Combrune wrote the brewing text (1784) detailing its use. The thermometer allowed for a good deal more consistency than the empirical methods in use, and it allowed detailed research into the dynamics of brewing procedures.

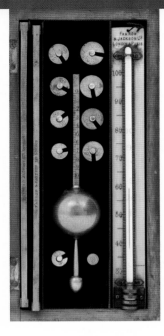

Antique Sikes Hydrometer by Farrow and Jackson Ltd. (London & Paris) Instrumentation was just as important as more muscular technology, helping with efficiency and consistency.

The Hydrometer

This is an instrument that measures specific gravity and is used to measure the amount of sugar and other dissolved solids in beer wort (the sweet liquid drained from the mash that is fermented to make beer). In 1785, John Richardson wrote the first book detailing brewing measurements made with the hydrometer, which had huge implications for the way beer was brewed and, more than any other technology, changed the way beer actually tasted by forcing brewers to formulate their recipes with yield in mind.

Yeast and Fermentation

Around 1680, the Dutch microscopist Anton van Leeuwenhoek was the first to observe and describe yeast cells. Three different scientists independently from around 1834 to 1835 revealed their living nature. Louis Pasteur penned his epic *Études sur la Bière* detailing the causes and prevention of "diseases" of beer in 1876. With Pasteur's help, Emil Christian Hansen isolated the first single-cell culture — as opposed to the mixed cultures that were then used for brewing.

While single-cell cultures make for a more consistent and, on average, better beer, their use only became widespread in the mid-twentieth century. Many brewers lamented the abandonment of more complex mixed-culture fermentation even as they acknowledged the necessity of doing so.

Refrigeration

This was a culmination of centuries of work by various luminaries. American Alexander Twining is credited with creating the first commercial refrigeration unit in 1859. German engineer Carl von Linde's advanced dimethyl ether refrigeration machines were installed in the Spaten brewery in 1873. Refrigeration offered an obvious benefit over ice cut from frozen rivers and lakes — until then the only form of cooling available. Not only were the logistics complicated, but natural ice was also becoming a health hazard, a result of pollution of the waterways. By 1890, artificial refrigeration was the norm for large-scale brewing everywhere.

Malt Kilning

Over time, there was a gradual transition from direct-fired, wood-fueled kilns to indirectly heated kilns fueled by coal, coke, or other fuels. By 1700, most English maltsters and brewers (who malted their own) had switched to indirect kilns making for smoke-free malts, although brown malt continued to be roasted by crackling hot wood fires into the mid-twentieth century (of course, smoked beers are today a specialty item in Bamberg, Germany). The most dramatic invention relative to malt kilning was the cylindrical roaster patented by Daniel Wheeler in 1817; this device forever changed the brewing and flavor of porter and stout, as a small amount of this much darker malt was more economical than the large amounts of brown and amber malts used previously. Crystal/caramel malt was a later (but prior to 1870) development of unknown origin.

Cold-Fermented Lager

Some time between 1400 and 1500, a cold-fermented beer called lager came into existence in Germany — or maybe Bohemia. How, when, and why is one of the great mysteries of beer history. The commonly told story has Bavarian monks fermenting in caves in the Alps, but this doesn't make a lot of sense. A mountain is not a great place to brew or sell beer. Barley comes from the fields far below, and that's where the customers are as well. So grain has to be hauled up and beer, in heavy wooden casks, transported down. Ice caves are a little too cold and rocky ones a little too warm.

The earliest mention of lager supposedly occurs in 1420, in records from Munich, but this is not well documented. Then, from the city of Nabburg in northeast Bavaria, bordering on Bohemia, we get this: "one brews the warm or top fermentation; but first in 1474 one attempted to brew by the cold bottom fermentation, and to preserve part of the brew for the summer." This seasonal preference must have

Lagering Casks, Pilsner Urquell, Czech Republic
While retired now, these large oak casks were the standard lagering
vessels for centuries.

been established by then, but in 1539 a ban on summer brewing in Bavaria gave it the force of law. However, the date seems a little late to explain the earlier mentions.

Lager yeast, *Saccharomyces pastorianus,* is a hybrid between an ale yeast and another yeast, *S. bayanus,* a cold-tolerant, osmophilic species first found living in birch galls in Patagonia, but more recently found in China and Tibet. Genomic data seems to indicate that this hybridization may have occurred multiple times, and it suggests that at least one "lager" strain is actually an ale and not a hybrid. The Patagonian discovery threw the time line of the whole story into question, but locating it in Eurasia means an appropriately early date is possible. Whatever the true story, by 1600 lager seems to have been pretty dominant in Bavaria and nearby regions such as Bohemia. Lager developed into a rollicking beer culture and put the Bavarians on the beer map.

Because of its landlocked situation — as well as being host to a good deal of political turmoil over the centuries — Bavaria was a little late to the industrialization party. But by the mid-nineteenth century, things were heating up, and the improvements of motive power, instrumentation, and kilning were all put to good use. Much of what we think of as classic lager styles were reinvented in the middle of the nineteenth century. Progress in microbiology pioneered by Pasteur, followed by the yeast work of Emil Christian Hansen, were especially well received by lager brewers. With their clean, pure flavors, lagers benefit from the consistency of single-cell cultures, so German brewers were quick to adopt them. English brewers of the day tried them out and because of their short brewing cycle found them unnecessary; mixed cultures are still employed today in some English breweries.

IN THE TOWN OF PLZEŇ IN 1842, a number of things came together to create a beer that would eventually dominate the world market beyond anybody's dreams. The beer, Pilsner, was a confluence of ingredients, technology, and a business plan just right for the times.

Community leaders thought it would be a good idea to build a sizable brewery to make lager beer and capitalize on the lager boom and the extraordinarily high quality of the malt and hops of the region. The story goes that a brewer named Josef Groll actually flubbed the recipe, and instead of a dark Munich-style beer, a much paler beer gushed forth, but this seems very unlikely for a number of reasons. I think when the historians have dug a little deeper, we will find that the parts and pieces were all there before 1842, and probably the beer, too, on a small scale. What the town fathers of Plzeň did was bet big on it, perhaps seeking to trade on the raging popularity of the English pale ale that seemed to be everywhere in those days. In any event, the pale, crisp, effervescent Pilsner beer was a huge hit, bringing its little hometown worldwide celebrity.

Bavaria joined the German union in 1871, and soon sought to impose its restrictive beer purity law; shortly after 1900 the *Reinheitsgebot* (German Beer Purity Law) had the force of law across Germany. At the time, northern Germany was white-beer country. Its beers had more in common with Belgium than they did with Bavaria. Beers brewed with a proportion of wheat, often smoked, sometimes sour, and using herbs such as coriander and sugars such as molasses and honey were very popular. Beers from that time, such as grodziskie (grätzer), lichtenhainer, kottbusser, Broyhan Alt, and gose can be lovely beers, and craft brewers are taking notice. There is a minor fad going on for gose, and some of the others are being brewed occasionally as well. Polish homebrewers are taking a special interest in grodziske, a Prussian ale brewed from 100 percent smoked wheat malt, going so far as to interview former brewery workers and resurrecting the correct yeast strain. Of all the northern German ales, only Berliner Weisse and the lovely specialty ales of the Rhine valley, Kölsch and Düsseldorfer Alt, have survived in any meaningful way in their home territory.

By the time World War II started rumbling up, all the classic Germanic lager styles as we know them today were pretty well set in stone.

Belgium and France

The picture is different in Belgium. Modernization came in fits and starts, beginning in the mid-nineteenth century. By the end of the century, most of the large-scale breweries were making Bavarian-style lagers, of which Stella Artois is the best-known example. Written accounts of the time describe many of the historically Belgian breweries as being small and dispirited.

Belgium's original beer culture revolved around wheat beers. Even those considered barley-malt beers, such as *l'orge d'Anvers* (barley beer of Antwerp), often had a dash of wheat

and oats in the grist. Many of these ancient styles are familiar to us today: witbier, lambic, and Flanders brown (although today this style is brewed without wheat), but many more that were popular in their day have disappeared: *bière de Mechelen*, *Peetermann*, *diest*, and many others.

Belgian beer has taproots that go back to the Middle Ages. Those dancing peasants in the Bruegel painting are most likely drinking something along the lines of lambic: the sour, wild-fermented beer of the Brussels region. Witbier also has a long pedigree. But many of what we think of as ancient and characteristic beers, such as Trappist beers, Belgian pale ales, and saisons, are actually inventions of the twentieth century. What you may have heard isn't always the real story.

Belgium has been through a lot. Wedged between vying superpowers, it has been dominated by the French, Dutch, Germans, Spanish, and Austro-Hungarians. Two devastating world wars were fought on its soil, and these brought with them calamitous foreign occupations.

Spices
Following an ancient tradition, many Belgian-style beers contain subtle combinations of exotic spices such as coriander, bitter orange peel, grains of paradise, cumin, and star anise.

THE BELGIANS LOVE TO DRINK BEER. Figures published in an 1851 book by Georges Lacambre state that "For a population in the neighborhood of four million individuals, [Belgians] brewed no less than eight or nine million hectoliters of beer per year," without exporting a great deal. This works out to a little over a pint a day (actually 0.58 liter) per person,

A Fifteenth Century Brewery
Stained glass from the Cathedral of Notre Dame, Tournai, Belgium, c. 1500.

Operation of the Brewery, **Jean-Louis-Joseph Hoyer (1762–1829), watercolor**
On a medium scale, brewing remained a very hands-on process.

OPERATION DE LA BRASSERIE

about twice what it is today. (If you're wondering, the Czechs are today's biggest beer drinkers, at just over 0.4 liter per person per day.)

The Belgian brewing industry was at a low point around 1900, and then came World War I. Despite the hardships, Belgian brewers managed to rebound. The 1920s and '30s saw the introduction of the strong, high-gravity luxury beers that form our impressions of Belgium today. Miraculously, the ancient lambic style managed to survive.

Belgium has never had a beer purity law. This means there was never a purge of the ancient spices, herbs, and sugars that were once widespread in European brewing. Coriander, orange peel, cumin, grains of paradise (a pungent, peppery spice), and many kinds of sugars find their way into Belgian beers, often in quite subtle ways. However, the aforementioned Lacambre notes casually that these "are English spices," and they were indeed common in eighteenth- and early-nineteenth-century English recipes, especially those brewed on private estates. This historical complexity only adds to the appeal.

Belgian brewing is subject to the same kind of Pilsnerization and consolidation that afflicts many of Europe's traditional brewing regions. But thanks to a strong export market — half of Belgium's beers leave the country — the scene abounds with fascinating artisanal products and is also starting to be populated with forward-thinking artisanal brewers injecting some fresh creativity. For a beer lover seeking new experiences, Belgium is a wonderland of the highest order.

THE NORTH OF FRANCE, particularly the region of Nord, which borders Belgian Flanders, has a beer tradition that blends into Belgium's. Many small breweries

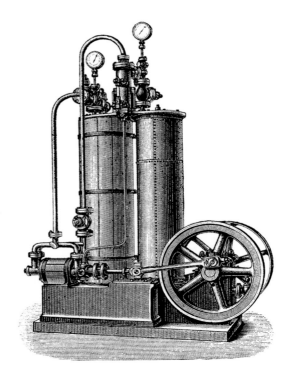

Linde's Ice Machine, c. 1880
Early refrigeration equipment may have looked ungainly, but it changed the seasonality of brewing forever.

were brewing their own top-fermented interpretations of the blondes, *bières de mars* (Märzens), and bocks that were popular as lagers elsewhere in France. These, especially the double versions, have been reborn as the *bières de garde* we know today.

Farther south, France's lager beer barrel was the Alsace-Lorraine region that bordered Germany to the east. By 1871, when Germany annexed the region after the Franco-Prussian War, Alsace was brewing most of France's beer. Louis Pasteur was among those enraged by this act of war, and he set about to do his part to rebuild the French brewing industry bigger and better with superb, world-class beer, which he called "the beer of revenge." He published his famous *Études sur la Bière* in 1876, which demonstrated the causes of beer spoilage and suggested methods for preventing it. This work was of enormous importance and had effects far beyond France, to every corner of the industrialized beer world.

North America

The first colonists to America brought with them a taste for beer. But brewing was extremely difficult in the New World for a number of reasons: Barley didn't grow well in southern regions such as Virginia or in northern New England. Imported malt was expensive and only occasionally available. People continued to make the effort in the seventeenth and early-eighteenth centuries, but after many generations, people's tastes change, and with beers made from molasses, dried pumpkin, and as one ditty says, "walnut-tree chips," it's not hard to see why. Easy access to cheap spirits helped rum and whiskey displace beer in most regions, and hard cider was easy to make on the farm. By 1800, per capita consumption of spirits was 10 times that of beer, in gallons. When you figure it based on the amount of alcohol consumed, it's more like 200 to 1.

Beer was never suited to the frontier, and those wide-open spaces dominated America for a long time. Brewing takes a cooperative climate and a lot of infrastructure, especially a steady source of clean water. Beer ingredients are heavy and difficult to transport overland, and the same is true of the finished product. Whether it was West Virginia or North Dakota, whiskey, rum, and cider were the logical choices for most.

In whatever manner people were getting their alcohol, small beer remained important in early America. George Washington's famous recipe of a little molasses and a handful of bran are probably typical. He was a commercial-scale distiller and had access to imported Madeira and other products for serious imbibing, but still, small beer was vital to the functioning of his estate. The idea was to add just enough flavoring to make it palatable as a source of safe water for slaves, servants, and master alike. After the Revolution, Thomas Jefferson saw beer as a temperate path for a spirits-soaked populace and began brewing experiments at Monticello, but ultimately nothing much came of this.

The exception to this dearth of beer was in Pennsylvania and parts of New York and Massachusetts. Wherever there were Germans or Dutch, there was a demand for beer, and these immigrants settled into lands that were

A Brewery at Monticello?
Thomas Jefferson penned this plan for a small brewhouse at his estate in northern Virginia. As far as is known, it was never built.

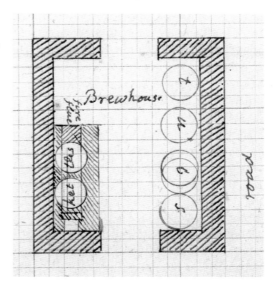

able to provide the raw materials for their favorite drink. The Dutch arrived in New Amsterdam (New York) in 1630, and brewing commenced there just 2 years later. Brewing was an important industry; the first paved street in the city was Brouwer (Brewer) Street. Brewing continued after the Dutch ceded New Netherland to the English in 1664, but the center of gravity shifted south. Philadelphia became the Milwaukee of its day: a brewing center famous for its porter and ale right up to the lager revolution.

Canada, having never severed its ties to Britain, maintained its own version of an Anglophile beer culture, at least in Ontario.

1800s

Political chaos occasioned by demands for democratic governments in Germany and Bohemia displaced many in the 1840s. Those flooding into America had a strong affinity for beer, a "culture of pleasure," as writer Maureen Ogle (author of *Ambitious Brew*) puts it. For them, a world without the joys of a few lagers in the garden on a Sunday afternoon was just unthinkable. They were men of ambition, skill, and great determination, and they set about rebuilding their beer culture here from scratch.

Many brewers remained small and were happy serving their local communities, but others had grander plans. Colonel Pabst, August Busch, and the Uihlein brothers of Schlitz dreamed of brands spanning coast to coast. This was a fairly ridiculous idea at the time, for there were few products of any kind with this sort of wide distribution. But as new technological improvements came along, these men were quick to seize on them as a way to achieve their goals. Steam power, refrigerated railcars, pasteurization, the telegraph, and artificial refrigeration were among these tools.

The business vision and organizational skills required to make this happen are awe inspiring.

AMERICA OF 1890 was filled with a sense of its own destiny, but it was still trying to coalesce as a people after half a century in which wave after wave of immigrants came ashore from Germany, Ireland, Italy, and elsewhere. While each had its own community, the order of the day was to become a "real American." One path to a shared culture turned out to be national brands of products made in modern factories that were rock-solid consistent wherever they were found. National brands such as Heinz pickles, Folgers coffee, Del Monte canned foods, and Coca-Cola are a few, but there were many more. There was an element of modernity in all this (something, happily, that we've gotten away from), but in those heady days, sliced bread (1928) really was the greatest thing.

The same impulses drove people's taste in beer. In the middle of the 1800s, rich brown Munich lagers predominated. Toward the end of the century, pale, crisp Pilsner and other Bohemian-inspired beers started to catch the imagination of the public. Beyond the fact that this quenching style is a natural fit with the warm climate of much of the United States, the addition of corn or rice compensated for the high-protein barley's proclivity for throwing a chill haze, and these beers were seen as simply more modern and fashionable than their heavy brown predecessors. By the beginning of Prohibition, pale lagers ruled the roost.

EARLY 1900s

It's hard to overestimate the effect that the double whammy of war with Germany followed by Prohibition (the two are not unrelated) had on the brewing industry and especially brewing shortly before this disastrous experiment in social engineering, only 756 were open a year after Prohibition was repealed, and many of these were destined to fail.

A whole generation grew up viewing alcohol as forbidden fruit, which makes it all the more tempting, but in a dirty, creepy sort of way. Quality plummeted. Worse, because brewing could only take place in utterly corrupt locales such as Chicago, spirits began to take hold nearly everywhere else, with the cocktail capturing the imagination of the drinker as a sophisticated, modern tipple. Although the beer industry regained its footing by the late 1950s, beer in America still suffers from this ravaged thinking many decades later.

Competition from the soda business was also a factor. From $135 million in sales in 1919, it had grown to $750 million by 1947, and double that a decade later. Soft drinks filled a need for a crisp, refreshing, temperate beverage — the role in which beer had held sole sway for thousands of years.

When Prohibition ended, beer started its slow climb out of the hole. Dark Munich-style lager was pretty well finished by then, replaced by crisp Pilsners lightened with additions of rice or corn. Consumption shifted away from saloons to the home. Before Prohibition, 75 percent of beer had been draft rather than bottled. By 1945, this had reversed, and three-quarters of all beer was packaged and increasingly sold to take home. This meant that beer was not only more available to women, but they also became involved in its purchase.

Illegally Filling Kegs, c. 1933
While alcohol was technically illegal during Prohibition, there were many loopholes, and in towns like Chicago, corruption allowed brewing to grow to a massive scale with little interference from the law.

the beer culture in the United States. German-Americans basically went underground. The beer gardens were shuttered. The royal family of England changed its name from the House of Saxe-Coburg and Gotha to the House of Windsor. Of the 1,300 or so breweries that were

THE FIRST CANNED BEER was released by the Kruger Brewing Company of Newark, New Jersey, in 1935. The new cans were light, were quick to chill, and took up less room than bottles in the refrigerator, all

MID-1900s

The other inescapable story in the last century of brewing is of consolidation. The United States had 4,131 breweries in 1873. A century later there were barely over a hundred. This is not unique to the brewing industry, or to the United States. It is a fact of business that over time the efficiencies of larger operations combined with national marketing, the vulnerability of weak producers, and the need to acquire cash for growth all lead toward the big getting bigger while small producers fall by the wayside.

For reasons related to consolidation and the relatively mature stage of the market, the 1950s and '60s saw a hotly contested race to the bottom in terms of beer quality and price. Bargain brands appeared, and then came ultrabargain brands, the low end of which scraped against the federal government's requirement that beer contain at least 50 percent malt. The real low came first with store brands, and then with generic beer that came in cans with no branding at all.

A NUMBER OF DIFFERENT ADDITIVES were used to make these discount beers more palatable. Cobalt salts were found to dramatically improve beer foam, and this was hailed as a godsend until people started getting sick and the product was withdrawn. By the late 1980s, most of these additives were gone for good, and it should also be noted that not all breweries resorted to extreme means to slice the price.

All this financial pressure put a great deal of strain on the production process. As malt content lowered, it became difficult to produce a product that resembled beer closely enough to deserve the name, and brewers were pressed to move the beer more quickly through the production cycle. Continuous fermentation was, and still is, an obsession among those

GIs Celebrating the End of the War with Cans of Beer
WWII brought enormous changes to the way beer was packaged and consumed. Early "cone-top" cans could be filled on a regular bottling line, but they were quickly phased out for cheaper options.

of which was very appealing to women. When masses of GIs returned home after World War II, having enjoyed canned beer in the intense arena of war, cans were a comfortable fit at home. They were a big hit.

Cans, by the way, are neutral as far as their effect on the product inside, even though by the 1980s they were snobbishly viewed as a low-class marker for the "Joe Six-Pack" life-style. At first made of steel, and now of aluminum, cans are lined with a beer-inert coating and have the real advantages of being totally opaque and recyclable. Canned craft beers have proliferated and are growing faster than craft beer as a whole.

modernizing beer production. In this process, wort is fed into one end of a fermenter, and finished beer comes out the other. Like a conveyor belt oven, this solves a lot of problems inherent in batch brewing. Brewers at Schlitz thought they were on to something big when they flipped the switch on their continuous fermenter in 1973, and they were. But the first batches of beer proved to be highly buttery and quite unacceptable to the consumer. This huge misstep coincided with a conviction for illegal "pay to play" that brought intense government oversight, dooming the brand to hide forever in the shadows, like a thing undead.

THE FINAL PART of the American industrial beer story is the success of light beer. The idea had been kicking around for some time. Miller bought the sleepy brand Lite, which had initially been Gablinger's and then part of the Meister Brau family. In 1975, Miller did the same thing to Lite that its parent company, Philip Morris, had done to Marlboro a couple of decades before: Take a female-oriented brand and restage it with a huge shot of testosterone, this time with aging sports stars, the cowboys of the day. *Blam!* Lite and its many

imitators shot to the top of the charts, exceeding regular beer in barrelage by 2005. Like any successful product, Lite had simply seized the moment and presented its product to a market segment thirsty for its particular qualities.

The trend toward light, pale beer reached its low point with the introduction of Miller Clear in 1993. This water-clear beer, stripped of all color and much of its flavor by a carbon filtration process was, thankfully, a step too far. It quietly slipped into the dark closet of failed brands.

Worldwide Beer in the Twentieth Century and Beyond

In Europe, similar economic and consumer-preference factors have been at work over the past century, but the specifics have played out differently.

Consolidation and thinning the market of weaker players are factors, but because there was no one catastrophic purge as the United States had with Prohibition, this has taken much longer — a death by a thousand cuts. Europe's classic brewing nations have a near-fanatical fan base for their traditional products, such as real ale or all-malt lager. These fans are by no means in the majority, but they are in some places organized and very vocal.

Even in that holy ground for beer geeks, Belgium, Pilsners account for 70 percent of the market. Over the past century, that style has bulldozed many local specialties out of

BEER

NET CONTENTS
12 FL. OZ. 355 ml

No-Name Beer
Things got so bad by the 1970s that there was a market for beer so cheap it didn't even have a brand name.

existence. For now, Germany still has its extensive network of local breweries, but most make similar products and the pressure for consolidation is on. In a way, we in the United States are lucky to have gotten through the worst of it a lifetime or two ago. When we hit bottom in terms of brewery numbers and interesting beers in the late 1970s, we had no beer culture, so we did what Americans are best at: reinvention.

Nonetheless, pockets of real, character-rich beers have managed to survive, even in Pilsner-drenched Germany. I'm now getting e-mails from people in Germany experimenting with "radical" brews. From the cheery session beers of the Rhine to the Weissbier of Berlin and Jena to the beery amusement park that is Bamberg, in northern Bavaria, there are specialty beers worth talking about, and their stories will be told in chapter 11.

In some places, such as Italy and Denmark, where there is not a recent history of meaningful local traditions, small brewers have built an interesting beer scene from scratch. At the moment, Italy seems to be on a Belgian-inspired path, while the Danish craft-beer scene is starting to resemble the hop-spattered playpen of American craft brewing. There's been lots of action in Japan since the government lowered the minimum brewery size to a reasonable level. Despite business, regulatory, and economic difficulties, craft breweries are popping up in Latin America, with especially lively scenes in Brazil, Chile, and Mexico gaining rapidly. It's a very exciting time for good beer.

ENGLAND'S CAMRA MOVEMENT

The classic product of England's breweries has long been naturally carbonated cask or "real" ale. By the late 1960s, this was being threatened by large brewers seeking to "modernize" the product by substituting filtered, artificially carbonated kegs or bulk cellar tanks filled from brewery tanker trucks. In 1971, the Campaign for Real Ale (CAMRA) was organized to fight this trend. It seeks to use public and political pressure to ensure that real ale remains a viable choice in Britain's pubs. It also produces publications and conducts a number of real-ale festivals in Great Britain, including the Great British Beer Festival every August. Membership in 2016 was listed at 175,000.

Despite their moral rectitude and formidable constituency, CAMRA has been unable to preserve real ale as the national drink, and it now lags behind lagers and keg beers as a specialty product, with just 17 percent of beer sold in pubs as of 2013; it is available at less than half of the nation's pubs. Economic forces and consumer attitudes can be battled, and may even be shifted a bit, but ultimately larger forces will always win out.

America, 1970 to the Present

It's hard to imagine now, even for those of us who were there, just how destitute the American beer landscape was back in 1977. At that time there were fewer than 50 brewing companies with less than 100 breweries, fewer than at any time in the past 200 years. There were still a few regionals, several of which are thriving today, but at that point they were turning out a bland and timid mix of products aimed at an aging customer base. The few that still brewed a seasonal bock beer usually just spiked their pale lager with a dash of caramel color. Nobody seemed to care about the *product*.

To be fair to the honorable family men who rode these institutions into oblivion, the twentieth century was pretty hard on breweries, especially regional ones. Changing patterns of behavior and a shiny new national culture meant that there just wasn't any real need for them, and the struggle for existence after Prohibition had turned into a decades-long cannibalistic orgy of price cutting, product cheapening, and consolidation. There was some pride here and there, but there honestly wasn't much to base a culture on.

About that time, way off in a quiet corner of San Francisco, a young man with an inquisitive spirit and deeper pockets than most came upon one of the last of these local breweries still making a historic and interesting product. The brewery was Anchor, and the beer was Steam. In 1965, Fritz Maytag bought the Anchor brewery and invested his life in making it mean

---

Anchor Brewing
While technically Anchor is the last survivor of a once widespread tradition, its 1971 reinvention of its Steam Beer made it the first craft brewery in modern times.

something again. Most see the ground-up reformulation of their iconic Steam Beer in 1971 as the beginning of the modern craft beer in America. It's fitting that this first craft brewery was also a living link to our authentic beer traditions and has the kind of historic cool that you can't just go out and invent.

W HILE FRITZ MAYTAG was busy rescuing San Francisco's Anchor Brewery, there were a number of other things happening. Young Americans had been experiencing the classic beers of Europe firsthand, either while stationed in the military or backpacking around. The *Whole Earth Catalog* came out, and even though there was scarcely a word about beer in it, for many of us it pointed a way to a kinder, gentler mercantile future of interesting, handmade products in every category, a theme that resonates just as strongly today. Michael Jackson was hard at work on his groundbreaking *World Guide to Beer*, first published in 1977. Books on homebrewing were leaking out of England, calling for such strange ingredients as treacle, and Fred Eckhardt published a small but technically detailed book called *A Treatise on Lager Beer*. Homebrewing was still illegal, an oversight in the law written just after Repeal, but nobody seemed to care too much. It's hard to overstate the importance of homebrewing as a source for the ideas, passion, and people that make craft beer happen. Without it, the beer scene today would look very different.

The first actual microbrewery was New Albion Brewing in Sonoma, California, which Jack McAuliffe opened in 1976. It didn't last long, but by then homebrewing was getting hot, and with a steady supply of guys brewing and friends saying, "Dude, that is great beer. You really should open a brewery," there were

eventually plenty of them that did just that. A trickle turned into a flood, and by the early 1990s there were hundreds of packaging breweries and brewpubs brewing a huge range of charming, and occasionally magnificent, beers.

By the early '90s, craft beer was growing at 45 percent per year and was attracting some unsavory types, and by that I mean people who were looking only at the money aspect of craft brewing, which was not enough for a venture to succeed. Not a single brewery that tried to start large was successful. By the end of the decade there had been a shakeout, but the upside was that there was a lot of nice used equipment available for a cheap price.

T HE CRAFT-BEER INDUSTRY is a lot more sophisticated today. Beer quality is high, marketing is correctly understood as helpful in getting the story out, and business acumen has caught up with the passion for beer, without overtaking it. Growth has settled into a robust 10 to 15 percent a year, and the category now commands about 11 percent of the U.S. beer market by barrelage, around 19 percent by dollars (2014 figures). North America is home to the most diverse, creative, and delicious beers on the planet. The late author Michael Jackson was fond of shocking European audiences with that observation.

For well over 100 years, the direction of the brewing industry was determined by its largest players. Today, with big beer stagnant and craft beer continuing to blossom, this is no longer the case. I hope we are headed for an era in which the beer market becomes something along the lines of the selection-rich wine category; when you hear August Busch IV say, "The future of beer in America is all about choices for the consumer," you have to just dig down deep and prove him right.

The Beer Marketplace

Since the earliest times, beer has been sold in a highly regulated system. The Code of Hammurabi threatens alewives with drowning in the river for cheating customers; today's punishments can be nearly as draconian. For thousands of years, governments have felt the need to keep beer contributing to society — as a taxable article and an alcoholic beverage — while not allowing it to do too much mischief. Because of corruptible human nature and what's at stake for all involved, it's inevitable that these efforts can be, at times, misplaced.

In the United States, many aspects of alcoholic-beverage regulation have been left to the individual states, especially when it comes to selling it.

Sophisticated Craft Beer
Despite the burgeoning popularity of IPA, craft brewing began as a way to restore some variety to America's beer market.

After some serious excesses in the brewery-owned saloon system before Prohibition, a three-tier distribution system was set up in most states after Repeal. With exceptions often made for brewpubs and occasionally for small-packaging breweries and wineries, alcoholic beverages must flow from brewer (or importer) to distributor to retailer. In many states, distributors are protected by franchise laws, which set the limits and obligations of the relationship between these parties.

The positive side is that franchise laws give distributors incentive to invest in the brands they carry, knowing that the brands can't be pulled without cause by a capricious brewer. But the downside is that this investment doesn't always happen, and distributors have been known to lock brands into a sort of dungeon where they are neither supported nor allowed to move to a distributor who will get behind them. Over the years, franchise laws have led to a considerable amount of discontent, and they are constantly in play in state legislatures as both sides struggle to move the balance point in their favor.

Most level heads in the beer industry see a need for distributors. One great argument in favor of the three-tier system is that it keeps the retail system out of the direct control of brewers. For a peek at brewery control of retailing, one need only look to England. There, brewers historically controlled the vast majority of pubs, either through direct ownership or through loans with exceptionally generous terms. In that situation, the marketing strategy becomes spending your budget in making your pubs as comfortable and showy as possible to attract drinkers. This has led to some real dazzlers, but it usually limits the beers available to a handful of a single brewery's products, with the requisite "guest" beer tossed in, often from a sister brewery's portfolio. After the Monopolies Commission forced English breweries to divest, control was snapped up by a small number of large multinational corporations that tend to do business with the largest breweries and keep consumer choice limited. If you've ever tried to find a locally brewed product in an American chain restaurant (and who among us hasn't?), you know what I mean.

America is so completely dominated by the large players (Anheuser-Busch had 46 percent

A Real Ale Hand Pump on the Bar of the Euston Flyer, King's Cross, London
The glory of many English pubs was financed by breweries, who insisted on exclusive sales of their products — or owned the pubs outright.

of the U.S. beer market as of 2014) that their ownership of pubs could easily be used to restrict consumers' access to smaller brands.

For startup breweries, distribution is a difficult issue. Early on, most are still getting their footing, trying to find out who makes up their market and struggling with the complexities of the business. In general, distributors are happier with somewhat more mature brands that have already had the kinks worked out in the production and marketing areas. In many states, breweries under a certain size are permitted to self-distribute. Distributors see this as violation of their bedrock right to the three-tier system, but it is arguably better for them to let very small breweries incubate on their own until they are ready for a more sophisticated step up into the market.

Liquor laws in the United States are a crazy quilt of sometimes senseless regulations that differ wildly by location. There are wet, dry, and damp counties (places where alcohol is available only at restaurants or private clubs), a county in Maryland that *is* the distributor, and many other practices that would be laughable if it weren't for the fact that they can seriously cut into your ability to enjoy legal products in the manner of your choosing.

Thanks to a slowly thawing political climate and a lot of hard work by enthusiasts and professionals working together, some of the old laws are falling victim to rationality. Alcohol-content restrictions for beer in North Carolina and several other states have been removed, and the anticompetitive package-size restrictions in Florida have been lifted. There is plenty more to be done, and neo-Prohibitionist forces are always trying to turn back the clock, so all of us who enjoy good beer need to be vigilant and ready to fight for it. The Brewers Association keeps a list of those who have expressed interest in maintaining their access to good beer and calls upon them as needed to provide grassroots pressure on beer-related issues. If you'd like to get on the list, go online to www.craftbeer.com.

Beer is a great mirror of history. It always amazes me how much of a story every beer has to tell. When I hold up the glass and think about it, every aspect of this malty, hoppy, foamy brew is a consequence of a remarkable chain of events that began some 10,000 years ago. That's a deep drink.

From *Let There Be Beer!*

Joe and his buddy sat down in one of the bare wooden drinking stalls in front of the long polished beer board in the Hofbräu-Haus, a bar as long and polished as life. A straight and narrow road to heaven.

Joe's pal held up two fingers and sung out, "*Zwei dunkels*, Fritz," to the waiter, a pleasant little German gnome, shorter than the boys, active as the yeast in beer.

Came the beer. Joe saw upstanding Würzburger for the first time, and was completely conquered. There was no such drink in the world as that — the foam was like whipped cream, you could eat it with a spoon.

— Bob Brown, 1934

CHAPTER 2

SENSORY EVALUATION

Why taste beer? Wouldn't the world be a better place if we could simply drink, enjoy, and relax? Of course there are times when an uncritical approach is just the ticket. But there are many other situations in which a more focused and structured approach is called for.

BREWERS LARGE AND SMALL must constantly evaluate their beers for consistency, freedom from flaws, and suitability to their slice of the market. Even for small brewers, implementing a structured sensory evaluation program can pay back big-time in the marketplace. Other members of the beer trade also need to tell good from bad, style from style, police their own operations, and try to determine which beers will offer the most irresistible thrills to their customers. And even for casual tasters, taking the time to develop proper tasting technique and vocabulary may elicit greater insight, meaning, and pleasure from every beer.

Understanding Our Senses

Sensation starts with stimulation and ends with perception. At the interface where our senses meet the outside world, sensory nerves fire in specific ways when stimulated by a host of different chemicals, sending signals on a wild ride through several processing stations and into some ancient and often very emotional parts of the brain before moving upstairs into our cognitive brain. Starting as simple coded signals and running through several processing steps, eventually the signals start to express themselves as thoughts, memories, and finally, language.

Taste and smell or, in technical terms, gustation and olfaction, form our chemical senses, aided by certain mouthfeel sensations. It's an exquisitely tuned system honed by hundreds of millions of years of evolution and undoubtedly predating "higher" senses such as hearing and vision. Just about every creature on the planet has some capability in this area. For a long

time, scientists had a prejudice against these life-sustaining senses, thinking them primitive and not worthy of study. The last few decades have revealed just how wrong they were.

Our senses help us navigate through the sublime and dangerous world in which we live. The chemical senses give us information about food and drink: nutritional content, edibility/toxicity, ripeness, and more. In addition, olfaction is important as a communication tool, as anyone who has ever seen a dog marking a tree can figure out. It has recently been discovered that the sense of taste may have another hidden role as a first line of attack against pathogens. Taste cells can be found all through the gut and nasal cavity as well as in several organs and even in the bones. It appears that certain bitter proteins on the surface of bacteria can stimulate these taste cells to release compounds that directly or indirectly begin an assault on the invaders, acting much more quickly than the immune system can.

Because the chemical senses are extremely ancient, they are processed in ways that are quite different from sight and sound and can often seem alien and illogical to us. Taste signals, for example, go first to the brain stem, the most primitive part of the brain responsible for controlling our heartbeat and respiration. It's the brain stem that makes the qualitative decision on whether this is something we like — or don't. Olfactory signals find their way to the amygdala and hippocampus, other ancient parts of the brain involved with emotion and memory. While it seems weird to us, it makes perfect sense. Sometimes aromas represent threats or opportunities that must be acted upon with force and speed. Emotions create direct action, often beyond the control of our thinking brain. A monkey in the forest smells ripe fruit; he has no need for the name of the species. All he knows is to move to that spot to repeat the feast he enjoyed last season.

It is frustrating for us, especially as we are trying to come to grips with being good tasters. We want our brains to be logical; they are not. We want to turn aromas into vocabulary words, but our brains are not structured to make that easy. In many ways, coming to grips with the strangeness of our own self is at the core of the process of mastering tasting. We are so accustomed to linguistic and visual learning that we struggle when we have to do things a different way.

I promise you, however, that it is possible to train these unseen corners of yourself and put their unique talents to use for our purposes. But you will have to learn to lay back, relax, and let them do their thing, and listen closely when they speak.

SMELL, TASTE, AND MOUTHFEEL are the main senses we use to interact with beer, but other senses also have input into the tasting experience. If you learn to make good use of them, they will tell you just about everything you want to know about a beer. While they are separate senses, our brain puts them together for us in ways that are generally useful, but this can also make it more difficult for us to really separate the senses. We all have some idea about what "flavor" is, but in reality it's not a sense at all, but an impression created by a combination of sensory inputs from the three chemical senses, possibly influenced by other senses and even cognitive processes like brand image.

Hence, one has to learn to be attuned to the senses separately when necessary and be precise in the use of language. We often say something smells sweet, but this is simply not possible; sweetness is purely a tongue taste. The reality is that for things like caramel, chocolate, and vanilla, our everyday associations are so skewed to sweetness that we can't help but describe them in those terms. So part of training yourself as a taster is "untraining" your brain from so helpfully synthesizing all of these things, and then learning to peel apart the layers.

The Sense of Taste

Like the rest of our chemical senses, taste evolved to give us important clues about good and bad things in our environment and guide us toward nutritionally desirable foods and away from potential poisons. It is so important to our survival that it is wired into the brain via three separate paths, so if one becomes damaged there are still two backups for the job — the same amount of redundancy built into spacecrafts.

If you look at your tongue, you will see that it is covered in small bumps. These are not taste buds but papillae, and embedded in particular groups of them are the buds themselves. Each of us has between two thousand and eight thousand taste buds on our tongue, with lesser quantities elsewhere in the mouth, as well as in other places in the body, where they play very different roles. Each taste bud is a cluster of sensory cells around a central pore that allows liquid to enter and contact the cells. Each sensory cell is sensitive to a particular set of chemicals. There are about 40 different receptor types currently identified in humans, and more than half of those are specific for bitterness. However, more seem to be identified all the time.

The Old Tongue Map
An erroneous product of nineteenth-century quackery, it has proven difficult to purge from the textbooks.

A New Tongue Map
While there are three different taste-sensitive regions on the tongue, the front half of the tongue is equally sensitive to all tastes. Bitterness is perceived a little more intensely in the circumvallate papillae across the back, and the foliate papillae on the sides are slightly more sensitive to sourness.

umami   salty   bitter
sour   sweet

The tongue map, as we all learned in grade school, is supposed to show the areas of sensitivity to various flavors: sweet up front, sour along the sides, and so on. It's a lie, having very little to do with physiological reality. The tongue map began with phrenology, the pseudoscience of translating the bumps and valleys of the skull into moral proclivities, and was later perpetuated by some enthusiastic charting of dubious data. The tongue map has wedged itself into our common knowledge base and has proven very difficult to dislodge.

While there is some slight localization of flavor on the tongue, most of the tongue is sensitive to all six flavors (see illustration, right). The tongue is covered with filiform papillae, the smallest bumps you can see and feel. These contain no taste buds and are purely mechanical. There are different groups of papillae containing taste buds in specific areas of the tongue. The larger bumps interspersed among the filiform papillae on the front two-thirds of the tongue are the fungiform (mushroom-shaped) papillae, and these are a little more densely packed at the margins. Each has a number of separate taste buds nestled into its sides, not its top. With only slight variations, these taste buds are equally sensitive to sweet, bitter,

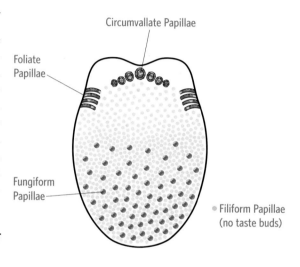

Circumvallate Papillae

Foliate Papillae

Fungiform Papillae

Filiform Papillae (no taste buds)

sour, salty, and umami, as well as the newly discovered tastes such as fat.

Across the back of the tongue is a row of large circumvallate papillae; along the sides, toward the back of the tongue, are the foliate papillae. The circumvallate papillae seem to be especially sensitive to bitterness, sweetness, and fat, which is why swallowing is regarded as part of the beer-tasting process; the cells in the foliate are somewhat more sensitive to fat and especially to sourness, which is why a sip of lemon juice (or a sour lambic) triggers a sharp localized sensation to the sides of the back of the tongue. It has also been discovered that acidity at high levels can trigger a painful mouthfeel sensation.

One cellular detail is especially important for tasters: acid and salt trigger relatively simple mechanisms that respond instantly. Sweetness, bitterness, and all others operate through a two-step process incorporating something called a G protein-coupled receptor. The upshot is that these taste responses are a little slower to register than salt and sour. Being aware of this helps us understand the way a sip of beer unfolds over time.

Sweet Beer
Beer styles such as doppelbock, milk stout, and Scotch ale often have considerable residual sweetness.

The Basic Tastes

SWEET

This familiar sensation evolved to alert us to food items with a lot of nutritive value in an environment where they used to be fairly sparse. Even premature babies automatically respond to sweet tastes with suckling. Now that sweet foods and drinks are within an arm's reach, this sensation serves us rather poorly. Some deep, dark corner of our brains still thinks that sweet foods are good for us, so we overconsume.

There is nearly always some sweetness in beer, although it only becomes a major player in a few rich styles such as Scotch ale, doppelbock, and milk stout, in which there is a significant amount of residual sugar. Alcohol, at high levels, can also taste a bit sweet. Sweetness is important in most beers as a balancing element, although it may be upstaged by hop bitterness, roasted malt, or acidity.

SOUR

These sensors detect hydrogen ions, as all pH meters do. Acidity (or lack thereof) is a pretty reliable indicator of ripeness in fruit and is also a marker for spoiled food, so there may have been some evolutionary utility along those lines.

The cellular mechanism is fairly simple, which is one reason for the lightning-quick reaction we have to acidic foods and drinks. Beer is a moderately acidic drink, normally with a pH of 4.0 to 4.5, but with the exception of the sour Belgian beers (at pH 3.4 to 3.9), acidity plays a supporting rather than a starring role. One place to really pay attention to acidity is in fruit beers, where it has a great deal to do with the brightness of fruit character.

This non-traditional cherry lambic has only a hint of bitterness and lots of sweet and sour flavors, unlike most beers.

SALTY

These taste buds respond to sodium ions and also to some extent to potassium. These salts are vital to many cellular processes and must be obtained from the environment. In beer, salt does not commonly play a role, but when it is present — either from mineral-rich water or added intentionally — it makes flavors richer and bigger.

BITTER

From the earliest days of beer, bitter herbs have been used to balance sweet malt, add to its refreshing qualities, and lend a substantial weight to the drink. Historically, the fondness for bitterness in beer comes and goes in waves, and boy, are we ever riding a crest right now.

Bitter tastes usually play only minor roles in cuisine, so beer really stands apart from other foods and drinks. Bitterness is an acquired taste, and we can see that as we watch our friends journeying into craft beer. There is a good reason for their hesitance, though. Bitterness is a signal to be on the lookout for something poisonous.

The bitter taste in nature. The first plants to evolve were probably easy prey. As they came under attack, they evolved defense mechanisms, including thorns, thick husks, and toxic substances. It must have felt like a great victory, but it was short-lived, as animals quickly developed the ability to recognize poisons such as strychnine, cyanide, and alkaloids. To be effective, these perceptions needed to be coupled with a call to action: one that was powerful, instantaneous, and aversive. The sense of bitterness was born.

And so the dance went on, and animals evolved the ability to recognize a huge range of bitter chemicals. The plants evolved to discover that a convincing decoy was as good as the real deal and began to produce perfectly harmless chemicals, such as the ones found in hops, that were just as effective at triggering the bitter-aversion mechanism in animals, keeping most plant eaters away.

Bitterness genes. The bitterness receptor genes — called TAS2R — are highest in plant-eating animals and much lower or absent in carnivores. At present, 25 bitterness receptor genes have been identified in humans. The more genes, the more potentially toxic chemicals can be detected, although the receptors may have other purposes. Bitterness receptors have been found in the entire length of the human gut, and in other nonobvious places such as the lungs and the nose. It is known that some of these send signals to the brain in a way that can affect behavior, at least in rats, and taste receptors in the gut and pancreas are involved with insulin release in response to blood sugar. Bitter receptors in the nose react to chemical markers of some pathogenic bacteria.

Because we have a lot of different receptors, we can perceive differences in certain types of bitter tastes. The clean, soft bitterness of hops suits beer perfectly, at least to our modern tastes. The sensations offered by gentian and wormwood are piercing and can be unpleasantly dry. The mellow bitterness of hops, coupled with their preservative power, may be an important reason they so completely dominate the world of beer.

Beer's bitterness is not all about the hops, though. Dark malts are plenty bitter. The Maillard reaction — the source of most color and flavor in beer — produces chemicals that lend their characteristic malty-to-roasty aromas but also converts phenolic acids into chemicals called lactones that can be strongly bitter in darker malts, just as they are in coffee.

Hop Cone
For more than a thousand years, hops have provided a bitter counterpoint to beer's malty backbone.

It's a slow bite. Bitterness can take a fair amount of time to fully register on our tongues. If you taste a moderately bitter beer of, say, 40 IBU against the same beer spiked to 120 IBU, the first 10 seconds will feel exactly the same. It takes a while for the bitterness to grow on your tongue, and it will build and build for nearly a minute. You really almost have to watch the clock as you try this, and force yourself to pay attention for far longer than you are probably accustomed. I recently sat in a room full of professionals going through this exercise without an up-front explanation, and watched close to half the room fail at telling them apart. It's harder than you think.

A specific level of bitterness is hard to pinpoint, even by trained tasters. Our accuracy may be no better than about 20 percent, so a 40 IBU and a 50 IBU taste pretty similar.

So watch how beer's bitterness provides a bit of a roller-coaster experience as it clack-clack-clacks its way up to the maximum, then lingers a moment and begins the long glide down. All that time, other beer flavors are weaving in and out: acidity up front, then sweetness and any astringency interacting with the bitterness, pleasantly or not. You have probably noticed that bitterness really blasts your palate, so after a massively hoppy beer or two it may take a while for your palate to recover. If you're staging a tasting or dinner, keep this in mind.

It's also important to separate hop aroma from the bitterness on your tongue. They are physiologically different things, but aroma and taste do not live in entirely separate silos in our brains, so it takes some effort to pull them apart.

Also remember that bitterness is always in context with the rest of a beer, so if you compare two equally hopped beers, the maltier one may seem less bitter than the other. Brewers know this when seeking balance in their recipes. We tasters should be aware of this as well, and always be wary of relying on numbers to tell us how we should feel about any given beer. Be aware that IBU levels on beer labels are often based on a brewery's calculations rather than an actual chemical analysis, and bitterness begins to decline even before the beer is packaged.

Bitterness in beer. This comes from five hop chemicals known as alpha acids, which are extracted and chemically transformed, or isomerized, by the heat of boiling. All hops produce a similar bitter sensation, albeit in varying degrees. Those with a higher proportion of one alpha acid, cohumulone, are reputed to have a coarser bitterness, but this is hotly debated. When offered to the market, the bittering power of hops is stated in a simple percentage of alpha acids, with values ranging from about 2 to 20 percent.

In theory, hops used purely for bittering should all taste about the same after their unique oil profiles are blown away by the hour of vigorous boiling typical of a brew. Brewers have a hunch that's not the case, and they typically choose bittering hops that complement — or at least don't contradict — the character of their aroma hops.

Brewers engaged in the bitterness arms race are starting to hit real limits. The solubility of hops decreases as the concentration increases, making it difficult to reach superhigh levels, especially in light of the high price of hops these days. Common wisdom in the industry once held that 100 BUs was pretty much the max, but some recent beer analyses have come in well beyond that. However, there is some debate about the linearity of the common assays used and what they are actually detecting way up at the high end of the scale. There is currently a beer on the market that has been measured at 658 IBU, although there are questions about the chemical and sensory meaningfulness of this. Above a certain level, more hop bitterness simply might not be detectable. No matter the chemistry, that level is clearly in the realm of the silly.

UMAMI (GLUTAMATE)

Although this flavor has been acknowledged for over a thousand years, it wasn't until the year 2000 that a genetic basis for the receptor was discovered, establishing it as a primary taste detected by the tongue. The Japanese *umami* translates as "deliciousness" in English, and this word sums up a savory, meaty quality found in many foods and occasionally in beer. The sensations originate with a group of amino acids, the subunits from which proteins are formed. Inosinates, guanylates, and glutamates are mainly responsible and are derived from many different types of food. Umami is found in aged meat, oily fish, mushrooms, fermented foods (especially soy products), aged cheese (as much as 10 percent by weight in Parmesan), ripe tomatoes, seaweed, and many other foods.

Umami starts to become noticeable in beer only after prolonged aging. First, a rich meatiness may show itself, and with enough time, flavor notes reminiscent of soy sauce might show up. It's not well studied at this point, but umami is an important player in beer and food pairing.

KOKUMI

A sister to umami, kokumi is another taste that indicates the presence of protein-rich material. Rather than being detectable as its own flavor, kokumi enhances sweet, salty, and umami flavors and for this reason has been much studied as a food additive. It also may be perceived as enhancing mouthfeel "thickness." It's not clear what the implications are, but in a 2015 Japanese study, peptides that can be sensed by the calcium-channel receptors on our tongues were identified in beer but not in sake or wine. Glutathione, present in beer as a product of yeast breakdown, is strongly kokumi.

FAT

This is the most recently discovered member of the taste family, having been added only with the discovery of its receptor in 2005. Like sugar, this receptor seeks out nutritionally loaded foods and can wreak havoc in the modern French fry–accessible world. It's not clear if this receptor plays any role at all in beer tasting, as beer is a fat-free product.

AND MORE . . .

Recent discoveries suggest that there could be quite a few more identifiable taste receptors. It appears that we may have the ability to detect calcium, some metals, carbonation (via an enzyme and a sour receptor), water, and perhaps even alcohol. And although we don't perceive the tastes directly, we may be able to taste carbohydrates such as starch and dextrins, and even be able to discriminate between them in some hidden way.

A HIGHLY SIMPLIFIED MAP OF THE BRAIN'S TASTING SYSTEM

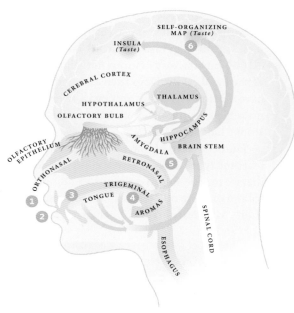

1 Orthonasal olfaction. Odors travel into our nose and trigger responses from sensory cells embedded in the upper part of the nose.

2 Taste. Sensors on the tongue and elsewhere relay signals about basic tastes through the brain stem and on to higher centers.

3 Mouthfeel. Touch and pain sensors in the mouth give added information about the texture and character of food and drinks.

4 Glycoside release. Enzymes from saliva and resident microbes split these specialized molecules, releasing aroma in the mouth.

5 Retronasal olfaction. An outward breath through the nose gives another chance to perceive aroma.

6 Flavor. Our brains put it all together for us in a synthesized sense called "flavor."

Aroma and Olfaction

Our olfactory system senses a wide range of airborne molecules. It's a vastly more complex system than taste. Humans have around 20 million olfactory neurons in the upper part of the nasal cavity. Dogs such as bloodhounds have 10 times as many and bears even more, making us relative olfactory lightweights in the animal kingdom.

Humans have about a thousand different receptor types. Recent research has suggested that we may be able to discriminate among one trillion or more different aromas, although our ability to identify or describe them is vastly less proficient. With a limited set of receptor types, combinations of signals create the wide range of perceivable aromas. Each odorant stimulates a particular set of neurons, each of those at a different intensity, making for a wide variety of possible aromas. Rather than the classic "lock-and-key" model, it appears that scent molecules nestle into dishlike pockets with sensitive proteins on their surface. This structure means a number of different chemicals can affect each pocket in different ways and also that the same molecule could also interact with a number

---

The Intoxicating Aroma of Beer
Without its vast array of aromas, beer would be a lifeless and monotonous drink.

of different pockets. This creates a large set of data that is mapped to our olfactory cortex; our brain interprets the patterns and sends the results along as distinct, specific aromas.

In addition to purely chemical sensitivities, it appears that we may also be able to discriminate between chemicals that are differentiated by isotopes of the elements within them, suggesting that some olfactory cells are able to "read" the energy levels at which the molecules vibrate.

Importantly, the sense of smell is wired into our brains differently from other senses. Rather than proceeding right away to the thalamus, which is a gatekeeper to higher centers of cognition, olfactory signals are routed to some very old and unconscious parts of the brain: the hypothalamus, seat of appetite, anger, and fear; the hippocampus, regulator of memories; and the amygdala, an important center for emotion.

WE PERCEIVE AROMAS in two different ways. The first is what you might expect: smells coming in through our noses when we sniff. This is called orthonasal olfaction. While still containing strong emotional and memory components, it also has an analytical side that allows us to make sense of our aromatic environment. Second is a type of olfaction known as retronasal. This involves aromas coming up through our nose from the back of our mouth and throat. It is different for several reasons. First, the food or drink has been chewed up and warmed, releasing a good deal of aroma. While in the mouth, it is subjected to the actions of salivary enzymes and to those oozing out of the complex mix of bacteria also residing there. These enzymes break down many chemicals, but the group of interest here are glycosides, complex molecules that consist of sugar molecules bound to other chemicals, in this case aromatic ones. When the glycosides are broken down, they release their aromatic partners and liberate a good deal of aroma into the mouth. This is especially important with hop aroma. It is known that much of hop aroma added to the beer is lost during fermentation as copious amounts of CO_2 gas carry it away. Glycosides stay intact until they hit our mouths, where they release a pleasant blast of flavor.

Finally, in retronasal tasting, our brains combine aroma with taste and mouthfeel sensations, combining them into a perception of flavor rather than simple aroma. This flavor also seems to be processed in such a way as to trigger impressions of familiarity, preference, and dislike, and may also be connected with satiation, the sense of having had enough to eat.

I would not be bothering you with all this neuroanatomy if it weren't genuinely practical beer-tasting information. Aromas can elicit powerful psychological responses in the form of memories and emotions, but we struggle with vocabulary. Having that name literally on the tip of one's tongue is a common and frustrating experience. We're all pretty bad at it at first, but with practice you can coax up an old memory from a particular aroma and often linger long enough to make sense of it. Is it Grandma's house? The kitchen, food? What's in the backyard? Are those flowers? Roses? And then, *bam!* Like a bolt, it comes to you. The best approach is always to just blurt out whatever weird thought or descriptor pops into your mind. It's almost never wrong, so don't edit or second-guess those impressions. This kind of mind expansion also makes for very entertaining personal growth, by the way.

FROM A BREWER'S POINT OF VIEW, these charged psychological experiences offer great leverage for art. If you can formulate a beer that will regularly conjure up happy childhood memories of, say, oatmeal cookies, you can create powerful affinities, even if your audience is not aware of the connection. I tell my recipe formulation students, "As an artist, it's your job to mess with people's heads." It's great to have this kind of tool in your pocket.

Understanding Ourselves

In the strange world of sensory experience, two plus two rarely equals four. Although we are exquisitely sensitive and better than machines for many tasks, we are far from perfect in some very interesting ways.

First, we all vary in our sensitivities to different chemicals. A beer that may seem sickeningly buttery to one taster may be comfortably caramelly to another. Phenol in certain forms is vile in beer, adding an electrical-fire stench, yet up to 20 percent of people may be totally blind to it. If you're a brewer, this should be a very scary thought to you. Most good tasters I know try to get a grip on this either by actually calibrating their palates using a series of different concentrations of specific aroma chemicals or simply by paying attention when doing critical tasting and comparing their own reactions to those of their peers. If you're always the one person at the table who can't pick up a certain aroma, there's a good chance you have a lower sensitivity to it than others.

Each of us has dramatically different sensitivities to every taste and aroma and may assign wildly differing levels of pleasure or distaste to the sensations. A beer that seems harmonious, pleasant, and balanced to one person might taste harsh and unpalatable to another. Our whole life's tasting experiences persist strongly in our memory, modulating every taste and sip. Culturally, biographically, and genetically, each of us is absolutely unique. We all inhabit utterly different worlds when it comes to our senses.

Just as our personal histories affect our responses to certain aromas, so do our cultural affinities. Some sensations are universally good or bad: the love of sweetness, the repulsion to rotting meat, and the sensitivity to musty smells, all of which are among the most powerful odorants known. But many sensations, such as the bitterness discussed earlier, are acquired tastes that affect us according to our genes and how we've been brought up, as well as how open-minded we are about seeking their pleasures.

In general, women are somewhat more sensitive tasters than men and also do better with flavor vocabulary. As we age, we become less sensitive, but fortunately this can be more than compensated through training and experience, so there is hope for those of us among the unyoung.

LET'S START at the simplest place we can — the intensity of various tastes on the tongue. There are just a few of them: sweet, sour, salty, bitter, umami, and a handful of others. One might think that if we're going to find any common ground, it should be here, right?

Well, yes and no. There are shared experiences — just look at the harmonious way cuisines develop and the tremendous attachment people have to them. On the surface, we seem to be pretty similar, but when you start digging, the differences between us can be vast.

We are all differently sensitive to tastes on the tongue, and we are particularly divergent when it comes to bitterness. As a dark and brooding sensation is meant as a warning against ingesting potentially toxic materials (think strychnine, cyanide, alkaloids), bitterness is an acquired taste because we are genetically programmed to be suspicious of it.

About 20 percent of people — somewhat skewed to the female side — are exquisitely sensitive to bitterness. It's one characteristic of a group labeled as "supertasters," and as you can imagine, this sensitivity plays a huge role in our preferences at the table. At the other end of the scale, 40 percent of us are labeled "nontasters," who are much less sensitive to all tastes, especially bitterness. The remaining 40 percent of us fall into the middle section. These differences are driven by two copies of a particular bitter receptor, which each comes in sensitive and insensitive versions. Two copies of the sensitive one and you're a supertaster; none and you're a nontaster, with the rest in between.

The wine world has spent years humiliating anyone who didn't just love big, inky, tannic wines. As a result, supertasters often had to conceal their preference for sweeter, less tannic wines. After some soul-searching, there is now some interest in accommodating those more sensitive tasters. Some wine clubs are even having people fill out questionnaires to help identify their "vinotype." Perhaps we may get to a point when we can talk about "zythotypes" with beer drinkers.

We have the same sensitivity differences with aromas. Perhaps 10 percent of the population is blind to one or more beer off-flavors such as diacetyl or DMS, while others may be highly sensitive. I'm personally sensitive to musty/earthy aromas; others I know are supersensitive to metallic, diacetyl, and other aromas. Formal training helps lower these

SENSORY ENHANCEMENT PRACTICES

- **Take a walk** or drive around with your windows open, and really pay attention to how smells change from location to location. I think about half of tasting skill is just being able to concentrate. I especially like Chicago around lunchtime.

- **Next time you order a beer,** make a few notes on your napkin about aroma, flavor, texture, and aftertaste. Real beer geeks carry around a notebook, like birders do. It isn't too important that you save the notes; it is the act of recording them that's important.

- **Go to a wine tasting.** Sometimes getting away from our comfort zone jolts us into a state of higher awareness.

- **Judge homebrew!** Club competitions are all over the place, and they're always looking for help. Being forced to go through a few flights of beer in a structured way in the presence of other, more experienced tasters is by far the best way to improve your tasting skills, and you'll make new friends as well.

thresholds, bringing sensitivity up to the physiological max. Taste panel QC programs train and calibrate their tasters; strong or weak responses to specific stimuli are accounted for in the panelists' scoring. One reason I so strongly recommend beer judging as a training tool is that competition judges get a sense of their own sensitivities and blindnesses in comparison to others at the table. If your response generally differs time after time, then you learn to take that into account in the way you judge.

ENORMOUS CULTURAL DIFFERENCES also exist in taste. Our perceptual world is shaped by the continued accumulation of tastes, textures, aromas, and sensory experiences, making us walking libraries of those past sensations. These are not passive memories but active mediators shaping our experiences in ways we are just beginning to understand. As with language, our sensory experiences transform our brains, affecting perception. The differences from culture to culture can be pretty dramatic.

What's more, your adult self is very different from the juvenile you — you can probably remember fights over broccoli or brussels sprouts as a child, their mild bitterness amplified through the lens of an immature perceptual system. Children are known to be several times more sensitive to bitterness than adults. And with diminished chemical senses, older people might add two or three times the amount of salt to a bowl of tomato soup as middle-aged ones.

Our bodies and brains also change throughout the daily cycle. Biorhythms may seem like a crock of new age pseudoscience, but there is real science behind the notion. Our palates are most attuned in the morning, which is why brewery taste panels are usually conducted

then. And what kind of mood are you in? Are you hungry? Thirsty? Those change your perceptual bubble as well.

Not surprisingly, your experience level also changes the way you perceive things. I've observed that newer beer enthusiasts tend to focus on a few key factors — hoppiness or roastiness, for example — and then are more likely to seek out that particular factor. Perhaps this explains some of the scores on the popular beer rating sites that favor intensity rather than balance or complexity. With experience, beer lovers expand their vocabulary and interests.

WITH A LITTLE EFFORT, tasters learn to evaluate the style appropriateness of a given beer. Highly experienced tasters can do two very different things simultaneously: deconstruct the beer into its component tastes, aromas, and even ingredients, and develop an opinion about the beer as an integrated whole. You generally don't see highly experienced beer tasters chasing crazy bitterness. In my experience, a lot of great brewers relish nothing more exotic than a well-brewed Pilsner or pale ale.

If you're feeling much less sure about yourself after reading all of this, good. Awareness of our own tasting abilities and preferences and sensitivity to the needs of those around us are signs of a mature and capable taster.

Multisensory Perception

Outside our individual variabilities, more weirdness may be found in other phenomena that affect the way flavors and aromas are perceived. While we may think we know a particular aroma or flavor, in reality it may change according to its concentration or context, present itself differently, and affect the flavors of other things in the mix.

Some chemicals change character as their quantity increases; that is, if you add more and more of something, you don't just get a stronger version of the same thing; it transforms into the smell of something else. One chemical, o-amino-acetophenone, smells like malt in parts-per-billion concentrations, like tacos in parts per million, and enough like Concord grapes in parts per thousand that it actually is used in grape soda. This is an extreme example, to be sure, but consider a fruity ester, ethyl acetate. At low levels, it contributes a pleasant fruitiness to ales. However, when a certain threshold is reached, it presents itself as a strong solvency smell, just like nail polish, of which it's one component.

Another example is the "matrix effect," which involves interactions between flavors that either change each other or give rise to new sensations altogether. Coffee is usually cited as the classic example. Despite the fact that there are over a thousand identified flavor chemicals, none of them taste exactly like coffee, and no one really knows what is responsible for "coffeeness." This is a common phenomenon in the Maillard reaction, or caramelization, important in cooked meat and in beer, where kilned malts contribute so much flavor and aroma.

Matrix effects may change the way single chemicals are perceived as well. In pale beer, DMS (a sulfur compound that can cause off-flavors) comes across as creamed corn. In darker beers, however, DMS presents as more of a tomato juice aroma — very useful to know if you're judging dark beers.

"Masking" is a phenomenon in which the presence of one chemical hides the flavor of another. In beer, carbonation and acidity mask hops, and high levels of ethanol can mask some characteristics of oxidation. Vanilla is a well-known masking substance, having the ability to round the rough flavor edges off just about anything.

"Potentiation" is just the opposite. It occurs when the presence of one chemical enhances or magnifies another. The effects of salt and pepper on food are the most familiar examples; umami is another. Beer itself can enhance other flavors, which is why it can be great for cooking and as a food companion.

Mouthfeel

"Mouthfeel" is a catchall term referring to sensations in our mouths that are not taste or aroma. Beer impacts the nerves in our mouth with a number of textures that add depth, please the palate, and aid in its ability to harmonize with food. These are sometimes called trigeminal sensations, after the nerve that sends signals about heat, cold, texture, and certain chemical sensations such as mint, chile, and astringency in the mouth. This is amazing evidence that our sensory systems use all kinds of tricks to squeeze out the most information possible from every little sip.

Beer presents a range of mouthfeel sensations found in no other beverage. Many are quite pleasant — think about the tingle of carbonation or beer's slightly weighty body. Others, such as creaminess, may be appropriate or not depending on the beer style. Some can be pretty negative. The dryness of astringency is rarely welcome except in very small doses, where it can crisp up the finish and add to beer's refreshing quality. While mouthfeel sensations abound in beer, one must search them out to experience beer in every glorious dimension.

L ET'S START WITH BODY, that sense of weight on the tongue or sense of density that every beer has in one degree or another. Many people assume that beer's body comes from unfermented sugars or starches, and these do contribute a sense of sweet richness in styles such as doppelbocks or Scotch ales that

---

Foam, Fabulous Foam
Certain proteins in barley provide structure for beer's lingering foam.

contain a lot of unfermented carbohydrates. However, beer's body comes from a network of proteins contributed by its main ingredient, malt. Dispersed in liquids under the right conditions, proteins intertwine to create a state of matter known as a colloid. By forming a sort of 3-D fishnet, these proteins entrap water and increase viscosity. Every schoolkid is intimately familiar with colloids in the form of gelatin dessert, its wiggly, wobbly blobs of sweetly colorful water miraculously held together by a pinch of protein. Beer is the exact same type of colloid, albeit much less dense.

This colloidial structure turns out to be responsible for the persistence of the beer foam lingering atop our pints. The same web of proteins stretches out to form the skins of the bubbles, trapping CO_2 gas.

C REAMINESS IS CLOSELY related in feeling to beer's body and is sometimes described as "oily." This common and important character of wheat beers and those using oats or rye is the familiar slippery texture of oatmeal. It comes from complex, gummy carbohydrates called glucans and pentosans that are present in grain. As they can make sparging difficult and reduce yield, maltsters take care to reduce them to low levels, but they can be plentiful in unmalted grains and also in malted versions of rye, oats, and wheat. The next time you enjoy a hefeweizen, oatmeal stout, rye IPA, or Belgian-style witbier, look for this creamy quality. If it's not there, something's wrong.

On the opposite side of the spectrum, you'll find the sharpness of tannins or the bite of astringency. In most beers they are minimal, but when present they can become obtrusive. The sources and causes vary. Most plant material, whether barley husks, hop cones, grapes, or wood, contains substances called polyphenols, which serve various functions in plant cells. One role is to taste nasty to help make the plant unappetizing to herbivorous animals. Depending on the specific varieties and brewing conditions, astringent polyphenols can find their way into beer and in large doses can be quite unpleasant.

ASTRINGENCY comes late in the taste of a beer, after the sweetness of the malt has diminished, sometimes changing a clean bitterness into mouth-puckering raspiness, leaving you with a desire to scrape the offending tannin off your tongue with the nearest available sharp object.

TANNINS are present in grains, concentrated in the husks and outer layers of the malt kernels. The levels vary by variety and growing conditions: moderate climates seem to produce the least; more polyphenol is present in either hot- or cold-climate barley, which are frequently six-row varieties. These have slimmer kernels contributing more husks relative to the weight of the whole grain. Brewers know to choose their malt carefully.

Polyphenol extraction in brewing is very sensitive to pH, increasing dramatically as the water becomes more alkaline, so controlling water chemistry is crucial for making smooth beers without harsh aftertastes. Hops also contain tannic material in their leafy bits. Hoppy beers can be harsh and unpleasant if brewed with water containing too much alkaline mineral.

Adjuncts are a mixed bag. Corn contains very little tannin, but rice has a noticeable amount. Beers such as Budweiser that incorporate rice as an adjunct are often thought of as having an especially crisp bite — one of the defining characteristics of that brand. Since they make their products entirely from rice,

sake brewers are very sensitive to the smack of tannic astringency. The main measure of sake quality is how much of the outer part of the rice kernel has been milled away. The most expensive sakes use pinhead-sized pieces from the very center of the rice grain, as it has the least amount of tannin, making these luxurious drinks exceptionally smooth as well as expensive.

Fruits, herbs, and spices also contain some tannin, but more often than not its effect is overshadowed by the more intense qualities of those ingredients, such as acidity or spicy aromas. Wood — especially the oak most commonly used for barrels — contains plentiful tannic material, which is used in winemaking to add weight to red wine, creating an important element of balance and helping it pair well with rich, meaty foods. Bourbon-barreled beers are often so strongly flavored that the tannic finish is obscured, but wild and sour beers such as lambics and Flanders red ales typically display a soft oaky-tannic finish.

CARBONATION has to be included in any discussion of mouthfeel. Although simple in nature — just CO_2 gas dissolved in liquid — it has a major effect on the character of beer. Its evolving bubbles tickle our palates, and it is likely that carbonation is a tongue taste just like sweet or bitter. The physical motion of the bubbles brings turbulence into our mouths, scrubbing away fat and other rich tastes in food.

Brewers fine-tune carbonation as appropriate for the style and particular beer. Traditional British cask ale carbonation tends to be pretty low, adding just a prickle of brightness and lifting malt and hop aromas out of the glass. Low carbonation is a very important characteristic in this style, allowing the full flavors to show through. Ale carbonation tends to be higher outside Britain. Because it is served cold, lager needs to be a step higher yet. In general, the beers of Belgium, especially the abbey types, tend to be highly carbonated, boosting aroma and a sense of dry drinkability beloved by drinkers there. The gueuze form of lambic is champagne-fizzy, while traditional straight lambic may be just about dead flat. German-style wheat beers also get a heavy charge of carbonation, which seems to balance the milkshake creaminess that is their other essential mouthfeel quality.

With the richness of malt or the blast of hops found in modern beers, mouthfeel may never be the first thing anybody thinks about when sipping their favorite brews. However, it pays to keep it in mind when tasting critically or just for fun. Its subtle charms add a lot of depth to our favorite beverage, and without it we would be faced with something far simpler, less balanced, and much less compelling. And how would your mouth feel about that?

Visual and Multimodal Perception

Beer really is quite beautiful. Humankind has been singing the praises of its deep, clear color and white, creamy foam for thousands of years, and we get no less pleasure from it today. From the glass on the table to the smells of the beer frothing up, to the sights and sounds of the barroom and beyond, our world usually feels solid and reliable enough.

It is an illusion, however — nothing more than a projection created by our highly fallible perceptions. Ancient wisdom makes a point of it; modern science increasingly verifies this unsettling truth. While seeing is believing, it may not always tell us the truth.

Of all of our senses, we rely most confidently on vision. After all, we drive cars, take aim at our prey, choose a mate, and take on many other tasks with a pretty high degree of visual confidence. Our eyes provide a spectacularly detailed view of the world, but they are not immune to being tricked, as any simple optical illusion demonstrates. When it comes to food and drink, our reliance on vision is a huge problem, because it can force (or lead?) us to taste and smell what we see, whether it's actually there or not.

All our senses are deeply intertwined, working in parallel to combine multiple threads of information into a single picture. If we see dark colors in a beer, for example, we almost always find dark flavors, even if they're not there. This can happen even if we make a conscious effort to avoid it; isolating a single sensory input is not easy. Furthermore, the visual system is wired to higher centers of consciousness in ways that the chemical senses are not, giving it the power to be a bit of a bully. However compelling they may be, visual clues tell you nothing about beer's thousand-plus aromas, tastes, and mouthfeel sensations. Focusing on aroma and taste becomes easier as you develop your vocabulary and technique, but it takes some practice.

Research has shown that when wine judges are presented with white wine tinted with red pigments, their responses are not the expected peach and citrus, but bramble and berry. This is why it is not unheard of for wines and occasionally beer to be judged in black glassware. While you're laughing at the silly wine people, don't forget we're just the same. Before there was craft beer, dark or bock beer in the United States was usually made by squirting a little caramel color into a pale lager, and consumers found them satisfying enough back in the day. I know I did.

FOR ANY PARTICULAR SHADE of beer, there are limitless ways to create it. Brewers can choose from dozens of malts, from ghost-pale to nearly carbonized. Not only does each shade of malt have a different set of flavors, but malts of the same color can have dramatically different flavors depending on the specifics of its kilning. With any style of beer, there are many different ingredient routes to get to the same color.

Experienced tasters try not to be too distracted by what they see. Beer competition score sheets rarely assign more than 10 percent of available points to appearance, but anyone who has ever judged a flight of beers knows the powerful seduction of which our eyes are capable. A beer that is too light or dark for its style will distort the experience. This trick is used in reverse with black IPAs, which have a deep chestnut color but if done right have very little roastiness — our brains manufacture it for us anyway. Have someone pour one blind for you and see for yourself.

We Drink with Our Eyes
Tasters have to be aware that our eyes can bully our other senses into tasting things that aren't there.

So whether brewing or presenting beer, we all need to understand the importance of visual clues and attempt to get them right whenever possible.

There is a lot of mumbo jumbo out there about wine and beer glasses, and whatever physics and physiology might ultimately prove, one thing is certain: presented with the same drink in two different glasses, the glass perceived as more "special" will definitely cause people to take notice and extract more pleasure from its contents. When I'm doing conducted tastings, I often use wineglasses. Every time, I get some raised eyebrows and such comments as, "Oh, beer in a wineglass?" I firmly believe people take beer a little more seriously in a context that demands they approach it differently from the way they normally might. Belgian brewers have made glassware an important part of their beer experience for quite a while, to their great advantage.

All of this points to the importance of great presentation, and recent research into the realm of cross-sensory perception shows that sometimes even details that seem insignificant can have a noticeable effect. A strawberry, for example, will taste sweeter on a white plate than a black one, and sweeter on a round plate than a square one.

Cognitive Factors

Other kinds of information can profoundly change the way we experience foods and drinks. Simply reading the word "salt," for example, causes activity in the brain where the salty sensation is actually processed. I don't know if it's been done, but if you presented beer enthusiasts with two identical pale ales, one labeled as 30 IBU and the other 60 IBU, I would bet actual money that a significant majority of tasters would find the 60-labeled beer to taste more bitter. We all like to think that we're above such manipulation, but it's been shown time and time again that we are not.

As social creatures, we have a strong desire to adapt ourselves to the group; our chemical senses are only too happy to play along. A few words on the label, some comments on RateBeer or from a persuasive tablemate, and we will often find the suggested flavor, whether it's there or not. This is the reason beer judging is usually done in silence until scoring is finished, with discussion afterward.

It has been proven that presenting information about the price or an expert's scoring of a wine will change the reported quality and preference by tasters. Other factors such as brand prestige and rarity are equally persuasive. By selectively focusing on these kinds of information, we further modify our perceptual bubbles.

Marketers have known for decades that packaging is not just about functionality or conveyance of basic information. Brands and their histories set the stage emotionally and create expectations that prime the consumer to be satisfied by the product. Call it deception if you like, but marketing and packaging can actually change the way a product tastes to us. This is why serious competitions are always judged blind, and it is a compelling reason for suspicion about online ratings sites. It might be a good exercise to take a few of your favorite beers, plus a ringer or two, and have somebody serve them to you blind. You might be surprised at your genuine, untainted reaction.

How do we stay strong when our senses lay such traps for us? First, be aware, and always try to keep the senses aimed where you can get the most information. The second is to really focus on the sensations and let the information flood in. Aroma particularly benefits from a very open and accepting mind. Collect and record your impressions first and categorize them later; always try to be open to unexpected sensations. Keep that big model of reality in your head as detailed and up to date as possible. This open-minded attentiveness is at the core of successful tasting but, come to think of it, is actually a pretty good way to live your life in general.

Someday you, too, may be called upon to spread the word about great beer. A well-traveled palate, solid tasting technique, and great vocabulary will be your best tools for guiding people through their beer experience. Having a keen awareness of all the parts and pieces of a given beer allows you to present the most relevant parts to your audience, and it allows them to develop confidence as educated tasters. I need hardly mention how much more gratifying your own beer experience will be.

The Tasting Act

As beer enthusiasts, we know the difference between simple, enjoyable drinking and a more serious activity called tasting. Drinking is mindless and unstructured, while tasting has rules. Drinking comes naturally, while tasting requires training and effort. Mastering the latter opens a lot of doors and steps us up in seriousness and prestige in the world of beer.

But what does that mean, exactly? Tasting's goal is to retrieve as much information as possible from that beer before you. Tasting typically has a purpose or a desired outcome, and these can vary widely. Brewery taste panelists doing quality control are on the lookout for off-flavors and any deviation from the flavor specifications of the beer. For beer-serving professionals, beer quality may focus more on problems caused by the beer's age or draft system issues.

No matter the situation, we are all working with specific tools and structures of our minds and bodies. With good technique, training, and practice, we can extract quite a lot of information from even a small sample of beer. A few simple rules and practices make the job manageable.

Let's start with the glass. A white-wine glass is ideal, but millions of beers are sampled and judged every year with clear plastic airline cups. Whichever you use, don't fill them more than about a third full, as it's important to leave some headroom for aromas to collect.

Make sure the beer is at an appropriate temperature, with lagers and lighter ales several degrees above freezing and heavier beers at a cool cellar temperature, remembering that beers will warm up quickly when poured. If a beer is too cold, just clutch it in your hand with a lot of skin-to-glass contact, swirl gently, and it will warm quickly.

Put yourself into tasting — rather than drinking — mode. Recently, I was lucky enough to spend 3 days with the Cicerone staff under the tutelage of Dr. Bill Simpson, the executive director of Aroxa, a company that makes flavor-spiking samples for brewing and other industries. His first instruction for us was to take the sample cups with the beer in them and swirl them counterclockwise at 45 rpm. "This is for your muscle memory," he said. "I want your brain to know that whenever you do that, you're in tasting mode." The speed and direction were a little unnatural, providing a Pavlovian cue to our inner brains.

We have to work with a number of different brain parts to be successful, and not all of them are under our conscious control. Many, like the amygdala, create the shadowy world of our emotions. You have to trick them when you can and have faith that they will catch on with practice, which they eventually do. The little trick with swirling the glass is just one technique.

A prompted tasting sheet can nudge you to pay attention to every facet of the beer and may even suggest specific flavors to be on the lookout for, but even a blank sheet of paper is helpful. The simple act of writing down words forces us to be more detailed in our tasting, while looking at the words we've written recycles the ideas through our brains in different pathways and adds another layer of understanding and memory to the experience. Pencils in hand, we're ready to taste. Tasting in a quiet place with a minimum of distractions is also very helpful.

Pour the beer. Bounce it straight down the middle of the glass to get a little foam going. Focus. Can you smell anything while it's sitting on the table? Try picking it up and gliding it past your nose, a technique called a "drive-by tasting." What can you smell? Strange as it seems, there are some highly volatile chemicals in beer that are best smelled from a distance and in brief bursts, lest your nose become acclimated.

Next, get the cup right up to your nose and have a couple of short sniffs. What do you notice? Consider the full range of beer vocabulary, and try to categorize what you're experiencing: the bready, malty, biscuit, caramel, burnt sugar, toast, and roast spectrum of malt; or perhaps the herbaceous, floral, or fruity notes of hops; or the spicy, fruity, or wild notes of yeast. If you're really not getting much, try holding one hand over the top of the glass and swirl gently, moving your hand away and taking a sniff. If the beer seems cold, warm it up a little. If you find the aroma triggers a memory, follow it back to the source — perhaps a candy store, Grandma's kitchen, or another childhood memory. Quite often, this is enough of a trigger to pull a specific vocabulary word out.

Pouring a Taste
Don't be afraid to kick up a little foam, and the goal is to fill about a third full for critical tasting.

| tabletop | drive-by | swirl | short sniff | the taste | retronasal |

Tasting Types and Techniques

Different aromatic chemicals in beer respond to different techniques. Be aware of these, and add them to the techniques in your tasting skill set.

The object is to move from general terms to specific aroma terms and, when possible, individual chemicals. With training and experience this gets easier, but if you're a novice, just let your impressions take you where they may and try to be as specific as you can.

Take a moment to observe the beer after you've made some notes about the aroma. Is the foam plentiful and stable? What's the clarity and color? Is it appetizing? However, remember that visual aspects of the beer are limited and can be misleading.

Now, a sip. With the beer in your mouth, pay attention to the way flavor changes second by second. Acidity registers right away, then sweetness chimes in, and — wait for it — there's the bitterness, building slowly. With a really hoppy beer it may take a minute or more to get the full effect. Don't be in a rush to swallow. Let the beer warm in the bottom of the mouth, and then let it slip slowly down your throat. As you do, breathe gently out your nose with your lips closed. This is retronasal olfaction, a very important part of the process, and quite different from smelling through your nostrils.

It's also important to try to tease apart tongue tastes such as sweet, bitter, and sour from aromas. It seems as though it should be an easy task, but to paraphrase *Star Trek's* Dr. McCoy, we're not machines, dammit. Our brains conflate taste and aroma, especially once the substance is in our mouths. It takes a special effort to pull them apart.

So what's going on? In a retronasal taste, the beer has been attacked by salivary and bacterial enzymes, releasing aroma. Your brain combines this aroma with taste and mouthfeel information, creating the more complex sensation of flavor. Learn to pay attention to this retronasal impression, as you often pick up a lot of valuable information with it.

Don't forget the texture or mouthfeel of the beer. Beer's colloidal network of proteins adds viscosity, contributing to beer's body, and gummy carbohydrates such as glucans create slick, creamy textures. Carbonation is an obvious characteristic. In stronger beers, alcohols may be perceived as "hot" or prickly on the tongue.

After the beer has left your mouth, the taste continues for a while, with lingering bitterness and perhaps other sensations such as astringency or the warmth of alcohols. A taste of beer has a beginning, a middle, an end, and maybe even an afterglow. Every part is crucial. A really great beer smells and tastes great all the way through.

The importance of practice can't be overstated. To become really good, you have to engage regularly in some formalized tasting activities. The Beer Judge Certification Program (www.bjcp.org) is well worth checking out. While they don't conduct regular classes, they do have free study materials available, and people in an area who are planning on taking their exam often form ad hoc study groups that meet regularly to taste beers and discuss styles.

There are formal classes offered at brewing schools, universities, and culinary schools. Classes are the best way to learn about specific beer flavors such as diacetyl or dimethyl sulfide (DMS). You'll encounter them along the way if you judge regularly, but it's helpful to go through a training session with those chemicals spiked into beers at a really obvious level, as it gives you an instant familiarity and some idea of what to look for in the context of real beer. You can even get a group together to share the cost of the sample spikes from Siebel, Aroxa, or elsewhere and do this yourself. It's definitely eye-opening.

BE PREPARED TO SETTLE IN for the long haul. There is no quick shortcut to mastering this fine and peculiar art. I've been at it for more than 25 years, and I am constantly humbled; I rarely walk away from a tasting without learning something utterly new. It's a lifelong pursuit, one in which you really never reach your destination but just get a little better, bit by bit. With some experience you do develop some confidence, and that makes it more fun, of course.

Just keep at it. Someday soon you'll be sitting at dinner and absentmindedly pick up your water glass, give it a counterclockwise swirl, and dive in for a series of critical sniffs before you snap back to reality. At that moment you'll know — you're a taster.

CHAPTER 3

BREWING AND THE VOCABULARY OF BEER FLAVOR

Every sensation found in a glass of beer has its origins in the decisions made by the brewer and maltster during its manufacture. The light nuttiness and hints of raisiny fruit? That's lightly kilned pale ale malt and a dab of crystal malt. The tangy, green perfume of hops? That's the result of the careful choice and deployment of prized aroma hops in the brewhouse, and perhaps in the fermenter as well. And all of this complexity is shaped by the mysterious workings of a particular strain of yeast under certain conditions.

THE ABILITY TO DECONSTRUCT a beer, to get inside the head of a brewer, is what separates serious from casual tasters. To those who understand the way the brewing ingredients and process create flavor, beer is an open book. An understanding of ingredients and the brewing process is the foundation of your practical beer-tasting experience. The goal is more pleasure and a better understanding of what's in the glass. To get that, we're going to have to get down and dirty with the brewing process.

The gleaming stainless megabreweries of today are doing essentially the same things with malt, water, hops, and yeast as the simple wooden and clay vats of the ancients. The process seems pretty simple, and the fact that it can be carried out to extremely high levels of art by people in their basements and garages with a few oversized pots and pans speaks to this. But however simple it may appear, the biochemistry is mind-bendingly complex. Our goal is to *really* know beer. And for that we've got to go deep and learn everything that's going on behind this beautiful, shimmering liquid.

Coming to Terms with Vocabulary

The best guess right now is that beer contains between one thousand and two thousand aroma chemicals. Although no one can ever hope to learn to recognize every single one of them, getting a handle on beer's flavor vocabulary is one of the most important tasks we must accomplish as tasters. Putting the right word on a particular aroma is crucial to identifying specific aromas and communicating with others. If you're finding it difficult, welcome to the club — *everybody* struggles with vocabulary. Like naming the colors of the rainbow, it ought to be as simple as child's play, but it turns out to be frustratingly tough. Science tells us that this is not poor memory or lack of sensitivity or diligence. The problems are far deeper.

First, we don't really have descriptive words for many of the smells we find in beer. We do pretty well with malt, as the chemistry of malt kilning is the ubiquitous Maillard reaction — source of most of the same bready, caramelly, toasted, and roast flavors in beer as it is in food — so malt vocabulary is easily drawn from food vocabulary, which suits the task just fine. Hops are more challenging. With more than four hundred identified aroma compounds, we are still stuck using such nearly useless words as "spicy" (a code word meaning it smells like Czech Saaz hops). Yes, some hops do smell a bit grassy, herbal, citrusy, or a bit like berries, cat pee, or tropical fruit, but only to a certain extent. We struggle to build a bridge from these vivid and distinct aroma memories to the confusing chemical stew that is hop aroma.

Our brains do not easily form words from aromas. For beer tasters, it would be really helpful, but this parlor trick never supplied any evolutionary advantage, so our neural wiring remains inadequate for the task in many ways.

One particular problem is organizational. To translate perception into language, it needs to be organized within some logical framework, or encoded semantically, like the rainbow for colors, as mentioned above. We can group aromas into broad categories, such as floral or spicy, but organizing them more precisely can be a challenge. The semantic organization of aroma terms is not a tidy filing system but somewhat messy and poorly understood. Evidence suggests it may occur at a level far below our conscious awareness and possibly

BEER AROMA SPIRAL

This simplified spiral organizes beer aromas by type, with broad categories broken into more specific aromas. Tasters should learn to go from general to specific as they work to identify aromas in a beer. For more detail on beer aroma vocabulary, see the charts on pages 351–55.

includes a strong emotional component. Try organizing that.

If that weren't trouble enough, it has been shown that language can actually interfere with the tasting process. As we struggle to familiarize ourselves with the commonly used vocabulary and link it to what we find in the glass, evidence suggests that words may alter our perception of aromas, especially when we are new to the tasting game. We tend to fixate on those vocabulary terms as we understand them, and if we don't find them when tasting, we tend to ignore other impressions that don't perfectly fit the description. This varies by flavor. Some are easy. Diacetyl, to name one, really fits its buttery-smelling description quite well, but other beer aroma chemicals only loosely match their vocabulary words. Acetaldehyde is a great

 ## DECONSTRUCTING A BEER

Aroma: Derived from ingredients such as malt and hops but modified and augmented by yeast.

Head: From the medium-length proteins present in malt and adjunct grains such as wheat, oats, and rye. Affected by mashing, hop iso-alpha acids, and possibly filtration.

Color: Primarily from kilning of malts chosen for the brew but affected by mashing and boiling specifics, and even to some degree by fermentation and filtration.

Carbonation: Carbon dioxide (CO_2) gas, a by-product of fermentation by yeast.

Body: Proteins from malts, affected by the brewing fermentation and filtering procedures; sweetness from malts, brewhouse decisions, and fermentation.

Mouthfeel: Sensations relayed by nerves in the mouth that can detect textures, chemical heat and cold, astringency, and more.

Flavor: A synthesis our brain puts together from aroma, taste, mouthfeel, other senses, and even our expectations. Much of its complexity comes from aroma, but it is experienced in a different way.

Alcohol: More fermentable material means more alcohol, along with everything else.

Taste: Sensations on the tongue, primarily. Sweetness, bitterness, and acidity are the most important ones in beer.

example. Its most common vocabulary term is green apples, and some people do get this. But it also resembles overripe apples, wet grass, pumpkin guts, avocado, or latex paint and sometimes comes with a bit of a solvency quality as well. No wonder this one is elusive for many tasters. So you have to learn the words, but be open-minded, and don't let them totally drive your experience.

As we learn aromas in various contexts and concentrations, we swap out the training wheel vocabulary words for more sophisticated and richer internal tagging. This means no amount of rote learning of words and chemical formulas can turn one into an experienced taster. A book like this can help lay the framework, but ultimately we are all on our own to make the effort to build an internal map of the aromatic wonderland that is beer, aroma by frustrating aroma.

Beer and Brewing Ingredients

Beer is an agricultural product, but the overwhelming majority of brewing's raw materials — barley and hops — are bought and sold as commodities. This is very different from the world of wine, in which grapes sitting mere yards away from each other can be dramatically different for reasons of microclimate, soil type, exposure to the sun, and other variables. In wine, the hand of nature is foremost. But in brewing, it's the hand of humans that is clearly visible, and that for me is one of its greatest fascinations. There are a few instances when terroir (the characteristics bestowed by soil, climate, plant breeds, and other local factors) really matters in beer, and we'll get to that later.

Paint is paint; it is the hand that guides the brush that matters. It should be your goal to get to know brewers through their art: their beers.

The choices begin with the maltster. Through a series of steps, the most fertile and uniform barley is coaxed into springing to life. As it does, it radically changes. Through a fantastically complex series of enzyme-driven transformations, the seed readies its starch reserve to support a new plant, unaware that the maltster has other plans. The particulars of this controlled sprouting have a huge effect on the brewing character of the malt and the flavor of the beer. At the desired point, heat is applied to stop the process, and it is during this kilning process that the malty flavors of beer are created — from the most delicate, breadlike graininess through dozens of shades of caramel, amber, and toasty brown, to the inkiest espresso of black malts.

And we haven't even started brewing.

Yet the choices go on throughout the entire process: recipe formulation, brewhouse procedures, yeasts, fermentations, carbonation, filtration, packaging, and much more. Hundreds of little steps work together with tradition, technology, market demands, and sometimes just the high-spirited determination of the brewer to put a particular beer in front of you.

Managing this complexity with a deft hand requires a unique personality. The very best brewers I've known exhibit a mix of curiosity, creativity, and willingness to take risks, coupled with a near-fanatical obsession with every tiny detail; unique people, to be sure, and among the beer world's great treasures.

While the details of brewing may seem technical, I can assure you they are the heart and soul of any beer. Start looking for them the next time you hoist a brew, and you'll find them just jumping out of the glass.

WATER

Beer is mostly water. Of course, it's going to have an influence on the flavor.

First of all, water — actually called "liquor" when destined for brewing — is not flavorless. To get into your sip of beer, water sometimes has to travel incredible distances over long time spans. Along the way, it has come in contact with soils, sand, rocks, and other matter. Because water is an unparalleled solvent, it dissolves various minerals on its journey. These show up as ions — components of molecules that split apart and float freely in water's magic solution. Some you can actually taste. The hard chalkiness of carbonate, the palate-expanding roundness of chloride, the plastery tang of sulfate all lend their character to beer.

But water minerals bring more than flavor to beer. The ions in brewing water are chemically active and have important effects on the brewing process. Each type of beer and brewing process has its ideal water. It wasn't until the late 1800s that brewers learned how to adjust the chemistry of their local water. Before that, they were limited in the types of beer they could brew by their local water's characteristics, which was one important factor in the evolution of many of the classic beer styles.

Water *Does* Matter
Water has flavors of its own and plays an important role in the chemistry of brewing.

SENSORY VOCABULARY
SULFATE

TYPE: Flavor, aroma

DESCRIPTORS: Plaster, drywall, sulfate

THRESHOLD IN BEER: Varies; rarely more than subtle

APPROPRIATENESS: May be noticeable and pleasant in some pale ales and IPAs brewed with high-sulfate water, as are the beers of Burton-on-Trent, England, and rarely in Dortmunder lager

SOURCE: Calcium sulfate ions in brewing water

NOTE: While water has a very important effect on a beer's character, it is not always overtly tastable. The plaster-of-paris aroma referred to here may be an expression of a mix of sulfur dioxide and hydrogen sulfide originating in high-sulfur water.

LIMESTONE, a common type of bedrock, is composed mainly of calcium carbonate (sometimes magnesium carbonate in a similar rock called dolomite). Water traveling over, under, or through limestone often dissolves some of the stone as it passes by. Pure water can't do this. It is only when the atmospheric gas carbon dioxide is dissolved in water that it becomes acidic enough to pick up some of the mineral, creating a slightly alkaline hard water. Since limestone is common, so is hard carbonate water, but it is not ideal brewing water for many beers. In pale beers, its alkalinity gives hops an unpleasant astringent bite and affects the chemistry of the mash. It is only with the addition of dark malts — themselves somewhat acidic — that this chalky alkaline water starts to work. And when you keep the hop rates down — bingo! You have a winner. The famous dark beers of Munich and Dublin are two such examples.

GYPSUM, or calcium sulfate, is a less common mineral but is key to an important beer style. After first becoming famous for a dark sweet beer called Burton ale, brewers in nineteenth-century Burton-on-Trent, England, were delighted to find their well water was just the thing to brew an evolving style of crisp, dry, and very hoppy beer called India Pale Ale. Even today, in a well-kept draft Bass, you can sometimes get a whiff of that plaster/drywall nose, a characteristic called Burton stench or snatch.

SALT (SODIUM CHLORIDE) can be found in perceptible quantities in some brewing water. The complex minerally water of Dortmund, Germany, is a famous example. Salt may be added on purpose, as in the case of the German white ale, gose, that's undergoing a bit of a renaissance in the United States.

Small amounts will make the beer taste just a little richer and fatter. It's easy enough to try by sprinkling in a few grains and letting it dissolve in your beer or even in a glass of water.

For some beers the best minerals are no minerals at all. Brewers in the Czech town of Plzeň coupled their extremely soft water with an elaborate mashing procedure to create one of the world's classics, Pilsner. Mineral-free water is not well suited for most beers or brewing methods, but of course, with very soft water it's easy for a brewer to simply add the needed minerals. Some brewers strip their water of incoming minerals and rebuild to suit the style. The methods for this are time consuming and can be expensive, so they tend to be most often used where the local water is really problematic.

It is important that water for brewing be of good drinking quality, which means free of organic contaminants, pesticides, heavy metals, iron, sulfur, and other noxious stuff. Even if not harmful to humans, some minerals — iron, for example — can be toxic to yeast and contribute to haze formation or add unpleasant tastes. Iron, when present in beer, gives a bloody, metallic flavor. Tiny amounts of metals such as copper and zinc are vital for yeast nutrition, so much so that workers in a new, all-stainless megabrewery had to replace a six-foot length of stainless pipe with copper to ensure healthy conditions for its yeast. Zinc is often added as a yeast nutrient.

Bottom line: the charming advertising mythology about northern waters or pristine mountain springs is just a big, beautiful lie.

SENSORY VOCABULARY
METALLIC

TYPE: Taste, aroma*

DESCRIPTORS: Metallic, bloody, iron, coppery, bitter

THRESHOLD IN BEER: 0.15 ppm (iron)

APPROPRIATENESS: Never

SOURCE: Iron, copper, or occasionally other elements present either in the water source or from antiquated brewing equipment. Some metallic flavors are thought to be a result of the oxidation of lipids (fats), which may in turn be catalyzed by metal ions. Iron can't be smelled directly, but it interacts with lipid oxidases present in or on the body, causing them to break down and release 1-octen-3-one, which has the characteristic musty iron smell. If you suspect the presence of iron in beer, a useful trick is to rub a little on the back of your hand; this causes more of the aromatic chemical to be released, magnifying the smell when you sniff your hand.

It has not yet been determined whether metallic flavors in the mouth are tastes or trigeminal sensations such as electrical effects.

THE MAGIC OF BARLEY

Barley is the perfect brewing grain. Not only does it contain a large reserve of starch that can be converted into sugar and a husk that makes a perfect filter bed, but barley also contains the tools — in the form of enzymes — to do the job without adding anything but hot water. The Neolithic people 10 millennia ago knew just what they needed to make beer, selectively replanted wild grasses with just the right qualities, and in relatively short order came up with domesticated barley.

Barley's unique enzyme system makes it a perfect brewing grain, as it allows the stored starches in the dense kernels to be split into simple sugars that the yeast can transform into alcohol. Enzymes are key to many aspects of the brewing process, which would be quite impossible without them. The crucial jobs of malting, brewing, and fermentation all rely on enzymes, which are specialized proteins that assist chemical reactions.

For a chemical reaction to happen, an energy barrier must be crossed, kind of like lifting something over a wall. Enzymes reduce the energy needed to change from one chemical state into another. In brewing, starch must be broken down into simpler sugars. While this is possible using the brute force of strong acids or high temperatures, enzymes present in barley have the ability to make these reactions happen with very modest inputs of heat. We'll be seeing enzymes in many parts of the beer-making process.

Barley for brewing comes in two forms, two-row and six-row, so named for the obvious fact that when looking down from above, there are either two rows of kernels or six. Two-row types yield plumper kernels and prefer cooler climates, while six-row kernels are less rotund and are usually grown in hotter, drier locations. From a brewer's point of view, one important difference is the level of protein, which is important in brewing for several reasons. Protein creates and sustains beer's head, is responsible for beer's viscous sense of body, brings a suite of useful brewing enzymes, and, when broken apart, yields nutrition for the yeast.

But it's not all good. Too much of the wrong kind of protein can cause problems in beer, mostly in the forms of chill haze (a visual cloudiness) and instability on the shelf. For

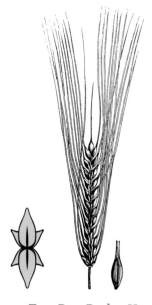

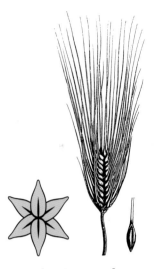

Two-Row Barley Head
(top and side views)

Six-Row Barley Head
(top and side views)

The seeds of this plant have been used to brew beer for 10,000 years. These two types of barley used in beer vary in how many kernels they have at each node around the center stalk. Two-row produces plumper, lower protein kernels, better suited for all-malt beers.

this reason, all-malt beers are most commonly brewed from two-row malt, while six-row is traditionally used in mass-market American-style beers, for which the additional enzymes are used to break down the starches in corn or rice grits, which have no enzymes of their own.

MAKING MALT

The malting process begins by selecting high-grade barley and soaking it in water for 2 to 4 days, until it reaches 40-plus percent water content. This rehydrates the kernel and activates the enzymes within, readying the grain for growth. Then the barley is placed in a cool place and kept well aerated, as the seed needs oxygen at this point. Rootlets appear at one end, and a shoot called an acrospire grows hidden under the husk.

When this sprouting has reached a certain point, the maltster stops the process by applying heat. The length of the shoot is a reliable indicator of the state of the malting process, a measure known as modification. In well-modified malt, the shoot is allowed to grow to the full length of the kernel. Most modern malt is fully modified and can be mashed with relatively simple brewhouse procedures. In the past, not all malt was well modified, which left small "flinty" ends. These flinty bits don't yield their extract easily and need more intensive mashing — usually including a short boil — to gelatinize and fully release their starches.

At this point, the wet, unstable, and relatively flavorless grains are headed for the kiln. Indirect heat is used to first dry the grain, then to toast it. Kilning is the source of nearly all malt flavor, even in the palest malts.

THE MAILLARD REACTION, sometimes called "nonenzymatic browning," is the term used to to collectively describe the chemistry of browning. It is important to understand the chemistry of browning, because it's such a big player in beer flavor, appearance, and aroma. The Maillard reaction describes all commonly encountered browning during cooking, including the char on your burger, the caramelly golden goodness of sautéed onions, and the roastiness of coffee and chocolate.

The specifics are hideously complex, but here's what you need to know: If you take some form of sugar or carbohydrate, combine

MALT FLAVOR VOCABULARY

This chart breaks the most commonly encountered flavors of malt into five broad categories, then subdivides each category into a color range from light to dark. Note that the colors shown approximate the range in which the specific flavors are typically found. Each wedge shows only the color range where those flavors are found. The °Lovibond arrows point toward the beer color in SRM.

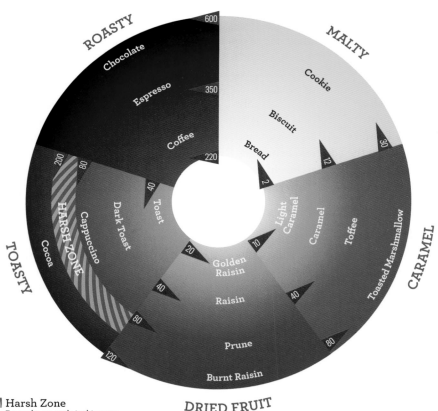

Harsh Zone
Few malts are made in this range, as they tend to be too harsh and pungent.

► Grain Color in °Lovibond
(for EBC: multiply × 2)

it with some nitrogen-bearing material (typically derived from protein), and add heat in the presence of moisture, you get a host of browned flavors, aromas, and color. The color components are known as melanoidins, and they are large, colored molecules with either a reddish or yellowish cast. They have no discernible aroma. It's probably important to note that the term "melanoidin" is often used to refer to all the flavors of Maillard browning, but this is incorrect. Kilned malt aroma comes from small, ring-shaped molecules called heterocyclics, which contain side-chains with sulfur, nitrogen, or oxygen attached to their hydrocarbon rings. These are very potent odorants, with thresholds in the low parts-per-billion range or below.

In Maillard browning, every different combination of sugars, starches, and type of nitrogenous material will produce slightly different end products. What's more, each slight difference in time, temperature, pH, moisture level, and other variables will create a different flavor profile. It's possible to produce two different malts of similar color but with different flavors simply by varying the moisture content during kilning. Roast it dry, and you get the sharp toastiness of a malt called "biscuit" or "amber." Roast it moist, and you get melanoidin malt, known for its cookie to toffee richness.

When you start combining malts in a beer recipe, the same principle applies. There are many ways to produce a brown beer. For example, large amounts of a modestly colored malt or a pinch of deeply roasted malt will produce beers of the same color but with dramatically different flavors. Pay attention to all of this, because in terms of understanding malt aroma and flavor in beers, Maillard browning is the big one.

CARAMELIZATION refers to a simpler browning process; it is what happens when you put sugar in a pan and let it cook until it develops color. Because this process requires sugars rather than starch, it's only

MALT TYPE AND BEER COLOR

This chart gives a rough idea of the amount of color contributed by varying amounts of different malt types in beer recipes.

Percent of Recipe

100	100	30	100	5	20	5	20	1	20
Pilsner, Lager	Pale Ale, Vienna	Munich, Mild Ale		Amber/Biscuit, Melanoidin, Pale Crystal		Medium Crystal		Black, Roasted Barley	

formed to any important degree in crystal/caramel malts. These malts are stewed prior to kilning to encourage breakdown of starch into sugar so that when they are heated to their desired color, a lot of caramel develops. This shows up as a wide range of caramel, raisin, prune, and burnt sugar flavors.

Grain color is expressed either in degrees Lovibond (United States) or EBC (European Brewery Convention) units; EBC units = 1.97 degrees Lovibond.

Malt Types

Malt kilning results in a wide range of colors, from below 2 degrees Lovibond for the palest Pilsner malt to over 500 degrees Lovibond for the deepest-roast black malt. This range gives the brewer a huge color palette from which to choose. Maltsters and brewers organize the various shades of malt into several categories according to how they're made or used, as follows:

Base malts. These are kilned lightly enough that they can serve as the entire brew. In even the darkest beers — stout, for example — base malt will be most of the grain bill. Pilsner, pale, Vienna, and Munich are included in this category, although the darker ones may serve as color malts rather than base malts in certain beers.

COLOR: 1.2 to 15 degrees Lovibond ● ● ● ● ●
PILSNER: The palest malt available
PALE ALE MALT: Classic for pale ales, but many other uses
VIENNA MALT: Continental malt produces amber beer, such as Oktoberfest
MILD ALE MALT: Classic as base for dark British ales
MUNICH MALT: Will brew deep amber beer; sweet and caramelly, hints of toast

"Kilned" or "color" malts. These are used in small amounts, perhaps up to about 20 percent of a recipe. The amber/biscuit and melanoidin malts fall into this group, as does brown malt.

COLOR: 15 to 200 degrees Lovibond ● ● ● ● ●
AROMATIC/MELANOIDIN/DARK MUNICH: Brown and amber beers; sweet and caramelly
AMBER/BISCUIT: Sharp, brown, toasty flavor
BROWN MALT: Classic for porter; smooth to sharp roastiness
PALE CHOCOLATE: Various uses; medium-sharp roastiness

Crystal or caramel malt. This is a special type of process in which the wet malt is "stewed" at around 150°F (66°C). The result is a glassy, crunchy texture and a range of caramel, raisin, or burnt sugar flavors noticeable even in small amounts — potent flavors that can easily be overdone. Crystal malts, especially around the 60 Lovibond (120 EBC) color range, are strongly implicated in beer staling, creating a distinctive "leathery" oxidized note. Although rare, extremely dark caramel malts in the 170 to 210 Lovibond (340 to 410 EBC) range have pleasant chocolaty aromas. A special crystal/caramel malt with very little color, called dextrin malt, is often used to contribute body and head retention in paler beers. The specifics of the kilning process are crucial to developing particular flavor character. Every maltster makes his or her crystal/caramel malt a little differently, so any two, even if they're of the same color, may taste quite different.

COLOR: 10 to 210 degrees Lovibond (Dextrin malt: 1.2 to 2.5 degrees Lovibond) ● ● ● ● ●
(All manufacturers make a range of colors. There is no common terminology except numbers.)

Roasted malts and grains. These include chocolate and various shades of black malts. They really do have very similar aromas and flavors to coffee, chocolate, and other highly roasted foods. It's counterintuitive, but it's important to understand that as the color increases, the flavor intensity of roasted malt actually decreases. The darkest black malts are the softest and most chocolaty, while the paler chocolate malts are actually the sharpest and most pungent. This makes sense if you realize that at higher temperatures, a lot of the flavor chemicals are destroyed or volatilized away, and some debittering processes actually accelerate this effect. Typical use is 10 percent or less of the grist.

COLOR: 180 to 600 degrees
  Lovibond ● ● ● ● ●
CHOCOLATE: Sharp roastiness for darker beers
BLACK: Classic for modern porters and stouts
RÖSTMALZ: German black malt, sometimes dehusked for smoother flavor
ROAST BARLEY: Roasted, unmalted barley is classic in Irish stouts

ADJUNCT GRAINS

While barley malt is by far the most dominant grain in most classic beer styles, brewers since ancient times have recognized the brewing value of alternative, or adjunct, grains. There are many reasons for using adjunct grains. Wheat beers, oatmeal stouts, and rye beer styles all call for specific grains in addition to malted barley. In the case of American-style industrial lager, corn, rice, or various forms of sugar are added to lighten the flavor; this usually results in lightening of the cost as well. With a few exceptions, the cheapest beer has the highest adjunct content. In parts of long-ago England, the poor folk who couldn't afford the premium stuff were called "grouters," after a thick, cheap oat ale.

IN TODAY'S BEERS, adjuncts are more about texture than flavor. All tend to be less assertive in aroma than barley malt. Wheat, oats, and rye all add creamy texture and great head retention to beers, and they are often called to that task even in beers for which these qualities are not openly acknowledged. Some claim to be able to detect a lemony spritziness from wheat, but I've never found this myself. Corn and rice always thin out a beer. Their paucity of protein means they contribute fermentable sugars but not a great deal else. Nonetheless, it is possible to detect a delicately husky rice "bite" in Budweiser and a subtle creamy corniness in many beers such as Miller Genuine Draft that use corn as a primary adjunct.

Malted specialty grains such as wheat and rye can be added directly to the mash without the special cooking procedures required for raw adjuncts, but their lack of husk sometimes requires that extra filtering material such as rice hulls be added to aid runoff of the mash. Pregelatinized grains are available, most commonly as flaked products such as oatmeal. These can be added directly to the mash without precooking, although rice hulls are recommended here as well. Raw, unmalted grains need a cooking procedure to gelatinize their starches. I'll discuss this process in more detail shortly.

> The wheat is like a rich man,
> That's sleek and well to do,
> The oats are like a pack of girls,
> Laughing and dancing too,
> The rye is like a miser,
> That's sulky, lean and small,
> But the free and bearded barley
> Is the monarch of them all.
> — A. T.

The Art of the Recipe

Before a drop is brewed, the brewer must decide what's going into the beer. How strong will it be? What's the desired color? Bitterness? Primary flavors? Balance? Sneaky, subtle background elements? Wacko specialty ingredients?

Most brewers decide on these and other characteristics first and then determine how much of what ingredients will cause the desired beer to materialize. Parameters such as gravity — the amount of sugars and other solids in the unfermented wort — come first. One, two, or as many as a dozen or more malts can be combined into a brew. Calculating gravity is easy. Each malt has a certain potential yield, and every brewhouse and mash procedure has a certain efficiency, which, after some experience, is usually well understood by the brewer. So it's just a matter of totaling things up. Color calculation is not so straightforward, as color does not add up in a linear fashion, and there are some differences in the way colors of different malts are measured. But there are formulas that take these differences into account when formulating recipes.

Hops need similar consideration. The brewer must plan for both aroma and bitterness, which work at cross-purposes. To extract bitterness, hops must be vigorously boiled. This drives off the volatile aromatic oils, so hops are usually added early for bitterness and late for aroma. Each variety has a certain amount of bittering substance, varying by region and year. Every hop shipment contains an analysis that indicates its bittering potential at harvest, but hops are a highly perishable product, so they lose bittering power and aroma, even when stored at cold temperatures. So the brewer has to decide how much of which hop to add, and when, to produce a specific amount of bitterness and aroma in the beer. This can be done manually, but increasingly it is worked out with computer programs.

BALANCE is very much a subjective quality and doesn't lend itself particularly well to numerical calculation. A measure called a bittering units to gravity units (BU to GU) ratio (see pages 112–114) can be helpful; it's a numeric expression reflecting that, at any given perceived level of balance, the amount of hop bitterness needs to increase as the gravity rises. What constitutes an appropriate balance varies by drinker and beer style, but in even the maltiest doppelbock or Scotch ale, there is some anchoring hop bitterness. The most tongue-slappingly hoppy double IPA should have at least some maltiness to back it up.

We normally think of balance as being simply about the play of hop bitterness against the sweetness of malt, but there are many other elements involved. Dark malt, for example, plays on the bitter side of the equation along with the hops. A deft touch can create a three-way balance of toasty malt, hop bitterness, and sweet malt, which makes for a very lively experience as you drink. In specialty beers, the balance can be altogether different. Acidic beers depend on sour against sweet or woody, as hops are usually subdued. Such elements as smoke, chiles, fruit, herbs, and spices can all come into balance play.

The word "balance" is the industry term, but I personally find it a little static. In our perception, there is no real balance, just a constant shifting of focal point, so from a brewer's point of view, the kind of dynamic contrast that comes from playing different elements against one another is a better notion.

Brewers use the same kinds of techniques that chefs — or any other kind of artist — use: contrast, harmony, layering, surprise. The best brewers have a twinkle in their eye and the ability to reach right out to give us an experience, not just a glass of beer.

If you do it right, brewing is about ideas. A big impression can be made with brute force, but sometimes a whisper speaks louder than a shout. In the end, all great beers tell a story.

 INGREDIENT TASTING

Conducting this type of tasting is how brewers familiarize themselves with the flavors of brewing ingredients. It's nothing more than laying out a number of different types of malts, hops, and waters, and letting everybody taste or smell each one. You can sample them all at once or taste one category per session. All the ingredients can be found at your local homebrew shop (or through mail order if necessary). Here's how to do it.

Malt

Gather a pound each of Pilsner, pale, Munich, biscuit, a couple of crystal malts of different shades, and a black malt. Lay these out and let everybody smell, then taste them. If you're feeling ambitious, fill some coffee cups with some of the paler types, crushed coarsely, and pour over 170°F (77°C) water to cover. Note the aromas and sweetness that develop in the next few minutes. You are brewing!

Hops

Purchase several different hop varieties in small quantities. Recommended varieties are Saaz, Hallertau, Kent Goldings, and Cascades, which will give you a sense for their use in Czech, German, English, and American craft beer, respectively. Whole hops are preferred, but pellets are okay. Lay them out on plates (the pros use purple paper, as it enhances the hops' green colors), and rub a small amount of each, in turn, between your palms to liberate the aromas; then cup your hands and smell. Unscented hand wipes or rubbing alcohol for use between each hop variety is definitely recommended for this. Don't bother tasting hops or making teas, as neither really works.

Water

Buy bottles of several different water types, and taste. Distilled water is just pure wetness; Evian is a hard, alkaline (carbonate) water with a little tooth to it and a minerally body; plain carbonated water such as Perrier demonstrates the powerful effects of carbonation, with its familiar bubbly texture and the bit of acidity that affects beer's flavor. Also put a little table salt in part of the distilled water to demonstrate that taste. Measure ⅛ teaspoon, then use one-eighth of that amount in a quart, which should get you into the 85 ppm range. It should taste rich and full but not particularly salty.

Mashing and Runoff

At the core of brewing is a magical porridge-making process called "mashing." Crushed malt is mixed with hot liquor (apprentices were fined tuppence if they called it "water"), and this mash is allowed to stand. In just a few minutes, enzymes present in the malt convert starch from the grains into sugars. The resulting sweet liquid — called "wort" — can then be drained off.

The quality of the malt crush is crucial. Too coarse, and the mash gives up little of its sugar; too fine, and the husks that are supposed to serve as a filter bed are useless, and you get what is, for all practical purposes, vegetable concrete. A full-size malt mill has up to six rollers and can weigh several thousand pounds, so this is something brewers take very seriously.

There are several enzyme systems in the mash that serve different functions. Each has a preferred temperature range and other optima, including pH, mineral ions, concentration, and more. Each is most active at a specific temperature; below that, they don't work, and at just a bit higher temperature they are destroyed by heat, ending their activity.

Some enzymes break down complex gummy carbohydrates such as glucan and pentosan in the mash. Others break down proteins into smaller parts of varying lengths — the smallest are critical for yeast nutrition. Midsize proteins are important for body and head formation. Large proteins need to be broken up to keep them from causing haze and instability in the finished beer.

THE MAIN EVENT is the conversion of starch into sugar. Starches are polymers of sugars, meaning they are large molecules strung together from a number of smaller molecules of glucose. In the mash, enzymes liberate maltose, a two-unit sugar, plus some longer ones with varying degrees of fermentability. The brilliance of the enzyme system in malt is that there are two enzymes working at slightly different temperatures. One enzyme creates a fully fermentable wort; the other makes wort that cannot ferment as completely. By varying the mash temperature, the brewer can adjust the fermentability of the wort, and therefore the sweetness or dryness of the beer.

At 145°F (63°C), highly fermentable wort is produced, making for a dry, crisp beer. At 155°F (68°C), the wort will have a good proportion of unfermentable sugars, resulting in a sweet, rich beer. In practice, most beers are mashed somewhere between these extremes. This is a dramatic simplification of what actually happens, but it gives you an idea of the importance of the decisions the brewer makes in the brewhouse.

Once the mash has done its work, the temperature is raised, ending enzyme activity and locking the ratio of fermentable to unfermentable sugars, a step called "mashing-out."

There are a number of different mash procedures in use today. Most basic is a single infusion in which hot water is mixed with the grain and allowed to stand for about an hour. A variation of this is called a "step infusion" or "upward step mash." In English-style beers, there may be just a couple of steps, but in some rustic methods, as used in Finnish sahti, multiple small steps are used, from room temperature to nearly boiling. Most complex of all are the traditional German decoction mashes. In this method, about a third of the mash is removed

Lautering the Mash
Brewer Brad Landman checks the progress of the grain-rinsing process at Wynkoop, Colorado's first brewpub.

from the tun, raised through a series of steps, and boiled briefly before being returned to the tun to create an overall temperature rise. Decoctions come in one-, two-, or three-step versions, the most complex of which takes more than 6 hours to execute. These are rare now, for reasons of time and energy use, but their addition of layers of rich caramelly flavor to beer still has value.

At the end of the mashing process, it's time to separate the sweet wort from the matrix of husks and chunks known as "spent grain." Most breweries use a lauter tun, a vessel with a perforated bottom, although sometimes the mash tun itself also serves this purpose. As the sweet wort is run off into the kettle, more hot water is added to the top of the mash, a process called "sparging." The whole runoff process takes about an hour.

Hops

Once in the brew kettle, the wort is quickly brought up to a boil, and the first load of hops is added.

Let's pause for a moment and consider what this unique plant has given to the beer world. A climbing vine in the nettle family and closely related to marijuana, hops have been cultivated since ancient times, although they didn't regularly find their way into beer until about a thousand years ago. The parts useful in brewing are the cones, and despite the fact that many brewers call them flowers, they're actually catkins or, botanically, strobiles.

Hops are cultivated between latitudes 35 and 55 degrees in both the Southern and Northern Hemispheres, as they need specific summertime day lengths to trigger cone production. They are large, showy plants and make nice ornamentals, despite their vulnerability to pests and diseases. In the Old World, the most prized varieties are tied to very specific locations: the Saaz gets its spicy character from the orange soil in western Bohemia; the herbal Hallertau grows in its namesake district in northern Bavaria; and in a region just a short jump southeast of London, the East Kent Golding develops its twangy green spiciness, prized for 2 centuries in the finest pale ales. Worldwide, there are easily more than two hundred varieties of hops, with more coming every day.

America grows its share of hops, nowadays near Yakima, Washington, and elsewhere in the Northwest, although a nascent industry is coming back to the Great Lakes region that used to be America's hop heartland. Classic European varieties grown in North America don't taste the same as those from their homelands, but they still have desirable brewing qualities. Varieties that do come closer to European "noble" hops (discussed later in this chapter) have also been developed.

Inside the hop cone there is a small internal stem, or strig, holding the leafy parts of the cone together. All around the strig are tiny golden globules of the pungent waxy substance lupulin. This contains the bitter resins and aromatic oils so valued in beer. The bitter resins can be divided into alpha and beta acids, the alphas being the more important of the two and the measure used to describe a hop's bittering power. Alpha acid content for hops ranges from around 2 percent for the least bitter aroma hops up to nearly 20 percent for high-alpha types.

SENSE AND NONSENSE IN BEER ADVERTISING CLAIMS

Beer advertisers often use the following terms and concepts to sell their beer. Here's my take on them all.

Water
You hear descriptions such as "sky blue" and "Rocky Mountain." Brewers need great water, and yes, there was a time when they had to brew with the local water as it was, so the better the water, at least theoretically, the better the beer. Most modern breweries treat their water to make it suitable for whatever type of beer they're brewing.
Verdict: Doesn't hold water.

Beechwood-Aged
A century ago, most American breweries aged their lagers in "chip tanks" with a pile of wooden slats in the bottom. These are stripped of any wood character before going into the tanks and impart no wood flavor to the beer. Their real purpose was to provide additional surface area for the yeast to settle on, and this may have benefits for the conditioning of the beer. Anheuser-Busch has continued to find it is worth the considerable trouble for their yeast and their beers, but few breweries feel the same these days.
Verdict: Nice nod to tradition, but not what it sounds like.

Krauesened
This is the process of adding some freshly fermenting beer to another batch nearing the end of maturation. The idea is that the lively yeast will hasten the reduction of unwanted "green" flavors such as acetaldehyde and diacetyl from the beer. It's an old method, and it really works.
Verdict: Usually a good thing, but because it requires freshly fermenting wort at just the right moment, it is difficult to employ in small breweries whose brewing schedules are generally less regular than large ones.

Reinheitsgebot
This timeworn Bavarian law forbids anything other than hops, malt, water, and yeast in lager beer. As far as I'm concerned, most beers on the planet

SENSORY VOCABULARY
CHEESY
(ISOVALERIC ACID)

TYPE: Aroma

DESCRIPTORS: Stinky cheese; stinky feet

THRESHOLD IN BEER: 0.7 ppm for isovaleric acid

APPROPRIATENESS: Never

SOURCE: Formation of organic acids during improper storage of hops. Also may be one of the many aromas of a bacterial infection. Rare in commercial beer but still occasionally encountered. In large amounts, it may be a sign of an infection, most commonly of *Brettanomyces*.

would probably be improved by this limitation, but there are many legitimate instances in which beer can be improved by sugar, herbs, spices, and other "forbidden" ingredients.
Verdict: Maybe.

Draft in a Bottle

This is an indirect slam against pasteurization, which its detractors say affects the beer negatively, although the beer literature says the differences are slight. "Bottled draft" beers are often filtered in some special way (see below) and then kept refrigerated right through the point of sale, which is generally better for beer.
Verdict: You be the judge.

Cold-Filtered

This is specifically a Miller product claim, but the technology is licensed from the Japanese brewer Sapporo. The idea is to remove yeast and spoilage bacteria while not stripping away proteins, color, and other valuable properties.
Verdict: Subtle, very subtle.

Brewed Longer

Although there are many parts of the brewing and fermenting process that may benefit from a little more time, this term always reminds me of marketing guys trying to fathom what the guys in the rubber boots are actually doing, and then turning it into something the consumer might see as a benefit. I've spent too much time at ad agencies — and breweries — to believe otherwise.
Verdict: Nonsense.

Craft-Brewed

While this should properly refer to small, independent breweries making highly flavorful and creative beers, the term is unenforceable, and maybe even a little difficult to agree on. However, there are clear instances in which large industrial breweries slap "craft-brewed" onto the label in the hope that a little microbrew mojo will rub off on them.
Verdict: Read the fine print. Know your brewery.

This old botanical print details the showy beauty of
all parts of the hop plant.

SENSORY VOCABULARY
HOP BITTERNESS

TYPE: Taste

DESCRIPTORS: Bitter, hoppy

THRESHOLD IN BEER: 5 to 7 ppm (5 to 7 international bitterness units or IBU)

APPROPRIATENESS: Always to some extent; may be up to 100-plus IBU in some extreme beers

SOURCE: Isomerized hop alpha acids; should be clean, pleasant, without harsh, woody, or astringent character

NOTE: The current hop arms race has brewers creating beers claiming 1,000 IBU. Self-inflicted pain and bragging rights aside, it is an open question as to whether chemical analysis can be correct at these levels, never mind whether the human palate is even capable of discriminating among such stratospherically bitter brews.

ALSO IN THE LUPULIN are hundreds of aromatic oils, each with its own character. Every variety and growing location produces hops with a unique mix of these oils. Floral to resiny, minty to spicy, hop aroma is a great tool for adding personality to beer. The characteristics seem to fall into national groups. German hops tend to be herbal, sometimes almost minty, while English hops bring a healthy dose of fresh green grassiness. The celebrated Saaz hop has a clean, refined character that's quite distinctive but incredibly difficult to describe — often tagged with the inadequate term "spicy." American hops are all over the map, but the most characteristic varieties veer off into the piney/resiny, floral, and citrus. There are some beer styles — American and English pale ale come to mind — in which the only meaningful difference between them is the choice of hops. Aroma hops are a powerful tool.

There is a group of European hops historically called "noble," usually used for aroma in lager beers. These are the Saaz plus the German Hallertauer Mittelfrüh, Tettnanger, and Spalt. There is a chemically defined requirement for this exclusive club, but as new aroma varieties have been developed, the rules have been extensively gerrymandered to limit the group to the original clique. No doubt these are all great hops, but surely they are not the only varieties truly deserving of the name these days.

In addition to aroma hops, there are high-alpha varieties that have been developed in the past hundred years with ever-increasing amounts of bitterness. These are sold by alpha acid pounds, so they tend to be more of a commodity item. However, some crafty American brewers have seized on the rustic, grapefruit charms of varieties such as Chinook and Columbus and have used them to create bigger-than-life pale ales and other beers.

There are many dual-use hops combining moderate alpha acid levels with pleasant aromatics. Breeding programs worldwide are always working on new varieties, seeking higher alpha acid, better yield, disease resistance, and other qualities. A recent focus has been on breeding for aroma, and hops have been released with berry, white wine, passion fruit, lemon-lime, pear, and many other delicious aromas not formerly found in hops. The landscape has changed as well. New Zealand and Australia are producing some excitingly luscious hops, and even Argentina is experimenting with hops not grown there before, with some exciting results. There are aroma-forward breeding programs in Germany, Slovenia, France, and other European countries as well.

With the popularity of IPAs around the world, consumers are becoming increasingly familiar with such hop breeds as Mosaic, Galaxy, Mandarina Bavaria, Citra, and others. Many more are on the horizon, lucky for us.

SENSORY VOCABULARY
HOP AROMA

TYPE: Aroma

DESCRIPTORS: See Hop Aroma Vocabulary Spider Chart, opposite.

THRESHOLD IN BEER: There are hundreds of different oils; for some, thresholds are well below 1 ppb; for others, it may be 100 times that.

APPROPRIATENESS: Style dependent; should be absent in some; absolutely critical to other styles

SOURCE: Aromatic oils from hops; technically, terpenes, sesquiterpenes, ketones, and alcohols. Can be extracted during boil, postboil, or via postfermentation techniques such as dry hopping. Also may be added as solvent-extracted pure or blended oils, but these often come across as one-dimensional.

NOTE: The term "spicy" is often used as a code word for Saaz and similar hops that have no other obvious distinctive aroma characteristics.

As noted above, hops are usually added in stages. To extract bitter substances, a vigorous boil is essential. In a process called "isomerization," hop alpha acids are rearranged chemically into a form with more bitterness, as well as solubility, in wort. The longer the boil time, the more bitterness, but after about 2 hours it

Hops off the Vine
Freshly picked cones are leveled off in the drying house, or oast, at Kitchenham Farm, Bodiam, England.

is subject to diminishing returns and may cause other problems (see page 87). Vigorous boiling drives off volatile oils, so if hop aroma is desired, more hops must be added toward the end of the boil.

BREWERS MAY ALSO MAKE one or more "flavor additions" with 15- or 30-minute boil times, which add a mix of bitterness and aroma. Hops may also be added after the boil has ended to emphasize aroma. Special devices called "hop backs" or "hop percolators" can be loaded with hops and the hot wort run through it on its way to the chiller.

HOP AROMA VOCABULARY SPIDER CHART

Hop aromas are particularly challenging, as the hundreds of essential oils don't neatly correspond to familiar foods. However, it is possible to identify several key families of aromas, which can then be further subdivided into more specific terms. Each hop actually contains all these flavors; it's their proportion that determines a hop's overall impression.

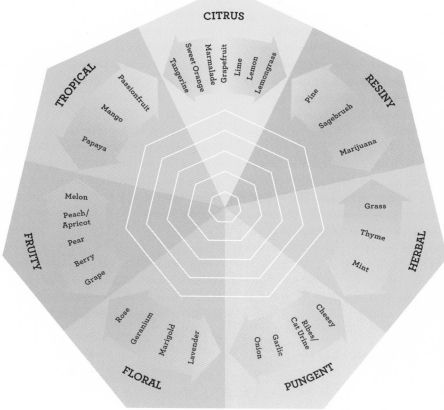

This spider chart shows aroma families with more specific descriptors further in. In addition to laying out aromas, a spider chart can be a helpful tool and is often used for recording hop aroma profiles. Dots are drawn on the "spider web" at the center, with stronger aromas (1–5 scale) farther from the center and weaker ones closer in. At the end, the dots are connected and an overall shape is created, reflecting the aroma makeup of the hop.

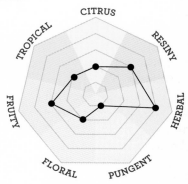

LIGHT, LOW-CARB, AND DRY BEER

Brewers have a number of tools at their disposal to affect the caloric and alcoholic content of their beer. Traditional brewing techniques always yield a wort with some unfermentables, but industrial fungal enzymes don't have this limitation and are put to use in a number of styles, the unifying feature of which is a very low level of residual carbohydrates. The terminology can be confusing to the public and beer aficionados alike, and it shifts as the market changes. These are strange animals for those accustomed to full-bodied, all-malt beers. Here's a summary.

Light Beer

This starts with a low-gravity recipe, then fungus-derived enzymes are used in the mash to convert any remaining starches into sugars. This means there are no residual carbohydrates in the beer, as they all have been fermented into alcohol. Light beer is lower in alcohol and calories than regular beer.

Ultralight/Low-Carb Beer

This is made in a similar manner to light beer. In the United States these are breathtakingly light beers aimed at dieters and the workout crowd. The starting gravity is much lower than a normal beer, and so is the alcohol content. All the carbohydrates have been turned into alcohol, so there are none remaining in the beer, which keeps the calories low as well. In Europe, low-carb beers are primarily aimed at diabetics.

Dry Beer

Again, the process is similar, but this time the brewer starts with a normal-strength wort. However, because the same extreme methods are used to turn all carbohydrates into fermentable sugars, which then are fermented into alcohol, dry beer is a little higher in alcohol than regular beer.

Ice Beer

This is the same idea but formulated into a stronger beer. There is almost no residual carbohydrate content, aided by the addition of highly fermentable sugars to the wort to boost the alcohol content.

Regular, Light, Ultralight, and Ice Beers
This chart gives original and finishing gravities for three of these superattenuated styles, with regular lager and a craft-brewed American pale ale for comparison.

	American Pale Ale	Regular Lager	Light Lager	Ultralight/Low Carb	Ice Beer
	ABV: 5.7%	ABV: 4.9%	ABV: 4.2%	ABV: 2.8%	ABV: 5.9%
Original Gravity:	1.053	1.044	1.030	1.020	1.041
Finishing Gravity:	1.011	1.007	0.9985	0.999	0.996
Apparent Attenuation:	78.5%	83.6%	105.1%	105.1%	110.2%
Real Attenuation:	64.3%	68.5%	86.1%	86.1%	93%
Alcohol by Volume:	5.7%	4.9%	4.2%	2.8%	5.9%
Calories/12 oz (355 mL):	171	140	96	64	130

% ALC/VOL

WATER

RESIDUAL

A technique called "hop bursting" uses minimal hops in the boil, adding all or most of the hops at the end of the boil or afterward in the whirlpool. This creates a beer with massive aroma but without overwhelming bitterness. Hops may also be used after fermentation, in conditioning tanks, or even in serving casks. This is known as "dry hopping," and it is often used in American IPAs and other styles in which hops are front and center, as well as in traditional English cask pale ales and IPAs.

Brewers have been working to reduce the time and improve the efficiency of the dry hopping process. Some breweries are now using external infusers, sometimes called "torpedoes," that are closed filter-type vessels with a screen to hold the hops. As beer is pumped through, it picks up aroma from the hops much more quickly than when the hops are simply dumped into the tanks. Better yield with fewer hops is another huge benefit. This type of system works with other flavoring ingredients as well.

A Rolling Boil

Once the kettle is full, it is brought to a vigorous boil. This accomplishes a number of things. First, it sterilizes the wort, which prevents the beer from being taken over by bacteria and wild yeast. Second, as noted previously, boiling isomerizes the hops' alpha acids, making them both bitter and soluble. And third, it coagulates excess protein with help from the tannins (polyphenols) present in the vegetative parts of the hops. This produces flakes of protein very much like egg drop soup, known as the "hot break," removing long-chain proteins that would otherwise cause instability or chill haze — the harmless but unsightly cloudiness that can appear when beer is served very cold. The boil also puts an end to any enzyme

activity remaining from the mash and locks in the ratio of fermentable to nonfermentable sugars. Direct-flame heating of kettles may also add some caramelization.

Another important thing that happens during the boil is the creation and expulsion of a chemical called dimethyl sulfide (DMS). At temperatures above 140°F (60°C) the s-methyl methionine in the malt is turned into DMS, which usually has an aroma of creamed corn. It's a very volatile chemical, so it can be expelled easily during the boil, but as soon as the boil stops, DMS starts to build, making it important to get the wort chilled as quickly as possible. The hot wort is now susceptible to picking up oxygen, which can cause problems later.

SENSORY VOCABULARY
DIMETHYL SULFIDE (DMS)

TYPE: Aroma

DESCRIPTORS: Creamed corn, cabbage, vegetal, green beans, canned asparagus; in dark beers, more like tomato juice

THRESHOLD IN BEER: 30 to 50 ppb

APPROPRIATENESS: Usually not appropriate, but acceptable in small amounts in pale lagers

SOURCE: Created in boil from s-methyl methionine (SMM), a precursor found in grain and usually symptomatic of brewhouse problems; may also be a symptom of infection, especially when found in large amounts

Hop particles and hot break are usually removed by running the wort tangentially into a settling tank, a technique that creates a whirlpool, concentrating the hot break and hop into a shallow pile, allowing the wort to be drained, leaving the crud behind. Then, the wort is cooled as rapidly as possible. In addition to the DMS and oxidation problems noted above, the beer may also be subject to microbial contamination if cooled too slowly. Typically a counterflow heat exchanger is used. Through a series of thin plates, hot wort flows in one direction and cold water in the other. The wort then emerges at fermentation temperature. This sudden chilling creates a "cold break," precipitating protein and some lipids (fats). In some larger breweries, this cold break may be removed, but it often remains in the wort in craft breweries.

SENSORY VOCABULARY
OXIDATION
(TRANS-2-NONENAL)

TYPE: Aroma/flavor

DESCRIPTORS: Papery, stale, cardboard, shoe box

THRESHOLD IN BEER: 0.05 to 0.25 ppb

APPROPRIATENESS: Never; symptomatic of over-boiling or poor brewhouse technique; also common in stale beer and increases as beer ages

SOURCE: Created by oxidation of lipid (fat) malt components during mashing, boiling, or other brewhouse activities where contact with air is possible, and magnified by time as beer is stored

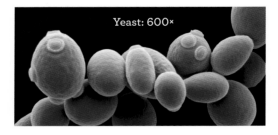

Yeast: 600×

Yeast and the Magic of Fermentation

Brewers make wort, not beer. Only yeast can make beer. The specific biochemical pathways are amazingly complex, but here are the basics: yeast metabolizes sugars and creates ethanol, carbon dioxide, and a host of other chemicals in much smaller amounts.

Yeast is a single-celled fungus that has been cultivated since ancient times for both brewing and baking. In the brewing world, there are two main families of yeast responsible for ale and lager fermentations. Ale, or top-fermenting, yeast is a species called *Saccharomyces cerevisiae*. Genomic data conclusively shows that lager yeast is a second, closely related species, *Saccharomyces pastorianus*. There is considerably more genetic variation among ale yeast strains, as you can easily detect in even a cursory survey of ales. Other yeasts and even bacteria are involved in some specialty beers, but the vast majority of beers are fermented with one of these two yeast species.

Yeast cells are fantastic little chemical factories. They must find food, metabolize it into energy, synthesize proteins and many other molecules necessary for life, rid themselves of waste, and reproduce. Think of them as little sacks of goo with membranes porous enough to allow some molecules through, as well as specialized gates or ports that allow the entry of specific molecules when appropriate. All of this chemistry is taking place inside certain structures, or just floating freely. The yeast must go through many steps to reach each of its goals, and some of the intermediate products it creates are aromatically potent enough themselves to be important aroma and flavor components of beer. The higher the temperature, the faster all of this chemistry happens. And because yeast does not always work efficiently, at higher temperatures some of the intermediate products leak out of the cells and into the beer.

At low temperatures, relatively fewer of these by-products are created; as the temperature rises, more are created. This explains the main flavor differences between ales and lagers. Lagers, fermented at 40 to 45°F (4 to 7°C) and conditioned at near freezing, have a relatively clean, pure flavor without fruity or

 ## TERROIR IN BEER

"Terroir" is a term used to describe the sum total of the effect of a region's location on a wine or other traditional product. Climate, soil, moisture, geology, micronutrients, and more are involved. Terroir doesn't just jump out of a glass of beer, though, as it does with wine. You have to know what you're looking for.

Heirloom Malts

Certain classic English malt varieties are very difficult to cultivate but have flavors that normal commodity malts just can't match. First among them is Maris Otter, long prized for its complex, slightly nutty flavor. Other varieties to look for are Halcyon and Golden Promise. In the Czech Republic, a strain called Hana is valued for production of undermodified malts for classic Pilsners. Klages, once widespread in the American Northwest, is a rare malt now that it has largely been replaced with Harrington, a malt with better agronomic characteristics, such as yield and disease resistance.

Noble Hops

The clean, neutral hoppiness of the Saaz only comes through if the hops are grown in the bright orange "cinnamonic" soil of the Blšanka (Goldbach) Valley, the traditional Czech growing region, and this is also true of the other noble varieties grown elsewhere. As with wine, many

factors, such as climate and soil, play a role in the subtlety and refined character of hops from their traditional growing areas.

Water

As noted earlier in this chapter, water chemistry is now under the control of the brewmaster, but characteristic water types do sometimes shine through. One of the most famous brewing waters is the mineral-rich borehole water from Burton-on-Trent, England, which adds a crisp dryness and plastery nose to many Burton beers. Dortmunder Export beers, now rare, relied on local water with a mix of sulfate, carbonate, and salt for a unique, minerally flavor.

Wild Yeast

In wild-fermented-style lambic, brewers depend to some extent on local microflora to inoculate the beer and begin fermentation. Because the old cherry orchards in the area just south of Brussels that harbored wild yeast are long gone, the process has changed somewhat. It is now believed that many of the formerly "wild" microorganisms reside in the brewery's barrels, but brewers still expose the cooling wort to the night air of the region. Brewers elsewhere have attempted to create their own wild-fermented beers, with varying degrees of success.

spicy aromatics. Ales, normally fermented well above 55°F (13°C), have loads going on, with fruity esters, spicy phenols, and higher alcohols, as well as other compounds.

One important chemical produced by yeast — even at low temperatures — is diacetyl. This familiar buttery compound is one step in an elaborate protein synthesis. Its precursors have relatively little flavor, but diacetyl is so buttery that it was used in microwave popcorn until it was found to cause respiratory problems in the workers exposed to large quantities of the chemical. At warmer temperatures, yeast will reabsorb diacetyl and turn it into flavorless chemicals. This step in the brewing process — a several-day elevation of temperature during conditioning — is called a "diacetyl rest." This is common practice with lagers and is also often employed in ale fermentations.

SENSORY VOCABULARY
BUTTERY (DIACETYL/ 2,3-BUTANEDIONE)

TYPE: Diacetyl (2,3-butanedione) is a buttery-smelling aroma chemical, part of a group including a related chemical called 2,3-pentanedione, collectively known as vicinal diketones, or VDKs.

DESCRIPTORS: Buttery theater popcorn; in larger amounts, butterscotch

THRESHOLD IN BEER: 10 to 40 ppb (diacetyl), depending on the beer and on the taster's sensitivity

APPROPRIATENESS: Sometimes pleasant at very low levels in English-style ales

SOURCE: Precursor leaks out of yeast cells during amino acid synthesis and is then converted into diacetyl in the beer. In larger amounts, it may be

a sign of stressed or mutated yeast. In very high amounts, it may be a sign of bacterial contamination and is especially common in dirty (infected) draft lines.

YEAST IS VERY SENSITIVE to temperature variations, and it will often produce markedly different beers at only slightly different temperatures. It is also sensitive to physical parameters such as tank depth and geometry. Yeast needs a proper nutrient mix and an adequate number of cells per unit of beer (which varies with the strength of the beer) to ferment properly. Yeast also needs oxygen to create more yeast, a process that happens before fermentation begins in the beer. This, it should be noted, is the only acceptable time in the brewing process for oxygen to be in contact with beer.

There are hundreds of brewing strains stored in yeast banks around the world. Larger brewers usually have their own proprietary strains; smaller brewers can order from dozens of strains available through commercial brewer's yeast suppliers. Often, if one can read between the lines, the particular pedigrees of specific strains can be gleaned from the catalog descriptions. For a fairly comprehensive list and description of the types of brewer's yeast, have a look online at one of these websites: Wyeast (www.wyeastlab.com) or White Labs (www.whitelabs.com).

A MEASURED AMOUNT of healthy yeast is added to the oxygenated wort in a carefully sanitized fermenting vessel. The yeast takes in the oxygen and begins to make more yeast by "budding" off new cells. This takes several hours, and during this time there is very little actual fermentation happening. At the point when all the available oxygen is used up, the yeast turns its attention to the sweet wort. First, because it's easier, the yeast eats the small amount of available glucose (a simple sugar that is its preferred food) and then begins to metabolize the maltose. This tiny ravenous beast can throw a thick, rocky head more than a foot high onto the surface of the fermenting beer and generate so much heat that tanks must be cooled to avoid runaway temperatures.

This violent process takes between a day and a week, depending on the temperature, wort strength, yeast vigor, and other factors. This is generally called the primary fermentation. When the maltose is eaten up, the yeast will turn to the next longest sugar, maltotriose. At this point, things slow way down.

SENSORY VOCABULARY
ESTERY/SOLVENT (ETHYL ACETATE)

TYPE: Aroma

DESCRIPTORS: Fruity at low quantities, but in larger quantities it comes across as nail polish remover or solvent; sometimes more evident as an eye-watering sensation rather than an actual aroma

THRESHOLD IN BEER: 18 ppm

APPROPRIATENESS: In small amounts, it is an important contributor to fruity aromas in beer. In larger amounts it may be a sign of too-high fermentation temperature, improper wort aeration, or other yeast stress. Often found in very-high-alcohol beers.

SOURCE: Formed during fatty acid synthesis, and then leaks out of yeast cells. Most common in beers with alcohol content over 10 percent, from stressed yeast. Very high amounts may be

a result of bacterial contamination (especially vinegar-forming *Acetobacter*) and are frequently encountered in wood-aged beers such as Flanders reds.

SENSORY VOCABULARY
CLOVE, ALLSPICE (4-VINYL GUAIACOL)

TYPE: Aroma

DESCRIPTORS: Clove, phenolic

THRESHOLD IN BEER: Around 1 ppb

APPROPRIATENESS: At detectable levels only in German weizens and some Belgian-style ales

SOURCE: Formed during fermentation from precursor, ferulic acid (interestingly, also a precursor to vanillin), formed during malt kilning

A few beer types require very specialized yeasts to create the appropriate flavor profile. Bavarian Weissbier, a.k.a. hefeweizen, uses a unique yeast that produces a clove aroma, along with banana and bubble-gum fruitiness. The Belgian farmhouse ale saison employs a unique strain thought to be related to red-wine yeast. This strain is most notable for its ability to thrive at temperatures up to 90°F (32°C), which is very high compared to normal ale yeast. It's a low-ester and high-phenol producer, giving a unique black-pepper spiciness that is a cornerstone of the style. It is one of the great delights of Belgian beer that many styles rely on highly individualistic yeast strains.

Then there are beer styles that rely on different species of yeast, and even bacteria, for their unique taste and aroma profiles. All of these listed below are dreaded contaminants in most breweries; brewers bold enough to bring them under their roofs need to take extraordinary measures to prevent their escape and the consequent fouling up of the whole place. Here are a few of them:

Brettanomyces. A slow-growing yeast that may be endemic to oak wood. Plays a role in lambic, some saisons, and traditional English old ales. Has barnyard or horsey aromas. Metabolizes maltose. Can be used alone to (slowly) ferment a beer. Also seeing use among adventurous brewers in North America.

SENSORY VOCABULARY
BARNYARD, BRETT (4-ETHYL PHENOL)

TYPE: Aroma

DESCRIPTORS: Horsey, horse blanket, barnyard

THRESHOLD IN BEER: Around 420 ppb

APPROPRIATENESS: Commonly found only in *Brettanomyces*-affected beers

SOURCE: Produced by *Brettanomyces* yeast; may be accompanied by 4-ethyl guaiacol or more peppery phenols

Pichia and Candida. Film-forming yeast similar to those in sherry; minor player in lambic but also occurs as a spoilage organism.

Lactobacillus and Pediococcus. Related genera that do the job of souring lambic and Berliner Weisse. Depending on the species, can also create a lot of diacetyl (buttery) and goaty, sweaty socks–reminiscent aromas.

Acetobacteria. Transforms alcohol into acetic acid but requires oxygen to do so. Adds vinegar or pickle aromas but may also create a fair amount of ethyl acetate (see page 91). Common in oak-aged beers and important to the aromas of lambics and especially Flanders-style red/brown ales.

SENSORY VOCABULARY
GOATY (CAPRYLIC, CAPROIC, CAPRIC ACIDS)

TYPE: Aroma

DESCRIPTORS: Goaty, animal, sweaty socks, sweaty

THRESHOLD IN BEER: 8 to 15 ppm, depending on specific chemical

APPROPRIATENESS: Generally unpleasant; sub-threshold may add earthy complexity

SOURCE: Part of a large family of organic acids with animal aromas common in many foods and beverages

SENSORY VOCABULARY
RANCID BUTTER, VOMIT (BUTYRIC ACID)

TYPE: Aroma

DESCRIPTORS: Rancid butter, vomit, sour, putrid

THRESHOLD IN BEER: 2 to 3 ppm

APPROPRIATENESS: In very low quantities may add a pleasant funk but usually quite a negative aroma

SOURCE: Common in wild fermentations and lactic beers, especially in sour-mashed beers, also caused by bacterial contamination in beer

After the early stages of fermentation, beer begins a process of maturation or conditioning. During this time, raw "green" flavors are mellowed by the yeast's continued metabolic activities. Errant molecules are roped back into the yeast cells and changed into something less obnoxious. During this time, yeast and other particles in the beer slowly settle out. Stronger beers take much longer to condition than everyday ones. Normal English-style ales might not need even 2 weeks before they're ready to drink, while a barley wine might take 6 months or more to reach proper condition. Because everything is moving in slow motion at near-freezing temperatures, conditioning a lager takes much longer. The average is 4 to 6 weeks, but a big doppelbock may take 6 months or more.

SENSORY VOCABULARY
ESTERY/BANANA (ISOAMYL ACETATE)

TYPE: Aroma

DESCRIPTORS: Banana, circus peanuts

THRESHOLD IN BEER: 1.2 ppm

APPROPRIATENESS: In small amounts, it is an important contributor to fruity aromas in beer. In larger amounts, it may be a sign of a too-high fermentation temperature, improper wort aeration, or other yeast stressors. Often found in very high-alcohol beers.

SOURCE: Formed during fatty acid synthesis, then leaks out of yeast cells. Common and desirable, if not out of control, in Bavarian weizens.

SENSORY VOCABULARY
HYDROGEN SULFIDE

TYPE: Aroma

DESCRIPTORS: Rotten eggs, sewer gas

THRESHOLD IN BEER: Below 1 ppb

APPROPRIATENESS: Occasional whiff in a lager acceptable

SOURCE: A metabolic by-product of yeast, especially certain lager strains. Stressed or mutated yeast may produce this chemical, sometimes as a result of copper deficiencies. Large amounts of hydrogen sulfide can be indicative of bacterial infection, especially of *Zymomonas*.

NOTE: This is a very volatile compound and may be detected when a beer is first tasted, but then it seems to vanish.

SENSORY VOCABULARY
SULFUR DIOXIDE (SULFITE)

TYPE: Aroma

DESCRIPTORS: Burnt matches, pungent, burning sulfur

THRESHOLD IN BEER: 25 ppm

APPROPRIATENESS: Occasional whiff in a lager acceptable

SOURCE: A metabolic by-product of yeast; most commonly a symptom of too-young "green" beer; certain lager strains are known for this. Stressed or mutated yeast may produce this chemical, and it may be symptomatic of nutritional deficiencies.

SENSORY VOCABULARY
OTHER ESTERS

TYPE: Aroma

ETHYL HEXANOATE (also known as ethyl caproate)

> **DESCRIPTORS:** Ripe apple, hints of aniseed

> **THRESHOLD IN BEER:** 0.37 to 0.21 ppm

PHENYLETHYL ACETATE

> **DESCRIPTORS:** Honey, sweet, flowery, roses

> **THRESHOLD IN BEER:** 3.8 ppm

ETHYL BUTYRATE

> **DESCRIPTOR:** Pineapple candy; classic in some *Brettanomyces* strains

> **THRESHOLD IN BEER:** 300 ppm

GIVEN ENOUGH TIME, beer will usually clear itself just fine. But because brewing is a commercial activity, it is sometimes necessary to speed things up a bit. A process called "fining" is often used, in which a gelatin or other substance is put into the beer to "pull down" yeast and other flotsam. Isinglass, the dried swim bladders of certain fish, is the traditional English fining, but gelatin works along similar lines. Silica and special plastic microspheres (PVPP/Polyclar) may be used to remove chill haze. A newer product called Clarity Ferm or Brewers Clarex prevents chill haze and, because it is an enzyme that attacks specific amino acids, has the additional benefit of reducing gluten to below the 20 ppm international standard for "gluten-free."

Filtration is a more powerful tool, but it can be too effective. In theory, a filter can be set to remove the finest particulates and bacteria. However, in practice, if a filter is too restrictive, it can remove color, hop bitterness, and body- and head-forming proteins from the beer. The so-called cold-filtration process that Miller licensed from Sapporo seeks to avoid these problems, but it is an expensive and complex process suitable only for megabreweries. Another solution for larger breweries is a centrifuge, which spins out particulate matter in a highly controlled way and may be used on its own or as a prefilter.

It should be noted that filtration will not speed up beer's maturation. Too-early filtration can lead to "green" beer aromas, especially of acetaldehyde and possibly diacetyl as well.

In many beers, the yeast is not completely removed through filtration. If some yeast is left in the beer when it is put into the bottle or cask along with a small amount of sugar and left to ferment, the additional carbon dioxide produced will be trapped, providing natural carbonation. Live yeast in the bottle or cask actually scavenges the dreaded oxygen, keeping the beer fresh tasting longer. Products that are naturally carbonated in the serving cask or bottle are called "real ale." This is the traditional method used for English ales, but many Belgian ales and American craft beers are bottle conditioned, too.

SENSORY VOCABULARY
ETHANOL/ETHYL ALCOHOL

TYPE: Aroma, sensation (warming as you swallow)

DESCRIPTORS: Alcoholic, sweet, warming

THRESHOLD IN BEER: Around 6 percent

APPROPRIATENESS: In normal-strength beers, usually not detectable

SOURCE: The main product of yeast fermentation (with carbon dioxide)

SENSORY VOCABULARY
HIGHER ALCOHOLS/FUSELS

NOTE: Four fusels are listed here, but in reality there are many more. It is rare for beer tasters to be able to pick out these individual compounds because there is a mix of fusels and (let's hope!) they rarely are the primary aromas in beer. They are normally perceived as harshly alcoholic on the nose and sometimes hot and peppery on the palate.

TYPE: Aroma

APPROPRIATENESS: Usually not detectable in normal-strength beers but adds to overall character; elevated in higher-temperature fermentations

SOURCE: Yeast metabolism

2-PHENYLETHANOL

DESCRIPTOR: Roses

THRESHOLD IN BEER: 45 to 50 ppm

1-PROPANOL/N-PROPANOL/PROPYL ALCOHOL

DESCRIPTORS: Sharp, musty, rubbing alcohol

THRESHOLD IN BEER: 600 ppm

ISOBUTANOL/ISOBUTYL ALCOHOL

DESCRIPTORS: Winelike, ethereal, unaged whiskey

THRESHOLD IN BEER: 80 to 100 ppm

ISOAMYL ALCOHOL

DESCRIPTORS: Fusel, ethereal, fruity, banana

THRESHOLD IN BEER: 50 to 60 ppm

Real-ale casks are delivered to the pub while still fermenting. It is the pub's responsibility to manage this process and determine when the beer is fit to serve. This is a challenging process, but aficionados feel the extraordinary texture and subtle flavors of real ale are worth the effort. For more on real ale, see pages 161–68.

At the opposite end of the spectrum is pasteurization. In this process, the finished beer is heated for a short time to temperatures high enough to kill any remaining yeast and bacteria, typically 2 to 3 minutes at 140°F (60°C). Some studies have shown that "cooked" flavors of pasteurized beer can be detected by expert panels, but they clearly pose no problem for the millions of people who regularly consume pasteurized beer. Flash pasteurization before packaging is generally regarded as being kinder to beer flavor. In this method, the beer is heated to 161 to 165°F (72 to 74°C) for 15 to 30 seconds. Either method ensures the beer will never spoil, but at a cost of being artificially aged by the heat of pasteurization (equivalent to several weeks in the bottle before ever leaving the brewery). Almost all keg beer sold in the United States is unpasteurized, which is the reason it should always be kept below 38°F (3°C).

A similar debate rages over carbonation. In most breweries, carbon dioxide gas is dissolved in beer, either in-tank during conditioning, or postfiltration just before bottling. More rarely, the tanks are simply closed toward the end of fermentation and fitted with a bleeder valve that allows carbonation to safely build to the desired level. Proponents of the latter method claim a finer bead and tighter head results, but it's a very subtle point and not generally agreed on.

SENSORY VOCABULARY
ACETALDEHYDE

TYPE: Aroma

DESCRIPTORS: Green apple, overripe apple, wet grass, raw pumpkin, latex paint, avocado; sometimes a little solventy as well

THRESHOLD IN BEER: Around 10 ppm

APPROPRIATENESS: Should never be detectable

SOURCE: Formed in the metabolic process as the yeast rids itself of waste carbon dioxide from its precursor pyruvate. A common symptom of too-young, "green" beer. Most acetaldehyde is eventually taken up by the yeast and converted to ethanol. Unwanted oxygen in the package may also be responsible for detectable acetaldehyde levels; it's also common in beers with extended wood aging, such as Flemish sour brown and red ales.

SENSORY VOCABULARY
MERCAPTAN (METHANETHIOL, ETHANETHIOL)

TYPE: Aroma

DESCRIPTORS: Rotten, garbage can, drainpipes

THRESHOLD IN BEER: 1.5 ppb (methanethiol)

APPROPRIATENESS: Can contribute some meaty complexity, but if noticeable can be an unpleasant off-flavor

SOURCE: Yeast breakdown (autolysis); fairly common in lager because of its extended aging on yeast; can also be a sign of bacterial contamination

Packaging and Beyond

In a brewpub, packaging can be as simple as just racking the beer over to a serving tank. But for most breweries, packaging can be one of the most challenging aspects of production. It is telling that of the three-volume set of books published by the Master Brewers Association of the Americas, the packaging volume is by far the largest. The equipment for bottling is large, complex, and expensive. Operating a bottling line is a high skill. Poorly packaged beer can suffer from a number of problems that customers can actually taste in the glass.

The most important potential problem is oxygen. Too much in the brewing process and the beer can develop stale, cardboard flavors; in the package, oxygen may create elevated acetaldehyde levels. There is no generally agreed-upon low limit for oxygen in the bottle. It's always bad to some degree, and brewers can become obsessed with getting the numbers down. Sierra Nevada switched from twist-off to regular bottle caps with a special lining, because tests showed that the pry-off caps kept the oxygen out a little better.

The other most common packaging problem is really a marketing choice. Clear or green bottles offer no protection from the wavelengths of blue light that cause beer to become skunked (see Sensory Vocabulary: Skunky [3-methyl-2-butene-1-thiol or 3MBT], page 100). Brown bottles provide excellent protection from sunlight or the fluorescent tubes that typically cause skunking. But as an English brewmaster, holding his beautiful clear bottles full of skunky beer, declared, "Yeah, but they look bloody great, don't they?"

It should be pointed out that Miller uses a specially processed hop-bittering extract called Tetra Hop that removes the offending precursor to skunking. As an interesting side benefit, Tetra Hop actually improves the foam stability of beer, and other brewers are looking at it specifically for its foam-enhancing properties.

HOW BEER STALES

While drinking beer is supposed to be about pleasure, tasting beer sometimes involves a certain element of pain. Beer is not always perfect. Not every beery flavor is delicious, and as tasters our job is to make note of every sensation we find, not just the happy ones. Beer is a fragile product that is vulnerable to the whims of nature and easily tainted by tiny wild beasts, poorly tended tap systems, and, more than anything else, the passage of time.

Stale beer is the brewing industry's number one technical problem, costing millions of dollars every year. Staling turns beautiful freshly brewed beer into a disappointing soup of blandness punctuated by notes of cardboard, decaying apples, and other unpleasantness. There is probably more funding and experimental science going on in this area than in just about any other aspect of brewing. And why not? Every brewery — but those that exclusively brew wild and sour beers excepted to some degree — must deal with the issue of stale beer in the market. The stakes are high.

The life-sustaining air that surrounds us is deadly for fresh, delicious beer. Even though oxygen and time are the major villainous actors, the stage is set long before bottling day, reaching all the way back to the chosen breeds

CANS VERSUS BOTTLES

Cans, long the symbol of mass-market blandness, are hot right now. The craft-can phenomenon started in hiker-friendly Colorado and has spread throughout the United States and beyond over the last decade. In terms of energy use and recyclability, cans have a lot of benefits. Their compact form and low weight means almost twice as much beer can fit on a truck as when it's in longneck bottles. Aluminum is valuable and easy to recycle, so it is reused at a very high rate compared to glass.

The bottom-line question is, "Are cans better for the beer?" With the caveat that any package is only as good as the machine that fills it, cans do have some advantages. The seal around the rim is a better barrier to oxygen, the main culprit in beer staling, than a bottlecap's plastic liner. As a result, shelf life may be a little longer for cans. And it is obvious that a sheet of metal forms a perfect barrier to the light that causes skunking, although it should be said that brown bottles also do an adequate job. On the flip side, all beverage cans have an epoxy liner containing large amounts (up to 80 percent of the epoxy) of a chemical called bisphenol-A, or BPA, which is thought to be an endocrine disruptor and has been implicated in high blood pressure. Some of this chemical does find its way into the bodies of those who eat and drink from cans, but at present, questions remain about how much of a health risk it poses. Efforts are under way to find an acceptable substitute, but progress has been slow.

of barley and the conditions under which they were grown. Being only a dabbler in this complex and highly technical area, I will attempt only a brief summary and hope no actual brewing scientists are reading.

While brewers typically place a 6-month shelf life on their products, the reality is that most of us can taste deterioration much sooner than that. The tasters at New Belgium Brewing Co. are so finely trained on stale flavors that they can differentiate between Fat Tire fresh off the bottling line and the same product just 1 week old. Even if we can't identify specific off-flavors, we often grapple with beers that just seem a little dull and drab, lacking the bright, fresh aromas and that sense of life we value so highly. Hops are especially vulnerable to the decay of freshness over time. Both bitterness and aroma fade, perhaps by as much as half in just a few months.

Beyond the simple wasting away of fresh, bright flavors, other changes pile on layers of weird fruitiness, beeswax, and unwelcome sweet breadiness, topped off by a flavor that is universally described as wet paper with nuances of shoe box, often accompanied by a drying, astringent finish. This wet-paper flavor is caused by an aldehyde — trans-2-nonenal — that is the most characteristic flavor of a beer in the final throes of old age. This paperiness may be apparent in the aroma but is usually more obvious in the taste, especially at the finish. It's not pleasant.

Other aldehydes and several esters accumulate over time, obscuring beer's more subtle aromas. Overripe apple can be common, along with a sickly sweet honey/beeswax note and sometimes a hint of aniseed.

For the übergeeks out there, here's a little more detail: Oxidation of lipids, or fats, is one of the prime movers here, but there are many

CLEANING AND SANITIZING

Cleaning and sanitation are of supreme importance in brewing beer. The late homebrewer and scientist Dr. George Fix used to say, "You can't sanitize dirt," which gives you an idea of the relationship between the two. Special chemicals and, in larger breweries, mechanized spray-down cleaning equipment are available to do the job, but it is the ever-vigilant eye of the detail-obsessed brewer that really makes cleanliness happen. And there's always some elbow grease involved.

Poorly sanitized equipment can provide a safe harbor for quite a number of offensive bugs that can get into beer at various stages, along with unwanted flavors, aromas, and more. Bacteria and wild yeast often produce large and unpleasant amounts of aroma chemicals that cultured yeast makes only in desirably modest quantities. *Lactobacillus* and *Pediococcus* are the most notorious, but there are many others in the gang.

compounds in malt, hops, and beer that play active roles in the process. There aren't a ton of fats in malt, but as they oxidize into potent flavor chemicals, a little goes a long way. Some dark malts (and caramelized wort as well) are rich in chemicals that act as reductones, absorbing and later releasing oxygen. The caramel/crystal malts are especially suspect in this process, and those in the middle of the range (about 60 °Lovibond) seem to be the most problematic. Beyond the weakening of aroma and bitterness, hops create other problems, as pigments known as carotenoids morph over time into something called damascenone, which has a sort of currantlike fruitiness that is not as pleasant as it sounds.

Various types of barley and malts differ in their vulnerability to oxidation and staling, but no matter the recipe, brewers must be careful during brewing not to offer the hot mash or wort easy access to air, as exposure to oxygen in the brewing or packaging process lays the groundwork for staling later. This is so important that packaging managers are sometimes given bonuses for keeping oxygen pickup at acceptably low levels. This is one of the biggest differences between small, semimanual bottling equipment and larger more sophisticated bottling lines, as equipment quality can dramatically affect the shelf life of packaged beer. Heat is also the enemy, as it accelerates all the chemical reactions to which beer is susceptible. Beer will age twice as fast at room temperature as it will at cellar temperatures. Just a few hours at elevated temperatures can add months' worth of aging.

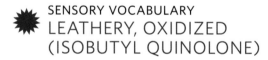

SENSORY VOCABULARY
LEATHERY, OXIDIZED (ISOBUTYL QUINOLONE)

TYPE: Aroma

DESCRIPTORS: Old leather, saddle, tobacco, aged barley wine

THRESHOLD IN BEER: 20 ppb

APPROPRIATENESS: Common in aged beers and, when combined with sherrylike oxidized components, can be part of a pleasant aged-beer flavor profile; inappropriate in nonaged beers

SOURCE: Oxidation of malt components; seems to be especially prevalent in beers with a high percentage of midcolor (40–80 °Lovibond/80–160 EBC) crystal/caramel malts

SENSORY VOCABULARY
HONEY (ETHYL PHENYLACETATE)

TYPE: Aroma

DESCRIPTORS: Honey, beeswax, sweetish aroma

THRESHOLD IN BEER: 160 ppb

APPROPRIATENESS: A positive component of honey beers but a very common indicator of oxidation in nonhoney beers; often quite noticeable in stale imported lagers

SOURCE: Oxidation component of stale beer

SIGNS OF STALENESS AND AGING

As beer gets older, its flavor changes (for more on this, see pages 177–80). Lighter beers change fastest, and higher temperatures accelerate the process.

First, hop aromas begin to dull, and there is the sense that the beer is just tired out. Papery or cardboard oxidation aromas start to become evident. The beer might display a waxy, appley, or honeylike aroma that's different from fresh malt. Hop bitterness also decreases. When they are extremely stale, pale filtered beers start to throw a little haze or have "snowflakes," both of which develop from proteins coming out of solution.

Unfiltered or bottle-conditioned beers contain yeast, which is a pretty good scavenger of oxygen. As a result, this type of beer ages a little more slowly, but a bit of yeast in the bottle is no panacea. The same group of off-flavors found

Brown is the only color of glass that can protect beer from the skunky aromas caused by blue light interacting with certain hop compounds. Cans and ceramic bottles offer good protection. Green and clear bottles offer no protection.

in filtered beers will show up in these as well. Yeast itself can also contribute its own flavors as it breaks down and releases chemicals from inside its cells. These may taste soapy or a bit toasty like vintage champagne, or perhaps a bit brothy like soup stock. With beers aged for years, some umami tastes may show up as a bit of soy sauce flavor.

SENSORY VOCABULARY
SKUNKY (3-METHYL-2-BUTENE-1-THIOL OR 3MBT)

TYPE: Aroma

DESCRIPTORS: Skunky, rubbery

THRESHOLD IN BEER: 0.05 ppb

APPROPRIATENESS: Never

SOURCE: Formed by the reaction between blue light and hop-bittering compounds (isohumulones). May happen in a matter of seconds, even in a fluorescent-lit cooler case. Brown bottles are good, but not perfect, protection.

SENSORY VOCABULARY
STALE HOPS (BETA DAMASCENONE)

TYPE: Aroma

DESCRIPTORS: Black currant, Ribena (black currant soda), grape jelly

THRESHOLD IN BEER: 25 ppb

APPROPRIATENESS: Never

SOURCE: A breakdown product of carotenoid pigments in hops. A common sign of staling in hoppy beers.

In a beer with a high alcohol content, aging can be beautifully graceful, as bright hoppy or fruity flavors fade to a dry, burnished maltiness, sometimes with a sort of leathery tang or a pleasing port or sherry character. These qualities develop only after several months in the bottle and can continue to evolve in a delicious way for years if the beer is strong and well brewed and properly stored. Additionally, oxidation often shows up as a sort of leathery aroma that can be quite pleasant in the right context, which is to say stronger and darker beers. However, hop flavors fade and may pick up an unpleasant black currant aroma. Years-old beers display tastes of umami (see chapter 2), a result of broken-down proteins, as well as soy sauce flavors of similar origins. A few years ago I tasted a Yorkshire beer that had been carefully aged since 1958, and it tasted as if it were only a few years old. Such beers are quite rare these days, although older literary references abound with descriptions of beers that were decades old and fine as any liquor. We'll talk about how to properly age beer in chapter 6.

Sadly, however, the vast majority of beers are like flowers blooming in the sunshine. Each has its brief moment, and then, poof, they become reminders of the swift passage of time and of the importance of seizing the moment and enjoying every sweet, fresh, delicious drop.

SENSORY VOCABULARY
SOLVENTY-STALE (FURFURYL ETHYL ETHER/FEE)

TYPE: Aroma

DESCRIPTORS: Stale-solventy, chemical

THRESHOLD IN BEER: 6 ppb

APPROPRIATENESS: Never

SOURCE: Develops during aging from precursors formed during malt kilning and in combination with sugars and amino acids in the boil; a pretty consistent marker chemical for beer staleness. As with most stale flavors, FEE develops faster at higher temperatures.

SENSORY VOCABULARY
AUTOLYSED

TYPE: Aroma, flavor

DESCRIPTORS: Autolysed, muddy, soy sauce, Marmite, umami, soap

THRESHOLD IN BEER: Varies

APPROPRIATENESS: Generally not pleasant; acceptable in older, stronger beers

SOURCE: Various lipids and amino acids, the results of the disintegration of yeast cells

SENSORY VOCABULARY
MUSTY/MOLD (TRICHLOROANISOLE)

TYPE: Aroma

DESCRIPTORS: Moldy, corked

THRESHOLD IN BEER: Less than 0.1 ppt (parts per trillion!)

SOURCE: In cork-finished bottles, may be the result of tainted corks or mold-tainted malt. Moldy aromas may migrate through plastic hoses in wet brewery locations and also contaminate empty bottles and cans during storage. Amazingly potent odorant! Generally tolerated as rustic earthiness in cork-finished beers but scorned as an awful flaw in wine.

OTHER musty/moldy compounds that can taint beer include geosmin (earthy, beetlike), 2-ethyl fenchol (earthy, with patchouli top notes), and many others; usually they are formed in damp locations and are imparted to the beer or brewing ingredients through plastic or wood, or via contaminated packaging materials.

SENSORY VOCABULARY
CHLOROPHENOL

TYPE: Aroma

DESCRIPTORS: Band-Aid, adhesive tape, disinfectant

THRESHOLD IN BEER: Less than 0.5 ppb

APPROPRIATENESS: Should never be detectable

SOURCE: Commonly a reaction of residual chlorine or chloramine in brewing liquor reacting with phenolic compounds in malt and wort. Also a common problem at the point of service if chlorine or bromine sanitizers are incompletely rinsed from glassware.

OTHER SOURCES OF OFF-FLAVORS

When the beer leaves the brewery, it is subject to a host of woes. Time and temperature are the enemies, but so are vibration, indifference, and laziness. Keeping beer fresh in its home country is difficult enough, but the challenges multiply when beer is shipped across the globe. It is pretty standard practice to put a 6-month shelf life date on beers that are staying close to home. Beers destined for export often double that to a year. It's a dirty little secret that this is wildly optimistic for normal-strength beers (under 6 percent volume). No matter how sophisticated the brewery, most beer deteriorates noticeably in a matter of weeks, and expert panels can tell the difference a week or two makes. Consumers have less acute palates, but almost anyone who has made the effort to compare a truly fresh beer with a 3-month-old product could likely tell the difference, even if he or she couldn't articulate the particulars. It makes you realize what a minor miracle a great-tasting beer really is when you finally get one in your hands.

Mishandling at the point of service poses several flavor problems, and these are almost entirely beyond the reach of the brewer. Tap lines are subject to exactly the same sanitation and infection issues as breweries, especially the buttery/hazy contamination of *Lactobacillus* and *Pediococcus*. Oxygen-loving *Acetobacter* can live in beer taps and introduce vinegar aromas in the first few pours of the day. A regular and rigorous program of line cleaning can prevent this, but not all bars and restaurants go by the book in this regard. At a minimum, a good cleaning every other week should prevent major problems. The most fanatical publicans clean their lines weekly. Incompletely rinsed glassware sanitizers can produce a Band-Aid aroma of chlorophenol or bromophenol.

It can be worth your while to take a tour of a brewery to see up close how all this brewing actually happens. There are a lot of technical details covered in this chapter, but as I've tried to make clear, these kinds of decisions are the heart and soul of brewing and really are what makes one beer different from another. Think about these decisions as you sip and your beer will tell you a story.

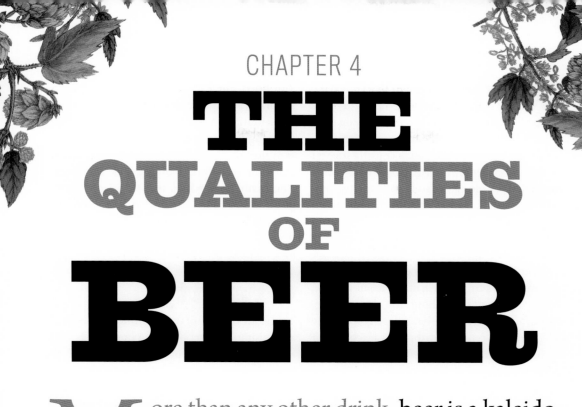

CHAPTER 4

THE QUALITIES OF BEER

More than any other drink, beer is a kaleidoscope of colors, flavors, strengths, balance, and other attributes. We have already seen the huge range of flavors and aromas contributed by ingredients and the brewing process. In this chapter, we'll see how those add up and present themselves in a finished beer.

WHAT KIND OF VARIABLES are we talking about here? First comes strength, both in terms of alcohol and the even more important measure of gravity, which is the amount of dissolved solids (mostly sugars) in the unfermented wort. More malt brings more alcohol, along with a host of malty, caramelly, toasty, and roasty flavors, depending on the recipe. More malt requires more hops, and that ramps up flavor even more. You can see how this adds up.

Beer is a whole rainbow of color. No other beverage goes from palest straw to inky black, surely offering something for every taste, mood, and moment. We have already seen how different malt types contribute to a rich mix of flavors in beer. Here, we will look at the way color is measured and described.

Bitterness may be minimal or quite confrontational, and when you layer on floral, spicy, herbal hop aromas, you have another dramatic way that beers can vary from one another.

Because there are so many variables and brewers have a need to be able to tightly control them, it is important to have objective measures that can be expressed numerically. Numbers aren't everything, but words are just not as specific or objective as a numerical system. For reasons of consistency, economics, quality control, judging, and even matters such as taxation, numbers are essential.

I don't think you need to run out and buy an ultraviolet spectrophotometer to determine the bitterness value of every beer you drink (although they're pretty cheap on eBay), but it is important to be fluent in the numerical language of beer. After working with these measurements for a while, one develops a pretty good idea of what a 1.065 gravity, a 44 IBU bitterness, or an 8 degree SRM color actually drinks like. Practice makes perfect, but nobody ever complains about practice with beer.

Gravity

This is the density of wort or unfermented beer and is simply a way of saying how much sugar and other dissolved solids are contained in the beer. There are two main numerical systems used to describe this in beer. First is degrees Plato, which is expressed as a percentage by weight of the dissolved solids. A 10 degrees Plato wort contains 10 percent solids, a 12 degrees Plato wort contains 12 percent, and so on. Older books may mention a scale called Balling, which was the standard of the day until Professor Plato fixed it up. Plato is used by all German brewers and by lager brewers worldwide, but it is not the only scale. The Czechs still use the Balling scale, as he was one of their own. If you've heard the term "Brix" in

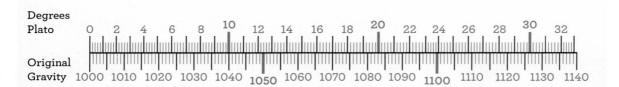

Original Gravity and Degrees Plato
This chart shows the relationship between these two different systems used to express wort density.

connection with wine, it's just about the same scale as Plato, but that term is almost never used in brewing.

The British use a scale called original gravity (OG). This is the specific gravity relative to water — the ratio of the weight of the wort to the weight of the same amount of pure water. Our 10 and 12 degrees Plato worts would have original gravities of 1.040 and 1.049, respectively, meaning they are 1.040 and 1.049 times as heavy as pure water. Sometimes the decimal point is omitted as a matter of convenience. English ale drinkers still look for the gravity on the tap handles as a way of gauging how strong (and how expensive) a particular beer is. Because so much of the early homebrewing literature was English, many American homebrewers still think in terms of original gravity, and this is also common among brewpubs and other small-scale brewers.

It figures that the Belgians would have an oddball scale of their own: Belgian degrees, sometimes called *degré Régie* in the old books. To make sense of this scale, used mostly in reference to abbey-style beers, just remove the "1.0" from the specific gravity. For example, a 1.050 beer becomes a Belgian 5 degrees beer, a 1.080 beer becomes 8 degrees, and so on. Be aware that for many Belgian beers, these numerical designations were based on recipes from decades ago, and as beers change over time, these numbers should be considered approximate rather than accurate.

GRAVITY IS MEASURED in various ways. The simplest is with a hydrometer, which is a floating tube, usually of glass, with weights at the bottom and a thin glass tube at the top with a scale inside. The higher it floats, the higher the number that appears at the liquid line, which is how the instrument is read. Liquids, like all other materials, expand and contract according to temperature, which means the density of liquids changes with temperature. As a consequence, hydrometers are always calibrated for a particular temperature. Higher or lower than this, corrections must be made.

In 1785 a brewing scientist named John Richardson was the first to publish the results of brewing experiments with a hydrometer. He fairly well turned the brewing world on its head, but that is a story that belongs in the porter section (see pages 249–50).

An instrument called a refractometer uses the refractive, or light-bending, power of sugar to make an accurate measurement of gravity. A drop is placed inside, the lid is closed, and the gravity is read on a scale through the eyepiece. However, once the beer is fermented, the alcohol's higher refractive power distorts the measurements, so the refractometer is mostly a brewhouse, not a cellar, tool. High-precision measurements are made with a special vessel called a pycnometer that has a known and very accurate volume. It is weighed empty, then filled; the weight of the bottle is subtracted, and the weight of that volume is converted

Hydrometer
This simple tool floats at different levels depending on the density of the liquid, giving brewers a rough idea of the potential strength of their beers when fermented.

DRINKABILITY: WHAT IS IT?

Large brewers know that their customers value drinkability above almost everything else, and they have done a lot of research in the area. Despite this, it's still a difficult quality to define precisely. In the words of August Busch III, "You stop drinking because you know it's time to stop but you don't want to: that's drinkability." This quest is one thing driving the very low hop bitterness levels in mainstream beers. Anything that has taste will fatigue the palate, so malt is removed and replaced with corn or rice. Smoothness and freedom from aftertaste also count, which is why water is highly drinkable.

The drinkability attribute plays an important role in serious beer as well. There is no question that the 7 percent hop bombs emanating from the West Coast are, for most people — even craft-beer lovers — not all that great as session beers and are perhaps meant to titillate more than beguile. There is something quite remarkable about a beer of ordinary strength with enough personality and depth to keep you interested, but with enough subtlety to keep you charmed right to the bottom of the third pint.

into a gravity number. This is a laboratory procedure and is used only in labs and larger breweries. The guy on the brew deck in the rubber boots rarely needs such precision.

Gravity is a rough measure of the amount of alcohol that may end up in the finished beer. A good rule of thumb is that a 1.050 beer will be in the neighborhood of 5 percent; a 1.060 beer will be around 6 percent, and so on. However, this is a very rough measure, as differing worts have varying degrees of fermentability, and yeast further complicates the picture.

Alcohol and Attenuation

Ethyl alcohol (ethanol) is the main product of fermentation. There are two ways of expressing the amount of alcohol: percent by volume and percent by weight. The former is the current international standard, and that includes the United States. But between 1933 and 1990, the United States used the alcohol-by-weight standard. After the disaster of Prohibition, American brewers were eager to showcase their products as temperate beverages, so they chose the measurement system that gave the lowest numbers. A 3.2 percent beer by weight is actually a 4 percent beer by volume. Canada and the rest of the world stayed with the percent-by-volume measurement, and this is perhaps responsible for the legend that imported beer was so radically, mind-bendingly strong compared to domestic brew.

NOT EVERY WORT of the same gravity will yield a beer with the same alcohol content. The degree to which sugars in the wort are converted into alcohol is affected by the brewing process, sugar and adjuncts used, yeast strains, fermentation temperature, and other variables. The brewer has a lot of control over these processes in the brewhouse, where a hotter mash will produce a less fermentable wort and a cooler mash a more fermentable one.

Now we need to deal with the slightly confusing concept of attenuation and the different

ALCOHOL STRENGTH BY BEER STYLE

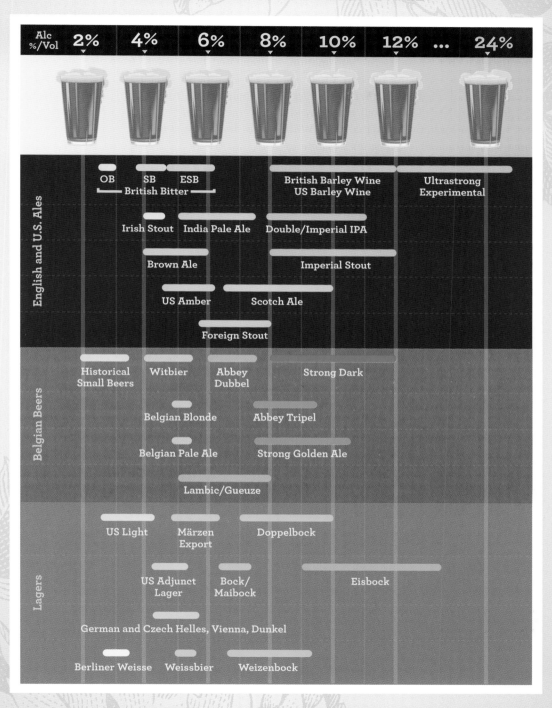

Alc %/Vol	2%	4%	6%	8%	10%	12%	...	24%

English and U.S. Ales

- OB SB ESB
- British Bitter
- British Barley Wine / US Barley Wine
- Ultrastrong Experimental
- Irish Stout India Pale Ale
- Double/Imperial IPA
- Brown Ale
- Imperial Stout
- US Amber Scotch Ale
- Foreign Stout

Belgian Beers

- Historical Small Beers
- Witbier Abbey Dubbel
- Strong Dark
- Belgian Blonde Abbey Tripel
- Belgian Pale Ale Strong Golden Ale
- Lambic/Gueuze

Lagers

- US Light Märzen Export Doppelbock
- US Adjunct Lager Bock/Maibock Eisbock
- German and Czech Helles, Vienna, Dunkel
- Berliner Weisse Weissbier Weizenbock

ways it may be measured and expressed. Most often, the brewer divides the finishing gravity by the starting gravity and subtracts that number from 100 to come up with the apparent attenuation. This gives useful information, but it is not a reflection of the true situation. Because alcohol is lighter than water, any alcohol present makes the terminal gravity readings appear lower than they actually are. With some very fermentable beers, it's possible to get higher than 100 percent apparent attenuation. To get "real attenuation," actual alcohol content must be measured. This is normally done by distilling the alcohol out of a small sample, so it's a bit of a cumbersome procedure and usually done only by larger breweries. All

but the largest craft breweries usually get along fine working with apparent attenuation.

Less attenuated beers are heavier and sweeter and have less alcohol than highly attenuated beers made from the same gravity wort. Highly attenuated beers have more of their extract turned into alcohol, and the extreme end of the scale encompasses low-carb, dry, and light beers.

Beer Color

Because we are such visual creatures, we are very sensitive to small differences in appearance, way out of proportion to the flavors. So getting color right is of extreme importance

BEER COLOR SCALE

Degrees SRM	2	3	4	6	9	12
	Pale Straw	Straw	Pale Gold	Deep Gold	Pale Amber	Medium Amber

Degrees SRM	15	18	21	24	30	40+
	Deep Amber	Amber-Brown	Brown	Ruby Brown	Deep Brown	Black

Beer colors as delineated on the American beer color scale, SRM. European (EBC) beer color numbers are about double SRM values.

to brewers. Despite many years of experimentation to create a more detailed view of beer color, the current measurement scale is a single numerical scale of light and dark. Because beer is a reddish liquid, it is most opaque to blue light, so that color gives the most sensitive readings and is the type of light used for measuring beer color. Technically speaking, beer color is 10 times the optical density (absorbance) in a 1 centimeter sample cuvette, as measured by a 430 nanometer blue light, typically in a spectrophotometer. This is the American Society of Brewing Chemists (ASBC) color standard, called the Standard Reference Method or degrees SRM. The ASBC is the organization that oversees analytical standards for brewing in the United States.

BEER COLOR AND BEER STYLES I: LIGHT BEERS

Arrows indicate the range of colors for commonly encountered beer styles.

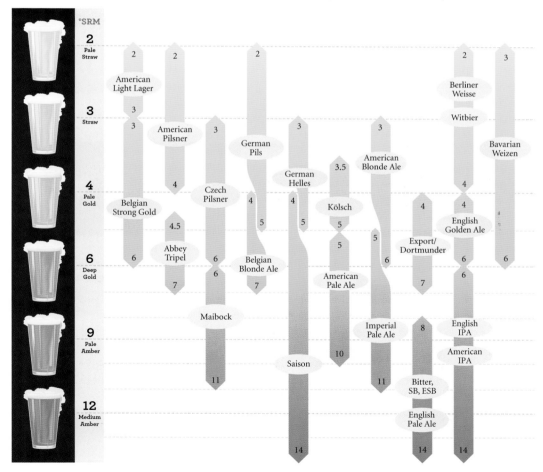

ORIGINALLY, BEER COLOR was determined by using a set of colored glasses devised by Joseph Lovibond in the late nineteenth century. A device similar to a stereoscope was held up to the light, beer samples were poured into a sample holder on one side, and then the operator would slide in different-colored glasses until a good match was found. Happily, when the spectrophotometric method was developed, the colors matched almost perfectly — which is why you still see beer color described as degrees Lovibond, and nobody gets too bent out of shape about it.

The Europeans use a different scale, the European Brewery Convention (EBC), the European equivalent of the ASBC, which, after recent efforts to coordinate with U.S. brewers, now reads approximately double (SRM × 1.97 = EBC) the American degrees SRM scale.

There is no generally agreed-on verbal description of a color scale for beer. In the chart on page 108, I have picked the most common and neutral terms available and paired them with sample pints that approximate the colors named.

Beer color varies a little between red and yellow. A method called "tristimulus" measures beer color in the same red, green, and blue wavelengths that the eye is most sensitive to, but this is only rarely used in brewing.

Spectrophotometer

This device measures how a specific wavelength of light is attenuated by a sample. In beer, it is used to measure color and sometimes other things.

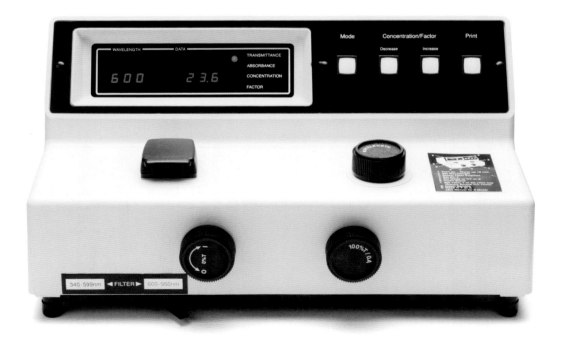

BEER COLOR AND BEER STYLES II:
MEDIUM AND DARK BEERS

Arrows indicate the range of colors for commonly encountered beer styles.

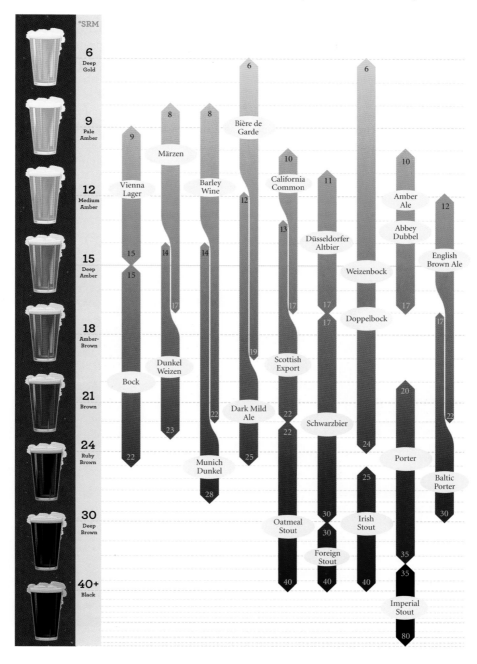

°SRM

6 Deep Gold

9 Pale Amber

12 Medium Amber

15 Deep Amber

18 Amber-Brown

21 Brown

24 Ruby Brown

30 Deep Brown

40+ Black

Hops, Bitterness, and Balance

Although hops contribute quite a complex aroma to beer, the only measurement routinely made is of a simple scale of bitterness. This is a measure of the bitter alpha acids from the hops, isomerized and dissolved during the boil. International bitterness units, or IBU, are the parts per million (ppm or mg/L) of iso-alpha acids in the finished beer. The laboratory analysis is done with reagent chemicals and an ultraviolet spectrophotometer. It's not too difficult to do, but the equipment is fairly expensive. Most small brewers calculate their IBUs during the recipe-formulation process and get an outside laboratory to do a proper analysis when they need accurate numbers.

Beers range from about 5 IBU to well over 100 IBU. The human threshold for the perception of bitterness in beer is about 6 IBU, and 6 IBU is also about the limit of human discrimination between different levels of bitterness.

Hop bitterness is absolutely critical to balance malt sweetness, even in the maltiest beer

BITTERNESS BY BEER STYLE

Bitterness is an important aspect of beer style. This chart shows some of the more common styles, measured in international bitterness units (IBU).

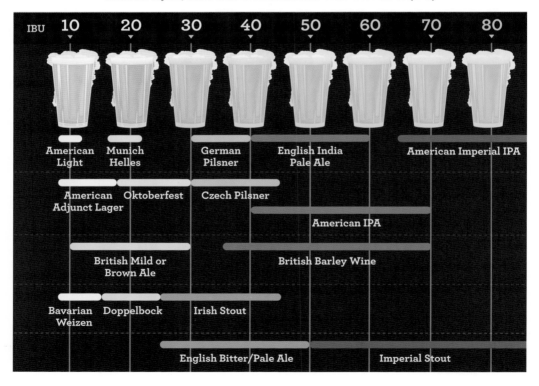

IBU | 10 | 20 | 30 | 40 | 50 | 60 | 70 | 80

American Light
Munich Helles
German Pilsner
English India Pale Ale
American Imperial IPA

American Adjunct Lager
Oktoberfest
Czech Pilsner

American IPA

British Mild or Brown Ale

British Barley Wine

Bavarian Weizen
Doppelbock
Irish Stout

English Bitter/Pale Ale

Imperial Stout

styles. The interplay between taste elements is very important for drinkability. Few beers are perfectly balanced; there's usually a tilt to one side or another. With malt, the paler types are perceived as purely malty, but this is a result of caramelization during kilning; flavors and aromas such as caramel, nutty, malty, and all the various types of roastiness may also be present in a beer. Some of these malt flavors can be very sweet and cloying and need hops to balance them, but roasty malt flavors often come down on the bitter side of the equation.

Bitterness from hops cuts sweetness and adds a refreshing quality. One way of measuring beer balance, at least as it applies to sweet malt versus hop bitterness, is the BU to GU

RELATIVE BITTERNESS (CICERONE BU:GU RATIO)

Bitterness tastes stronger in a weaker beer, so it's really the ratio of bitterness to original gravity that matters. The chart shows international bitterness units against gravity units — the two most significant digits of the original gravity (1050 = 50 gravity units).

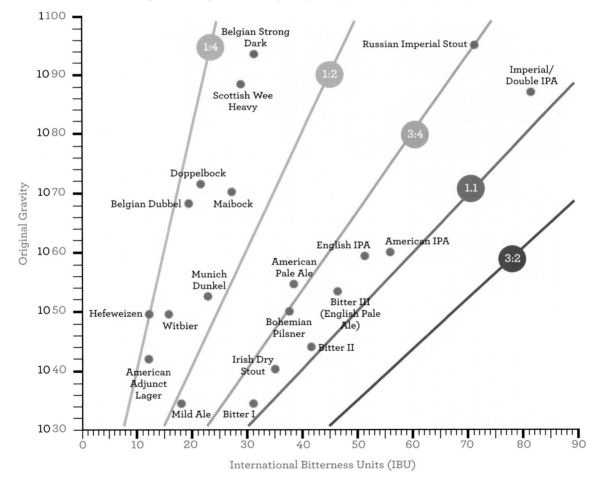

(bittering units to gravity units) ratio. (The BU is just the IBU we've been talking about.) Fifty IBU, for example, may be quite a lot of bitterness, but it sure tastes different in a big malty barley wine than it does in an English bitter. The GU is the wort's original gravity with the 1.0 removed: 1.050 OG becomes 50 GU. If you plot some familiar beer styles showing BU against GU (see chart on page 113), the differences pop into focus.

It is important to keep in mind that this BU to GU ratio only expresses the sweet malt versus bitter hops balance vector, and although this is the major sensory player in beer, there are many others; for instance, toast, roast, fruit, smoke, acid, and carbonation.

As for hop bitterness, once in the beer it's all pretty much the same. Hops express their considerable individuality through their aromas.

Haze and Beer Clarity

Since ancient times, people have praised the virtues of luminously clear beer. Today, clarity is a desirable aspect of almost all beer styles regardless of their origin. The important exceptions are noted below.

A perfectly clear beer requires expertise and vigilance on the part of the brewer. Malting, brewhouse procedures, fermentation, conditioning, filtration, and packaging all play a role. And this can all be for naught if the beer gets mishandled down the chain of distribution, as most beers of normal strength will throw a haze if they become old enough or are mistreated. Haze can be measured, but the numbers are never used in beer style specifications.

SOURCES OF HAZE IN BEER

Chill haze. This is the result of malt-derived proteins precipitating in the beer when chilled. It is often seen in unfiltered (or lightly filtered) craft beers, where it is felt that the cosmetic downside is a worthy trade-off for the added complexity of an unfiltered beer. Chill haze is totally flavorless and vanishes as soon as the beer warms up a bit.

Yeast haze. This may be either deliberate, as in the case of hefeweizen (see at right), or a consequence of a sloppy pour or shaken bottle of a sedimented, bottle-conditioned beer. In the hefeweizen, yeast may also contribute a slight bready yeastiness. In an aged bottle-conditioned beer, the yeast sometimes imparts a slightly muddy taste, which should be avoided if possible. Wheat beer kegs are often stored and shipped upside down, then turned over for serving, dispersing the yeast in the beer.

Starch haze. In certain archaic traditions, the brewing process is conducted so as to leave a fine opalescent "shine" to the beer. See Witbier/Bière Blanche/White Ale on page 299.

HAZE AS AN INDICATOR OF FLAWED BEER

Old or mishandled beer. A haze, often accompanied by small "snowflakes" of precipitated protein, is a common feature of seriously old beers, especially in pale imported lagers. Multiple cycles of cooling and warming accelerate the process.

Infection. Many beer-spoilage organisms will throw a haze. Dirty tap lines, a breeding place for *Lactobacillus* and *Pediococcus* bacteria, are an all-too-common culprit.

PURPOSEFULLY HAZY OR CLOUDY BEERS

Most barley-malt-based beers are designed to be served crystal clear, but a common feature of many wheat beers is a certain cloudiness. This goes back to the Middle Ages, when beers were divided into two classes, red and white. In addition to their paler color, the reference to "white" likely refers to their haziness.

Hefeweizen. The word *hefe* means "yeast," and indeed yeast is added to the bottles of this spritzy German wheat beer. Part of the pageant of serving this beer from the bottle is the dollop of dregs swirled atop the thick, creamy head. If you really must have your Weissbier clear, ask for a Kristal.

Berliner Weisse. This sour wheat beer may show a haze from the protein-rich wheat that makes up 50 to 60 percent of the recipe. In the photo below, it's dosed with the traditional green woodruff syrup, although raspberry syrup is also popular.

Witbier/Belgian white ale. This ancient style has a starchy sheen, a result of turbid mashing techniques — or a handful of flour tossed into the kettle.

Kellerbier. This little-known specialty is usually a pale German lager, served in its *bierkeller* directly from the aging tanks, without filtration. At least one bottled version is imported into the United States, and a few craft brewers have tried their hand at it, naturally.

"East Coast" IPA. A recent U.S. variant on IPAs has been a very cloudy version often brewed with wheat and/or oats. While the haze is attributed to the lack of filtration, there have been reports of brewers adding wheat flour to the kettle, which creates a lingering haze.

Hefeweizen is a wheat beer with *hefe*, or yeast, which gives a cloudy appearance.

Berliner Weisse in a classic goblet, flavored and colored by woodruff syrup.

FILTRATION: DREAM OR NIGHTMARE?

This is a very complex topic for which there is no simple answer. On the plus side, filtration is a fast and efficient way of removing yeast and other material that might otherwise contribute to instability and shorten the shelf life of certain beers. Bright, fresh beer at affordable prices is the benefit. Filtration is often used to speed up what happens naturally.

Like so many aspects of brewing, proper filtration requires a wise and experienced brewmaster. Well-filtered beer can indeed be a thing of beauty. The downside is that over-filtered beer may sometimes be stripped of color, body, head retention, and flavor, leading the drinker into bland land.

EVALUATING CLARITY

Unless the style specifies haze of some sort, all beers should be bright and clear when served. With pale beers, it's easy. In darker beers, haze may be masked by the color. As a rule, if you can't see it with the naked eye, it's not a problem, but some aficionados when evaluating dark beers for clarity use a small flashlight and observe the beam as it illuminates any suspended haze. When you look for clarity, remember to wipe the glass first, so you're not mistaking condensation for haze. And also allow craft beer to warm to the higher end of appropriate serving temperatures, as chill haze may disappear.

Carbonation and Beer Foam

The foamy, effervescent nature of beer has fascinated us since the very beginnings of our long love affair with it. Beer is the only beverage with real foam, a result of beer's unique protein structure. It's not just the drinker that takes foam seriously. It is one of the most technically complex and well-studied aspects of brewing, and its proper management starts with decisions made way out in the farm fields.

Foam is all about beer body. Proteins in beer form what is called a "colloid," a loose protein net that ties the whole beer together. You can actually taste or, rather, feel this as a fullness on the palate. It is very similar in structure to a thin sort of Jell-O. This colloidal state affects the surface tension of the beer, which in turn is crucial for the formation and retention of foam. It's a Goldilocks thing: beer foam requires proteins that are "just right" in length; those that are either too short or too long won't do. Hops and yeast also play a role. As I said, it's a complex topic.

Wheat has the right kind of proteins to form a great head, and this is one of the desirable characteristics of any wheat beer. In fact, wheat and other grains such as oats and rye are sometimes collectively called "head grains" and quietly find their way into recipes in which a little help with the head might be needed: Kölsch and English bitter come to mind.

Some substances in the serving environment are deleterious to beer foam. Either detergent or oil will kill a head pretty quickly — a testimonial for beer-clean glassware.

POURING FOR GREAT FOAM

At home. To get the best head on a beer, pour boldly down the center of an absolutely clean glass. It will foam up, but this is good. Really. Allow it to settle, and then repeat until you have a full glass. By delaying gratification and allowing a large amount of foam to build up and then shrink, you have created a dense, creamy foam, filled with tiny, long-lasting bubbles. As a side benefit, you have knocked some of the excess gas out of the beer, and the result will be more like the smooth creaminess of draft beer.

The bar pour. The procedure above generally takes too much time to be practical for the impatient patrons of American taverns. The usual procedure is to tilt the glass at an angle and pour down the side, then when the glass is two-thirds full, straighten it up and pour on top of the beer already in the glass to achieve a ½- to 1-inch (1.5 to 3 cm) cap of foam.

Pour straight down and let it foam up

Let the foam settle

Pour, wait, and repeat until filled to appropriate level

Enjoy!

SELECTED BEER STYLES AND CARBONATION LEVELS

HIGHLY CARBONATED BEER STYLES

STYLE	VOLUMES CO_2
Belgian strong golden	3.5–4
Belgian abbey	2.7–3.5
Belgian gueuze	3–4.5
Bavarian hefeweizen	3.5–4.5
Berliner Weisse	3.2–3.6
American lager, adjunct light beer	2.5–2.7

LIGHTLY CARBONATED BEER STYLES

STYLE	VOLUMES CO_2
British cask ale	0.8–1.5
Straight lambic	0.5–1.5
Barley wines	1.3–2.3
Imperial stout	1.5–2.3
Super-high-gravity ales	0–1.3

NORMALLY CARBONATED BEER STYLES

STYLE	VOLUMES CO_2
Normal lager range	2.2–2.7
Normal ale range	1.5–2.5

O F COURSE, there would be no foam if there weren't carbonation in beer. Carbon dioxide is highly soluble in water-based liquids, and a good deal of it can dissolve in a cold beer. Compare it to nitrogen, which has minimal solubility. On those draft cans of stout, as soon as you pop the top the nitrogen leaves the beer, which is what it's designed to do. Open a regular beer, and rather than gushing out, the CO_2 stays in the beer, even though there's a tremendous amount of dissolved gas in there (as evidenced by what happens if you shake the can before opening).

In the United States, brewers discuss carbonation using a measure called volumes, an

The delicate veil of Brussels lace clinging to the glass is a sign of a well-made beer and a clean glass.

CARBONATION: NATURAL VERSUS ARTIFICIAL

For many, forced carbonation is the tool of the devil himself, and because of the crusading nature of the Campaign for Real Ale's (CAMRA) battle to preserve traditional ales, the debate takes on an ideological rather than a scientific tenor. The dissolving of gas in a liquid is largely a matter of physics, no matter how it got there. The longevity of the bubbles, however, is highly dependent on the protein chemistry of the beer, and so is highly dependent on the brewing process and the way beer is fermented and especially how it is filtered and otherwise clarified. Opponents often conflate forced carbonation with other woes: high adjunct content, serving at improper (too cold) temperatures, pasteurization, and over-filtration. These things do change the taste of beer and affect its head. It is possible that careless forced carbonation can reduce a beer's head-forming ability by over-foaming in the tank during the process and using up the valuable head-forming proteins. With proper care a well-brewed, unfiltered, *living* ale should do just fine with forced carbonation.

absolute measure not affected by pressure or temperature. However, as you can see from the graph on page 152, the three are related; the higher the temperature, the more pressure at any given volume. Elsewhere in the world, the percentage of CO_2 by weight, typically grams per liter, is a more common measure (1 volume equals 1.96 g/L).

Not all beer styles are carbonated to the same degree. Beers such as cask ales are only lightly carbonated, as beer was ages ago. Wooden casks in the old days could stand only so much pressure. It doesn't hurt that British ale tastes great this way, never mind the fact that a highly carbonated beer served at cellar temperature would be asking for trouble. Because we like 'em c-c-c-cold and because the carbonation adds to the crisp, refreshing quality, American industrial-style beers are highly carbonated. The chart on the facing page lists a few more of the beer styles that fall outside the normal range of carbonation.

Color, clarity, carbonation, and much more — the range of qualities that beer displays is truly dazzling. I think that's one of the things that make our relationship to beer so compelling. No matter how schooled you think you are, there is always more to discover. Beer has a language all its own, and it gives up its secrets only if you approach it the right way. Treat it with respect, and gaze deeply into its amber, bubbling depths. If you listen very carefully, it will speak volumes to you.

CHAPTER 5

TASTING, JUDGING, AND EVALUATION

I t should be clear by now that this is not a book about the uncritical guzzling of beer (not that this practice is without its pleasures). This chapter is about the various ways and settings in which we taste and the goals of such encounters. I hope in every case there is some pleasure in it, but that may be far from the expressed purpose. No matter the situation, the chemistry of the beer remains the same, and we all bring our own physiology and psychology to every interaction.

DEPENDING ON THE OCCASION, your relationship to the beer will be very different. In a casual, fun, educational tasting, you are the beer's friend, trying to size him up, and like any friend, you should be gracious and tolerant of faults. Try to pick out the best, and don't dwell on — or at least publicly acknowledge — the shortcomings.

In a competition, it's your job to give him a merciless grilling, stacking him up against the other beers and possibly some idealized notion of the style. You and your tablemates might disagree, which can spark a debate of near-metaphysical import over intention, purity of concept, historical details, and a quality I like to call "wonderfulness" — a summation of artistic and technical brilliance in liquid form.

In serious quality-control settings, great care is taken to remove any notion of like or dislike. The taster's job is to describe, without editorializing, in highly standardized language. In the simplest and most accurate of all these tests — the triangle — the taster's job is simply to pick which two of three samples are identical.

As a taster, you will be tested, too. In casual settings, knowing details such as starting gravity, IBU, or what color pants the brewer wore while brewing will get you big-time beer-geek cred. But that's nothing compared to the study and work needed to pass the Beer Judge Certification Program (BJCP, the sanctioning organization for homebrew competitions) exam and move up through the ranks, nail your Cicerone exam, or earn the industry standing that gets you a seat at the World Beer Cup (WBC). In industry quality-control settings, it is also standard practice to train and calibrate judges, so that their strengths and weaknesses can be factored into evaluations of the sample beers.

The Tasting Environment

No matter what the purpose of the tasting, the environment is critical. The room should be reasonably comfortable; beyond that, here are a few helpful guidelines.

Limit distractions. Generally, the job is to get rid of distractions, as tasting takes intense concentration. You don't want to break the samplers out of their reverie. As you go from casual to structured, this becomes more important. Too many rules are overly restrictive for a social tasting, but in the most critical tests judges are put into small booths, so there's nothing else in the world but them and their sample cups of beer.

So anything not essential to the occasion must go. You want to separate your group from the Junior Miss Hemisphere Pageant going on in the ballroom next to you (a true story). It is quite reasonable to request that cell phones be turned off or set to vibrate, and some competitions ban them entirely. Judges who have finished should be quiet or leave the room. Do everything you can to make it easy to keep everyone's attention. A little background music is okay for very casual events, but it should not be so loud as to impede conversation.

Consider lighting. Good light is always welcome. The ideal, rarely achieved, is natural, north light. Lighting is not always under your control at hired locations, but it is something to consider, especially for competitions.

Provide water. No matter what the event, unlimited amounts of drinking water should be available. Municipal tap water can sometimes have a distracting amount of chlorine, and raw or softened well water rarely makes the grade. Unless you have access to great mountain tap water, stick to bottled.

Dump it. I might as well come out and say it: dump buckets. Painful as it is to throw away beer, you have to make it easy for people at any kind of tasting to throw it away, or else you just cultivate chaos.

Jot it down. For casual tastings, a listing of beers makes it easy for people to take notes and look for the beers in a store later on. Make sure there's paper and some pencils available, and make sure they are mechanical rather than wood; I have more than once had the thought, "Man, this is a cedary beer," only to realize a split second later that I'm holding a pencil and the glass in the same hand. As I said, details count.

Keep score. Judging depends heavily on score sheets, which have been structured to put the proper emphasis on various attributes of the beer, from appearance to aftertaste. The sheets are like a road map, guiding the judges as they consider every dimension and put it all into perspective. Even novice tasters can benefit from this kind of discipline, and it's a lot of fun to run through a few beers on the tasting sheet opposite or on score sheets downloaded from the BJCP or WBC websites.

Eliminate unwanted odors. Wayward aromas can be devastating. Grandma's perfume can stink up a whole city block; bless her, but there are times when it's gotta go. A little perfume is okay in casual or even educational settings, but there is no conceivable reason you would want it near a judging, a competition, or a professional taste panel. Even scented hand soap or lotion can interfere as you hold the cup up to your nose. The Great American Beer Festival swaps out the hotel's soap with a scentless formula in bathrooms adjacent to judging panels. And ladies, lipstick can ruin a beer's head. The other most common olfactory contaminant is the kitchen. Make sure you know in advance where it is relative to the tasting, and how well the vent fans work. This is generally not a problem, but when it's bad, it really stinks.

TASTING TYPES AND THEIR REQUIREMENTS

	AROMA-FREE	NO SMOKING	QUIET	DRINKING WATER	DUMP BUCKETS	NOTEPAPER	SCORE SHEETS	BEER LIST	STYLE GUIDELINES	NONWOOD PENCILS	CRACKERS OR BREAD
Casual Tasting	Y	Y	-	Y	Y	-	N	Y	-	OK	-
Structured	Y	Y	-	Y	Y	-	N	Y	OK	Y	-
Educational Presentation	Y	Y	-	Y	Y	Y	N	Y	OK	Y	OK
Casual Competition	Y	Y	N	Y	Y	Y	N	N*	N	Y	OK
Competition	Y	Y	Y	Y	Y	Y	Y	N*	OK	Y	Y
Sensory Panel	Y	Y	Y	Y	Y	-	Y	N	OK	Y	N

Judges get "pull sheets" in categories for which it is important to know what special ingredients, such as fruit or spices, may have been used and should be expressed in the beer.

TASTING RECORD

DATE

TASTED BY

BEER

AGE OF BEER

TYPE/STYLE

PACKAGE

LOCATION

ALCOHOL/GRAVITY

AROMA

APPEARANCE

BODY & TEXTURE

AFTERTASTE

OVERALL IMPRESSIONS

SPECIFIC OFF-FLAVORS & AROMAS

- O Acetaldehyde
- O Aged, cardboard, leather
- O Barnyard
- O Cheesy
- O Chlorophenol (bandage)
- O Diacetyl (buttery)
- O DMS (creamed corn)
- O Earthy/corked
- O Estery/solventy
- O Goaty/sweaty
- O Metallic
- O Phenolic
- O Sulfuric/sulfidic
- O Yeasty/autolysed
- O Other

To download a printable version, go to the "Tools and Downloads" page of the "Books, Etc." section of http://randymosher.com.

We once made the mistake of holding a judge-certification exam in a house where several cats lived. This was not a problem except for the one individual who was spastically allergic to cats, and it was a total washout for him. I have some allergies myself, and because ingredients in beer sometimes trigger them, I try to remember to take my allergy meds before any serious tasting or judging.

Provide a palate cleanser. People have varying opinions on the usefulness of bread or crackers. Generally, when there is a chance that judges may become fatigued or when the beers presented are different enough from each other to require a palate cleanser, it is a welcome addition. Plain water crackers, matzo, or French bread are preferred. Avoid fatty crackers (most are), as the fat will ruin the beer's head if it gets into the tasting sample. Your nose can become fatigued as well, so sometimes small bowls of coffee beans are provided for the table. A sniff of these can reset your nose, and then you can get back to tasting.

Consider the glass. Tasting glasses are usually a bit of a disappointment. In an ideal world, all beer would be evaluated in stemmed white-wine glasses. These present beer beautifully, the inward taper holding aromas below the rim, and the stem keeping our sticky fingers from heating it up. In fact, there is an International Organization for Standardization (ISO) standard tasting glass, a diminutive stemmed tulip.

For a small number of judges with a limited number of beers in a controlled setting, using proper tasting glasses is possible. But the logistics of a large competition such as the World Beer Cup are challenging enough already, so just about all homebrew and commercial beer gets judged in plastic cups. The hard, crystal-clear cups of about 8- to 10-ounce (240–300 mL) capacity are the best. Plastic aromas usually aren't a problem these days, but do check. Avoid the milky translucent cups, as they can make it difficult to tell if a beer is sparkling clear. Opaque or colored cups won't do.

No matter the vessel type, it should never be filled more than one-third full. You need all that headspace to develop the proper aroma. Two to 3 ounces is all that is needed to give a beer a very thorough judging.

46 mm ±5

65 mm ±5

65 mm ±5

65 mm ±5

65 mm ±5

50 ml

ISO Standard Tasting Glass and Plastic Judging Cup
Research by the International Organization for Standardization led them to this glass (at left) for tasting wine and other beverages. Note the incurved rim and where the fill line is. For beer, a similar geometry works great, even at a somewhat larger size. Crystal-clear 10-ounce cups will also work for most tasting purposes.

Preparing and Tasting Spiked Beers

Beer contains many aromatic chemicals that can be either good or bad depending on quantity and context. Knowing a dozen or two of these is considered part of the knowledge base for beer professionals, from brewers to bar managers. In an educational setting, you want to deliver specific off-flavors in particular concentrations, beer by beer. While you may be able to round up some flawed beers for sampling, it's usually better to use a technique called "spiking," in which controlled amounts of specific chemicals are added to the beer. Dozens of chemicals can be spiked into beer, but general and beginner audiences only need to be familiar with about half a dozen that are the most important (see list below).

Clean, neutral, consistent beers work best as a spiking base. Light beers are *too* light and don't have enough "beer" aroma so they're easily overwhelmed by the spiking chemicals. Mass-market beers are usually used, but well-brewed craft brews will serve if they don't have too many strong flavors going on. One 12-ounce beer will serve six to eight tasters.

There are a couple of ways to do the spikes: you can use premixed spikes or mix your own. Various companies such as the Siebel Institute, Aroxa, and FlavorActiV make spiking chemicals that are easy to use, as they come in premeasured capsules or other containers that need only be mixed into a specific quantity of beer to reach a certain taste concentration, typically around three times the threshold value.

If you have some lab skills, you can purchase food-grade versions of the pure chemicals. Some spiking chemicals are present in small enough quantities to be used directly in the beer samples. Other more powerful flavors need to be diluted into stock solutions at 1:1000, 1:1,000,000, or more, before they can be squirted into the beers. I usually find vodka works well for dilution. A dispensing pipette (the kind that has a dial to set the amount that is picked up with a push of the button)

COMMON SPIKING CHEMICALS

CHEMICAL	DESCRIPTOR	THRESHOLD	SAMPLE CONCENTRATION
Ethyl Acetate	Solvent/ester	18 ppm	72 ppm (4x)
Acetaldehyde	Green apple, leafy	10 ppm	40 ppm (4x)
Isoamyl Acetate	Banana/ester	1.2 ppm	5 ppm (4x)
2,3-Pentanedione	Buttery/diacetyl	10–40 ppb	80 ppb (4x 20 ppb)
DMS	Creamed corn	30–50 ppb	160 ppb (4x 40 ppb)
Trans-2-Nonenal	Papery	0.05 ppb	0.20 ppb (4x)
Hop Iso Extract	Bitter	5 ppm (IBU)	25 ppm (5x) + base beer

For more on these individual aroma chemicals and their origins, see chapter 3.

is the best tool for the dosing. A capacity of 1,000 microliters (1 mL) is the most useful size for this.

A word of warning: Some of these spiking chemicals are not pleasant and will stink up your freezer pretty strongly unless stored in an airtight glass or metal container. And in their pure form, they may actually be flammable or otherwise dangerous. Any work with pure flavor chemicals should be done in a very well ventilated space. It's also a good idea to do your spiking in a wide plastic tub or tray so any spills or drops can be contained. Many, such as DMS, are not stable and will deteriorate within a matter of months. All keep best in the freezer as long as you have something to contain them properly. A metal box with a tight, waterproof gasket is advisable.

Note that 2,3-pentanedione is not as important in beer aroma as diacetyl, but since the workplace inhalation hazards of diacetyl have become known, it has become more difficult to obtain and so 2,3-pentanedione is often used as a substitute. If you can get diacetyl (2,3-butanedione), use it at the rate of 80 ppb.

Once you have the solutions, it's a simple matter to put on a fresh pipette tip and adjust the pipette to the desired amount of spike. If you're using twist-off beers, then just carefully twist off the cap. Don't use a bottle opener, because you're going to screw the cap back on

when you're done spiking. With the beer open, use the pipette to drop in the proper quantity of spike. Set the pipette down, and tightly twist the cap back on. For beers lacking a twist-off cap, you can use a homebrewing capper and fresh crowns. Don't forget to label both the caps and the labels with the spike name.

Whether you're mixing your own or using premixed spikes, always present a "control," or unspiked, beer to your tasters so they can go back and forth, comparing the control with the spiked samples. I usually use this as a refresher course on how to taste: tabletop, drive-by, swirl, sniff, taste, retronasal (see page 61).

We generally find that for most audiences, spikes between three and four times the threshold values seem to work best to introduce people to these aromas and flavors. For advanced training, tasters start at these levels and work their way down to their individual thresholds over time. As we all differ in our sensitivities to various aromas, it makes sense for serious beer tasters to get themselves calibrated.

Some off-flavors are more easily presented as regular beers than artificially spiked-up samples:

- **Skunkiness,** the smelly effect that light has on hops in beer, is simple enough. Just take a Corona or Heineken (or any beer in a clear or green bottle) and expose it to daylight for a few minutes; voilà, skunk!

Note that Miller products won't work (the chemical that causes skunkiness has been removed from their hop extract).

- **The clove-tinged aromas** that yeast adds to weizens can be simulated with a chemical called eugenol, but I find it both simpler and more accurate to just use hefeweizen.

- **Overaged beer** has an awful complexity that is complicated to simulate, but not that difficult to lay your hands on. It's a little indelicate, but you can ask at your liquor store if they have any out-of-date beer they're planning on sending back to the distributor.

Judging and Competitions

Competitions are an important tool in pushing forward the art and science of brewing. For most brewers, having an unbiased panel of their peers bestow a medal for a well-brewed beer is a soul-tickling thrill. These guys build their reputations — and sometimes get their raises — on these awards. It's as serious as beer gets.

There are many ways to select the winners, and every competition is different, but there are similarities in all approaches, as follows:

- Judges are carefully vetted, and their work is checked for completeness and vocabulary.

- Judging is usually highly structured, by means of score sheets and a specific methodology.

- Conditions are controlled in terms of lighting, aromas, noise, and other distractions.

- Beers are always presented blind, which means judges have to evaluate just what's in the glass and nothing else.

- Judging is structured so that judges don't unduly influence each other.

- Beers are presented in flights, usually of 8 to 15 beers, usually all in the same style category.

BEER MAY BE JUDGED purely on its own for flavor, balance, and other sensory characteristics, or against some agreed-on notion of what a particular style should be. The former is called "hedonic" judging, and judges simply score the beer based on how good it tastes to them. This is a perfectly legitimate means of rating beers as long as beers of similar styles are being compared. The bias is that no matter how sophisticated they are, judges in these contests tend to give higher scores to bigger, more flavorful beers, such as barley wines. As long as apples are compared to apples, there's no problem with this method.

In style-based judging, each beer is judged on how well it expresses the essential character of the style category in which it is entered. The style guidelines are similar to the ones in chapters 9 through 13 in this book, and a copy is present right at the table; judges will usually confer to make sure they all understand the style before actually judging. An enormous amount of work has been put into the guidelines to match historical styles with modern commercial practice and to structure the judging process to ensure a thorough, balanced evaluation.

Neither system is better, and each has its disadvantages. Judging to style inevitably means that some delicious beers are too light, dark, fruity, bitter or otherwise don't conform to published style guidelines. It doesn't matter

HOW DO YOU BECOME A BEER JUDGE?

Judging beer is by far the best way to hone your skills as a critical taster. Whether or not you're a brewer, you can participate in the Beer Judge Certification Program (BJCP). You study, take a test, and become recognized as a judge. Higher ranks are attainable with higher test scores and experience points. The BJCP itself (www.bjcp.org) is your best portal to all of this, but equally important is your local home-brew club. Many clubs run study sessions, and these invariably include lots of beer tasting, so they're as fun as they are educational. The American Homebrewers Association (www.homebrewersassociation.org) or your local homebrew shop can also help you get in touch.

If you want to dip your toes into judging gradually, sign on as a steward to be involved with all the behind-the-scenes work involved in getting judges their beers in the proper order and condition. There are often opportunities to "taste along" and get a sense of what the judging process is all about. Your help is always welcome.

The BJCP program allows judges to climb in ranks with experience, knowledge, and effort.

whether the brewer disagrees with the styles; they're the road map everyone must follow. On the other hand, hedonic judging fails to take into account the language of styles that brewers and drinkers use as a kind of code to communicate with each other.

In larger competitions, you will need more than one round to winnow a category with a large number of entrants down to a group that can be judged in a single, final round to determine the winners. Typically the senior judges from the preliminary round will get together and quickly rejudge the best from the former flights to determine medal status.

A TASTER'S NOTES ON JUDGING

The beer's on the table. The conditions are perfect. The stars are aligned. Now what?

Come ready to do great work. Be sure you understand what is required of you. Every competition has a solid framework and a certain style of organization. Things work best when everybody plays along. In some ways beer competitions are always a bit of an artificial construct, so just suspend judgment and play by the competition's specific rules.

For style-based competitions, it's your job to evaluate how well a particular beer represents the style as it appears in the guidelines. It's not in your judging job description to quibble with the guidelines — I've had plenty of those disagreements myself — but there's a time and place for that, and the judging table is not it. Be aware that there is a "heartbreak" beer in almost every flight: a really delicious, well-brewed beer you would like to just take home and snuggle up with but that for some reason fails to conform to the guideline. Sadly, it must be swept off the table.

With hedonic judging, you have a different kind of problem. Most judges are so used to the style-based structure that they may feel on shaky ground when going without it. It's important, however, to have a well-developed sense of what simply tastes good, as well as analytical skills. In the end, beer is supposed to be about pleasure.

Guidelines and score sheets always come along with a competition. With styles, it's routine to read the applicable category description before the flight begins so everybody is on the same page. Copies are provided in case you need to look up a fine point. The score sheet is your guide to the judging process. In addition to the details, be sure to check the general comments about what certain scores imply as far as beer quality, and make sure your numbers fit that standard.

There are written and unwritten rules for judging. Most of them are simple common sense and etiquette. It's a privilege to be allowed to evaluate someone else's beers. They put a lot of work into them, so try to be considerate. First and foremost, though, your job is to accurately describe the beer in front of you in as much detail as you can. Make a conscious effort not to influence other judges. This will occasionally require suppression of a gag, groan, or eye roll, but keep it to yourself for now. There will be time later for all of that.

Be productive. A lot has to be done in a short period of time. It's your duty to help keep it moving. Most homebrewing competitions try to spend 10 minutes per beer, but when you're new, this can flash by very quickly. It's important to trust your instincts and first impressions and let the score sheet be your guide. Don't hold up the process looking for that one perfect word. Remember, retronasal olfaction (see page 47) gives you another chance, and it may come to you later. Make your notes and get through the scoring, then circle back for a second whiff if you have time. Write notes of what you're tasting, but don't try to figure out what went wrong or how to fix it unless it's blindingly obvious.

Choose your battles. Sure, there will be disagreements over flavors or the fine points of a style, but it's a beer competition, not the final battle between good and evil. Everybody tastes the beer a little differently, so if you're the outlier, you need to acknowledge that others are at least as right as you are, come to consensus, and move on.

It's best to smell the beer before anything else, as there are aromas — especially sulfur-based ones — that are so volatile they may linger for only a minute or so before wafting away forever. Start with a drive-by, and proceed with a few quick sniffs. Give it a moment to sink in, as some aromas take a while to register. Be especially aware of any little memory flashbacks you have, as these can be valuable clues to identifying aromas.

If you're not getting much, try covering the glass with your hand and swirling. If the beer seems overly cold for the style, cup it in your hands as you swirl to help warm it up and release aroma.

Now have a good look at the beer, and make notes about color, clarity, head character, and retention. Be aware that the appropriateness of these qualities varies dramatically by style. Also be aware that these are not the most important characteristics of a beer, and they generally account for only a small percentage of a score. And honestly, there isn't all that much information to be gained by close visual scrutiny of a beer. Don't let your eyes trick you into tasting something that isn't there. Dark color may be just that. Are you *really* sure you're picking up that toasty note? It's easy to be fooled.

Take a sip, and let the liquid linger on your tongue and warm up on the bottom of your mouth. Pay attention to basic tastes such as sweetness and acidity, and wait a few beats for the bitterness, as it builds more slowly than other tastes. As the beer warms, aroma will be released. Wine tasters, because they normally spit out the sample, use a technique called aspiration. With beer warming in the bottom of the mouth, air is drawn through it, making a gurgling sound, and then the lips are closed as the air is gently expelled through the nose. This creates a retronasal impression. Since we normally swallow beer, you can skip this and just follow the usual retronasal technique of slowly swallowing, then making a gentle outward breath with lips closed. There is an additional technique that can sometimes turbocharge the retronasal taste: as you taste and swallow, hold your nose closed, then as the beer is going down the throat, let go of your nose and let out a sharp breath through it. Sometimes this will pick up additional subtleties.

Be complete and detailed. Are there off-flavors such as diacetyl or DMS? Is there any harshness or astringency, especially on the finish? Are there any papery or woody notes of oxidation, or unwanted acidity?

Be sure to give some attention to mouthfeel sensations: body, carbonation, astringency, and oiliness. What about the aftertaste? Is it quick or long? Smooth or harsh? Hoppy, malty, roasty? All of the above or something else? Again, take notes. Look for anything sticking out awkwardly.

Finally, do some higher-level analysis. If the beer is being judged to style, how well does it fit in terms of overall intensity, bitterness, malt character, and the overlay of fermentation? If it is a lager, is it free of fruity, estery aromas? How is the balance? Do all the parts seem to fit together? Is this a beer you would drink a pint of? Or two? Take to a desert island? Will you remember this beer in a year . . . in a good way?

Once you've written all your notes and scored the beer (if appropriate), only then can you discuss it with the other judges. Those discussions are best when the most experienced judges make an effort not to dominate the discussion, as even new judges have useful contributions to make — everybody misses a thing or two.

A SAMPLING OF COMPETITIONS

Great American Beer Festival and World Beer Cup. The Brewers Association, the organization representing America's craft brewers and homebrewers, runs these competitions. They are identical except that the Great American Beer Festival (GABF) is open only to American brewers and the World Beer Cup is a worldwide competition. GABF judging has been going on since 1981. The World Beer Cup began in 1996 and operates in even years only.

These are style-based competitions, and an extensive set of style guidelines (used by both organizations and available at www.brewers association.org) is updated every year based on feedback from judges and brewers. The categories in these competitions tend to reflect current commercial practices in the United States and abroad. All the judging takes place over 3 days. The scoring is not based on points; beers are brought to the tables in flights, and each flight is judged as if it were a best of show flight. The judges go through the beers one by one and make notes and add appropriate comments on a specially designed judging sheet. The first pass is done without discussion, to prevent judges from unduly influencing each other. Once everybody has had a

In addition to bragging rights, breweries know winning medals is a powerful sales tool.

journalists are included. It's a hot ticket: there is a waiting list, and many judges are on a rotation.

BJCP/AHA-sanctioned homebrew competitions. There are many of these Beer Judge Certification Program (BJCP) and American Homebrewers Association (AHA) events at local, regional, and national levels in the United States and abroad, and competitions are a valued part of the homebrew-club experience. Like the GABF, these are style-based competitions. The BJCP guidelines (available at www.bjcp.org) are similar to those of the GABF but are more focused on historical or "classic" versions of the styles, less influenced by current commercial practice, and get revamped only every 5 years or so. The numbers (but not the discussions) in the beer styles in this book are the 2015 BJCP numbers, and these are also used by the Cicerone organization.

The National Homebrew Competition, run by the AHA, is the biggest beer competition in the world. Entered beers go through a two-round process. The first round is split up and judged in multiple locations. Beers that make the cut are sent by their brewers to the second round, always held during June in conjunction with the National Homebrewers Conference.

Judging is very structured, using a 50-point scale, with a certain number of points allotted for appearance, aroma, flavor, body, and overall impressions. Whether the competition is large or small, winners are determined for each category, and then all the category gold medalists face off in one final best-of-show round. In contrast to the GABF, contending beers are opened one by one, and after a period of scoring and contemplation by the judges, elimination begins. Sorting out the best-of-show beers is complicated by the fact that they are all different styles. Judges may have to weigh

chance to form opinions about the beers, the discussion begins.

The most obviously problematic or out-of-style beers get kicked out first. Then it comes down to small problems with flavor or style or beers that just don't come together. The field narrows to a handful of beers. At that point, they are pretty much all in the style, so the judges must focus on less tangible attributes: deliciousness, nitpicky flaws, and the ability to create a positive impression. A flight usually takes between 60 and 90 minutes to taste.

Professional judges are preferred, although some exceptionally skilled homebrewers and the sheer power of a barley wine against the delicate beauty of a witbier.

BJCP/AHA-sanctioned competitions happen on a local level as well, from small competitions with fewer than a hundred entries to the gigantic madhouse (and I mean that in the best sense) that is Houston's Dixie Cup. In addition, there are a number of different regional circuits that tally up the points from a season's worth of competitions, just like NASCAR does. It's a rare club that doesn't hold a competition.

Mondial de la Bion. This beer festival started in Montreal but now has events in Strasbourg, France, and Rio de Janeiro as well. All have competitions associated with them; however, the judging method is a little unusual. Instead of a single style, each flight is a mix of different styles of similar weight, and each judge at the table judges different beers, which the organizers believe cuts down on discussion biases. If you're used to style-based judging, this can be a little disorienting at first, but when you get comfortable, it works just fine. The unusual feature of this system is that you are asked to guess which style the beer fits into, and then to rate it based on how much pleasure it gives as an example of this style. The method is definitely unconventional, but in my experience, the great beers still do very well here.

Beverage Testing Institute/World Beer Championships. The Chicago-based Beverage Testing Institute is exactly what the name says. It started out as a wine-evaluation program that expanded into beer and spirits in 1994. The company runs judging panels frequently and sorts beers by styles. However, this is a hedonic system, meaning judges are asked to evaluate beers on a 14-point scale by how much they like them. Naturally this results in some disparities from style to style,

but because the ranking is within each style, it doesn't matter. Beverage Tasting Institute (BTI) medals are based on achieving certain scores, which trigger bronze, silver, and gold medals. The company has been criticized for being too free with the awards, but this point-based medal system is pretty standard for most food and wine competitions.

International competitions run the gamut. Many, especially in Latin America, use the BJCP format, sometimes with a specially modified set of style guidelines. Other competitions, such as the multinational Mondial de la Bière and the Birra del'Anno in Italy, are as idiosyncratic as they get. If you ever get the chance to judge outside the United States, jump on it. It's a fantastic experience, and there are usually some enjoyable extracurricular experiences as well.

Taste Panels and Beer Evaluation

Breweries need highly structured systems for evaluating products, and although much of this work can now be accomplished with sophisticated analytical equipment, humans are still better at many aspects of assessment. Breweries may need to monitor their current beers for consistency or verify that the same beer brewed at different breweries all tastes the same. They may be looking to evaluate improvements to the beer or check consistency when raw materials, equipment, or brewing techniques are changing. And of course, when new products are created, those have to be tasted, too. Taste panels are usually selected from tested and trained brewery personnel, but when it comes to things like new products, it is important to use regular consumers as well.

There are many types of protocols. The most sensitive are those in which panelists are presented with beers that differ only in one respect. An example of this technique is called a "duo-trio," in which a reference sample is presented first, and then the panelist is asked to identify which of the next two beers is the same and which is different. In the "triangle," three beers are presented simultaneously, and the panelist has to pick the odd beer. And in a "paired comparison," the taster is asked which of the two beers is higher in one specific attribute — bitterness, for example.

Subjects may be presented with a series of beers and asked to rate any differences in specific attributes, often on a scale of 1 to 5 or 1 to 10. Other scales use a (−) to 0 to (+) system, with +7 or −7 as the extremes and 0 as neutral. Subjects might be asked simply to rank a series of beers, usually six or fewer, in order of some characteristic or preference.

With all of these approaches, there is a certain amount of statistical work that needs to be done to determine the validity and reliability of the results, as there is some chance that tasters will pick the right beer simply by chance.

In addition to statistics, there is a whole raft of psychological effects that need to be accounted for in any evaluation for which big money is at stake. It is well known that the order in which samples are presented affects the way they are evaluated, with the most honest appraisals going to the middle of the pack. Strong contrasts from beer to beer have an effect, which is why less intense beers are evaluated first. Beers that are all fairly similar tend to lull the panelists into thinking them more similar than they really are. Individual judges use the scale differently, too, with some using

SUGGESTIONS FOR TASTING TYPES

- **By style:** IPA, Weiss, etc.

- **By country or brewing tradition**

- **Craft versus traditional producers of classic styles**

- **Vertical:** Same beer, different years

- **By ingredient:** Hops, malt, etc.

- **By season:** Summer beers, etc.

- **A variety of yeast types:** Lager, ale, Weiss, Belgian

- **A comparison of tradition**

- **Similar ales and lagers:** Brown ale and Munich lager, for example

- **With food:** Cheese, chocolate, etc. (for details, see chapter 7)

the extremes and others sticking to the middle of the scale. Sometimes, the lowest and highest scores on any panel are tossed to smooth out the data. And of course, we are all susceptible to suggestion, either from prior expectations such as brand names or packaging, or from the opinions of other tasters, which is why those things are eliminated or avoided as much as possible in serious settings.

Presenting Beer for Judging or Evaluation

Any time a beer is to be evaluated in a serious way, every effort must be made to ensure that the beer arrives at the taster's lips in the best possible condition and with minimal distractions.

The first consideration is proper temperature. This is devilishly hard to manage, especially because the creator of the universe chose not to bless us with 50-degree ice. As a general rule, 40°F (4°C) for lagers and 50 to 55°F (10 to 13°C) for ales is about where you would like to end up, with stronger beers warmer than weak ones. The usual approach is to pull refrigerated beers out of the cooler an hour or so in advance of the competition and let them warm to their ideal serving temperature, or actually a little below, as the beers will warm a few degrees just by contact with the cup. This is one of the finer points of competition stewarding. An infrared thermometer is a useful tool for a competition organizer or head steward because with it he or she can take a beer's temperature just by pointing at it — much less messy than probe-type thermometers.

Judges should be aware of beer temperature. Too-cold beers will lack aroma, and some will throw a forgivable chill haze. Beers that are obviously a little too cold may be warmed up in the hands before rechecking the aroma.

Beer should always be poured just before tasting. Pour the beer right down the middle of the glass, wait for the foam to settle, and if needed, pour a little more, but never more than one-third full.

Some hypergeek judges like to carry a small flashlight or a laser pointer with them. This can help to evaluate haziness, especially in darker beers. It should be aimed either up through the bottom or through the side of the glass. If you can see the beam, that's the haze lighting up. My favorite tool for competitions is pretty low tech — a grease pencil. It's useful for writing entry numbers on beers that I want to keep on the table and come back to, so I don't have to keep them in order to remember which is which.

Organizers should be *organized*. Tasters should know what to expect. Plenty of information means the tasters and the beers will both get the best out of the experience.

Lighter-tasting beers — meaning less hoppy, less roasty, and lower alcohol — are usually judged first. A dozen beers per flight is considered a good maximum, although this is sometimes pushed a little. Make sure the tasters have adequate breaks and reasonable creature comforts.

Finally, it's important to understand limits. Formal tasting can be quite fatiguing, even if the amount of alcohol consumed isn't all that great. In a judging session with flights of 12 to 15 beers, a break is needed after every flight.

A Sampling of Tasting Events

Tastings fall into a wide range of formats, ranging from completely spur-of-the-moment thrashes to carefully planned and staged educational events. They may be large or small, formal or informal. The following list is by no means complete, but it should give you an idea of what's out there.

Reception-style tasting. Like a beer festival, these tastings are often mostly for enjoyment, with education as a secondary goal. In the most common format, there are 10 to 15 beers of either widely varying types or examples more narrowly chosen from a style or region or to illustrate a specific point. Bottled beers are usually placed in bus tubs with some (but not massive amounts of) ice. Attendees usually circulate and try beers at their own pace. With smaller groups, you can get away with people pouring their own; larger groups require pourers. There may be a program to suggest a particular tasting order or to suggest things to look for in the beers. A handout with some detail on the beers is very helpful. There may be some spoken introduction.

In many settings, it is important to match the beers to your audience. If you have wine drinkers in the crowd, serving a fruit lambic may be a way to entice them over to our side, or at least to get them to admit that all beer is not yellow and fizzy. I love to hear them say, "I *like* this. It doesn't taste like beer!"

Remember, with a general audience, people may have vastly differing experience and individual taste sensitivities. Not everyone may share your enthusiasm for a 100 IBU double IPA, so it's usually a good idea to have some creative-yet-approachable beers. It's okay to get people a little out of their comfort zone; that's what they came for. You can often push people a lot further than you might think.

Don't make assumptions about who will like what; my mother loved big, sweet dark beers. Just be careful with very hoppy beers. Just like chile heat, bitterness in beer takes some getting used to, so use a sensitive touch unless you have a well-seasoned audience.

Casual competitions. While not widely held, these can be a fun way of engaging the beer providers as well as the attendees, and the results can be meaningful. The key feature is that scoring is done by whoever attends the event and not by highly trained judges under controlled conditions. In a way, it's more of a real-world way of evaluating a beer, as it is more of a social situation in which people are enjoying and talking about the beers. The Chicago Beer Society has been holding one such event for almost 40 years. The current format is to have around a dozen draft beers, identified only by style. Attendees have a scorecard with room for notes and a tear-off portion to record their first, second, and third favorite beers; about 90 minutes is allotted to sample the beers in any order. After the ballots are collected, the identifying tap handles are installed and dinner is served. This type of tasting can be done with bottled beer, but it's hard to do for a large crowd because the beers have to be poured out of sight of the attendees, which means a lot of pouring and schlepping.

Beer and food events are another good way to involve brewpubs and breweries. The Chicago Beer Society holds an annual "Brewpub Shootout," featuring food and beers meant to pair with each other. Attendees vote on best beer, best food, and best pair. It's amazing how much energy breweries and brewpubs will invest if there's a chance of taking home an award. After 15 years of this event being held, there is quite a rivalry between participating breweries to take home the gold.

Casual tastings. These can take lots of different forms. Examples include a Weissbier brunch; an Indian buffet plus IPA-fest; a beer and cheese event with specific different pairings; or a high-end Belgian dinner with Belgian-inspired beers and steamed mussels, carbonade flamande, and other Belgian dishes.

Music-related events. If you live near a navigable body of water, you can move the whole affair to a boat and have a brews cruise. A blues band and a roast pig equal a Blues and Brews Cruise. Capital-F Fun!

Brewery tastings. This is one of the more common formats, as breweries know that the best way to sell beer is to get it into peoples' mouths. A typical lineup is six to eight samples, usually presented in a specific order from less to more intense. It's a good idea to provide a "welcome" beer that people can start drinking as soon as they arrive, as people sometimes are a little impatient and want to get going right away. Be aware of the total alcohol being served. A quantity adding up to between two and three standard beers (see chart on page 144) is about right for a 2-hour tasting. Make sure they know what beers they're tasting, what to look for in each, and how they fit into the bigger picture of the beer world. Some leave-behind material and a tasting sheet with space for notes are always welcome. You can get by with two glasses as long as the attendees have a dump bucket and rinse water. Pour the first and while talking about that, the second can come around. By the time the third beer is pouring, the audience needs to either drink up or dump.

Educational programs. These are usually presented in lecture or classroom settings. They can be on any topic, but those revolving around styles seem to be the most popular. For people studying for the Cicerone or BJCP exams, they're almost mandatory. Typically, the group focuses on a family of styles and tries a number of commercial examples, with perhaps some commentary from knowledgeable or well-traveled experts. Ingredient tastings

---

Brewery Tastings
Guided brewery tastings are the best way to get to know a brewery and its products in a short time.

and spiked beer samplings are other fun and useful exercises. Two- to 3-ounce samples are presented in a specific order. You often have to urge people to offer up descriptions to the rest of the class — nobody wants to get it wrong — but keep at them. It's important that people get comfortable discussing what they are perceiving. They are usually better at it than they expect to be.

Real-ale events have special needs, especially an accommodating host space, as the beers have to be set up by Tuesday for a Saturday event. It also takes a certain skill level to make sure the beers are in prime condition when the time comes to tap them. These events are best held when the weather is guaranteed to be cool so that beer temperature can be controlled by opening windows or lowering the thermostat. There are real-ale cooling systems, varying in complexity from ice blankets to circulating glycol, but these are expensive and very labor intensive and should be avoided unless absolutely necessary. The beer is served by gravity, which means only simple plastic taps are needed and not expensive hand pumps that add nothing to the beer in this situation.

A vertical tasting may take years of preplanning, but it offers a beer experience like no other. The idea is to taste one beer through a number of different years' releases, and for obvious reasons it only works well with strong beers that are fit for aging. It's amazing how different the beers can taste, even when the recipe remains unchanged. While breweries or bars sometimes hold back limited quantities of special beers for these events, a sizable group of enthusiasts is often able to put together a pretty good vertical tasting from what people have squirreled away in their private stashes.

Bottle-sharing meetups. These range from simple living room get-togethers to much larger affairs. The mother of all of these is Three Floyds' Dark Lord Day in Munster, Indiana, with its sea of E-Z Ups, each with a unique set of rare bottles. Your price of admission? A few of your own prized specialties. Don't be a hoarder. Beer is not meant to be kept indefinitely, and you sure can't take it with you, so bring those bottles out and share them with people who care as much as you do.

Social tastings are one of the great joys of being a beer fancier. Setting forth into a room full of beer enthusiasts to seek out and share new beer discoveries is just like being in church for me, but a whole lot more fun.

Most brewpubs and many packaging breweries regularly hold brewmaster dinners, which can be great places to meet the brewers as well as fellow beer fans, and they are a terrific way to get to know a particular brewery's beers and what makes them tick. And in my experience, they're even more enjoyable when you get involved and help organize them.

Setting Up Your Own Tasting Event

The simplest events are just social get-togethers with a little structured beer focus. You can ask people to either bring things, share the cost, or just take turns doing events. The important thing is to have a focus, and don't try to drink in the whole beer world at one whack. Preparing people with an introductory talk, reading from an authoritative book, or working with a set of tasting notes will help everyone get the most out of each event. Try to limit the number of different beers to 10 or so, as it gets overwhelming beyond that. Nice glassware adds to the experience, and often you can ask people to rinse and reuse the same glass (or two) all evening.

I was involved with the Chicago Beer Society (CBS) board for 20 years or so, and I remain a member. This all-volunteer organization has explored a number of different event formats over the years, learning what works and what doesn't. Much of the information I share in this section comes from my experience with this organization.

It's best to have food at events if you can manage it. It's the responsible thing to do, as it slows consumption, makes the occasion more social, and highlights beer as a gastronomic experience. Simple but substantial appetizers work well, such as artisanal cheeses or the pile of sausage we refer to as "alottagoddammeat," a term our beloved Hungarian butcher spit back at us in response to a request for $500 worth of deli trays for a CBS event.

Once you have a concept, the next step is to contact restaurants with a private room sized to accommodate your expected group and talk about what you'd like to do (including serving beer from outside sources) and what the costs will be (make sure to include tax and tip in your calculations). Liability insurance is also an important consideration. If your event is being held in a commercial space, your event may be covered by their insurance, but if not, the AHA offers liability insurance for clubs.

Then contact your local breweries and beer distributors about donating beer, possibly in exchange for complimentary tickets to the event.

You also need to check out your local laws regarding donation of beer. In many states direct donation of beer is illegal, and in that case the beer may need to be purchased. However, brewers might be willing to pay for tickets to the event, or offer a monetary donation to offset the cost of the beer. It usually makes a difference whether the event is for the benefit of a nonprofit. I can't advise you on specifics, but your local brewers and distributors will know what is allowable.

Promote the event like crazy over social media and good old-fashioned flyers at beer hot spots, and make sure to include cost, as well as the process and deadline for ticket purchases, in your promotional media. There are physical logistics to handle as well, the most difficult of which will be the transportation and serving of the beer. Some clubs have a pretty sizable collection of draft equipment; others may need to borrow some from the restaurant, local breweries, distributors, or homebrewers.

If your group is wary of taking on too much responsibility, consider partnering with a local group of brewers or your local craft brewers guild. These trade groups are sometimes happy to have someone else help take care of the details, and they may share the proceeds of a successful event in exchange for the organizing manpower.

Making the Most of Beer Festivals

Festivals hold a lot of allure. Acres of beers lined up for your tasting pleasure, a whole year's worth of pub crawling in just a few hours, being elbow to elbow with a teeming mass of beer fans wearing pretzel necklaces: nirvana!

But festivals can sometimes be a little overwhelming, with large crowds, too much choice, and uncomfortable conditions. A good strategy and a little self-restraint can go a long way toward making the event more enjoyable. Here are some tips.

Know your limits — of alcohol, heat and sun, being on your feet, and dealing with crowds. Be aware that brewers sometimes trot out their biggest, baddest beers for these events. This is great, of course, but you have to be respectful of high-alcohol beers.

Go when the crowds are lightest. Get there when it starts, or if it's a longer fest, pick a slow day. Know when to quit — I never mind missing the chaotic last hour. Some festivals will have a "private session," which may cost more but will be much less rowdy. These are well worth the money as far as I'm concerned.

Do your research. Find out who's making great beer before you get there. BeerAdvocate.com and RateBeer.com aren't the final word but can be very helpful.

Don't be afraid to dump. There's just no point to drinking a beer you don't like. You won't offend anybody.

Have a purpose. Focus on something, such as beers you haven't had before, a particular style, breweries you have never heard of, or finding the perfect session beer. Take notes. Discuss.

Talk to the brewers. Some festivals have brewery personnel stationed with their beers. This is a great opportunity to find out more about their beers, how they brewed them, how they think of them, what inspired them, and maybe even a few recipe secrets.

Volunteer. Events are often more fun when you are on the other side of the taps. You are usually working with other interesting beer fans or pro brewers and have the opportunity to spread the word of good beer to the crowd. It gives you a sense of purpose and is often rewarded by perks such as a private tasting, an after-event party, or swag such as T-shirts.

Check out the "extra" events. Many festivals have a dinner, tour, or other event within a few days of the festival. Book early; these usually fill up fast. Sometimes these are open to the public; sometimes they are limited to brewers and those involved in the fest, which is another great reason to volunteer.

Hydrate. Eat. Apply sunscreen. Make sure your body is well cared for.

Make sure you have a ride home when you need one. Some events have deals on taxis available.

FROM THE MOST FORMAL JUDGING to the simple joy of a fresh, delicious brew in a sun-dappled beer garden, the range of tasting experiences varies almost as much as beer itself. Once the beer is in the glass, it's up to you to decide what your relationship to it will be: advocate or critic, stranger or best buddy. Like any worthy pursuit, the beer-tasting experience is only as good as you make it. Summon all your senses and experience, and dive into it wholeheartedly. You'll find the experience that unfolds between you and your beer to be truly enlightening.

CHAPTER 6

PRESENTING
BEER

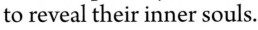

Beer is a fussy beverage. It doesn't like to be too warm or too cold. It shies away from the sun. It cares about the size, shape, and cleanliness of the glass it is served in and really responds to a great pour. In the whole constellation of different beers, each and every one is a prima donna, demanding just the right touch to bring out its best.

Beer has a generous spirit, so if you make any kind of effort at all, it will reward you with a rich and memorable experience. Sure, you can just grab a bottle and gulp it down — and there are beers made for this — but most beers need to be treated with a little more respect if you want them to reveal their inner souls.

A LUMINOUSLY BEAUTIFUL BEER suited to the mood and moment, of proper age and condition, with a creamy, long-lasting head, bursting with aroma, can be a delight to every sense. It is an experience that has moved people since the very beginning of beer, and it is every bit as exciting today. It's worth the small effort required to do it right. In this chapter I will cover all the aspects of beer's presentation, with the goal of making you, with a little practice, a master beer server.

Temperature

Nothing affects the beer in the glass more than the serving temperature. Flavor, aroma, texture, carbonation, and even clarity may change with temperature. It's not always easy to hit the nail on the head, especially when a large number of beers will be served, but it's always worth putting some effort into it.

To some degree, beer-serving temperatures are determined by tradition, but they do follow a certain logical pattern: Stronger beers should be served warmer than weak ones, and dark beers warmer than light. Lager beers are fermented cooler than ales and should be served cooler as well. American industrial beers have been formulated to taste best at lip-numbingly cold temperatures, but no specialty beer should ever be served at anything approaching these temperatures.

The proper range for serving beer is between 38 and 55°F (3 and 13°C), the specific temperature being very much dependent on the style (see box, opposite page). Too cold, and aromas just sit in the beer; if they don't become airborne they are not of much use to us. Too warm, and, well, we all know what warm beer tastes like. In practice it's very difficult to get it perfect. Come close, and you'll have a great experience.

CHECKLIST FOR A WELL-SERVED BEER

○ Beer at proper temperature

○ Correct glass for beer and occasion

○ Squeaky-clean, well-rinsed glassware

○ Good pour with a tight, long-lasting head

○ Correct quantity for the strength of the beer

○ Proper expectations of drinker

Infrared Thermometer
Although a little geeky, this type of thermometer will take a beer's temperature without touching it. Just point and shoot.

In a perfect world, retail establishments serving specialty beers should be able to control the temperatures and serve beers at temperatures appropriate to each style, but this is only rarely the case. It would be great to have one area at 38°F (3°C) for domestic and specialty lagers and another at perhaps 45°F (7°C) for specialty ales (maybe a tad warmer if you're concentrating on English-style ales), but this is pretty difficult to implement.

Real (cask) ale requires its own temperature control, unless you have a deep, dark cellar with a very constant temperature of 50 to 55°F (10 to 13°C). Most bars in the United States that serve real ale typically limit the selection to one or two at a time, so it doesn't take up too much space.

Quantity

With the dramatically different quantities of alcohol in beer these days, getting the serving size right is an important matter of both business and social responsibility. Whether it's friends or customers, one really needs to be careful about overserving people, and in a commercial setting selling pints of barley wine is not only reckless but misses an opportunity to maximize profits — important in any business. It takes just a little math, but the chart on page 144 should simplify things. The industry has a sort of fictitious "standard drink" corresponding to a 1.5-ounce (43 mL) shot of 80 proof liquor or 12 ounces of 5 percent beer, equivalent to 0.5 ounce (14 grams) of pure ethanol. It's not always followed, but it's a good guide nonetheless.

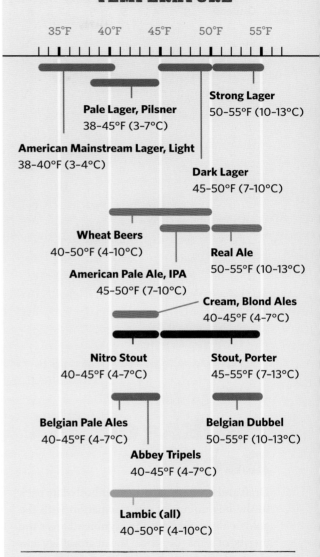

SUGGESTED SERVING TEMPERATURE

35°F 40°F 45°F 50°F 55°F

Strong Lager
50-55°F (10-13°C)

Pale Lager, Pilsner
38-45°F (3-7°C)

American Mainstream Lager, Light
38-40°F (3-4°C)

Dark Lager
45-50°F (7-10°C)

Wheat Beers
40-50°F (4-10°C)

Real Ale
50-55°F (10-13°C)

American Pale Ale, IPA
45-50°F (7-10°C)

Cream, Blond Ales
40-45°F (4-7°C)

Nitro Stout
40-45°F (4-7°C)

Stout, Porter
45-55°F (7-13°C)

Belgian Pale Ales
40-45°F (4-7°C)

Belgian Dubbel
50-55°F (10-13°C)

Abbey Tripels
40-45°F (4-7°C)

Lambic (all)
40-50°F (4-10°C)

NOTE: These are temperatures in the glass. Be aware that most of the major draft equipment companies recommend a 38°F (3°C) storage temperature for all beer types (except real ale), as higher temperatures may cause foaming.

AMOUNT OF PURE ETHANOL BY SERVING SIZE (OUNCES)

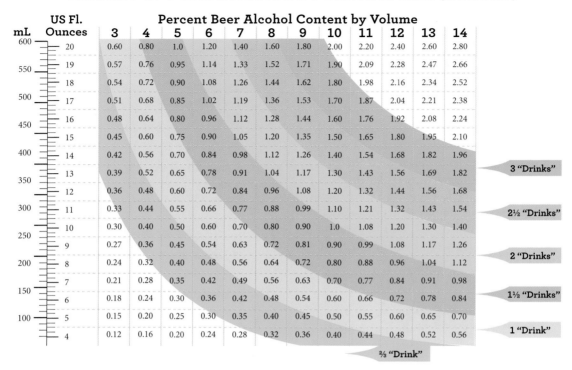

mL	US Fl. Ounces	3	4	5	6	7	8	9	10	11	12	13	14
						Percent Beer Alcohol Content by Volume							
600	20	0.60	0.80	1.0	1.20	1.40	1.60	1.80	2.00	2.20	2.40	2.60	2.80
550	19	0.57	0.76	0.95	1.14	1.33	1.52	1.71	1.90	2.09	2.28	2.47	2.66
	18	0.54	0.72	0.90	1.08	1.26	1.44	1.62	1.80	1.98	2.16	2.34	2.52
500	17	0.51	0.68	0.85	1.02	1.19	1.36	1.53	1.70	1.87	2.04	2.21	2.38
450	16	0.48	0.64	0.80	0.96	1.12	1.28	1.44	1.60	1.76	1.92	2.08	2.24
	15	0.45	0.60	0.75	0.90	1.05	1.20	1.35	1.50	1.65	1.80	1.95	2.10
400	14	0.42	0.56	0.70	0.84	0.98	1.12	1.26	1.40	1.54	1.68	1.82	1.96
350	13	0.39	0.52	0.65	0.78	0.91	1.04	1.17	1.30	1.43	1.56	1.69	1.82	3 "Drinks"
	12	0.36	0.48	0.60	0.72	0.84	0.96	1.08	1.20	1.32	1.44	1.56	1.68
300	11	0.33	0.44	0.55	0.66	0.77	0.88	0.99	1.10	1.21	1.32	1.43	1.54	2½ "Drinks"
250	10	0.30	0.40	0.50	0.60	0.70	0.80	0.90	1.0	1.08	1.20	1.30	1.40
	9	0.27	0.36	0.45	0.54	0.63	0.72	0.81	0.90	0.99	1.08	1.17	1.26
200	8	0.24	0.32	0.40	0.48	0.56	0.64	0.72	0.80	0.88	0.96	1.04	1.12	2 "Drinks"
	7	0.21	0.28	0.35	0.42	0.49	0.56	0.63	0.70	0.77	0.84	0.91	0.98
150	6	0.18	0.24	0.30	0.36	0.42	0.48	0.54	0.60	0.66	0.72	0.78	0.84	1½ "Drinks"
100	5	0.15	0.20	0.25	0.30	0.35	0.40	0.45	0.50	0.55	0.60	0.65	0.70
	4	0.12	0.16	0.20	0.24	0.28	0.32	0.36	0.40	0.44	0.48	0.52	0.56	1 "Drink"

⅔ "Drink"

This chart calculates alcohol quantity for a wide range of beer strengths and serving sizes.

Packaged Beer

Draft and bottled forms of beer both date back to the beginnings of our fascination with the golden elixir; perhaps the arguments over the merits of each do, too. The technology has changed, of course, but the discussion goes on. Which is best? There's no simple answer. Both can be perfectly wonderful storage vessels for beer, and each has its potential for trouble.

In the United States and Europe, most draft beer is unpasteurized and must be kept chilled for maximum storage life. Most people feel the taste and texture are a bit better than the equivalent bottled product.

BOTTLED BEER

Bottled beer comes in a number of forms (pasteurized, unpasteurized, and bottle-conditioned being the most popular), and you may not be able to tell exactly how it's packaged by looking at the label. Which form is best is very much dependent on beer type and how it will be enjoyed. Mass-market brewers and their consumers like the stability that pasteurization brings to mainstream beers, while craft consumers are happy to have the fresher flavor of unpasteurized beer.

Bottle-conditioned beers contain live yeast which was still active on bottling day, and a small amount of fermentation creates the carbonation but at the price of a small deposit of yeast. In most beer types — wheat beers excepted — yeast haze in the glass is not desirable. Not everybody appreciates the haze and slight earthiness that sometimes comes with that slug of yeast in the bottom of the bottle. So it's helpful if you can pour a whole bottle in one go and leave the yeast in the bottle. If you are serving small portions, especially from large bottles, it is usually best to decant the beer into a pitcher. From there you can pour at will.

The main drawback of bottles is their transparency, but not all bottles are created equal. Brown bottles offer reasonably good protection from the blue light that causes skunkiness, while clear and green bottles offer none. Some manufacturers who package in clear bottles use special hop extracts that have been processed to prevent their transformation into the skunky, lightstruck aroma.

The stability of any packaged beer is the result of a number of factors. First is the brewing process and the recipe, as there are some compounds called reductones that can be involved with oxidation, and different ingredients and details of the brewing process can affect how much potential there is for staling. Midcolored caramel malts, in particular, can

FORMS OF BOTTLED BEER

Bottled, then pasteurized. This is the most common bottled beer type. Many feel pasteurization dulls the flavor of beer, but this is a fairly subtle effect.

Flash pasteurized, then aseptically bottled. Practitioners feel this shorter but hotter form of pasteurization is gentler on the beer.

Micro- (cold) filtered, then aseptically packaged. This is supposed to give "real draft" flavor in a bottled product; it is not pasteurized.

Bottle-conditioned. Live yeast and some sugars are sealed into the bottle, left to ferment. Yeast produces carbon dioxide, which gives the beer its carbonation. Yeast provides oxygen scavenging and other protective effects. Considered "real ale."

contribute disproportionately to staling, but it's an incredibly complex part of brewing science. The amount of oxygen added during bottling is also important. The goal is always zero, but this is not practical. Generally, the larger and more sophisticated the bottling equipment, the lower the oxygen content. The exception is bottle-conditioned beer. Yeast is a ferocious oxygen scavenger, which gives a protective effect. Brewers conventionally bottling craft beers sometimes leave a tiny amount of yeast in the package, serving the same function.

Even the bottle caps have an effect. The standard lining material for many years was PVC, but this was relatively permeable to oxygen and caused some concerns of harmful chemicals leaching into the beer. For those reasons, PVC is being phased out. The few craft brewers who were using them are also phasing out twist-off caps in favor of pry-off caps that seal more tightly and allow less oxygen into the package. Increasingly, craft brewers are switching to oxygen-barrier or oxygen-scavenging caps.

CANNED BEER

Canned is pretty much the same thing as bottled. Once only for mass-market beers, cans have become part of mainstream craft beer, starting in 2002 when Colorado brewery Oskar Blues started using them. Just as with the big guys, craft customers appreciate the benefits of the light weight, unbreakability, quick chilling, and eco-friendliness of canned beer. It's currently a rapidly growing segment of the craft category. Some have questioned the safety of a chemical called bisphenol-A (BPA) that is used in the epoxy coating on the insides

Canned Craft Beer
Normally associated with mainstream lagers, canned craft beer has become a huge phenomenon and is still growing rapidly.

of cans, but the science is not particularly clear on this. A search for alternate materials is under way, but seems a long way in the future.

GROWLERS: DRAFT BEER TO GO

"Growler" is an old term for a container used to bring draft beer home from a bar. People would typically send their kid to a bar with the empty growler (typically a half-gallon tin pail with a lid) and a nickel — something unimaginable in today's world for numerous reasons.

Modern growlers are usually half-gallon (1.9 liter) glass jugs, although other sizes and shapes, including quart-sized "howlers," are increasingly common. There are some sophisticated metal growlers featuring vacuum insulation and even the ability to pressurize and use them like tiny kegs. And quart-sized cans called "crowlers" are also occasionally employed.

Growlers are most often filled in a somewhat haphazard manner by bartenders, who attach a length of plastic tubing over the end of the tap and fill into the growler through that. This wastes a fair amount of beer, knocks the carbonation way down, and introduces oxygen and unwanted microbes. As a result, shelf life is extremely short, perhaps just a matter of a couple of days. Dedicated counterpressure growler fillers eliminate nearly all of these problems. Although expensive, they are finding a lot of popularity in taprooms, brewpubs, and off-premises retailers who sell growlers, as they know their customers will be getting a better product. Shelf life is reported to be a month or more.

In the United States, state and local laws differ widely about who is allowed to sell growlers and under what conditions. Generally, growlers must be labeled in accordance with federal Alcohol and Tobacco Tax and Trade Bureau (TTB) regulations, although the law is fuzzy in some places. They also usually need to be fitted with some kind of breakable seal that, when intact, shows that the container has not been opened — important when you're taking one home in your car.

Draft Beer

Draft was once the overwhelming choice for most beer drinkers. Bottled beer was rare until the late nineteenth century, and draft dominated until after Prohibition in the United States, when beer began to be more frequently consumed at home. Craft consumers love its freshness and sustainability and have expanded its popularity.

A draft system in its basic form is a fairly simple thing. The beer, pressurized from the carbonation it received at the brewery, is contained in a stainless steel keg with a coupling valve that admits gas and allows the beer to leave. A tank of liquefied carbon dioxide fitted with a pressure regulator is connected to the keg through a specialized coupling, which allows gas to flow in while the beer flows out to the taps.

Multitap systems with long draws need glycol-chilled lines and mixed-gas pressure, adding a good deal of cost and complexity. One bar in downtown Chicago reportedly spent a million dollars on its 360-tap, 114-beer draft system. But no matter how fancy the system, the fundamentals are absolutely the same.

Despite the simplicity, devils lurk in that dark space beneath the bar. There are many ways to get it wrong: flat, foul, and foamy beers being the most prevalent. It takes a lot of fine-tuning to get the system into proper balance, so the beer is well carbonated yet not overfoaming. And once set up, it takes constant vigilance to keep it humming along properly and an aggressive cleaning schedule to keep the ever-present microbes from fouling up the works.

PERFECT POURS

A good bartender can make it look easy to pour a perfect beer, but it does take a lot of practice, and your draft system has to be properly set up.

U.S./International Pour

A 1-inch (2.5 cm) head is considered the ideal, but many consumers would rather have the beer instead of the foam. Still, at least ½ inch of tight, creamy foam is a beautiful thing.

Equipment: Standard taps, CO_2 gas only

Technique: Pour down the side until half full or more, then straighten up and pour for foam, lowering the glass if necessary to create a more impactful stream and additional bubbles.

Euro Pils Pour

Glassware everywhere in Europe is calibrated, usually with a line to show a specific volume. Any foam on top is a bonus. The beer is often poured with a fairly large amount of foam, allowed to settle, and then topped up in one or more steps. This process releases some gas and creates dense, creamy foam.

Equipment: Euro Pils taps with variable restriction, CO_2 gas only; fairly high pressure for a foamy pour

Technique: The first glass should be about half foam. Allow the foam to settle, top off with another foamy dollop, wait, then finish topping off, giving a full measure and filling the rest of the glass with dense white foam.

Chope (Brazil)

This creamy-topped pour is reserved for the characteristically light Brazilian mass-market "Pils," typically served in small (9 ounce/266 mL) Pilsner flutes, normally served lip-numbingly cold, sometimes well below 32°F/0°C.

Equipment: A special beer tap called a "creamer" faucet. Typically, beer from room temperature kegs is chilled through refrigerated coils.

Technique: Pour beer into a small chilled Pilsner glass within 1.5 inches (3.8 cm) of the top, and then push the creamer faucet backward to top it off with a blob of dense foam that rises above the rim.

Nitro Pour

This is the familiar pour of Guinness, created to emulate the soft, creamy texture of cask ale. While it does require a special faucet and mixed nitrogen and CO_2 gas, the beer must be specially prepared at the brewery. This technique requires

US/International

Euro Pils

Chope

Nitro

about half the normal carbonation, typically 1.0 to 1.4 volumes; any higher and the beer becomes a foamy mess. Then it is put under pressure with a blend, sometimes called G-Mix, of 25 percent CO_2 and 75 percent nitrogen. Because nitrogen dissolves poorly in beer, when the beer exits the faucet the nitrogen comes out of solution and brings some of the CO_2 with it as well. This causes the beautiful cascade of fine bubbles and creamy head that characterizes this style of pour.

Equipment: Nitro faucet and mixed gas

Technique: Just place the glass under the nitro faucet and flip it open. Some bartenders are known for creating shamrocks or other images with a drizzle of foam.

Real Ale Pour

This is far more than just a type of pour. Real ale is a treasured and ancient method of serving beer that was once on the verge of winking out. It is defined as beer that is unfiltered and unpasteurized, carbonated in the package from which it will be sold. While that definition also includes bottles, draft real ale arrives at the pub cellar still alive and must be carefully managed by the publican to bring it to the customer in the best condition. See pages 161–68 for more on real ale.

Equipment: Hand pumps if the beer is in the cellar; otherwise a simple gravity dispense with a tap directly from the cask is preferred.

Technique: How much foam is very much a matter of personal and regional preference, with those in the north of England generally preferring a nice ½-inch to ¾-inch (1.3 to 2 cm) blanket of dense creamy foam, while in the south, the head should be minimal.

Belgian Pour

Because these vary quite a bit, each one takes a different approach and should be poured into its own proprietary glass if available. With highly carbonated bottled beers, a glass with a lot of excess capacity is needed to accommodate the copious foam.

Equipment: Normal draft or bottles; water for rinsing is helpful

Technique: Prerinse the glass with cold water to keep foam to a minimum. With bottles, pour the whole beer at once, leaving the muddy yeast behind in the bottle.

Hefeweizen Pour

A tall, vase-shaped glass is classic. The theatrical bottle pour is detailed on page 117; the remaining yeast is normally added to intensify the haze.

Real Ale

Belgian

0.5 L

Hefeweizen

DRAFT SYSTEM FUNDAMENTALS

While there is plenty of biochemistry to be found in the world of beer, we'll be talking about something more basic here: physics, which describes the behavior of gases as affected by pressure and temperature, and their ability to become soluble in a liquid.

BOYLE'S LAW is at the heart of the draft system. It is an equation created by the seventeenth-century scientist Robert Boyle that spells out the relationship between the pressure of a gas and its temperature. As you know from grade school, gas is just a phase of matter whose molecules are bouncing around so energetically that they can't live together as a solid or a liquid. That molecular motion is driven by heat. Take a kettle of water, apply heat, and you make a gas called water vapor.

In the case of beer, we're mainly dealing with carbon dioxide, which has a low boiling temperature ($-109.3°F/-78.5°C$), making it a gas at room temperature. Compress it at several hundred pounds of pressure into a heavy metal bottle and it becomes a liquid, and that's our prime mover in draft systems: a tank of liquefied CO_2. Some specialized draft systems, such as the "nitro" systems, employ nitrogen gas as well, usually in mixed form. Nitrogen has a much lower boiling point and is also less soluble in beer than CO_2 and behaves differently in a number of ways.

When beer comes from the brewery, it is already carbonated, suffused with a specific amount of CO_2. Various terms are used to quantify this amount. In the United States the word "volume" is used to describe an amount of gas equal (at the ambient pressure and $32°F/0°C$) to the volume of the beer. Beer volumes are typically in the 2.2 to 2.6 range, with some styles, such as Belgian abbey ales and Bavarian Hefeweizens, over the 3 mark. Champagne is in the neighborhood of 5 to 6 volumes. On the other end, British cask ales are somewhere in the 1.1 to 1.8 range. The European standard unit for carbonation is grams per liter, a number roughly double that for volumes.

CO_2 is highly soluble in water, which is why it doesn't all come gushing out the moment you pop the top off that IPA. Even with the pressure released, most of the CO_2 just sits there, fortunately for us, helping create bubbles and foam and making our beer drinking a lively experience.

But gas gauges are calibrated in pressure, not volumes. To reconcile the two, we need to consider temperature. At any given volume of CO_2, as the temperature rises, the pressure will also. The mathematical formula is fairly complex, so most people just refer to the chart on page 152, which gives pressure for any combination of temperature and CO_2 volume.

BALANCE is the central operating principle in a draft system. The beer is under pressure in the keg; the amount of pressure is a combination of the amount of gas introduced by the brewery and the temperature of the beer. This pressure, which can be found on the chart on page 152, must ideally be matched by resistance created by various restrictions within the system. With insufficient restriction, the beer comes gushing out in a foamy mess. Balanced by the correct restriction, the beer pours as if it were gently lifted from the keg to the glass, full of carbonation and a controllable amount of foam for the sake of aesthetics.

Every length and diameter of tubing and vertical distance from keg to glass creates a specific amount of restriction, expressed in pounds per square inch (psi), as can be seen in the chart on page 155. For shorter runs,

A DRAFT SYSTEM AT ITS MOST BASIC

A kegerator is a self-contained chilling and serving device for beer. It really is the model for larger and more complex systems.

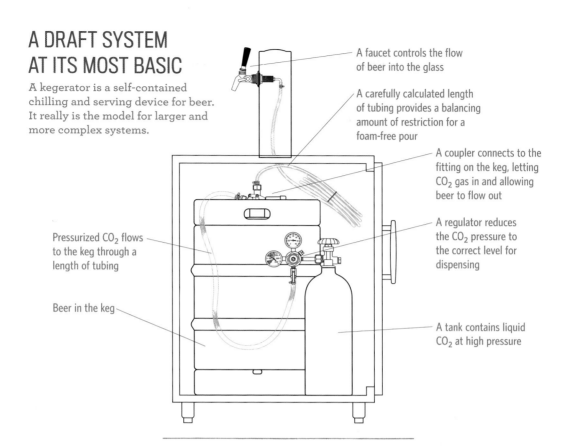

A faucet controls the flow of beer into the glass

A carefully calculated length of tubing provides a balancing amount of restriction for a foam-free pour

A coupler connects to the fitting on the keg, letting CO_2 gas in and allowing beer to flow out

A regulator reduces the CO_2 pressure to the correct level for dispensing

A tank contains liquid CO_2 at high pressure

Pressurized CO_2 flows to the keg through a length of tubing

Beer in the keg

just calculate the restriction from the vertical distance the beer must travel and then add the necessary length and diameter of tubing needed to bring the system into balance. For longer runs, higher amounts of restriction are unavoidable, even though larger diameter tubing is used, so the dispensing pressure at the keg needs to be raised to match the restriction to get the beer to flow, and that in turn often requires mixed gas in various proportions to give the necessary pressure without overcarbonating the beer.

Let's take a simple example: A pale ale is carbonated at 2.2 volumes and is being served at a temperature of 44°F/7°C. If we look at the volumes/pressure/temperature chart on page 152, we find that those two parameters will leave the container pressurized at 11 psi (0.76 bar). For ideal serving conditions, we need to balance this with an equal amount of system restriction. If the beer is being served from a cellar with a 14-foot (4.3 m) vertical difference from the beer to the tap, the force of gravity acts at 0.5 psi per foot, creating 7 psi of restriction. That leaves us needing 4 psi of additional restriction to create a balanced system. We'll get it from the tubing. With a little slack in the line, we need something like 17 feet (5.2 m) of tubing to reach from the keg to the tap, which means we need 0.3 psi per foot for the proper amount of total restriction. Stainless tubing that is 5/16 inch (7.9 mm) gives us exactly the right amount (see chart on page 155), but since this stainless is rather rare in draft installations, let's assume we'll use ⅜ inch (9.5 mm) vinyl at 0.2 psi/ft, which delivers 3.4 psi restriction for that 17 feet (5.2 m). This leaves us 1.6 psi short, so to get the total needed restriction we would need to lengthen the line by 8 feet (2.4 m) to a total of 22 feet (6.7 m), or add a choker line of smaller tubing — 2 feet (0.6 m) of ¼ inch (6.3 mm) would be about right.

The long coils in jockey boxes (coolers with beer taps and coils or cold plates inside) also create a lot of restriction, so these also need higher dispense pressures. If you're using pure CO_2 rather than mixed gas in that situation, always depressurize the keg back to its original pressure rather than leave it to sit overnight at high pressure and become overcarbonated.

Some beer faucets are fitted with a little lever on the side that varies the restriction a bit. This can be used to tweak the pour, but don't expect it to correct a badly unbalanced system.

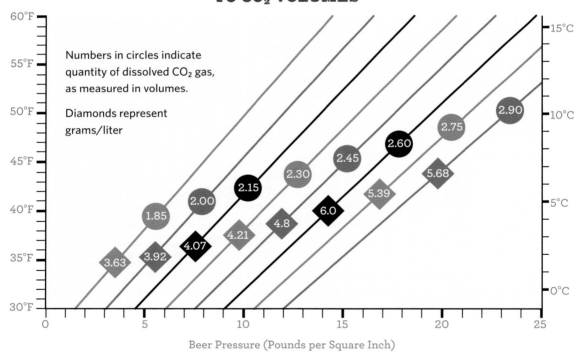

PRESSURE AND TEMPERATURE AS RELATED TO CO₂ VOLUMES

Numbers in circles indicate quantity of dissolved CO_2 gas, as measured in volumes.

Diamonds represent grams/liter

Beer Pressure (Pounds per Square Inch)

As anyone who has ever opened a warm beer knows, the pressure of beer's carbonation increases with temperature. Brewers in the United States use CO_2 "volume" to express the absolute amount of CO_2 gas dissolved in beer. Diagonal lines show volumes and grams/liter at any given pressure and temperature.

Brewpub Serving Tanks
This may appear highly complex, but a brewpub draft system is just a kegerator with very, very large kegs.

JOCKEY BOX COILS come in lengths from 50 to 120 feet (15.2 to 36.6 m) and in several different diameters. Longer coils often use larger diameter tubing but may add a shorter length of smaller diameter tubing to increase restriction. Restriction varies between 15 and 36 pounds (6.8 and 16.3 kg), but check with your manufacturer for your model's specific amount. Because of the pretty high restriction, beers served from jockey boxes often need to be served at pressures from 20 to 30 psi (1.5 to 2 bars) and may require some twiddling to get it right. If you finish the event and want to use the beer that's left in the keg, be sure to bleed the pressure back to the keg's original pressure to prevent overcarbonation.

DRAFT SYSTEM TYPES

Basic cold-room, direct draw. This is a common and simple system for smaller bars and restaurants. Beer is kept chilled and under pressure, while lines typically run a short distance through the back bar or directly to the tap from a kegerator. Unless they are very short, unrefrigerated lines may cause foaming and are not generally recommended.

Long-draw, refrigerated lines. When the point of service is a long way from the kegs, the lines can contain a good deal of beer. This makes it necessary to chill the lines to prevent warm beer and excess foaming. Typically, lines are run parallel in an insulated bundle with a chilling line contained inside, or through a tunnel or raceway that is refrigerated. Long distances create a good deal of restriction, which means higher pressures must be employed. This requires the use of mixed nitrogen and CO_2 gas to avoid the overcarbonation that would occur with pure CO_2.

Long draw, pump-assisted. When the runs are very long or when there is a considerable vertical distance to travel, the necessarily high pressures start to be a problem, so pumps may be added to the system to push the beer along. These are typically used in only the largest installations, such as sports venues.

Long-draw, compressed air. Some high-volume systems use compressed air to supply the pressure for dispensing. While this is generally not recommended, in some venues where huge quantities of beer are sold very quickly there's no time for oxygen to affect the beer, so compressed air is sometimes used in this situation.

Brewpub cold-room system with serving tanks. Small breweries that serve their own beer don't need to keg the batch. Beer is served either from jacketed, temperature-controlled tanks or unjacketed cellar tanks in a cold room. Outside of the fact that the sizes are much larger, the other parts of the system are pretty similar to those mentioned above, except that CO_2 is generally hard-piped from the brewery's bulk CO_2 cryotank. Since large tanks can't be pressurized as highly as kegs, pumps are often used to assist the delivery of beer.

DRAFT SYSTEM WORKSHEET

This worksheet can be used to calculate the total amount of restriction and pressure needed for a perfect dispense.

1) Find Pressure

Beer Temperature: _____   Volumes of CO_2: _____

(Most beer: 2.2 to 2.6 volumes; Belgian ales and Hefeweizens: up to 3 to 3.8 volumes)

Keg Pressure = _____ psi = Needed Restriction

2) Add Up Restriction List

Faucet: _____ = _____ psi or _____ bar

Height: lbs/ft _____ × _____ ft = _____ psi or bar/meter _____ × meters = _____ bar

Other 1: _____ lbs = _____ psi or @bar _____ = _____ bar

Other 2: _____ lbs = _____ psi or @bar _____ = _____ bar

Other 3: _____ lbs = _____ psi or @bar _____ = _____ bar

Other 4: _____ lbs = _____ psi or @bar _____ = _____ bar

    Subtotal: _____ psi or Subtotal: _____ bar

Hose: lbs/ft _____ × _____ ft = _____ psi or bar/meter _____ × _____ meters = _____ bar

    Total: _____ psi or Total: _____ bar

3a) If restriction with necessary length of hose is lower than pressure off beer in keg, add length or reduce diameter to create additional restriction to match beer pressure.

3b) If restriction with necessary length of tubing exceeds beer pressure, look at increasing tubing diameter and check the numbers. If the restriction still exceeds beer pressure, higher pressure must be applied to beer to bring the system into balance, but if using pure CO_2, this can lead to overcarbonation. In these cases mixed gas is often used.

DRAFT SYSTEM RESTRICTION SOURCES
AND QUANTITIES

TUBING

IN/MM	OD/ID*	MATERIAL	RESTRICTION
3⁄16"/4.8 mm	ID	Vinyl	3.00 lbs/ft (0.67 bar/m)
¼"/6.4 mm	ID	Vinyl	0.85 lbs/ft (0.19 bar/m)
¼"/6.4 mm	OD	Stainless	1.20 lbs/ft (0.27 bar/m)
¼"/6.4 mm	ID	Barrier	0.30 lbs/ft (0.067 bar/m)
5⁄16"/7.9 mm	ID	Vinyl	0.40 lbs/ft (0.089 bar/m)
5⁄16"/7.9 mm	ID	Barrier	0.10 lbs/ft (0.022 bar/m)
5⁄16"/7.9 mm	OD	Stainless	0.30 lbs/ft (0.067 bar/m)
3⁄8"/9.5 mm	ID	Vinyl	0.20 lbs/ft (0.044 bar/m)
3⁄8"/9.5 mm	ID	Barrier	0.06 lbs/ft (0.013 bar/m)
3⁄8"/9.5 mm	OD	Stainless	0.12 lbs/ft (0.027 bar/m)
½"/12.7 mm	ID	Vinyl	0.025 lbs/ft (0.006 bar/m)

*Outer diameter and inner diameter

COLD PLATE

12 ft/3.7 meters of 3⁄16"/4.8 mm tubing: 3.6 lbs/0.24 bar

18 ft/5.5 meters of 3⁄16"/4.8 mm tubing: 5.4 lbs/0.37 bar

CHILLER COIL

50 ft/15.2 m of ¼"/6.4 mm tubing: 15 lbs/1.02 bar

70 ft/21.3 m of ¼"/6.4 mm tubing: 21 lbs/1.43 bar

100 ft/30.5 m of 5⁄16"/7.9 mm tubing: 12 lbs/0.82 bars

(Note that some chiller coils use two different tubing diameters to manage restriction. Check with your manufacturer's specifications.)

Faucet: Negligible

Height of tap from middle of keg, per foot: 0.43 psi/0.015 bar

Height of tap from middle of keg, per meter: 1.64 psi/0.11 bar

Plastic mixer insert* per 6 inch/15.2 cm: 6 psi/0.41 bar (approx.)

A spiral plastic tube meant for mixing epoxy. Used by homebrewers who insert them in the dip tubes of soda kegs to add restriction without greatly extending the beer line.

Warm kegs with chiller. In much of the world, refrigeration is very expensive, making cold rooms for beer storage pretty uncommon, so in hot climates there is less draft beer in general. The one or two beers that may be on tap at a typical venue will be room temperature. To cool it to serving temperature, it flows through refrigerated coils usually chilled electrically, similar to a jockey box. Craft beer is making inroads in such places as Mexico, Brazil, and elsewhere in Latin America. Specialized beer bars in those regions increasingly make the investment required to keep their kegs cold, often showcasing the cold rooms with a window into the bar.

Kegerators and keezers. Kegerators, generally intended for home use, consist of a keg-sized refrigerator, with lines going to taps on the outside. "Keezer" (keg + freezer) is the name for a home-crafted version made from a chest freezer with a setback thermostat, and sometimes with a homemade riser between the chest and the lid that has holes for shanks or lines to run through.

Festival system. The typical system for events consists of ice-filled tubs for the kegs, with lines running through a jockey box containing a coil or plate chiller immersed in ice to standard taps on the outside of the cooler. Foaming is often a big problem, and the response is often to reduce pressure. Counterintuively, the solution is often the opposite. Because of their long lengths of tubing in the chiller coils, jockey boxes often provide a lot of restriction, so beer flow may improve if the pressure is increased.

Homebrew draft beer. Having fresh draft beer at home is a true luxury. While most homebrewers start by bottling, it can be a little tedious, so many step up to a draft setup. It's the same parts and pieces as any draft system: a keg, CO_2 cylinder, regulator, hoses, and some type of faucet. Most homebrewers use corny kegs, 5-gallon (18.9 L) kegs originally meant for soda. They feature quick disconnects for liquid and gas and a hatch-type lid that makes it easy to get inside to clean — the big point of difference from Sankeys and other dedicated beer kegs. Homebrewers typically serve through relatively short lines and as a result often don't have adequate restriction, so paying a little attention to system balancing can prevent foaming when serving.

TYPES OF DRAFT FAUCETS

- Standard
- Euro type
- Cobra tap
- Creamer
- With variable restriction
- Nitro/mixed gas (Guinness type)
- Picnic tap (pump and disposable gas cartridge type)
- Pigtail and zwickel (breweries only)

TYPES OF KEG COUPLERS

Sankey, Euro-Sankey. The standard Sankey (type D) is the most common type of keg coupler in North America. Beer comes straight up the center while gas flows in through the side. They're simple to use: simply insert, twist until it locks, pull the handle out a little to unlock, then push down until it clicks in place. The North American and European (type S) versions differ only by a couple of millimeters, causing annoying problems. If you have both in your kit bag, make sure they're clearly marked.

Slider. This European type is most popular with German breweries. It comes in two variations, "type A" and "type M," which differ only in the probe configuration.

Half-bell or ration. Type G, sometimes called "half-bell."

Guinness "type U" couplers. As one would expect, these fit mainly Guinness and its related brands.

Proprietary couplers for plastic kegs. These are often specific to a particular manufacturer. Note that with some systems, the coupler must stay on after tapping until the beer is gone.

DRAFT BEER KEG TYPES AND SIZES

KEG TYPE	SIZES
Stainless Sankey	½ bbl (15.5 U.S. gallons), ¼ bbl, 1/6 bbl (sixtel)
Euro-Sankey, etc.	½ hL/50 liters (13.2 U.S. gallons), 30, 25, 20 liters (7.9, 6.6, 5.3 gallons)
Plastic one-way kegs	A variety of popular sizes is available and varies by manufacturer
Corny kegs (homebrew)	5 U.S. gallons (18.9 L), 3 U.S. gallons (11.4 L)
Kölsch and Alt barrels	10.2 L (2.7 U.S. gallons)
Proprietary fractional kegs (with self-contained CO_2)	Various sizes but usually less than 5 gallons (18.9 L)
Golden Gate (discontinued)	½ bbl (15.5 U.S. gallons), ¼ bbl
Hoff-Stevens (discontinued)	½ bbl (15.5 U.S. gallons), ¼ bbl

DIN (EUROPE) KEG SIZES, MM

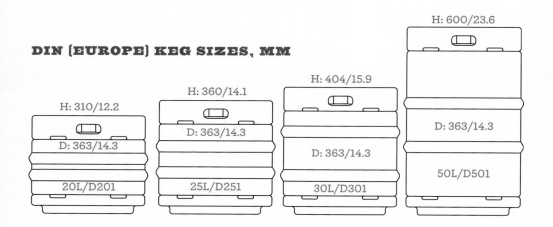

H: 310/12.2
D: 363/14.3
20L/D201

H: 360/14.1
D: 363/14.3
25L/D251

H: 404/15.9
D: 363/14.3
30L/D301

H: 600/23.6
D: 363/14.3
50L/D501

U.S. KEG SIZES, INCHES

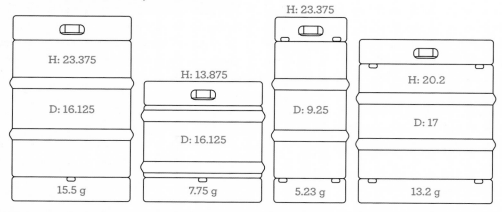

H: 23.375
D: 16.125
15.5 g

H: 13.875
D: 16.125
7.75 g

H: 23.375
D: 9.25
5.23 g

H: 20.2
D: 17
13.2 g

SPEED FILLING

The TurboTap is a patented device that attaches to a beer tap and improves the dispensing speed. It is basically a tube with parallel baffles that creates a nonturbulent, laminar flow that reduces foaming; at the bottom of the tube is a conical nib pointed upward into the beer stream that redirects the flow outward, again with reduced turbulence. When these devices are set up properly, they can fill a large cup of beer in a matter of seconds. They are obviously not needed everywhere but can dramatically shorten the lines of people waiting for beers in sports and music venues.

Bottoms Up cups are a different way to speed up pouring. The cups have a simple valve or flap on the bottom that opens to receive beer when placed on the filling device. Beer then flows from the bottom up, with little foaming. When the cup is lifted off the filler, the valve snaps shut.

SAFETY AND DRAFT SYSTEMS

Any time a gas is confined, its kinetic energy can be dangerous. A tank of CO_2 may range between 500 and 800 psi, and because it is in liquid form, that means there is a lot of highly compressed material ready to shoot out with terrifying force when the opportunity allows.

Gas cylinders are superdurable and rarely fail, but the valves screwed into them are relatively delicate. A fall or other rough handling can knock them off, with disastrous results. When the television show *MythBusters* tried this, the tank rocketed its way through two concrete block walls before stopping. So extreme caution is required. Handle them like babies, and always fasten them securely with a chain (not a bungee cord) to something vertical when in use. Never use them on their side or inverted, as this will cause liquid CO_2 to squirt through the regulator, which is not designed to handle liquid CO_2 and can fail spectacularly. It goes without saying that you should never tamper with a safety pressure-relief or rupture disc.

At high concentrations, CO_2 can cause asphyxiation. In very small quantities, it is harmless to breathe. Many workplaces require CO_2 alarms and other safety systems, especially for hard-piped systems.

Kegs are very heavy. A full U.S. half-barrel weighs 161 pounds (73 kg), which is more weight than the average person can handle alone. Beer delivery people do need to maneuver these single-handedly, but experience and extreme caution is needed, and even so, back injuries are common. Steel-toed shoes are also highly recommended.

Kegs do sometimes explode. Stainless steel kegs fail only under the most extreme circumstances. Over the last decade there has been a lot of interest in one-way plastic kegs for the many benefits they bring, especially when beer is shipped long distances. However, as this technology has developed, there have been a number of injuries — some fatal — involving explosions of plastic kegs. If you're working with these, always follow the manufacturer's instructions for cleaning and filling to the letter, and make sure your gauges and other systems are functioning properly. This technology is evolving rapidly, so we should expect them to become more common. Do your research, and choose one with a built-in pressure-relief device to prevent explosive failures.

DRAFT BEER TROUBLESHOOTING

Their tangle of hoses and valves can make draft systems appear complicated, but they're really pretty simple. While a full troubleshooting guide is beyond the scope of this book, there are a few general points that can be covered. Common sense and logically tracing the problem from source to tap usually identify the cause. Almost any flow or foaming problem can be solved by making sure that the connections and valve positions are correct and observing the general principle of pressure balancing.

Beer is not flowing. Check all your valves (including the gas bottle) and connections, and make sure there is still gas in the cylinder and beer in the keg. It's good to have a healthy mistrust of your gas gauges, especially if they've been in service for a while and have been knocked around a little, as most gauges contain a delicate brass tube inside that is easily damaged. It's not a bad idea to keep a couple of spares around and replace them whenever you suspect they're not reading correctly.

Beer is overfoaming. There can be many causes. First, double-check to make sure that the system has adequate balance for the carbonation level and temperature of the beer. If that looks good, try adjusting the pressure via the screw or knob in the center of the regulator. Counterintuitively, too-low pressure may cause the same kind of foaming as too high, so try more pressure first, not less. If the problem is persistent, turn the gas off, bleed the keg coupling, and try the faucet with no gas flowing. If the beer is still coming fast and foamy, it's possible the keg could be too warm or overcarbonated. If the beer has been tapped for a while and the dispense pressure is high, it's possible pressure has built up. Or it could be some problem at the brewery. It's rare, but it does happen. Certain styles such as hefeweizens and Belgian ales are highly carbonated by design, and they may require additional restriction to pour properly.

 ## SEND IT BACK! A DRAFT DRINKER'S BILL OF RIGHTS

No one expects you to drink a bad beer, so when you get one that's problematic you should feel well within your rights to return it and ask for another — *without* an argument. You have the right to beer that is:

- Beautiful, sparkling, and clear if the style is supposed to be clear (note that many craft and especially brewpub beers will have a little haze, especially when cold)

- Fresh and free from cardboard or honey oxidized aromas

- Free from off-flavors due to dirty draft lines or taps; sourness (in anything other than the specialty wild and sour styles for which it is appropriate) along with off-aromas such as butteriness, spoiled milk, or cheesy smells, can be a symptomatic of dirty lines

- Lively and fully carbonated

- Served in sparkling clean glassware appropriate to its strength and style (large areas on the inside of the glass where mats of bubbles cling are a sure giveaway of dirty glassware; another telltale sign is lipstick on the rim, which is just inexcusable laziness)

- Free from any taste of sanitizing solution

Beer pours okay but is relatively flat. In this case, the beer has probably lost some carbonation, either from incorrect pressure on its gas line over time or from a gas leak. It's a frequent occurrence when mixed gas (such as the G-Mix used for Guinness) is hooked up to normally carbonated beer. The beer will pour fine for the first day or so, but because there is not enough CO_2 even at the fairly high pressures used for mixed gas, the carbonation bleeds out of the beer.

Beer has weird flavors. These are a common problem. Buttery and/or vinegary aromas and acidic tastes are likely signs of a *Lactobacillus* or other bacterial contamination of tap lines that may also result in haze. If the problem goes away after pouring a few beers in rapid succession, it's the lines. If it's persistent, the brewery may be at fault. Be aware that root beers and some other sodas or flavored malt beverages may "flavor-stain" the lines, usually requiring their replacement.

For more details on draft systems, there are some great resources available, including the *Draught Beer Quality Manual* from the Brewers Association. Equipment manufacturer Micro Matic offers a 3-day Dispense Institute and a free, condensed online version. The Siebel Institute also offers a 4-day Draught Master class.

Cask (Real) Ale

The British beer preservation society, the Campaign for Real Ale (CAMRA) (see page 32) defines real ale as "a natural product brewed using traditional ingredients and left to mature in the cask (container) from which it is served in the pub through a process called secondary fermentation."

A hundred years ago, this was the norm for British beers. Brewed quickly, and rushed out to the pubs while still fermenting, real ale requires skilled and motivated cellar staff to make sure the beers arrive in the customers' glasses in perfect, bright, delicious condition. This is a very old way of doing things, and it has clashed pretty dramatically with the business realities of the past half century. CAMRA was formed at a time when brewers were pushing to eliminate cask beer altogether and move to kegs or cellar tanks filled by tanker trucks. Thanks largely to CAMRA, cask beer survives in Britain, although it is now more of a specialty than the norm.

KEG THEFT

American brewers estimate that stolen kegs cost the industry well over $50 million a year. With the price of metals such as stainless steel escalating, criminals find the easy pickings of loose kegs irresistible. And who pays for this? You do. There are legislative and public-awareness efforts under way to combat this, but the situation will remain problematic as long as the cost of the deposit continues to be just a fraction of the keg's true value. Each keg costs a brewer as much as $150, and the price continues to rise along with the price of stainless. And homebrewers, please get your kegs from legitimate sources. A deposit is not a purchase price.

ESSENTIAL DRAFT SYSTEM TERMS AND EQUIPMENT

Atmosphere. The mean atmospheric pressure at sea level, used as the metric standard unit of pressure and also known as a bar. One atmosphere is equivalent to 14.7 psi.

Bar. Same as atmosphere (above), the term used as the metric system unit of pressure. One bar is equivalent to 14.7 psi.

Blender/mixer (gas). A device that mixes pure CO_2 and N_2 gases for a desired mix. Used only in larger and more sophisticated draft setups.

Check valve. A simple device within a line or coupling that allows the flow of beer or gas only in one direction.

Chiller. Term for refrigeration equipment used to chill glycol.

Choker. A small-diameter piece of tubing that is sometimes added to a line to increase restriction.

Coil (cooling). A long (50–120 foot/15.2–36.6 meter) spiral of stainless tubing that, when immersed in ice water, cools beer to serving temperatures. Normally used in jockey boxes.

Cold plate. A zigzag of tubing embedded in aluminum that serves the same purpose of chilling beer as a coil but generally with less cooling capacity. Recommended for contact with ice but not recommended to be submerged in water. Often used in jockey boxes.

Corny. Short for "Cornelius," one of the manufacturers of soda kegs; corny kegs are now universally used as a homebrew draft serving vessel. Available in 3-, 5-, and 10-gallon (11.4, 18.9, and 37.9 L) sizes; the 5-gallon size is by far the most common.

Coupler (keg). The tapping head that attaches to the fitting at the top of the keg, allowing gas to flow in and beer to flow out. Different parts of the world favor different styles. As a result, imported draft beer in the United States often requires specialized couplers.

Creamer faucet. Specialized beer tap that pours normally when pulled, but when the handle is pushed backward it delivers pure foam used to top off a beer. Widely used in Brazil for their *chope* draft; nitro faucets generally also have a creamer feature.

Faucet. The tap at the point of service.

Gas cylinder. The thick-walled container used to store gas. In the United States, gas bottles are required to be tested and recertified every 5 years, and a test date is stamped into the metal near the valve.

Glycol. Short for propylene glycol, a nontoxic chemical used as the coolant liquid for remote chilling in beer lines and other beer service applications.

Jockey box. A cooler with a coil or cold plate inside and beer taps on the front, mostly used for festivals and other events. In many countries where cold rooms are rare, stationary coolers, often electrically chilled, are used to bring room-temperature beer down to serving temperature.

Keg. Stainless steel or plastic beer container used to hold beer under pressure.

Line. Tubing used in a draft system. Different sizes and types are often used for gas and liquid.

Manifold. A splitter, often with on-off valves, that feeds several gas lines from one source.

Nitro. Casual term for a mixed gas (CO_2 and N_2) dispensing system mimicking the rich, creamy foam of traditional cask ale.

Partial pressure. A physical phenomenon describing the behavior of mixed gas systems. Each gas has a fraction of the pressure, proportional to its content in the mix. It's a complicated topic, a little beyond the scope of this book.

Python. *See* Trunk line

Quick disconnect. Gas or liquid connectors for various parts of the system. Most commonly used for gas, they are used for both connections on homebrew-type corny kegs originally meant for soda.

Regulator. A device used to reduce the pressure of a gas. One is always attached to the gas cylinder to reduce the CO_2's high pressure. Secondary, or dropping, regulators are used in many systems to provide fine-tuning capability for each beer.

Relief valve. Any device to allow the safe relief of excess pressure; it is commonly fitted to gas cylinders, regulators, couplings, and certain types of kegs.

Restriction. A term indicating resistance from hoses, fittings, and other parts on the beer's liquid path to the tap that, when perfectly adjusted, balance the pressure in the keg.

Rinser. Bar-top device that sprays water into a beer glass when inverted over it and pressed down. Prerinsing a glass reduces the surface tension and makes highly carbonated styles less likely to foam.

Shank. A threaded fitting mounted through a wall or other barrier to get beer from one space to another. Typically, a beer tap is mounted on one end and the beer line is connected to the other.

Trunk line/trunk bundle. A parallel bunch of draft lines running from the cellar/cold room to the point of service. Typically refrigerated if the run is longer than a few feet.

Washers (gas and beer). Pretty simple, these are just small round gaskets that make a seal in fittings. Gas washers are fiber (one use only) or hard plastic and make a seal between the gas cylinders as they connect to couplers, shanks, and faucets.

Zwickel. A small tap fitted to a brewery conditioning tank, allowing beer to be sampled. It's often used in combination with a pigtail, a tight coil of small-diameter stainless tubing that reduces the foaming that would otherwise occur. The zwickel lends its name to an unfiltered version of a lager, most commonly sold only in brewery bierkellers, although a few release packaged versions.

Not-quite-finished beers are racked into casks and bunged with a wooden plug called a shive, then sent off to the pubs. Each cask has two openings: one on the head, which holds another plug called a keystone through which the tap is inserted, and another at the broadest point around the middle, which is on top when the cask is sitting on its side ready for service.

Once in the pub's cellar, a porous reed peg called a spile is driven into a hole in the shive, allowing excess carbon dioxide to vent. This may typically take a few days, sometimes longer, depending on the state of the beer when it arrives. When this venting slows down and the beer is deemed by the cellar master to be in prime condition, a gas-tight hard spile is swapped for the soft spile, allowing pressure to remain in the cask.

Once the cask is hard-spiled, a period of time, usually just a few days, is allowed for the beer to rest and drop free of yeast and other solids. Sometimes a fining agent, isinglass, is added, which speeds up the settling process. Hops may be added for aroma as well. When the beer is ready to serve, a plastic tap is pounded into the bung with a brisk whack. An inner wooden plug in the bung, the keystone, gives way and allows the tap to seat. If done correctly, very little beer escapes, but a timid hand with the mallet may only partially seat the tap and release a gusher of beer. The hard spile must temporarily be removed to allow air to enter, displacing the beer being served, but it is usually placed back in the hole when the pub closes for the night.

Beer served this way has a very limited shelf life, as the carbonation dissipates and the deleterious effects of oxygen and bacterial contamination take hold. Once the cask has been tapped, the ale must be consumed within a few

 ## ODE TO THE BARREL

The barrel is one of the barbarians' finest gifts to humanity. Invented around the year 0 CE, the wooden barrel has had a useful technological life of 2,000 years — so far. It is a testament to the cleverness of these forest folks that, save for the introduction of metal hoops a couple of centuries ago, the barrel continues in its original form and purpose even today. It is now only rarely used for beer, having been replaced by the metal keg after World War II, but wooden barrels are indispensable for all aged spirits and a good portion of all wines. In today's craft scene, barrel-aged beers are an exciting addition to the luxurious end of the beer world.

Barrel-Aged Luxury Beer
Used barrels impart the flavors of their previous contents, plus other flavors, to these rare and expensive beers.

Hand Pumps for Real Ale
Operating on the same principle as a bicycle pump, beer engines like these are the traditional method for raising beer from the cellar to the bar.

days. Seasoned aficionados can tell how long a cask has been on tap and may even prefer the somewhat softened flavor a little oxygen can impart. But at a certain point it all goes wrong, and the cask ale will turn flat and lifeless and will probably sour as well.

In most pubs, the beer is stored in the cellar, which necessitates some means of transporting the beer up to bar level. Hand pumps are traditional and are still preferred, because CO_2 pressure disqualifies the beer from being classified as real ale by CAMRA standards. These are large and showy but at their heart are simple devices much like a bicycle pump, with a cylinder, a plunger, and valves at either end. When the pump is pulled down, beer is drawn

up through the line, through the spout, and into the glass. A small plastic restrictor known as a sparkler is sometimes screwed onto the end of the spout. This forces the beer through a small orifice, releasing some carbon dioxide and helping to create a dense, creamy head of foam. Like so many things about British beer, the use of sparklers varies by region; the practice is much more popular in the north. It should be noted that hand pumps, although a highly visible part of the regalia of real ale, actually add nothing to the flavor or texture of the beer (with the exception of the sparkler); they are simply a means of bringing the beer up to the bar level from the cellar. For festivals and other situations where the casks are on the same level as the drinkers, simple gravity taps can be used to no ill effect.

CAMRA holds on to the old ways with a death grip. The transition from a mainstream product to a specialty one has been painful and continues still. But if it weren't for the tenacity of CAMRA, real ale might be only a memory. Sometimes, however, this conservatism is less than helpful. One problem with the traditional method is that the beer is exposed to air when the cask is broached. In 1995, CAMRA did a detailed study of the use of cask breathers, devices that replace air with a gentle blanket of carbon dioxide, which give casks a longer life in the pub. Blind tests showed that cask breathers did no harm to beer. CAMRA, however, chose to ignore its own research and rule in favor of tradition, disallowing their use.

Cask beer is a somewhat uncommon specialty in the United States, but it is growing slowly. Because of its complexity, it often comes about as a special relationship between like-minded brewers and publicans who have established a certain level of trust that the beer will be well cared for and pulled if it falls short of proper quality. A few breweries specialize in this, but

WARM AND FLAT?

Contrary to the oft-repeated first impression of American tourists, British ales should be served at cool cellar temperatures of 50 to 55°F (10 to 13°C), and with a lively, but not excessive, carbonation. The proper amount of head is subject to vigorous debate in the United Kingdom, and this standard varies by region — more head being appropriate in the north. Although the royally approved pint glass now has a fill line about an inch below the rim, just a few years ago the rim of the glass was the full measure, which led to endless gamesmanship from patrons, wary of any foam, who would down half the glass and then call for a "top up"!

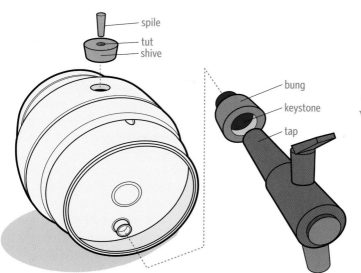

spile
tut
shive

bung
keystone
tap

Firkin
This 10.8 U.S. gallon (40.9 L) cask, the standard vessel for serving real ale, is a metal version of earlier wooden ones, with all the same working parts. Pin (5.4 U.S. gallons/20.4 L) and, more rarely, kilderkin (21.6 U.S. gallons/81.8 L) sizes are also used.

Real ale "in stillage" ready to be served from the cellar to the bar.

they are still quite rare and are often run by people with a strong English connection.

Despite the challenges, a pint of cask ale in perfect condition is a thing of rare beauty: cool, soft, creamy, and bursting with aroma, it is dangerously drinkable, pint after pint.

Cleaning, Sanitation, and Beer Service

Cleanliness always needs careful attention in brewing, and it is every bit as important when serving beer. Many a fine beer has been ruined by lack of diligence at the point of service. Drinkers aren't necessarily aware of all the things that can go wrong with a beer after it leaves the brewery. All they know is that they're holding a bad beer from a particular brewery, and guess whom they blame? Well-informed beer mavens look for patterns. Too many buttery beers at a bar might mean the establishment is not taking beer-line cleaning seriously.

When beer runs through plastic lines, a minute film of protein and other gunk sticks to the sides of the tubing, and this can be very difficult to remove. Beer lines are usually cleaned by pumping a hot caustic solution through them. A good beer bar will clean their tap

lines every 2 weeks, and some even more frequently. In the United States, responsibility for tap-line cleanliness varies. In states that allow it, distributors generally take responsibility for cleaning lines. In other states, this is seen as a gift that may unduly influence bar owners and is therefore prohibited along with other forms of pay to play.

Dirty or poorly cleaned glassware can cause dramatic problems as well, and these are all too often overlooked. Dirt may be hard to see in dim light, and it may be difficult to take proper care when the drinks are flying over the bar. Once the beer is poured, dirt on the glass reveals itself in telltale patches of bubbles clinging to the side of the glass. An old trick is to wet an empty glass with water, shake the excess out, and liberally sprinkle the inside with salt. The water will not adhere to the greasy or dirty spots, and without the water, the salt won't stick. So, where there is no salt, there is dirt.

In addition to the problem of dirt, glassware cleaning and sanitizing solutions are harsh and unpleasant tasting. A rushed rinse may leave a nasty phenolic taint, ruining an otherwise perfect beer.

Most commercial dishwashing detergents are petroleum based and may leave an oily film on glassware, which can interfere with a beer's head. Use special "beer-safe" cleaners for best results. Chlorine- or bromine-based sanitizers are pretty standard, and they do work well, but these powerful chemicals interact with

**Nor wanting is the brown October, drawn,
Mature and perfect, from his dark retreat
Of thirty years, and now his honest front
Flames in the light refulgent, not afraid
E'en with the vineyard's best produce to vie.**
— James Thomson, from his poem "Autumn"

polyphenols in the beer, creating chlorophenols or bromophenols, either of which can add a nasty Band-Aid or antiseptic aroma, ruining the beer. Consequently, I urge special caution to make sure glasses are well rinsed and completely odorless before they are filled with beer.

Sadly, many establishments fail to meet these criteria. Lack of training, short staffing, laziness, bad equipment, and more can be blamed. Do them a favor, and call them out when you get a less than perfect beer because of the condition of the glass.

The Beer Glass

Specialized beer-drinking vessels have been a treasured part of beer culture for thousands of years. They come in many sizes, forms, and materials, yet the goals have always been the same: deliver the beer to the lips in great form, in a pleasing, even celebratory way. They must fit the hand and suit the brew. If they dazzle the eye, so much the better.

Until the past 150 years or so, beer-drinking vessels were more commonly made of some baser material. Glass was a rare and expensive material, and its production depended on highly skilled artisans. Only the wealthy could afford glass. Regular folks drank from clay, metal, or even tar-coated leather vessels known as blackjacks. It wasn't until machine-made glassware became available in the second half of the nineteenth century that it became possible for everyone to enjoy the beer-enhancing qualities of glass drinking vessels.

Beer glasses range from a few ounces up to a full liter. Typically, the beer will be matched to the glass, with the strongest ones calling for the smallest glasses, for obvious reasons.

Contemporary beer-drinking glasses often have shapes very similar to earlier ones. The geometry of the glass affects the way beer looks, smells, and tastes, so it's not surprising that certain forms have withstood the test of time.

Clear glass is nearly always best, although subtly tinted colors can also be attractive (see Pasglass, page 171). Deeply colored beer glasses are rare. Designs such as faceting can add to the optical effects of the beer itself.

How the glass feels in the hand is also important. An outward taper or various types of ridges or bump-outs keep the glass from slipping out of the hand. For larger vessels, a handle is almost mandatory. Stems can accomplish an effect similar to that of a handle, as they allow one to hold the glass without transferring too much heat from the hand to the beer.

From an aroma standpoint, nothing helps a beer so much as having a narrower top than a middle. A wineglass is the classic example, although there are many beer glasses that share this feature. When served filled to the brim, this feature doesn't add anything, but as soon as the beer drops an inch or two below the rim, the inward taper holds the aroma inside the glass instead of letting it drift out into the room. The effects are obvious, even dramatic. Try a side-by-side comparison of a standard shaker pint (see page 173) and any red-wine glass. Fill both half full and try to give an honest appraisal of the aroma. I won't tell you what to find. But it can be striking.

An outward taper, as in a classic Pilsner glass, seems to have an effect on foam. The tapering shape serves as a wedge and gives the head on the top of the beer some additional support. An inward taper seems to force a head in on itself as the glass is filled. This has the effect of concentrating the foam, which results in a denser, creamier head.

HISTORICAL BEER-DRINKING VESSELS

◄ The Golden Tumbler of Lady Puabi

Northern Iraq, c. 2400 BCE

Found in a royal burial at the Mesopotamian city of Ur in northern Iraq and dating to 2400 BCE, this expensive vessel shows the status ancient people placed on their drinks.

▲ Golden Chicha Vessel

Siccan culture, northern Peru, c. 1000–1476

A corn-based beer called *chicha* was central to both ritual and daily life of people responsible for the sophisticated ancient cultures of northern Peru.

◄ Medieval Ceramic Drinking Jug

London, c. 1271–1350

Medieval drinking vessels used by ordinary folks were largely utilitarian.

◄ Bellarmine or Bartmannkrug jug

North Rhineland, c. 1575

Rotund jugs with faces, named for the equally ample prelate Cardinal Bellarmine, were used for wine and other beverages, as well as beer. They are usually also marked with a city seal.

Leather Blackjack or Bombard ►

London, sixteenth century

Pitch-lined leather tankards like this could withstand the rough-and-tumble conditions of earlier times. They were made from easily available materials and were unlikely to serve as a weapon in bar fights. Their use continued into the nineteenth century.

▲ Beaker Culture Beaker

Great Britain, c. fourth millennium BCE

Bell-shaped beakers are found all over Europe. The corded decorations suggest a connection of these people to the hemp plant.

Pasglass ▶

Northern Europe, seventeenth century

The tall, tapered form of this glass is the direct ancestor of the modern Pilsner glass. Like so many other glasses, this was meant for communal use and passed from drinker to drinker. The rings are part of a drinking game in which each drinker is expected to drink *exactly* to the line — no more, no less. The green cast is typical of the so-called forest glass and comes from iron and other impurities in the glass. Reproductions of these and other old styles are still made by artisans in the Czech Republic.

◀ Sterling Silver Pint Tankard

London, c. 1704–5, Philip Rollos (the elder)

◀ Chased Silver Tankard

London, c. 1670–75, Jacob Bodendick

Gentlemen (and ladies) drank their ale from luxurious mugs ranging from the simple to the ostentatious.

Beer Steins ▶

Germany and Austria, c. 1830–1900

Lidded beer steins are still made in a variety of sizes, materials, and personalities, and they keep the bugs out of your beer when you're drinking outdoors.

◀ Schnitt

United States, c. 1900

These stubby little tumblers were designed to hold a small amount of beer, which used to be delivered automatically as a chaser to whiskey. Versions with logos are highly sought after by breweriana collectors.

English Dwarf Ale Glasses ▶

c. 1760–1820

These delicate little glasses were designed to hold just a few ounces and were used to sip the strong "October" beers brewed on the country estates of the landed gentry. Although the size and proportion varied, they were decorated in many ways, with the engraved hops and barley design being one of the most common.

BEER FOAM has been prized since ancient times. Soap or oils inside the glass can degrade its delicate colloidal structure. Foam forms at nucleation sites, microscopic rough patches formed by dirt or scratches that can also serve as a pretty dramatic indicator of sloppy cleaning and can be cause for a good scolding of bar staff. Nucleation sites are sometimes added intentionally to cause a small stream of fine bubbles to be continually released, replenishing the head and releasing aroma at the same time — the Chimay goblet has a small Chimay logo etched with a laser into the bottom of the bowl for this purpose.

Foam has an especially dramatic effect on the way hop flavor manifests itself in beer. Because of their electrical and chemical nature, bitter hop compounds preferentially migrate to the head. The result is that the foam may taste much more bitter than the beer itself. Be aware of this if you are serving beer that is pushing your audience's hop comfort level.

How much foam is the proper amount? Most people feel that an inch is about right, although this is a culturally determined preference. The amount is also related to the level of carbonation in the beer. Many of the Belgian beers have loads of carbonation, and it's virtually impossible to pour a beer like Duvel without creating a big, fluffy head. For this reason, some of these proprietary beer glasses have a capacity about twice the size of the serving portion.

With the right beer, properly poured, you can create a rich, creamy head. To do so, pour the beer right down the middle of the straight-up glass (see page 117). Trickling down the side is for sissies and will result in a too-gassy beer with little aroma and a poor, quickly dissipating head. It's also important, especially with bottled beer, to release some of the carbonation. Too much fizz masks things such as hop aroma and fills you up quickly. There are places in Europe where drinkers are suspicious if the beer arrives too quickly because they understand what is needed to create a great head on a beer and are willing to delay gratification for a minute or two for the sake of a better experience.

With highly carbonated beers such as Belgian ales or Bavarian weizens, it may be beneficial to rinse the glass with cool, clean water before filling. This breaks the surface tension and allows these ultrafizzy beers to be poured without troublesome amounts of foam.

THE RIM is the final aspect of a glass. These may turn inward or flare outward (called "everted" by glassware experts). The shape of the rim changes the part of the mouth into which the beer is delivered, and a flared rim distributes the liquid more widely across the mouth, not just to the center of the tongue. This changes the way flavors are perceived in the mouth. The effects are complex, and I can't say there are simple rules about rim shapes that are universally true. I do personally find an everted rim (and a thinner edge) pleasant to drink from, as it matches the natural curve of the lip.

Much of the supposed benefits of the geometry of the myriad of highly specialized wineglasses derive from the pseudoscience of the tongue map, and it turns out this doesn't really work the way we were all taught in grade school (see chapter 2).

Practical qualities such as cost, stackability, and ease of cleaning play a huge role in deciding what glasses are used in eating and drinking establishments. Because of these considerations, we in the United States have gotten stuck with the worst possible beer glass: the shaker pint. Not only is the word *pint* a source of confusion — many hold only 14 ounces (414 mL), some only 12 (354 mL) — these were originally intended as half a cocktail shaker. They do absolutely nothing for the aroma or presentation of beer.

MODERN CLASSIC GLASSWARE

Shaker Pint Glass

- Standard in United States
- Not recommended for stronger or more exotic specialty brews
- This is called a shaker glass because of its original use in combination with a slightly larger metal cup as a cocktail shaker. It was never designed for drinking anything,

much less a beer. These were not used for beer until the 1980s, when they started being filled with craft beers. They were appreciated for their relatively large serving size, but they're not particularly attractive or flattering to the flavor and aroma of beer.

English Tulip Pint

Another twentieth-century glass. This one has found a home, especially for Irish stouts.

Nonick Pint

- Used for English ales since the early 1960s
- Good for low-gravity session beers
- Bump keeps rim from chipping and makes it easier to hold for stand-up drinking

Shaker Pint Glass

English Tulip Pint

Nonick Pint

Snifter

- Popularized in the twentieth century for brandy
- Good for barley wines and imperial stouts

Another not particularly ancient form, but with its deep, incurved rim and small stature, it is ideal for serving strong ales.

Stemmed Tulip or Poco Grande (Libbey)

- Inward taper holds aroma
- Outward flare supports the head and fits the lips

In many ways, this is the best of all worlds. Tulips like this are rare in history but start to show up in the late nineteenth century.

Tapered Pilsner Glass

- Narrow shape shows off pale color
- Outward-tapered shape supports head
- Footed design adds elegance and stability

The Pilsner glass we know today appeared in a similar form in the late Middle Ages, but it really didn't find wide acceptance until the 1930s, when its dramatically angular form reflected the Art Deco spirit of the age.

Weissbier Vase

- Large size holds foam
- Inward taper concentrates foam for a great head

The Weissbier vase seems to have evolved from the late medieval footed-beaker forms, but it probably didn't develop its modern curvaceous style until the twentieth century.

Snifter   Stemmed Tulip   Tapered Pilsner Glass   Weissbier Vase

A PROPER WEISSBIER POUR

Highly carbonated Bavarian weizens have their own special ritual of pouring and presentation. Use a tall, gracefully tapered vase glass with a fair amount of headroom above its half-liter (16.9 oz) capacity. The unique, traditional method of pouring will amaze and astound your friends.

First, rinse a very clean vase glass with clean water. Then uncap the bottle and invert the glass over it. With the glass in one hand and the bottle in the other, invert both, and hold at a steep diagonal angle. As the glass fills, keep the neck of the bottle just above the level of liquid in the glass. If you do it right, you'll get a full glass with foam right up to the rim. If you do it wrong, well, you may find yourself mopping beer off the table. The final step is to take the near-empty bottle and roll it back and forth on the table, then pick it up and dribble the yeast in a circular motion on top of the foam, where it will melt through and create a cascade of cloudiness through the beer.

A slice of lemon may be added, or not. Most of my beer-geek friends turn up their noses at it, but I think it makes a nice presentation. The story I heard was that Weissbier used to be a little more acidic than it is now, and the old-timers used to add lemon to bring the acid level up to the level they remembered and preferred. If you like lemon, I say go for it without shame.

Bolleke Goblet
- Inward taper concentrates head and aroma
- Smaller size is great for strong beers
- Famous in Antwerp, Belgium, and associated with De Koninck

Bolleke translates from the Dutch as "little ball," the meaning of which I will leave to you to derive.

Pokal
- Classic for bock
- Small size for stronger beer
- Outward taper supports head
- Short stem

The original pokals were often large and decorated in quite showy ways and fitted with removable (not hinged) lids. By the nineteenth century, they were most often associated with bock beers.

Updated Pokal
- Inward taper concentrates head
- Good general-purpose glass for high-class beers such as Belgian-style tripel, maibock, and imperial IPA.
- Stem keeps hand from warming beer

Bolleke Goblet   Pokal

English Dimpled Pint

- Appeared c. 1948
- Used for mild ale and bitter

This is a shortened, wider, handled version of the lens-cut "pillar" pale ale glasses that became popular around 1840 in England. They're quaint and comfortable, even if they're not antiques. The lens design makes a beautiful play of light on an amber-colored beer.

Bavarian Seidel

- Big glass for small beer, such as Pilsner, helles, and Oktoberfest

This seidel is just a glass version of the simple stoneware krugs that were used for centuries as drinking mugs. The optic circles first appeared in the mid-nineteenth century when machines for cutting and polishing glass became available; later, they were molded in.

PROPRIETARY GLASSWARE

The Belgians are mad for custom-made glasses emblazoned with the brewery's logo. There are bars in Belgium where, if all the logo glasses of the beer you want are being used, you need to have a different drink while you wait for an appropriate glass to be returned. I like the showiness of this presentation and what it says about how we should respect the beers. But I can't tell you that they all have been scientifically designed to perfectly show off the sensory properties of specific beers, and some are better than others. Many American craft breweries have been creating their own glasses as well.

English Dimpled Pint   Bavarian Seidel   Proprietary glass

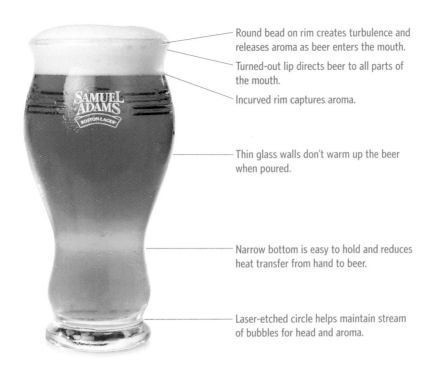

Round bead on rim creates turbulence and releases aroma as beer enters the mouth.

Turned-out lip directs beer to all parts of the mouth.

Incurved rim captures aroma.

Thin glass walls don't warm up the beer when poured.

Narrow bottom is easy to hold and reduces heat transfer from hand to beer.

Laser-etched circle helps maintain stream of bubbles for head and aroma.

Boston Beer Company's Jim Koch spent 2 years on a mission to make a glass designed to enhance the taste experience for his Samuel Adams Boston Lager. A functionally similar glass has recently been created by Spiegelau in collaboration with Dogfish Head and Sierra Nevada breweries.

Storing and Aging Beer

Beer is a very delicate product. As such, it is never a fixed thing but is constantly evolving. Every day during fermentation and conditioning it's a little different, and at a certain point it's deemed ready for shipment. But the beer keeps changing when it leaves the brewery, and for most beers these changes are not positive. Flavors fade, the death grip of oxidation takes over, and the subtle protein structure that gives beer much of its body and head-forming qualities simply falls apart. The more delicate the beer, the quicker these changes will degrade the drinking experience. In severely overaged beers, the collapsed proteins actually appear as little flakes that make it look like egg drop soup. A beer should not resemble a snow globe.

Heat is the enemy. All chemistry speeds up as the temperature rises. With beer, repeated cycles of ups and downs in temperature also have a negative effect, especially for the proteins, which is the reason that once cold, beer should be kept cold if possible. One or two trips in and out of the fridge won't kill a beer, but steady temperatures are always preferred over wild swings, even if that means a slightly higher average temperature.

Cellar-Aged Beer
Some strong beers can age in fascinating ways if carefully cellared.

The first thing to go is that nice fresh flavor, especially the hop aroma. Malt flavor dulls a bit and takes on a kind of sweet honey or waxy aroma. In ales, fruitiness gradually fades as esters are changed to other compounds. Bitterness declines, losing maybe half its punch in 5 or 6 months. This kind of time frame is beyond the "best by" date of most normal beers, though it is relevant to stronger beers and those that are designed to accommodate a little aging. Hoppy beers are especially vulnerable to the ravages of time, often displaying a blackcurrant aroma called beta damascenone.

That said, beers with less than 6 or 7 percent alcohol are never meant to age. Most beer is best when it leaves the brewery. Brewers do their best to control the conditions under which their products are handled, but in reality it's mostly out of their hands.

Most beers have some kind of date coding on the package. These may or may not be meant to be read by the drinking public, but by distributors and retailers to determine when the beer is past its designated shelf life. A typical code shows the date of bottling in the day, month, and year, plus perhaps some other information like a specific brewery or bottling line. There is no standard format, but fortunately, there is a wealth of information on the Internet, and there are also phone apps available to decipher brewery codes.

Freshness is a particular problem for imported beers, especially pale lagers. These beers command a premium here, but they just don't taste the same as in their homeland, even when the recipe is the same. In addition, some large brands customize a beer's recipe for the American market, usually with less body and less hop bitterness.

Importers swear to me that a high-volume beer such as Heineken can reach store shelves in a few weeks, but judging by their taste, this is just a dream for many brands, especially the lower-volume ones. The beer has a long journey: from brewery to docks to a ship across the ocean to the docks here, then through customs and off to the distributor's warehouse, and finally to the shelves in the store, with conditions in every leg of this voyage less than ideal.

Stronger beers can handle some age. It was the custom in eighteenth-century England to brew an extra-strong "double" beer to celebrate the birth of a son and then to drink it when he reached the age of 21. During the early- to mid-nineteenth century, porters and strong ales were commonly aged for a year or even two before being deemed fit to drink. And even

AGING TIME FOR VARIOUS BEER TYPES

BEER TYPE	PERCENTAGE ALCOHOL	MAXIMUM AGING TIME	
Belgian abbey dubbel	6.5–7.5	1–3 years	
Belgian abbey tripel/strong golden	7.5–9.5	1–4 years	
English or American strong/old ale	7–9	1–5 years	
Belgian strong dark ales	8.5–11	2–12 years	
Imperial pale/brown/red, etc.	7.5–10	1–7 years	
Barley wine and imperial stout	8.5–12	3–20 years	
Ultrastrong ales	16–26	5–100 years	

today, certain strong and wood-aged beers get this type of treatment.

DIY AGING

You can age your own beer if you have reasonable cellar conditions. The ideal is a cool basement without too much moisture. These are common enough in the East and Midwest; folks in the South and West either rent wine storage lockers or rig a setback thermometer on a refrigerator or chest freezer to create a cool environment. I have an unimproved basement room in Chicago, and I can report that it ages both beer and wine admirably. So there's no need to rig up fancy temperature-and-humidity-controlled vaults if you have a space with proper conditions at home.

Ideally, the temperature should remain in the 55 to 65°F range (13 to 18°C), although somewhat higher temperatures in the summer seem not to cause any real trouble. Again, daily temperature swings should be avoided if at all possible.

So which beers are best for aging? Ales primarily, with bottle-conditioned ones preferred, as the yeast provides a bit of a protective effect. These "live" beers undergo more complex changes and age more gracefully than filtered or pasteurized ones. There is rarely a need to age lagers, as these are normally brought to their peak of flavor at the brewery.

You should be looking at beers upwards of 7 percent alcohol; bigger beers will age even longer. Belgian dubbels will lose a little of their sweetness, dry out, and become a little more complex and elegant in a year or two. In beers with *Brettanomyces* yeast, such as Orval or Goose Island Matilda (which Orval inspired), the wild yeast continues to evolve fascinating barnyard overtones over the course of a year or two.

Sour Belgian-style beers are somewhat the exception to the strength rule. Many of these beers will age for quite some time, yet they rarely exceed 6 percent alcohol. Many, such as lambics, are aged for several years at the brewery, but the boisterous little party of microflora in the bottle will keep the beer evolving for quite some time. You have to like bold, sour beers to undertake this, as they get even more acidic as they age.

Some beers *need* some aging. The classic Bigfoot barley wine from Sierra Nevada Brewing is, in my highly personal opinion, a little overwhelming when it is young. Sierra Nevada owner Ken Grossman likes it "on the fresher side, up to a year old." But he also says, "I have tasted some Bigfoot up to 10 years old and have found it quite enjoyable, although a totally different beer." I buy a six-pack every year and usually don't crack one of the bottles until 5 years later.

As beer ages it dries out, becoming less sweet and more vinous. Somewhat counterintuitively, aged beer may become more sweetly malty on the nose as the fragile hoppy and fruity aromas dissipate. As aging progresses, rich leathery, nutty, or sherrylike oxidation adds another layer of flavor.

Yeast contributes rich, meaty flavors through a process called "autolysis," the same process that gives champagne its toasty aromas (autolysed yeast rarely manifests this toastiness in beer). The meatiness comes from the breakdown products of the yeast, such as glutamic acid, often manifesting as umami. In very old beers, sometimes soy sauce flavor notes are present, and if they get too strong they cease to be charming.

Cork-finished beers destined for more than a year of aging should be laid on their sides just like wine to keep the corks from drying out and leaking carbonation.

AGED BEER AND VERTICAL TASTINGS

Aged beers provide a great opportunity for a fun and educational vertical tasting, although this may require some serious advance planning. The idea is simply to compare the same beer from different years to try to understand how the beer has changed as it has aged. Sometimes there's a lot more variation than you'd expect.

If you have a large circle of beer aficionado friends, it may not be all that difficult to gather a representative sampling of some of the more widely available big beers such as Bigfoot, Rogue's Old Crustacean, and J. W. Lees Harvest Ale, as it seems that many beer maniacs have these little nuggets squirreled away. A number of bars have started vertical collections of stronger beers. These older beers can be fairly expensive, but with a group it can be easily worth the money to get the benefit of perspective over time.

Like any art, beer needs a proper context to be truly compelling. The effects of a thoughtful presentation are not smoke and mirrors; the details really do affect the quality of our beer experience, sometimes in very dramatic ways. The brewers who make great beer for us put their hearts and souls into it. Let's honor that artistry by doing all we can to bring it to the table in a way that allows it to really shine.

CHAPTER 7

BEER AND FOOD

Because it is nearly a food itself, beer's range of flavors, aromas, colors, and textures complement many kinds of fare, giving us plenty to choose from when seeking resonance. From a cheery, golden Pilsner to a brooding imperial stout, from a comforting malty Scotch ale to a bracingly hoppy India Pale Ale, beer is hands down the most varied beverage on earth. So whether it's a rustic handmade sausage or the loftiest tall-food masterpiece, there's a beer that's made for it.

EATING IS A MOST INTIMATE ACT. We experience food and drink not in the cold, hard light of reason but in a charged, emotional, and often mysterious world. The experience is more akin to the world of dreams than of reality, suffused with both delight and dread, and with uncontrollable memories and feelings that seem to come from nowhere.

Getting people to accept good beer is less of a challenge than it used to be, but we still encounter those who are deeply set in their habits and choices. The challenge is to shake them up and convince them to try new things. Nothing has that power like putting beer and food together in a single delicious mouthful. My most triumphant moments are when I hear someone say: "You know, I don't care much for blue cheese, and actually I hate IPAs, but that was really good together." A good pairing allows people to suspend their normal rules and open up to new experiences, changing them — at least in small ways — forever.

The power to change peoples' minds and behavior is where the money is. The wine industry has done a great job of this and made their beverage the center of the food and drink world, but beer is every bit wine's equal in capability and complexity. Many of us have been hammering away on this for a couple of decades or more, but there is still plenty of work to be done. Beer brings a lot to the table, but it takes actual beer and food in the mouth to make the point convincingly. So let this chapter be your guide to this compelling world.

What Are We Trying to Do Here?

To amaze people and change minds, we need to make sure people see beer as a beverage that is comfortable at the highest level of gastronomy. It's a big task, not because beer isn't up to it, but because we are challenging 2,500 years of blah-blah-blah about how wine is superior to beer.

Sommeliers, if you can get a beer or two into them, will grudgingly admit that wine has a long list of blind spots with food — many more than the well-known asparagus conundrum —that beer happily fills. Various experts have thrown up their hands trying to pair wine with soup, salads, vegetables, mushrooms, cheese, dessert, and every spicy cuisine ever created. Bring 'em on. Beer can cover all those foods with grace and delight.

Making this monumental change requires us to step up our game and deliver great experiences. To do this we need to be clearheaded about our goals, insightful about the fundamentals, attentive to the details, and flawless in

A cauldron of fat Beef and stoop of ale
On the huzzing mob shall more prevail,
Than if you give them with the nicest art,
Ragouts of Peacock's brains, or Filbert tart.

— William King

our execution. We all have a responsibility to help beer speak in the elegant voice we know it's capable of in the best circumstances.

So let's think about this great pair. Each partner should support and highlight qualities in the other and sometimes even transform them in some interesting, delicious way. There should be pleasing flavor combinations. The tastes on the tongue should play nicely with each other, and one half of the pair shouldn't be a bully and dominate the other. Sometimes a new flavor is created, and sometimes an old memory may be summoned. While in the United States we generally use the term "pairing," the Brazilians use the word *harmonizacāo*, or harmonization, which I think comes a lot closer to what the experience should be like — more fling than cozy partnership.

Beer and Food: The Perfect Match

You really can't ask for a better partner for food than beer. Its breadth of flavors, aromas, textures, strengths, and colors offers some compelling harmonies and appropriate contrasts to just about any imaginable dish. From sweet to bitter to sour, and tempting us with at least a thousand different aromas covering the better part of food vocabulary, beer offers far more to work with than wine. It's a rare dish that can't find its beery mate.

Since it's made from grain that has been kilned, beer smells like cooked food. Its bready, toasty, caramel, and roasty flavors resonate with many kinds of food. Hops add herbal, citrus, fruity, or resiny aromas. Yeast adds soft or strident fruitiness and spiciness ranging from the enveloping warmth of cinnamon and cloves to the crisp austerity of black pepper.

And then there are beers that actually do have spices in them, from hearty wassails to delicate witbiers, plus many other possibilities: fruit, nuts, coffee, chocolate, and the vanilla-soaked wonderfulness of a used bourbon barrel. Are you getting hungry yet?

BEER AND FOOD TRANSFORM EACH OTHER. Contrasting elements balance and sometimes blend into one another, like matter and antimatter, into a powerful, singular experience. These effects are often quite stunning and are at the core of a well-chosen match. To find combinations that really work and create memorable experiences, you need to pay attention to the effect each partner has on the other. Bitterness in beer can overwhelm delicate flavors, but it can also be just what is needed to balance rich or creamy foods, even the sweetest desserts. Carbonation, roastiness, sweetness, smoke, and alcohol also come into play as contrast elements. In food, sweetness, fat, the savory flavor of umami, and chile heat are all potential pairing elements.

Beer's lively carbonation tackles problems that make wine shrink in horror. Carbon dioxide bubbles literally scrub out your palate, which is sometimes helpful with intense or rich foods — cheese, for example. Fortunately, there is a range of available carbonation as well, from the slight tingle of British cask (real) ales to zippy Weissbiers and Belgian tripels.

Another tool we have to work with is our own familiarity with certain flavor combinations that normally have nothing to do with beer. A grilled cheese sandwich is an iconic combination of gooey cheese and the toastiness of grilled bread. When you pair a soft, creamy cheese such as a Camembert or Muenster with a toasty brown ale, you are conjuring this familiar sensation in an entirely new context. These familiarity-based pairs can be striking and memorable, as well as a lot of fun.

Be Mindful of Language

Choosing the right words is important. The theoretical underpinnings of food and drink combinations are a little messy, and that applies as much to wine as it does to beer. Science has only taken a serious interest in the chemical senses in the last few decades. For questionable reasons, taste and smell were long considered "base" senses of little complexity, unworthy of serious study. Over the last few decades the science has exploded, proving this attitude deeply wrong on all counts. But when it comes to what actually happens when food and drink get together in your mouth, there is very little research from which to draw fundamental rules. To push forward, we need to be as informed and logical as possible, learn from science when possible, and try to make sure that theory and practice support each other.

The messy state of food and drink pairing theory is reflected in the terminology in use. Lots of different words are tossed about, often with only vague meanings. This may not only reflect disagreement or disarray, but a lack of understanding of what specific interactions are occurring. What's happening with every bite and sip? Is it chemistry? Something at the chemical-sensory boundary, or higher processing of sensory signals? Integration with memory and emotion? Cognitive processing like language? We probably could answer yes to all those questions, and this only points out the enormous amount of work ahead of us if

Pair Like a Local
Pairing local beer and the region's cuisine is often a great place to start looking for successful match-ups.

TERMS USED FOR BEER AND FOOD INTERACTIONS

Resonant

Alternate Term: *Link, echo, connect, similarity, complementary*

The term "resonant" indicates an interaction based on aromatic similarity, either from shared aroma molecules or aromas in the same general family (e.g., citrus, spice, and caramel).

Affinity

Alternate Term: *Tangential, familiar, attraction*

Affinity is neither a diminishing nor enhancing relationship; not a general harmony based on aromatic similarity but deriving from familiar flavor combinations from our experiences with cuisine over a lifetime. Because of this, it has a strong personal as well as cultural bias built into it.

Synthesis

Alternate Term: *Synergy, blend, integrate, fuse, join*

Sometimes the affinity between flavors is so strong as to create a third flavor from its components, recalling something different. An example is in combining fruit and vanilla (maybe from a barrel-aged beer) to create a sensation of a fruity ice cream.

Overwhelm

Alternate Term: *Intensity mismatch, overpower*

This is a problem condition, when one partner is so strongly flavored that it largely obscures the other. This is different from balancing or masking, in that it happens with the totality of the pairing, and usually is viewed as something to avoid.

Balancing

Alternate Terms: *Complementary, opposing, equalize*

Many tastes interact in a way that seems to annihilate one another, and in a really dramatic match, it's almost like matter and antimatter coming together. Sometimes two strong tastes, such as bitterness and sweetness, can seem to nearly vanish when combined.

Masking

Alternate Terms: *Attenuation (diminishing), concealing, camouflaging*

It's not clear whether masking is exactly the same as balancing, but it seems to be a little different and perhaps not as dramatic in its effect. Vanilla, for example, is famously a masker, so this is clearly operative in the aromatic realm.

Cleansing

Alternate Terms: *Cut, clear, rinsing, scrubbing, flushing*

Cleansing is mainly due to the action of bubbles formed by carbonation, which quite literally scrub food from the palate. It's especially helpful with rich and fatty foods. This may also be a result of physical rinsing as in the case of carbonation, or the enhanced solubility of certain compounds in alcohol.

(continued on next page)

Like-Like Canceling
Alternate Term: *Sweet matches sweet*

Like-like canceling is well known in the world of wine, when sweet wines and foods are combined. It's a bit counterintuitive, but piling sweet on sweet is not necessarily additive, especially as we reach the tongue's upper limit and it starts to give diminishing returns on all that sweetness. Acidity may behave this way up to a point, although such pairs are much less common in beer than in wine.

Aggravating
Alternate Terms: *Inflaming, irritating, grating*

"Aggravating" describes a sort of negative enhancement, in which one element in a pair amplifies or alters the character of another in an unpleasant way. This is most notable with chile heat, which can be heightened by either alcohol or hop bitterness but can also happen with tannic or astringent mouthfeel.

Enhancing
Alternate Terms: *Amplification, augmentation, enriching, increasing, boosting, heightening, potentiation*

Enhancing happens when one partner increases the perceived intensity of one or more components of the other. It's a common occurrence; for example, when adding a little citrus or herbal element brings out a previously unnoticed similar character in the mix. Salt and pepper are commonly used to do this within a food dish, and they can have a similar enhancing effect on the flavors in beer. This can happen both with tastes and aromas and also with flavors.

Soothing
Alternate Terms: *Calming, softening, alleviating, lessening*

Soothing reduces heat or irritation and is usually used in the context of chile heat, which seems to be reduced or soothed by sweet, malty beer.

we really want to understand and master beer and food.

So we start where we can get a toehold: with the actual terms we use. If we can be analytical with them, perhaps they may point the way to areas where more research can be done. If we strip them down to their essentials, maybe we can be more clearheaded in our choices.

Just as with drinking beer, it is important here to separate different sensory processes: aroma, taste, mouthfeel, and that combined sensory experience we call flavor. Separating these sensations points out that many interactions occur mainly in one realm or another. Most of the resonant connections we find between beers and foods that share flavor characteristics have an aromatic basis. Much of the important work of managing contrasting elements is done with taste and mouthfeel. While taste and aroma do interact strongly in our brains, trying to think of them separately does seem to bring some clarity to the process.

Simple Beer and Food Pairing Guidelines

I am sorry to tell you that there is no equivalent to the "red wine with meat, white wine with fish" rule as far as beer goes. It's more complicated than that, but fortunately pairing beer and food is really all about common sense and taking a few things into consideration. There is nothing difficult or mysterious about the process. Follow a few basic rules, pay attention, and it is hard to go too wrong. Don't be too consumed with finding perfection — there is no such thing. But every now and then you will have a truly transcendent moment, which is what we are all looking for.

If you're not doing so already, start paying attention to the beers and foods you enjoy now: the crisp bitterness of a pale ale cutting the boldness of a grilled hamburger; the smoky silkiness of a stout balancing the creamy tang of smoked salmon; the bittersweet edge of a barley wine cutting through the sweetness of crème brûlée. Memorable pairs are there for the taking. All it takes is a little focus. To paraphrase an Eastern mystic, "Beer here now."

For those new to this pursuit, it can be a bit overwhelming. The guidelines presented here should give you a framework for thinking about beer and food and get you down to the very important business of finding great beer and food matches. As you practice, you will gain an intuitive grasp of the ideas here and develop your own repertoire of no-fail pairings to amaze and astound your friends. Of course, it helps to keep notes on your beer and food odyssey.

Many pairing approaches describe the results as a zero-sum game: the pair is either a contrast or a harmony. In my experience, it's a rare pair that really is one or the other. Almost always, pairings operate on multiple layers, with different sets of aromas and tastes operating simultaneously, although the first impression may highlight specific contrasting or harmonious flavor pairs. Sometimes the strongest connecting points will be secondary flavors, such as a touch of herbs or citrus rather than the bigger and more obvious flavors.

Taste and aroma are different things, and even though they often work together, they can also be seen working completely independent of each other, so the harmonies often occur most strongly in the aromatic realm, with the contrasts happening with the taste elements. I feel that thinking about everything that's going on when that beer and food hit your mouth, rather than simply focusing on a single thing, makes a more engaging and profound pair.

The following three-step process covers what I feel to be the most important considerations when choosing beer and food partners. I have tried to separate different phenomena and keep the language as simple as possible. Although there may be other valid ways of setting up a pairing, having used this approach for over a decade now, I can say with conviction that if you consider these three things you won't go far wrong.

STEP 1: MATCH INTENSITY

While one partner often will be a little more assertive than the other, delicate dishes work best with delicate beers, and strongly flavored foods demand assertive beers. A pair can tolerate a fair difference in intensity, but at a certain point one will overwhelm the other, an effect I call "Bambi vs. Godzilla." We're shooting for

Foods in Order of Increasing Intensity

Sushi, poached fish, fresh mozzarella cheese, white bread

Sautéed whitefish, chèvre, grilled vegetables, pretzels, butter käse, Brie cheese

Roasted chicken, spinach salad, pizza, fried fish, young Gouda cheese

Grilled pork chops, salmon, or portobello mushrooms; roast turkey; crab cakes, Gruyère cheese

Hamburger, barbecued chicken, ham, kielbasa, clothbound cheddar cheese, pâté

Fajitas, *guylás*, gumbo, soppressata, apple strudel, chocolate chip cookies, Pecorino Romano cheese

Smoke-roasted prime rib, cheesecake, pecan pie, aged Gouda cheese

Grilled lamb, *cevapcici* (uncased pork and beef sausage), blue cheese, carrot cake

Barbecued ribs, Texas mesquite-smoked brisket, Stilton cheese, chocolate mousse

Chocolate lava cakes, chocolate truffles, Parmigiano Reggiano cheese

pairings where each partner transforms the other, and that's pretty difficult if one totally obliterates the other.

What defines intensity of flavor? It is not any single thing, but the entirety of the flavor experience. In beer, it may be a combination of alcoholic strength, malt character, hop bitterness, sweetness, body, hop or malt aroma, acidic funk, roastiness, and much more. In food, richness (or fat), sweetness, cooking methods (such as roasting, grilling, or frying), and seasoning all play a role. We'll go into the particular dynamic of taste elements on the tongue below, but this step is simply about the overall impact.

STEP 2: FIND HARMONIES

These are flavors that are either similar or feel comfortable together for other reasons. They are most often found in the aromatic realm. It makes sense, because there are thousands of unique aromatic molecules in beer and food, so there are ample opportunities to find things that can relate to one another. In contrast, the tongue has just a handful of different taste sensations, and although they are really important in making a great pairing, they have a specific dynamic we'll discuss below. Aroma, not taste, is the place to look for connecting points.

Beer and food combinations work well when they share some common flavor or aroma elements. Because similar biochemical processes operate in a wide range of different contexts, you'll often find the same aroma molecules popping up all over the place: yeast and fruit can both produce fruity esters; hops, flowers, and citrus fruits share a range of tangy, aromatic terpenes; kilned malt, baked bread, caramelized onions, and grilled meat share toasty, roasty heterocyclic aroma molecules from the Maillard browning they all undergo.

Citrusy hop aromas

Citrus fruit, pepper, vinegar

BEER AND FOOD: COMMON FLAVORS

Here are some of the foods that share specific beer flavor and aroma profiles.

Herby hop aromas

Blue cheese, herb rub, salad dressing

Fruity yeast character

Wine- or fruit-based dressings, chutney, fruity desserts

Peppery yeast character

Black pepper, juniper, ginger

Spicy yeast character

Pepper, cinnamon, star anise, spicy dishes, chiles, barbecue

Honeyish malt or yeast character

Light caramel, fruit, honey, floral

Barrel-aged, vanilla, coconut aromas

Desserts with vanilla, nuts, coconut

Nutty malt flavors

Nuts, nutty Alpine cheese, aged sausage

Caramelly malt flavors

Sautéed or caramelized flavors of meat, onions, vegetables; barbecue sauce; aged cheese; caramel in desserts

Roasted malt flavors

Roasted or smoked meats; chocolate; coffee

Toasted malt flavors

Grilled or roasted meats, toasted nuts, bread, pastry

BEER AND FOOD: FLAVOR AFFINITIES

This chart points out harmonious relationships between some elements in beer and in food that are not necessarily similar in aroma.

MEATY
- woody/tannic
- smoky
- chile heat
- herbal
- caramel
- roasty/chocolaty
- spice
- salty

SMOKY
- meaty
- salty
- herbal
- chile heat

CHILE HEAT
- smoky
- meaty
- herbal
- spice

HERBAL
- woody/tannic
- smoky
- chile heat
- meaty
- floral
- toasty

WOODY/TANNIC
- salty
- meaty
- herbal

SALTY
- woody/tannic
- smoky
- caramel
- meaty
- buttery/creamy
- roasty/chocolaty

ROASTY/CHOCOLATEY
- caramel
- vanilla
- fruity
- spice
- meaty
- buttery/creamy
- salty

SPICE
- meaty
- citrus
- chile heat
- toasty
- caramel
- roasty/chocolaty
- cookie
- buttery/creamy

BUTTERY/CREAMY
- vanilla
- toasty
- citrus
- cookie
- fruity
- pastry/cracker
- roasty/chocolaty
- spice
- salty

CITRUS
- fruity
- spice
- buttery/creamy
- floral

TOASTY
- herbal
- spice
- fruity
- buttery/creamy
- pastry/cracker

FLORAL
- fruity
- spice
- citrus
- herbal

FRUITY
- citrus
- vanilla
- toasty
- floral
- pastry/cracker
- roasty/chocolaty
- buttery/creamy
- cookie

VANILLA
- fruity
- caramel
- roasty/chocolaty
- buttery/creamy
- cookie

COOKIE
- fruity
- caramel
- vanilla
- buttery/creamy
- spice

PASTRY/CRACKER
- toasty
- fruity
- buttery/creamy
- caramel

CARAMEL
- meaty
- salty
- vanilla
- cookie
- roasty/chocolaty
- pastry/cracker
- spice

Lucky us, as this gives us a huge range of possible connection points to explore. The deep, roasted flavors of imperial stout combined with chocolate truffles, or the caramelly flavors of an Oktoberfest lager paired with roasted pork are just a couple of examples, but there are countless others.

There are also flavor combinations that feel harmonious to us because of our personal and cultural histories. Bready, toasty flavors taste great with buttery ones to those of us who have grown up in Europe or the Americas, but this association may be totally alien to Asians, who have a limited exposure to dairy. Vanilla has a strong association with all things sweet in the West, but not so much in Asia.

I use the term "affinity" to describe this relationship. Because they are culturally and personally based, these affinities vary hugely by audience, and one has to be sensitive to this when putting together a pairing for a culturally diverse crowd. I've made an attempt to graph out some of the relationships I've grown up with, a result of my midwestern U.S. roots. The more different you are in terms of your cultural experiences, the more different this type of chart will look.

STEP 3: CONSIDER THE CONTRAST ELEMENTS

Sweetness, bitterness, carbonation, heat (spice), and richness — certain qualities of food and beer interact with each other in specific, predictable ways. Taking advantage of these interactions ensures that the food and beer will balance each other, with neither one hogging the limelight. These are specific interactions, taste by taste, and that's different from the overall matching of intensity mentioned above.

Food and Beer Interactions

The chart below lays out a specific range of interactions that happen between different tastes and mouthfeel sensations in beer and food. It shows what kind of interaction is most likely to occur. Most terms are explained on the next page, but a few need additional comments. "Neutral" means there is little or no interaction; "caution" means that although sometimes this combination can work in pleasant ways, there can also be problems, so proceed with caution.

		FOOD TASTE AND MOUTHFEEL					
		SWEETNESS	SPICINESS (CHILI HEAT)	FAT	UMAMI	ACIDITY	SALT
BEER TASTE AND MOUTHFEEL	HOP BITTERNESS	Balances	Balances	Caution	Masks	Masks	Aggravates
	ROASTED MALT BITTERNESS	Balances	Balances	Affinity	Affinity	Affinity	Neutral
	SWEETNESS	Like Cancels Like	Balances	Affinity	Balances	Caution	Balances
	CARBONATION	Cleanses	Cleanses	Cleanses	Cleanses	Cleanses	Cleanses
	ALCOHOL	Balances	Cleanses	Balances	Aggravates	Caution	Aggravates
	ACIDITY	Caution	Balances	Neutral	Like Cancels Like	Masks	Aggravates

Sweet, fatty, or umami-rich foods can be countered by various elements in beer: bitterness, sweetness, roasted/toasted malt, or alcohol, but each may operate a little differently. Carbonation is also effective at cutting richness, but it's a simple scrubbing action, perhaps aided by a sensation of brightness or acidity that comes along with it. Umami is the rich, savory basic taste found in fatty fish, aged cheese, meat, and ripe or cooked tomatoes and can be balanced by the same things in beer as are used to balance sweetness. But because umami is less intense in character than sweetness, it can get by with a lower level of matching intensity.

Spicy (chile) heat is another specific interaction. Hoppy beer will make hot food hotter. If you're the kind of hothead who would just as soon have capsicum injected directly into your veins, this won't bother you, so have at it. For the rest of us, a more balanced approach with some maltiness is always welcome. If you're leaning toward a hoppy beer with spicy food, make sure it has plenty of malt as well.

ADDITIONAL CONSIDERATIONS

The principles outlined above are the primary considerations. Here are a few additional thoughts about enjoying beer and food together.

Look to classic cuisines. The cuisines of beer-drinking countries offer many great beer and food combinations. Beer and cheese from the same region or even the same monastery may be an obvious choice, as is bratwurst with pale lager, but who would have thought to put stout together with oysters? Classic matches are tried and true and are a great starting point for further exploration. The Belgians have a near-obsession with beer and food and a highly evolved *cuisine à la bière*. Learning about

how they do things will give you lots of ideas for pairings.

Make use of familiar patterns. The flavor combinations in certain dishes are so familiar to most people that they constitute a common ground on which to build. If you can re-create or even evoke these recognizable flavor pairs in the new and different context of beer, you're halfway to acceptance (photo, opposite).

Practice makes perfect. Not every pairing works as expected, and this can be fun if you can appreciate the unexpected. If it's not so great, make a note of it and move on. Build on the things that work, and keep seeking out those magic combinations.

Up and down the ladder. A "ladder" in this context is a group of pairings based on some particular principle that may be the same throughout a range of intensities. Blue cheese and hoppy beer is a great example, and the pairing can work with a mild blue Brie with a hoppy Pilsner, a medium-intensity blue such as a Gorgonzola with a Belgian IPA, or all the way up to the top with Stilton and barley wine (see graphic on page 194). The fat-cutting power of bitterness and the harmonious herby linkup of hops and the blue mold apply at each level — only the intensity changes. So once you discover a pairing that works for you, leverage this by looking at similar flavors of greater or lesser intensity, and you may find you've got a lot of new pairings to work with.

Consider seasonality. Go lighter in the summer and heavier in the winter; the beers and foods of a given season pair very naturally and suit the mood.

Think beyond "matchy-matchy." Yes, chocolate and imperial stout taste great together, as do many other combinations of beer and food that share common flavors.

Affinity-Based Pairings

Cherry strudel + porter = chocolate-covered cherries

Soft Camembert cheese + a toasty brown ale = liquid grilled cheese sandwich

Burrata cheese + a fruity hefeweizen = peaches and cream
(Burrata is fresh mozzarella stuffed with cream and curds.)

Meaty, aged Gouda + imperial stout = roasted or grilled meat

HIGH INTENSITY

Barley Wine
Stilton

American IPA
Point Reyes Blue

Belgian IPA or
American Pale Ale
Gorgonzola Dolce

Bohemian Pilsner
Blue Brie

LOW INTENSITY

**A Pairing Ladder for Blue Cheese and
Hoppy Pale Beers**
The ladder to the left shows how the same
combination of flavors can work at various
intensity levels. Using ladders helps expand
your repertoire by allowing a single idea to work
with a number of different foods and beer styles.

And while there's nothing wrong with this approach, more experienced practitioners usually try for something more imaginative, often looking to affinities rather than similarities for that magic spark.

Tweak. Sometimes a lackluster pair just needs a small change to make it really wonderful. Encourage whoever's composing dishes to get creative, and make sure you help them understand the flavors in the beer so they can find food flavors to harmonize with them. Sometimes a simple green garnish, a dab of sauce, or a spritz of citrus can add one more link that makes the whole pairing sparkle.

When in doubt, go Belgian. If you are going to a dinner and you need a beer that would go with just about anything, I suggest a Belgian-style abbey dubbel or tripel. These have enough substance to stand up to just about anything, but do not have any overly aggressive malt or hop flavors that will overwhelm most foods. Besides, the big bottles make a nice presentation.

Remember, the above suggestions are just that — not absolute rules. Beer gastronomy was founded on creativity and experimentation. We hope you follow that spirit on your beer and food journey.

Beer through the Meal

Each part of the meal has a unique dynamic that offers both restraints and opportunities. Salads are ultimately flexible, appetizers need to keep it light, main dishes can be just about anything, and desserts require big beers to tame the sugar and other such flavors.

BEER WITH SALADS AND APPETIZERS

Crisp, refreshing beers are the best way to start a meal. Lighter wheat beer can be a perfect (if perhaps boring) match for simple greens, but the beauty of salads is that they're totally modular. By choosing more intensely flavored toppings, a salad can actually handle a fair amount of intensity in a beer, including some serious bitterness.

Salads can link with a beer's bitterness through the use of bitter greens such as arugula or radicchio. This bitterness can also be balanced by sweet elements in the dressing or a garnish such as sugar-glazed nuts or crumbled blue cheese, either of which will stand up to a fairly hoppy beer. The same goes for tomatoes, as ripe ones have a lot of umami, which can handle some bitterness. Aged cheese is another source of umami likely to be found sprinkled on top of salads. In addition to finding ways to celebrate and work with bitterness, all these add-ons can provide opportunities to link up with the beer in the aromatic realm.

Salad Ingredients and Beers by Intensity

Salad Ingredients	Beers
Aged cheese	IPA
Candied nuts	
Black olives	American pale ale
Radicchio	
Ripe cherry tomatoes	Saison
Avocado	
Dried cherries	English bitter
Marinated artichokes	
Fresh cheese	Bohemian Pilsner
Arugula	
Belgian endive	Witbier
Croutons	
Leaf lettuce	Helles

There is no simple rule with appetizers because they are such a disparate group. A simple shrimp cocktail is a very different beast from a cheese-stuffed fried jalapeño pepper, so the same rules about matching intensity, finding affinities, and dealing with contrasts apply. Look at the whole dish — protein, starch, preparation method, and sauce/garnish — and make a guesstimate of its overall intensity. This narrows down the range of possible beers, so you can then start looking for those harmonies. There are usually plenty of choices.

A character-filled blonde ale might be great with seared ahi tuna. A hoppy American pale ale can balance succulent appetizers such as cheese tartlets and bruschetta. Spicy saison is the perfect counterpoint to tangy New Orleans–style shrimp. A full-flavored red ale or amber lager can be an ideal mate to smoked fish — or you might choose to present it with a light-bodied, smoky-roasty stout. Aperitifs should present a fantastic experience without wearing out the palate. Look for beers that are light in body and are not ferociously bitter.

Beers for Light Appetizers

All-malt Pilsner

Belgian-style saison

Hefeweizen

Witbier

BEER WITH MAIN COURSES

There's a beer to suit every main dish, as long as you remember the rules: match intensity, find resonance and affinities, and deal with the contrasts. Like appetizers, main courses combine a main ingredient, cooking method, sauce, and garnishes, each with its own contribution to the overall intensity and character of the dish.

First, consider the main ingredient, often a protein. Lamb, for example, is a much heavier taste on the palate than chicken, so its intensity begins to build at a higher level from the start.

Second, consider the method of cooking. Poaching adds little of its own flavor, but roasting, sautéing, frying, grilling, and smoking give progressively more intense flavors. Because the chemistry of browning is basically the same in food as in the kilning of malt, it's a great place to look for common elements and affinities: bready, nutty, cookielike, caramelly, toasty, roasty. Different foods and

Beers for Hearty Appetizers

India Pale Ale

Fruit beer

Red rye ale

Belgian pale ale

British pale ale

methods of preparation add varying amounts of fat, and this demands a certain intensity in the beer used to balance it (see Food and Beer Interactions chart, page 191).

Third, consider any seasoning, sauce, or other element added to the dish. These dramatically change the character of the dish and may contain herbs, spices, fat, salt, sugar, acidity, chile heat, or all of the preceding. Seasonings and sauces present lots of opportunities for finding connecting points, but they can complicate the picture as well. Remember, there is no perfect match. Look for the most intense flavor elements on the plate (don't forget to consider sides or accompaniments), and make sure they're balanced by the beer, and then move on to making sure there are some common or affinity elements.

Barbecued ribs are a good example. Pork ribs by themselves have only a moderately intense flavor, but quite a bit of fat. When you pile on a spicy rub, a load of smoke, and browning of the meat from heat, some chile spice, and a final caramelly layer of sweet and tangy sauce, you have quite a mouthful. The sweet caramel aspect of the meat and sauce is the primary element, which provides a link to the caramelly malt flavors in beer. Because of their sweetness and richness, barbecued ribs are balanced by a beer that is dry on the palate, and a moderately high alcohol level and high carbonation will further help cut through this richness. Although several other beer styles may fit here, I like a Belgian-style dubbel. In addition to its other characteristics, dubbel also matches the dish pretty well in terms of overall intensity. This kind of analytical deconstruction of flavors is key to successful pairing.

BEER WITH DESSERT

Desserts work beautifully with beer. In case you missed that, let me reiterate: beer is fantastic with dessert! At first thought this might seem to be an odd fit, but when you think about the rich, sweet, caramelly, and roasty flavors that can be commonly found in both beer and food, it makes perfect sense.

Not just any beer will do, however. The sweetness and richness of desserts demand rich, full-flavored beers. For the most part, don't even think about pairing beers of less than 6 percent alcohol with dessert, and the "sweet spot" is probably higher than that. We tend to think about sugar as being a fairly bland flavor, and although it's true that it is not complex, on your tongue it explodes and takes over, which is why it needs a strongly flavored beer to balance it. The same is true for fat.

Fortunately, there are plenty of choices in dessert beers. You might pair a fruity dessert such as apple pie or apricot tart with a strong-but-crisp Belgian-style tripel. Bread pudding or a sugary pecan pie might play off something with similar qualities. The caramelly bittersweet charms of an old ale fills the role beautifully. Spice and citrus qualities in many beers work well with desserts that highlight similar flavors.

The sweeter the dessert, the better it will work with hop bitterness. Strong, highly hopped beers such as double IPA are ideal partners for supersweet items such as cheesecake, crème brûlée, or carrot cake. This is a dramatic balancing of a beer and food interaction, with each partner changing the way the other tastes. No matter how sweet the dessert, a hoppy beer will knock the sweetness right out of it. Likewise, even the most aggressively bitter beer can be totally tamed by a nice, sweet dessert. I always compare sugar

A Hoppy Ending
Hops are your friend when
it comes to dessert, as in
this pair that matches key
lime pie with a tropical,
citrusy IPA.

and hops to matter and antimatter, each negating the other.

Chocolate loves a dark beer. Milk chocolate is beautiful with Belgian-inspired strong dark ales or any strong beer without too much black roasty character. The purest, most intense expressions of chocolate, such as flourless chocolate cake or truffles, really do well with a huge black beer, such as inky imperial stout. But also remember that chocolate loves other flavors as well, especially caramel, nuts, and spices. So look to other big beers that have those affinities if you want to move beyond pairs where each partner tastes pretty much the same. Desserts with less chocolate — chocolate chip cookies and peanut butter cups come to mind — can do well with less roasty brews, such as a gutsy brown ale, Scotch ale, or weizenbock. Don't forget about white chocolate. It can be great with strong pale beers and sometimes even with fruit beers.

Fruit beers have an obvious affinity with fruit desserts. The acidity of a kriek or frambozen can cut the sweetness and creamy richness of something like a cherry cheesecake or raspberry coulis in the dessert.

BEER AND CHEESE PAIRING SUGGESTIONS

Orval Trappist Ale
with an ash-ripened, bloomy-rind goat cheese

Dogfish Head 90 Minute IPA ▸
with Golden Ridge Blue (a creamy, sophisticated blue with mushroomy overtones)

Flossmoor Station Pullman Brown
with ColoRouge Camembert (a deliciously gooey washed-rind cheese)

Lindemans Framboise
with Redwood Hill Fresh Chèvre (an earthy, creamy, fresh goat cheese)

Saint Arnold Fancy Lawnmower Beer (Kölsch)
with Fair Oaks Farms Triple Cream Butter Käse (a simple but indulgently creamy butter cheese)

However, seriously sour lambic-type beers are often too sharp and lacking body or structure, so they can come off as thin and screechy when paired with sugary foods. Beers that have a light caramelly toastiness often go great with fruit, as they bring pastry flavors that are obviously welcome elements in many desserts.

Barrel-aged beers are hugely flavorful, offering sophisticated tones of bourbon, vanilla, and sherry and are absolutely delightful with almost any rich dessert. There are also specialty beers with coffee, chocolate, hazelnuts, and many other ingredients that offer obvious possibilities for pairing.

BEER AND CHEESE

As Brooklyn Brewery's Garrett Oliver is fond of telling audiences, cheese is grass processed through a cow and modified by microbes. Beer is also grass processed through a microbe — yeast. So it is not surprising to find a wide range of common flavors from which to draw when seeking pairing possibilities. Cheese is also a great partner because, like craft beer, it is often

▼ **North Coast Old Rasputin Imperial Stout**
with Roth Käse Van Gogh Vintage Gouda (a rich and nutty 6-month Gouda)

Rogue Ales Shakespeare Oatmeal Stout
with Rogue Creamery's Smokey Blue (an explosive dry-textured blue with a nice smokiness)

Two Brothers Dog Days Dortmunder
with Canasta Pardo (a sheep's milk cheese with a delicate dusting of cinnamon)

Einbecker Mai-Ur-Bock
with Meister Family Dairy Horseradish Cheddar (every bit as zippy as you might imagine)

Schlenkerla Rauchbier Märzen
with Carr Valley Apple Smoked Cheddar (an American-style cheddar with a delicious bacony twang)

made by small, artisanal producers driven by passion, with strong creative and independent streaks that have correspondingly distinctive and delicious results.

Cheese can be tough to match with other beverages. Its intense, pungent, earthy, salty, and creamy aspects often overwhelm lesser beverages — although I'm not naming any names. Beer, with its mix of carbonation, hop bitterness, and roasty elements, can handle the mouth-coating richness of cheese just beautifully, if you observe the usual pairing guidelines previously noted.

Like beer, cheese comes in a wide range of intensities, from delicate to magnificently pungent. It's helpful to understand some of the basics of cheesemaking, as it clarifies a complex landscape. Animal type and breed set the protein and fat levels, along with the underlying flavor character. Water removal is one of the most fundamental aspects of cheesemaking and strongly influences the texture and concentration of the final cheese, as does the aging process. Bacterial and mold cultures add further aromatic characters and textural changes.

As with any pairing, the choice of beer partner depends first on intensity. I find that putting together cheese and beer pairings gets easier as the flavors get more intense. It's almost impossible to screw up a combination of a barley wine or imperial anything with a huge, well-aged cheese such as Stilton.

THE FRUITY AROMAS of hefeweizen make a nice match with the milky simplicity of fresh mozzarella. Fruit beers are excellent with a delicate ripened cheese such as Brie or chèvre. The herbal, hoppy nose of an IPA blends nicely with the complex aroma of blue cheese, while the bitterness cleanses the palate. Washed-rind cheeses, with their stinky

aroma and mild flavors on the tongue, work very nicely with medium-strength brown beers like English brown ales and dark lagers. Those same dark beers, perhaps stepped up a bit, work nicely with nutty Pyrenees sheep cheese and alpine types such as Gruyère.

Stout and cheddar make another great pair, as does smoked beer with a tangy, semihard cheese. Triple cream cheeses can work with

Anchor Old Foghorn Barleywine and Point Reyes Farmstead Cheese Company Original Blue

either a strong pale beer such as a Belgian tripel or with a doppelbock that will create a sort of chocolate cheesecake impression. The meaty richness of salty, well-aged cheeses works best with strong, dark beers such as imperial stout. This meat-plus-roast is a great example of a familiarity-based pair; when they come together in a beer-food pair, there is already a sense that they fit together.

GREAT CHEESE is worth seeking out. As with mainstream beer, Americans are rejecting the rubbery, plastic-wrapped grocery-store varieties of cheese. What passes in chain stores for cheddar, Muenster, Jack, Swiss, and all the rest are but limp imitations of the genuine thing. *Real* cheese is flavorful, funky, varied, sublime, and authentic. And some of the best stuff comes from some of the

NO-BRAINER, NO-FAIL BEER AND CHEESE PAIRINGS

A peppery saison +
- Brasserie Dupont Moinette
- North Coast Le Merle
- Southampton Saison

A creamy bloomy-rind cheese
- Sweet Grass Green Hill semiripened
- MouCo Camembert
- French Coulommiers

A toasty, deep brown ale +
- Dogfish Head Indian Brown
- Unibroue Chambly Noire

A nutty, firm sheep's or cow's milk
- Ossau-Iraty
- Comte St. Antoine

A big, hoppy pale ale +
- Firestone Walker Union Jack
- Bell's Two Hearted
- Victory HopDevil

A rich creamy blue or Gorgonzola
- Green Mountain Gore-Dawn-Zola
- Rogue Creamery Rogue River Blue
- Maytag Blue

A big or imperial stout +
- North Coast Old Rasputin
- Deschutes Abyss

A meaty, caramelly well-aged Gouda
- 4-year-old Dutch Gouda
- Roth Käse Van Gogh Vintage

Barley wine +
- Anchor Old Foghorn
- Three Floyds Behemoth
- Brooklyn Monster

Stilton or other intense, aged blue
- Colston Bassett Stilton
- Jasper Hill Bayley Hazen Blue

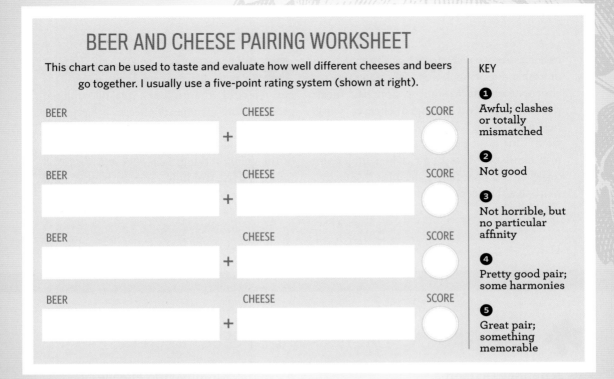

BEER AND CHEESE PAIRING WORKSHEET

This chart can be used to taste and evaluate how well different cheeses and beers go together. I usually use a five-point rating system (shown at right).

BEER		CHEESE	SCORE
	+		
BEER		CHEESE	SCORE
	+		
BEER		CHEESE	SCORE
	+		
BEER		CHEESE	SCORE
	+		

KEY

1 Awful; clashes or totally mismatched

2 Not good

3 Not horrible, but no particular affinity

4 Pretty good pair; some harmonies

5 Great pair; something memorable

smallest producers, whether they are staunch traditionalists or bomb-throwing renegades. In other words, great cheese has a lot in common with craft beer.

High-quality cheese is a delight to the senses and a joy to pair with great beer. Grocery stores usually have few cheeses of real interest, so you are much better off at a specialty grocery or gourmet store or, if you're lucky enough to have one nearby, a specialty cheese shop.

As in craft brewing, there is an artisanal cheese movement in the United States, and some of the resulting cheeses are the equal of anything found in Europe. They are well worth the effort and expense. In my experience, the cheesemonger behind the counter usually knows his or her stuff, and it is a good idea to ask for recommendations (and perhaps a taste)

as you are making your decision. Quite often these folks will have good suggestions for pairing beers.

Cheese is a great place to start off on a beer and food journey (desserts work well, too). Great cheese is not too hard to find, doesn't need extensive preparation before serving, and because it is one thing and not a mix of ingredients, seasonings, and cooking methods, it's a little easier to pair. As a subject of study, though, cheese is every bit as complex as beer, so I advise getting a good introductory text to help you understand the world of cheese.

The simplest way to hold a casual tasting is to gather a few friends together with four or five different types of cheese and have everybody bring some beers, then lay them all out and have at it. For a casual tasting, an ounce of each cheese per person is a good place to start; double that if they're big eaters. If you want bread or crackers, keep it really simple. Fine cheese tastes best at room temperature, so don't forget to let it warm before serving. Talk about what works and what doesn't. Sure, you are going to find some great pairs, but ultimately it is the process that is most meaningful. Oh, and don't forget to have fun.

Southampton Saison and Pavé d'Affinois (a soft, creamy ripened cow's milk cheese).

Staging a Beer Dinner

Beer and food events take many forms, but most typical is a multicourse dinner with a specific beer — or sometimes two — paired with each course. Ambitious dinners also attempt to include beer as an ingredient in each food course. These events are a good way to experience beer and food together and are also a great way to get to know the folks behind the scenes at your favorite brewery and to meet others who share your fan-club status. Most brewpubs and many packaging breweries regularly conduct brewmaster dinners.

You can create your own dinner party; just put some thought into which beers to serve with the courses. There are menus all over the Internet, and beer-specific cookbooks are another great resource; look for books by Julia Herz and Gwen Conley, Garrett Oliver, and Lucy Saunders.

Beer-centric cuisines such as Belgian or German are can't-miss options, or get a lot more exotic with what you serve: India Pale Ales with Indian cuisine, Thai food with German lagers, Mexican with Oktoberfest, barbecue with Belgian ales — possibilities abound.

Like any gastronomic experience, the proper setting and preparation can make the difference between an ordinary experience and an extraordinary one. Here are a few things to consider when planning your beer and food extravaganza.

What are we doing here? Make sure there is a clear plan that everyone in the room understands — from servers to guests. A printed list and description of the beers and their food partners is extremely helpful. Be sure to leave space for note taking, as this really increases attentiveness and information takeaway.

PAIRINGS FROM A
CHICAGO BEER SOCIETY'S
BREWPUB SHOOTOUT

The Onion Pub
- **Harissa-spiced beef** with fig jam and couscous
- **Abbey tripel**

TASTING NOTES:
The tripel cut the richness and soothed the spicy heat, while echoing the figgy fruitiness.

Goose Island Clybourn Brewpub
- **Duck pastrami** with brussels sprout sauerkraut
- **Barrel-aged doppelbock**

TASTING NOTES:
Beer linked with bready flavors and matched the richness of the cured duck. Tangy brussels sprouts provide fat-cutting sharpness.

Prairie Rock Brewpub, Elgin
- **Thai chicken lollipop** with spicy Asian sauce and baby greens
- **Double IPA**

TASTING NOTES:
The IPA brings a hoppy contrast to the richness of the dish but with enough malt to balance the heat.

Rock Bottom Restaurant & Brewery
- **Beer-braised brisket** with watercress and Asiago cheese in mini flatbread sandwiches
- **Dry-hopped American brown ale/winter warmer**

TASTING NOTES:
The rich, beefy taste resonated with the toasty beer, which had enough bitter crispness to cut the considerable richness.

Beer or food first? There's no hard and fast rule here, but if you're representing the brewery or the beers, it's obvious that you'll want to have people try them on their own for the first sip.

Taste from low to high intensity, but . . . Alcohol, hops, roastiness, and sweetness can all beat up your palate, so it only makes sense to put the more delicate beers at the start of the tasting. However, one long, slow ramp-up can be a little tiresome, so consider a break and possibly a palate cleansing beer that's crisp, bright, and perhaps tart or bitter, or accomplish the same thing with a food item. This allows peoples' palates to reset and refresh halfway through.

Consider a "welcome" beer. People don't always arrive at exactly the same time, and they generally are really ready for a beer the moment they walk in. To solve this dilemma, offer a half-glass of something bright, refreshing, and not too strong. That will give everybody time to arrive and settle before the main event begins.

Don't overdo it. Tasting too many beers can lead to palate overload. When planning a dinner, try to limit the number of beers to six to eight tasting portions. This means a maximum of about 4 ounces a pour; somewhat less for strong beers. Do the math on alcohol; a good range is the equivalent of two to three "standard" beers of 12 ounces at 5 percent alcohol by volume. And always encourage the use of public transportation, especially in a public tasting.

Present the beer in its best light. Serving temperature, proper and clean glassware, decent light, and a setting free from smoke or other distracting aromas should all be considered when preparing for any beer and food pairing event.

Think Creatively
Roasty or hoppy beers are the norm for
beefy dishes, but this fruity and spicy
tripel cuts through this dish like magic.

Swap 'n' dump. Just two glasses can get attendees through a whole evening. Pour the first, and bring the second while they are enjoying the first. By the time the third beer comes around, they'll either have to drink it or dump it. Remember to have some means of dumping glasses handy. Chlorine-free filtered water for drinking and rinsing is essential.

Cooking with Beer

With its wide range of properties, beer can be great in the kitchen. It may be used like other cooking liquids, but it does require a few considerations. Match the intensity of the beer to the dish, just as if you were pairing a beer with any other food. Bitterness in beer is like the junkyard dog — you always want to keep an eye on it. Low-bitterness beers are best for cooking.

Do not reduce beer, as even a slightly bitter one may become too bitter for the dish. Salt, acid, and sweetness all have the power to mask bitterness. Small amounts of one or more of these can cover up the bitterness without making the dish noticeably salty, sour, or sweet. Always remember to taste as you go.

Lighten up a batter. Beer adds lightness to batter used for deep-frying such items as fish or appetizers.

Beer suggestions: Pale or amber moderately hopped lager or ale

Deglaze the pan. A quick sauce for sautéed or roasted items can be made by using beer to deglaze the pan. Do not reduce the beer, as it may become excessively bitter.

Beer suggestions: Either delicate or intense, to match the nature of the dish, but low-bitterness is preferred. Tart fruit beers often shine in this role.

Dressings and marinades. Beer can make a great addition to salad dressings and marinades for grilled meat or barbecue. Acidic beers can substitute for vinegar in dressings.

Beer suggestions: Pale, low-bitterness beers for dressings; heartier amber or brown beers for marinades

Steaming or poaching liquid. Although mussels steamed in wheat beer is a classic, other great combinations are possible.

Beer suggestions: Witbier, Weissbier, other delicate and lightly hopped brews

Replace or augment stock in soups and sauces. Many beers can add richness to hearty soups or meat gravy. Don't make cheese soup without it!

Beer suggestions: Sweet stout, doppelbock, Scotch ale

Make dessert more luxurious. Strong, rich beers may be substituted for other liquids in cakes and pastries. Fruit beers add a complexity to fruit compote or sauce. Or make beer the star — drop a scoop of ice cream into a glass of imperial stout and voilà, dessert!

Beer suggestions: Sweet stout, doppelbock, Belgian strong dark ale, fruit beer

W E'RE EATING AND DRINKING all the time, so just start paying closer attention to the flavors, textures, and other sensations along the way. A little effort leads to big rewards, and pretty soon you'll develop the kind of repertoire that means always having the perfect sip ready for the next forkful. Like the great dance team of Fred and Ginger, beer and food are lively, supple partners that seem to have been made for each other. A beer and food match is always a great interaction, whether supporting, cajoling, caressing, or raising each other to lofty new heights. Beer and food just swing together.

DISHES PREPARED WITH BEER

- Roast pork loin with apples and cherry ale
- Braised pork shanks with dunkel lager or schwarzbier
- Duck glazed with doppelbock
- Roast salmon with witbier cream sauce
- Grilled steak marinated in red ale and green peppercorns
- Beef short ribs with stout or porter
- Roast chicken with dried apricots and weizenbock sauce
- Steamed scallops in witbier
- Gingerbread brown ale cake
- Chocolate imperial stout truffles, dusted with powdered black malt
- Barley wine–walnut ice cream

CHAPTER 8

ANATOMY OF A STYLE

There are those in the brewing community who chafe at the notion of beer styles. Beer is art, they say, and any attempt to limit it to preordained categories diminishes its greatness; styles are nothing more than a crutch for unimaginative minds.

But styles are a reality. They exist in history and in the marketplace, and in some places they have the force of law behind them. Brewers brew by them, consumers buy by them, and competitions are judged by them. Styles honor the past and give order to the present. Something has to go on that chalkboard behind the bar. Styles help people wrap their heads around the world of beer.

I LOVE CREATIVE BEERS that break all the boundaries. Just the same, rebellion is a little empty without something to rebel against; styles provide that kind of structure in wild abundance. The notion of styles adds a depth and dimension to the wide world of beer. Studying them brings into focus the less obvious aspects of beer, such as balance, cultural taste, changing fashions, and our notions of ourselves.

It's a bit like religion. You can choose to believe or not to believe, but the landscape is richer and more profound when all manner of unsupported ideas are tolerated. So I say: Bring 'em on!

Just What Is a Style?

A style is a collection of qualities that combine to form a single, identifiable whole. That one thing may turn out to be many things when you start looking closely, but it doesn't matter. Styles are all about consensus.

Our modern notion of styles really coalesced when professional and homebrewing competitions started in the 1980s. Once it was decided that beers were to be judged by styles, detailed guidelines needed to be developed, crystallizing what was known about them at the time — really a mix of current commercial practices and historical interpretation, as it was understood. Of course, with some styles, such as porter, dead in their original homelands, there was a lot of guesswork. Even today, some details are still being straightened out as new details come to light. So bear in mind as we romp through the landscape of styles that they serve many masters, and in different lights they may look very different.

First and most obvious among the qualities that define a style are objective measurements: color, gravity, alcoholic strength, bitterness, attenuation, and others. A beer style can almost be defined by these alone. On top of that are subjective sensory characteristics: aroma, flavor, texture, and mouthfeel, which complete the picture of what's in the glass — and what's in or out of the style box.

But this only scratches the surface. Sensory characteristics can't tell us the full story or explain how the style came into use, through whom, and for what purpose. At a deeper, richer level are the technological, geographic, and cultural foundations that gave rise to the more obvious points of the style. Understanding them and also seeing beer styles in their proper historical context are essential to grasping the bigger themes and essence of a style, and allow both brewer and drinker to celebrate them at a higher level.

Styles are indispensable for brewers and drinkers to share some common ground about what a particular beer is going to taste like. A style is marketing shorthand. What's easier to understand, "American pale ale" or "an amber-colored, top-fermented ale of 5 to 6.5 percent alcohol and crisp bitterness with the resin and citrus overtones of American hops"? Sure, that may be written in tiny type on the back of the label. But does anybody really read labels? Studies have shown that shoppers spend no more than a couple of seconds on an initial scan of packages on the shelf, so communication has to be nearly instantaneous. Styles really help with that.

Historically, many styles have developed spontaneously and only later get the name by which they have become famous. Dark brown ales were brewed in London for a generation before the name "porter" was applied to them sometime around 1725. "Stout" was a term used generically for strong beer in England as early as the late seventeenth century, but it didn't find common use until a generation later, when it came exclusively to mean a strong porter. Münchener beers were simply the local brew until they became popular elsewhere and then took on the city's name.

Other beers are the product of invention, not evolution. Pilsner dates quite precisely to 1842, when the city fathers decided to build a brewery and brew a pale lager, then a new idea. Bill Owens, the creative force behind one of the first latter-day U.S. brewpubs, lays claim

to the invention of the "amber" designation: "I had a dark and a light, and what was I gonna call that middle one? *Amber.*"

STYLES GO THROUGH CHANGES, generation by generation. What seems to be constant is that no one wants to drink his or her father's beer. It seems that each generation has to find its own way, even if it ends up pretty close to home. Newness has its own appeal, and tradition, while nice at times, doesn't always rule. Even since the first edition of this book, amber and red ales have become hoppier; the tawny, hallowed Oktoberfest has almost

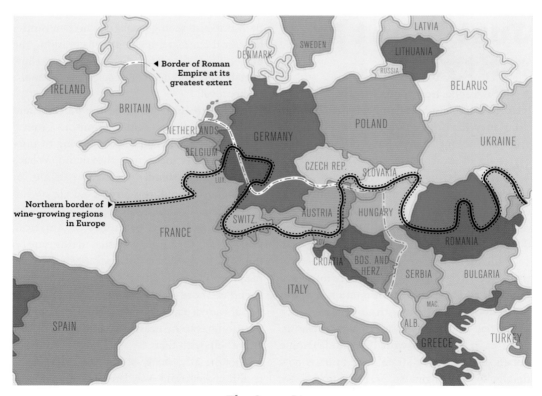

The Grape Line
This indicates the northern extent of grape cultivation in Europe and approximates the extent of the old Roman Empire (Britain excepted). Above the line, they were definitely beer drinkers.

entirely turned into a pale beer; and IPAs have gotten paler and more aromatic and at the same time spawned white, black, red, lager, and session versions — all in just 6 short years.

Whatever the other influences on the formation of a style — and there are many — it must be satisfying to the senses. All the parts must coalesce in a beer that looks, tastes, smells, and feels great. In the range of all possible beers, not everything is going to work. Taste differs in different times and places, but I've brewed quite a number of extinct historical beers and found them all quite delicious. Despite our differences, I feel that we share a lot in common about what we like in a beer.

In every culture you find different beers serving particular needs: hydration, nutrition (as in "liquid bread"), dining companion, and everyday drinking, as well as special occasion beers serving as luxury goods. Even in ancient Sumeria, weak, strong, extra-quality, and even diet beer all existed side by side. Beer is a part of culture, and it embraces the many tasks it is called on to perform.

Beer in Its Time and Place

You have to look at human activities in the broadest possible context to fully understand beer styles. There are places on the globe where barley grows well, regions better suited to other grains, and, of course, places where no brewing grains do well. This affects who will be making beer and from what. There is a line that cuts across Europe, north of which wine grapes don't grow; this roughly corresponds to the northern boundary of the old Roman Empire.

For reasons of agriculture as well as cultural patrimony, the lands south of that line have always preferred grape to grain. The Greeks, and the Romans after them, saw wine as civilizing and beer as a barbarian's drink, an attitude that has infected Western thought since those days. Happily, this is changing. Former beer deserts such as Italy have recently blossomed with some very exciting artisanal beers.

CLIMATE AND RAW MATERIALS

Barley and, to a lesser extent, wheat, have always been the preferred grains for beer, but a passable brew can be coaxed out of hardier grains such as rye and oats, which tolerate harsher climates and soils. Oat and sometimes rye beers used to be commonplace in England, the Low Countries, Scandinavia, and all the way up the Baltic Sea. Wheat requires a specific climate and very good soil, and there's always competition from the bakers for raw material. So in various times and places you find wheat beers more tightly regulated than barley beers, sometimes banned in difficult years or assigned to a royal monopoly, as in eighteenth-century Bavaria.

Hops have a narrow range of latitudes where they will produce cones. In England, for example, they do stupendously well in the south but less so farther north. The rate of hopping in English beer tends to follow this tilt. Hops are a compact, high-value crop and have been shipped great distances for centuries. Following the trail of hops is another way to make sense of beer styles.

As any farmer can tell you, weather is unpredictable. Beer's raw materials are subject to this uncertainty, and the results are shortages and high prices. The net effect of bad growing years is that brewers either cut back or look for substitutes. Sugar was forbidden in beer in England prior to around 1825, when a couple of inadequate barley crops led first to the temporary and then to the permanent (in 1847) allowance of the use of sugar and other adjuncts for brewing.

GEOLOGY AND WATER

In addition to climate, one must also consider geology. The bedrock of a region has a big influence on the chemistry of the local water. As it flows through rivers, lakes, and aquifers, it dissolves minerals that affect the hardness and acid-alkaline balance, both of which have a strong influence on the brewing process. Prior to the late nineteenth century, water chemistry wasn't understood well enough to be manipulated, so brewers in a given place had to brew a beer that worked with the local water.

Although it's a complicated subject, the most important vector to understand is that hard, alkaline water is best for dark, malty beers. Hoppy beers require either hard and acidic (gypsum/sulfate) water or soft water. The brown beers of London, Dublin, and Munich were all created in cities with chalky, hard water. The crisp hoppy brews from Plzeň and Burton-on-Trent, famous since the mid-nineteenth century for bitingly bitter pale ales, each took full advantage of the local water.

SEASONAL CYCLES

Before refrigeration made brewing a year-round venture, climate enforced a seasonal brewing cycle. The demand for agricultural labor meant that workers were often unavailable for brewing in the summer. And then there's the heat. With no means to limit fermentation temperature and a very high count of airborne bacteria and wild yeast, summer's heat produced beers that soured very quickly,

Burton-on-Trent, England
Canal improvements, c. 1800, made this town the brewing powerhouse of northern England.

so only the essential thirst-quenching small beers were brewed. Winter was the proper season for brewing.

Storage conditions were not great either, and by summer, last fall's malt — and especially hops — were pretty tired out. Common practice was to brew stronger beers at the end of the brewing season — March or maybe April — that could mature through summer and be consumed in the fall to celebrate the harvest. This cycle was similar across Europe. England's most prized beer in the old days was a strong "October" beer, and a similar but slightly lower quality "March" beer was also made. For at least a couple of centuries, the French brewed and enjoyed bière de mars. Märzen lager was the original Oktoberfest beer and, though fading, still exists in Munich. The Germans in Saxony had a celebrated erntebier (harvest beer), with many similarities to modern-day Altbier.

Bock beer is another brew with fascinating seasonal connections. Born in Einbeck, the story goes, this strong beer was brought to Bavaria and its name was eventually corrupted from *einbeckisches* to *einpockisches bier* and eventually was shortened to bockbier. The word *bock* is the German word for male goat, prancing symbol of priapic fertility, whose natural season is spring. Religiously observant monks, looking for a loophole to the denial of Lenten fasting, studied the rules and decided that God somehow overlooked banning beer along with meat, and so took full advantage. To show their gratitude, the monks at Paulaner — then a monastery, not a commercial brewer — cooked up an extrastrong version of bock in 1773 and named it Salvator. This name served as a generic name for the style for a couple of centuries, until they decided to take their trademark back. Such jumbled mythology highlights the enormous task facing beer-style researchers.

We still can follow the flow of seasons with our beers. A beer that can be tossed down to quench thirsts in the heat of summer fails to satisfy in the dreary gloom of February. The promise of spring creates a different mood from the breezy desiccation of fall and demands a different sort of beer.

Paulaner Salvator
First created by monks, the name "salvator" was once generic for the doppelbock style until the secularized brewery began defending its trademark.

THE YEAR IN BEER

New Year's. Pop a Belgian-style tripel as an alternative to the same boring old champagne when the year changes. The next day, nourish your soul and your head with a nice yeasty weizenbock.

The last twelve interminable days of January. Nothing makes the time fly like a vertical tasting of your favorite barley wine or imperial stout. Take care to avoid the tasting becoming a horizontal one.

Valentine's Day. Loads of choices! Try Belgian strong dark ale with milk chocolate or an imperial stout with something really hot and sinful such as lava cake with a touch of spicy ancho chile inside. If your sweetie wants to walk on the pale side, how about a Belgian strong golden ale with a white chocolate version of Black Forest cake? Who says beer guys and gals can't be romantic when it counts?

Lent. Personally, I don't have a lot of experience with self-denial. I'd go with a bock or doppelbock, the proven remedy for mortification of the flesh. And they do taste great at this time of year.

Easter and more pagan expressions of the vernal equinox. Easter beers used to be big business in Scandinavia and elsewhere in northern Europe. We'll have to be content with something pale and slightly strong, provided we can crack open the maibock a little early. Open up a bottle of raspberry lambic when Aunt Ruth comes to brunch.

The first really nice day of spring. Even though I sometimes do it, I think there is something wrong with drinking Weissbier indoors. So I am greatly relieved to be rid of my guilt when it's finally nice enough to sit outside in some makeshift beer garden and enjoy a dunkel weizen in the chilly sunshine.

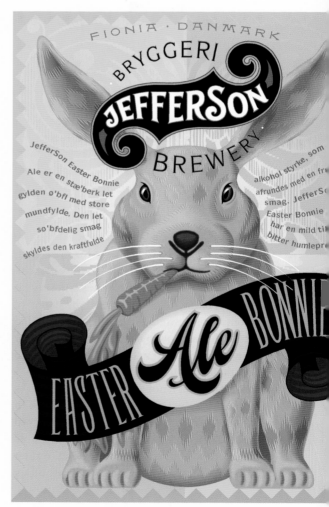

May. Go for a maibock, if there's any left from Easter.

June. Let's just call it India Pale Ale month.

Fourth of July. Let the national frenzy take hold and honor honest-to-God U.S. of A., lawn-mowing beers, both great and small. There are many to choose from: pre-Prohibition Pilsners, Kölsch, steam beer, cream ale, American wheat ale, and craft-brewed malt liquor.

St. Swithin's Day, July 15. Yes, there really is one, and its history involves an interesting story about great torrents of water. I recommend a light beer.

Dog days. Still hot. Time to break out the big thirst-quenching guns: witbier, English summer ale, classic German Pilsner, hefeweizen — in large glasses, please.

Back to school, or whatever. Still warm and sunny but change is in the air. It's the perfect time for a nice saison, but many beers suit the season: British bitter, Irish stout, schwarzbier, gueuze. Wait till the end of September and you can taste them all and much more at the Great American Beer Festival in Denver.

Oktoberfest. You really need a suggestion here?

Halloween. Pumpkin beer is a natural at this time, but see if you can score one of its scarier variants: pumpkin barley wine, pumpkin weizenbock, or pumpkin imperial porter. Better than pie!

Turkey time. Try a tripel with the succulent bird, roasted to perfection — but toss a pint of Scotch ale into the bottom of the pan when you start roasting. The tripel will go nicely with pecan pie, but for pumpkin pie, a strong brown ale will be better.

Christmas Eve. I hear the old man is partial to drinking imperial pale ale with his chocolate chip cookies.

The holidays. The English had their wassail and many other hot compounded drinks that can make you the life of the party if you don't burn the house down. There are many festive beers inspired by the rich, spicy flavors of Jolly Old England. But honestly, at this time of year just enjoy all the big celebratory beers available and give yourself incentive for some serious New Year's resolutions.

Technology and Beer Styles

Technology has a huge influence on beer. But while progress in other areas, such as aviation, shows the level of technology is clearly in line with the quality of the product, the effect of technology on beer is more complicated and doesn't always result in more delicious beer. A knowledgeable guy with little more than a bucket and a pinch of yeast can brew beer good enough to make you weep, but it takes technology to be able to do this consistently and, especially, economically. Every new technology brings with it changes that may not have been on the mind of its inventor, thereby influencing the styles for which it is employed.

THE EVOLUTION OF HEATED KILNS

In preindustrial times, malt was sometimes dried simply by spreading it on the attic floor, but more commonly, heated kilns were used. These early malt kilns were direct fired, so that the hot combustion gases passed over the malt and gave it a smoky aroma. By 1700, improvements in kilning technology meant most European beer was no longer smoky. However, the rustic touch of smoke is still enjoyed today in Bamberg and northern Bavaria, and in the ancient homebrews of Gotland, Sweden. A century ago smoke-touched beers were more widespread, with beers such as grodziske (grätzer) and lichtenhainer thriving in northern Germany and Poland, and these are starting to be revived. Even Strasbourg, France, had a smoky beer before lager got rolling there in a big way.

Smoke wasn't the only issue in early malt kilning. It's fairly easy, with simple equipment, to make amber- to brown-colored malt. Getting it really light or dark poses more of a challenge. In 1817, Daniel Wheeler patented a drum roaster with an iron cylinder that contained the malt, keeping it separated from the fire. Even today, it is called black patent malt. Black malt changed porter forever. Just a

Smoky Beers
While we love their rustic charm these days, brewers distanced themselves from smoky kilning processes as soon as they could.

generation before, a brewer named Richardson had written a book detailing his observations on brewing aided by a hydrometer. Surprise! All that brown malt is making the beer nice and dark, but it has a lot less fermentable extract per quarter (a volume measure) than pale malt, so the brewery accountants were climbing all over themselves to get the brewmasters to use more pale and less brown, to reduce cost. Although it

was not strictly legal, the government seemed to look the other way as porter and stout were colored by caramelized sugar, at least until Wheeler came along with his patent. Books covering this tumultuous period of change in these popular beers often lamented the fact that you couldn't get "real" porter anymore.

Similarly, it took sophisticated indirect kilns with good temperature control to produce malt light enough to brew what could truly be called pale beers. While air-dried "white" malt had long been available in England and on the Continent, it wasn't until the mid-nineteenth century that very pale, or Pilsner, malt was produced in any serious quantities.

When or where caramel or crystal malt was invented is a bit of a mystery. The intensely rich malt used in many modern beers doesn't show up in the old books until about 1870, so it played little role in the creation of most of the classic European beer styles. It found an early role in the creation of low-gravity English bitters, where its chewy, caramelly character lends heft to what are very low-gravity beers. Crystal eventually found its way into many classic styles, but it had little to do with the beginnings of most of them.

VESSELS AND INSTRUMENTS

A very challenging task in early breweries was the big job of heating water, mash, and wort. Metal vessels are still among the most expensive parts of the brewhouse, and they were only used when nothing else would serve. Wood will hold water just fine, but you can't put a flame to it. In ancient times, heated rocks were dropped into the mash or boil to raise the temperature. Later on, a brewer with a small kettle could remove some of the mash, boil it, and return it to the rest of the batch for a temperature step-up. This process, known as decoction,

Malt Roaster, c. 1850
Patterned after the revolutionary device patented by Daniel Wheeler in 1817, roasters like this made black malt possible and ushered in a new era of very dark beers.

figures heavily in traditional German and Czech styles of lagers, where it adds a unique and delicious caramel touch.

Instruments other than the hydrometer also had their influences. Brewers had long been able to control mashing temperatures by the seat of their pants, either by carefully pro-portioning boiling water with cold and making allowances for seasonal variations in tempera-tures or by observing the way water behaves as it is heated. At a certain point on its way to a boil, the blanket of mist clears, but before the surface starts to roil from the heat, there is a brief moment when a calm, glassy surface lets the brewer see his reflection. This is at about 170°F (77°C), which is in the neighborhood of the right point to make the mash. Even with a lifetime of practice, this technique must have

been approximate, so it's hard to say how much fine control there was over the temperature of the mash and therefore the fermentability of the wort. Being able to fine-tune temperature at every stage is critical if you want to make beer consistently and efficiently. Using tem-perature measurements also allowed brewers to discuss the most critical parts of the brewing process using a common language.

As soon as brewers understood how tem-perature affected the brewing process, they developed a keen interest in controlling it. This led to temperature control of fermenters, usually accomplished by passing cold water through pipes suspended in the tanks. In the 1870s, refrigeration technology became prac-tical for brewing. At that point it was possible to brew a beer year-round instead of during just

Copper Kettles
Copper is so traditional that the brewing kettle itself is often simply called "the copper."

the coolest 6 months. And eventually, beers appeared that were meant to be consumed ice cold. Among these crisp, pale, highly carbonated beers were sparkling and cream ales, as well as American adjunct Pilsners.

PASTEURIZATION

Louis Pasteur had an effect as well. While the nature of yeast was discovered by others, Louis Pasteur, in his 1871 *Études sur la Bière,* identified the "diseases" of beer and worked out practical methods for avoiding them. He also figured out a method for rendering beer and other products microbiologically stable by heating — or pasteurizing — them using a specified time and temperature regimen. Pasteurization greatly increased the shelf life of bottled beer, and this, in conjunction with refrigeration, made a massive distribution network possible and brought beer to places like the southern United States, where it had previously had been scarce and inconsistent.

THE BOTTLE'S ROLE

Draft beer had always been modestly carbonated, as the wooden kegs could hold only limited amounts of pressure. Bottles handmade of glass or clay existed, but these were heavy and unreliable. It wasn't until about the last third of the nineteenth century that machine-made bottles capable of holding serious pressure came on the market. This led to new, highly carbonated beers. Gueuze, a blended and bottled form of lambic, came into being shortly thereafter. Berliner Weisse enjoyed a huge popularity in the nineteenth century in its very heavy stoneware bottles. In Scotland (mainly as an export to America), Australia, and the United States, bottled sparkling ales were all the rage. And let's not forget modern industrial lager.

Packaged Beer
While people in the old days sometimes bottled up a little beer, things didn't really scale up until the late 1800s.

PERHAPS THE BIGGEST CHANGE all this technology brought was that beers were no longer so closely tied to the materials and conditions at their points of origin. There were plenty of cultural reasons that certain beer styles stayed in particular areas, but by 1900 or so, there were few technological ones. With certain styles — Pilsners, for example — being brewed internationally and slowly morphing into something very different, the pure and authentic expression of a style often depended on the bullheaded intransigence of the original brewers. I'm all for creativity, but it's a lousy way to preserve tradition. The power to make anything, anywhere changes the tradition equation dramatically. Today, with tinkering of the classics, such as Oktoberfest and Bohemian Pilsner, by the geniuses in the marketing departments, it falls to passionate and historically informed brewers elsewhere to preserve a style in its truest form. Like animals in a zoo, the styles may eventually be released back into their wild habitat, but for now, the task is simply to save the species.

Laws, Taxes, and Beer Styles

The government has had its sticky hands on our beer since the earliest days, and our desire for beer is so strong that we usually let them get away with it. The famous stone stele upon which is chiseled the 2225 BCE Code of Hammurabi, the world's first written laws, includes a regulation about how tavern owners should charge for beer. In medieval Europe, beer tax made up half or more of the municipal revenue in such places as Bruges. Before the advent of hopped beer, tax was in the form of the *Gruitrecht*, which was the right to sell a highly marked-up seasoning mixture to the local brewers, who were required by law to use it. Later, when hopped beer came about, the tax was levied on malt and hops. The *Reinheitsgebot*, the much-vaunted Bavarian beer "purity" law, was created mainly as a tax-enforcement law, forcing the brewers to use the taxed ingredients.

WHEN BREWERS ARE TAXED ON MALT, there are often additional laws specifying how much must be used for beers selling at specific prices to ensure that drinkers get the strength of beer they're paying for. These regulations were common in northern Europe for hundreds of years. When the hop tax is high, brewers are cautious about their hop use. In Britain, repeal of the hop duty in 1862 coincided with a growing popularity of highly hopped pale ales.

British breweries today are taxed on alcohol content, which means there is constant pressure to keep their beers as weak as possible, and of course this fits with the British style of session drinking.

Through the middle of the nineteenth century, the Belgians had a unique tax system based on the volume of the mash tun. Because the tax was on the size of the vessel regardless of how much malt was in it, this law encouraged brewers to fill the tuns to the brim and above, affecting the beers. The government also allowed the use of a second tun for unmalted grains. Taxed at less than the full volume, brewers were eager to fill that one, too, leading to the classic recipes for both witbier and lambic, which use unmalted wheat in a peculiar mashing scheme.

TAXATION OF ALCOHOL DIRECTLY dates to the end of the nineteenth century. Typically there are tiers with progressively higher taxes as alcohol increases, as with the class I, II, and III system used in parts of Scandinavia. Wherever this is done, the beers get redesigned as brewers bump them down to fit into the lowest class that they think customers will tolerate. Many beers in Germany that had been table strength (4 to 5 percent alcohol by volume) were dropped into the *schenkbier*, or small beer, category when it was created in about 1890, bringing them more into the 2 to 3 percent alcohol range.

There is also often a beer versus spirits battle that ultimately affects beer styles. In most times and places, the government will tax beer at a lower rate to discourage the use of spirits. When the Belgian government banned the on-premises sale of gin in 1919, it inadvertently created a market for strong beer to fill the hole in the marketplace.

WAR AFFECTS BEER in profound ways. It can create shortages of ingredients and equipment, and the resulting beer is not very good. This wouldn't be such a problem if people didn't get so damned used to it. It seems the affected beers never bounce back well from such catastrophes. And for the soldiers, war is a transformative event; the beers they shared with their soldier pals became a part of lifelong patterns. Canned beer was the beneficiary of such male bonding during World War II.

Brewers and governments sometimes work together when it comes to appellations. These are protected categories of products that limit how and by whom the beer may be brewed when labeled as a particular style. Trappist ales, for example, are not a style but adhere to a set of rules governing what a true monastic brewery is, and this determines who is allowed to use the *Trappiste* designation (see chapter 12). Lambic has its own set of rules. In Germany, many styles have upper and lower limits on the gravity of the wort, and brewers of Oktoberfest beer must be located within the city limits of Munich. America is largely free of these types of rules.

Pressures of the Beer Business

Controlling costs and being competitive in the market influence much of what happens on the brewhouse floor. American brewers first started using adjuncts to thin the body of the beer and dilute the protein to levels that could be manageable in packaged beer, but eventually they caught on that adjuncts such as corn and rice are cheaper than barley malt. American brewers after World War II went through an orgy of product cheapening as the inexpensive beer segment exploded. Today the cheapest bargain beers contain up to half adjuncts, the maximum allowed by law.

Our cultural attitudes affect what we eat and drink, and these swing in long arcs. We are now enjoying the civilized benefits of a pendulum swing back to the pleasures of more specialized and authentic foods and drinks. As an often unruly group of immigrants, the people of the United States tried to find ways to come together into a single nation. Finding common language in mass-market, "modern" products was one way to do this: Campbell's Soup, Wonder Bread, and American cheese. They're still on the shelves, but they're in decline. The bright, soulless rationality of these industrial icons no longer holds so much appeal. Many of us would rather have our bread unsliced, our cheese moldy, our coffee freshly roasted, our beer dark and maybe just a little bit hazy as well. Irrationality can be a beautiful thing, and I hope we can keep pushing the pendulum for a long, long time.

A FEW NOTES ON THE FOLLOWING STYLES
AND SUGGESTED BEERS

Once you start dividing the beer world into styles, there are decisions to be made. Large brewing competitions slice the style pie into very thin slivers to reduce the number of beers in a category to a manageable size. Many styles that warrant separate categories in competitions are minor variants of each other that share common history, brewing ingredients, and more. In this book, I have treated certain styles — pale ale and bitter, for example — as a close-knit family rather than as a bunch of individual entities. My aim is to clearly describe the styles and to elucidate the relationships among them.

Styles themselves are moving targets, changing with market tastes and economic pressures. There is a tug-of-war between current and historical styles, with some beers, such as Oktoberfest, rapidly morphing into something different, even as some small brewers dig up and rebrew historically inspired examples for the market. I have generally taken the conservative approach and cast a wide net, keeping the classic historical point of view in mind when defining styles and setting parameters.

The numbers in this edition are courtesy of the BJCP's 2015 style guidelines. I have sliced and diced the categories a little differently from the way they do, to emphasize similarities and common families, as this is an educational overview rather than the finely delineated categories needed in large beer competitions.

I have chosen a mix of European classics and American craft-brewed beers as examples, the latter almost always being a little more in-your-face than their European inspirations. I've tried to pick beers that are widely available, and from different regions. Smaller, local craft breweries and brewpubs often make dazzling examples of many styles, so please take the time to seek them out.

I've picked these beers to illustrate specific aspects of beer styles. There are many terrific beers that bend the rules a little, so they don't fit here. And never forget that there are a huge number of excellent beers that have nothing to do with any particular style. Sometimes these can be the most fun of all.

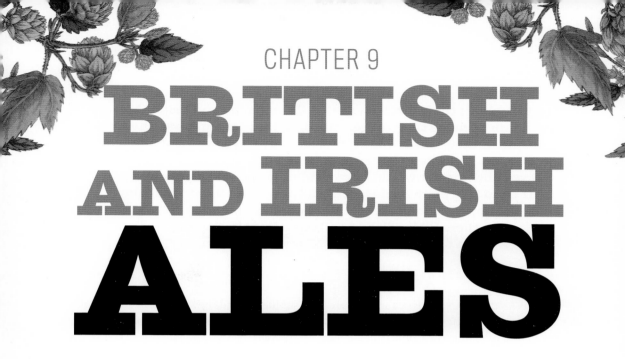

CHAPTER 9
BRITISH AND IRISH ALES

The inhabitants of Great Britain and Ireland have been beer drinkers for a very long time. Traces of cereals and honey, a common ancient mixture, have been found in Scotland on potsherds dating to about 3000 BCE. Elsewhere in Scotland, there is more evidence that the original Pict inhabitants enjoyed beer spiked with such things as heather, meadowsweet, sweet gale (a.k.a. bog myrtle), cranberries, and a dangerous psychotropic herb called henbane. Scholars believe it is entirely possible that these brewing traditions originated in place and may not have been transferred from regions to the east.

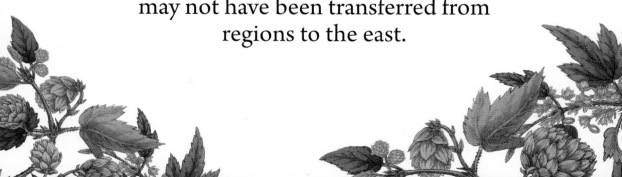

They talk about their foreign wines — Champagne and bright Moselle —
And think because they're from abroad, that we must like them well,
And of their wholesome qualities they tell a wondrous tale;
But sour or sweet, they cannot beat a glass of old English Ale.
D'ye think my eye would be as bright, my heart as light and gay,
If I and "old John Barleycorn" did not shake hands each day?
No, no; and though teetotalers at malt and hops may rail,
At them I'll laugh and gaily quaff of old English ale.

— J. Caxton, from the song "A Glass of Old English Ale"

IN ADVANCE OF THE ROMANS, there was no great Celtic invasion, as is often suggested. But over time the Gallic tribes, later identified as the Celts, did seep into Britain, and with them came a long-established beer tradition. The Greeks and Romans had plenty of encounters with the Celts in the east, as well as in France and Italy. Classical writers record their fondness for drinking and their shockingly indiscriminate beverage choices, befitting the "barbarian" moniker. Imported Italian wine was a luxury product in early Britain. The Romans called beer *cerevesia*, likely derived from the Celtic word *korma* or *curmi*. Honey is mentioned as being employed in some beers, which likely would have meant they were stronger and more luxurious than everyday beer.

Starting in 55 BCE, Julius Caesar introduced Roman culture onto this already complex scene. He notes that in Kent (Cantium) people lived as the Gauls did, but farther north was a culture less familiar to him and much more beer-oriented. Beer was immensely popular among troops hired to protect the Roman frontier, as these were not Italian but Germanic auxiliaries. These troops may have some things in common with the people they were there to subjugate, and they may have actually reinforced Britain's beer-drinking ways.

There is plenty of documentary and archaeological evidence for beer and brewing in Roman Britain. As always, details about the beer are scant, but it is known that barley, wheat, and spelt (a kind of grain intermediate between the two) were used and that dedicated malting and kilning facilities existed.

St. Brigid is said to have turned her bathwater into beer.

Rome never conquered Ireland, allowing them to maintain their native brewing traditions and meld them with early Christianity as they moved into the monastic age. St. Brigid, in particular, had some fantastic powers, turning water into beer for the benefit of the ill and multiplying beer for an Easter celebration at a time when grain was short.

Beer in the Middle Ages

The Romans finally left the British Isles in the fifth century. At that time, there was a lot of raiding into England by the Picts from Scotland and the Scots, who were the original inhabitants of Ireland. After appealing to Rome for help and receiving none, Briton leaders turned to Anglo-Saxon mercenaries. They decided they liked the place just fine and stayed, against the wishes of their hosts. King Arthur's mythic success at Badon Hill was a rare victory in an ultimately unsuccessful effort to drive them out.

The Anglo-Saxons brought a new wave of beer drinkers, along with their tradition of communal drinking in mead halls. The saga *Beowulf* mentions four types of beverage: *win* and *medo*, clearly wine and mead; *beor*, which despite its seeming similarity to the word "beer" probably refers to another honey beverage; and *ealu*, which is the early form of the present English word ale and indicates a beverage made from grain.

Documents in the early Middle Ages mention "clear ale," "Welsh ale" (which was sweet and may have included honey), "double-brewed ale," and "mild ale" (the meaning of which is unclear in context). Later on, the term "mild" referred to a beer that was relatively fresh and had not undergone an extended aging period.

HOPS SHOW UP in English herbariums in connection with drink as early as the ninth or tenth century. Hops, of course, don't become widespread in English brewing until about 1500, but by the fourteenth century, there was a distinction being drawn between unhopped ale and hopped beer. By the early fifteenth century, hopped beer had established a significant beachhead in Kent and elsewhere in southeast England.

Even in late medieval times, recipes show the use of some proportion of wheat. There were also oat beers that were made cheaply and sold to a poor class of clientele called "grouters," after the grain and spice mix that was used to season it. Such beers are actually related to the great family of white beers that spread along the North Sea coast of Europe and had their last refuge in the British Isles in late nineteenth-century Devon and Cornwall.

By the tenth century, taverns start to become an important locus of Anglo-Saxon beer culture, but little is known about who was doing the brewing. Outside of the monasteries, beer

> **Her ale, if new, looks like a misty morning, all thick; well, if her ale be strong, her fire good, her face fair, and the town great or rich, she shall seldom sit without chirping birds to bear her company, and at the next churching or christening, she is sure to be rid of two or three dozen cakes and ale by gossiping neighbors.**
>
> — Donald Lupton, *London and the Countrey Carbonadoed*, 1632

THREE LIESE PAS- SANT

Louse Hall.

You laugh now goodman twoshoes but at what
My Grove my mansion house or my dunn hatt
Is it for that my loveing Chin and Snout.
Are mett because my teeth are fallen out?
Is it at me or at my ruffe you titter?
your Grandmother you rogue nere more a fitter

Is it at foreheads wrinkle or cheekes furrow
Or at my mouth so like a Cony-burrough
Or at those Orient eyes that nere shed teare
But when y Excisemen come thats twice a yeare.
Kisse me & tell me true and when they fayle,
Thou shalt have bigger potts and stronger ale.

production was a domestic activity, primarily performed by women; this would remain so for several hundred years, until brewing increased in scale and prestige enough to become thoroughly commercialized and mainly an affair of men. The early women brewers were called brewsters or alewives. Brewing at home was a legitimate way to bring in a little extra money and was especially helpful for women who were widowed or otherwise in difficult circumstances. Just as in ancient Sumeria, where women were also the brewers and tavern keepers, alewives with beer available for sale would hang a broom or a small bush — an ale-stake — above the door. The practice may have its roots in the use of twisted or braided

---

Mother Louse, Alewife Proprietor of Louse Hall, near Oxford, England
Mother Louse represented the end of an era when alewives supplied beer to local residents.

---

twigs to entrap yeast and preserve it between batches.

FOR CENTURIES, possibly as far back as the Norman Conquest, the English have had some form of price control on their ale. A legal device known as the Assize of Bread and Ale fixed the price for specific measures of beer based on the prevailing price of malt; it also specified how much malt was to be used for single and double beer and, therefore, how strong each type of beer could be. The assize was retooled to increase revenue several times, but it stood in place until 1643, when it was replaced with a stepped system that greatly increased the tax on strong, expensive beers and was a forerunner of the current excise system.

For nearly a thousand years in England, beer has been sold only in measures certified by royal gaugers. The old documents are full of violators being put to the pillory or ducking stool for tampering with the measures, selling

You laugh, my goodman twoshoes, but at what —
My grove, my mansion house or my dun hat?
Is it for that my loving Chin and Snout are met
Because my teeth are fallen out:
Or is it at my RUFF you titter;
Your grandmere, you rouge, ne'er wore a fitter.
Is it at Forehead's wrinkle or Cheek's furrow,
Or at my Mouth, so like a Coney-Burrough,
or at those orient eyes thet ne'er shed Tear.
But when the Exciseman comes, that's twice a year?
KISS me and tell me true, and when they fail,
Thou shalt have larger Pots and stronger Ale.

— David Loggan

in uncertified measures, and other crimes. For Americans accustomed to buying beer by the glass, the seeming fixation on a full measure seems obsessive until you realize how deeply ingrained it is in the English culture.

Full Measure
Drinks in England and the rest of Europe are guaranteed to be a specific quantity, due to centuries of government control of weights and measures.

Toward the Modern Era

The sixteenth and seventeenth centuries saw the development of the roots of modern British beer styles. As is so often the case with a conquering army, the old unhopped ale didn't vanish outright but was transformed, little by little, into a hopped beer. Even a small amount of hops gave the beer a good deal more stability, and when combined with a lot of alcohol, beers could be aged for a year or sometimes much longer.

During this time, country estates became larger and more efficiently run, and since beer was a specified part of wages for employees, a brewery was needed for smooth functioning of the enterprise. Country estate or "house"

breweries typically produced three strengths of beer: "small beer" of around 2 percent alcohol, to which everyone had nearly unlimited access; "table beer," which we would recognize as normal strength at between 5 and 6 percent; and "March" or "October" beers of 8 to 10 percent, named for the months in which they were brewed. It was a point of etiquette that there was no special grade of small beer for the family; everybody drank the same small beer. There were stronger beers as well. A "double beer" of 10 or more percent alcohol was sometimes brewed and laid down to mature for special occasions.

The domestic-scale recipe given by Elizabethan chronicler William Harrison (*The Description of Elizabethan England*, 1577) is a barley-malt beer with 5 or 6 percent each of wheat and oats, showing those grains still in use in mainstream beers of the time. Referred to as "headcorne," they were likely used to enhance the beer's head, a task for which wheat is still employed in English beers. This recipe also makes use of about three-quarters of a pound per barrel of hops, a reasonable quantity by modern standards. Harrison likely got the recipe from his wife — she was the brewer in the family.

By the time industrialization began, the strong amber beers of the countryside had the reputation of being superior to commercially brewed beers. Landowners didn't have the same economic pressure as common brewers and so could use more malt and hops and likely a better grade, too. Also, they were homebrewers and could brew whatever pleased them. They paid less tax than public brewers, which gave them further advantage.

Another important feature of the era was the distinction between "mild" or "running" ales and aged "stale" beers, whose long residence

in wooden barrels or tuns encouraged a long, complex secondary fermentation, picking up fruity and earthy aromas and probably tangy flavors from the microorganisms that lived in the wood. Such beers rightfully deserved the term "old" ales, as the aging really did impart unique flavors to them. This formerly universal practice with strong beers is now a rarity in Britain. Guinness still blended a small portion of this stale, aged beer into every stout it made, until a couple of decades ago.

THE EIGHTEENTH CENTURY was a challenging time for beer in England, despite advancing technology and breathtaking increases in the scale of industrialization. Coffee and tea were replacing small beer for all but the poorest folk, and gin roared into popularity with such force as to upset the social fabric because of high levels of consumption. As with Prohibition in the United States, attempts to restrict alcohol led to rampant bootlegging and all the problems that come with pervasive criminality. Many brewers illegally incorporated medicinal ingredients, which were narcotic or toxic, for added zip: *Cocculus indicus* (a bitter berry from Southeast Asia containing a potent, dangerous stimulant) and bitter bean (a bitter spice from the Philippines containing strychnine). It wasn't until the early nineteenth century that this mess was cleaned up.

Despite, or perhaps because of, this turmoil, brewing became concentrated in the hands of fewer but larger operations, and this consolidation continues to this day. London was at this

---

**Seeth grains in more water, while grains be yet hot,
And stirre them in copper as poredge in pot,
Such heating with straw, to make offal good store,
Both pleseth and easeth, what would you have more?**

— Thomas Tusser, "Pointes of Good Huswiferie," 1557

time the undisputed brewing center of the kingdom. By 1701, London's 194 common brewers made twice as much beer between them (on average, about 5,000 barrels each) as the 574 common brewers elsewhere in the country, but it should be noted that public brewing was at that time concentrated in the south.

In late-seventeenth-century London, a beer called "amber" or "twopenny" was the last remaining vestige of unhopped ale. It did have a modest charge of hops but much less than the new, hoppy chestnut brown ales that would soon be called "porter."

The old books abound with paeans to the fine strong beers of the day, and although the nicknames were numerous, the plainer description tended to be "brown" or "nut-brown" ale. Despite the difficulties of the eighteenth century, this era exemplifies for many the classic period for beer in Jolly Old England. There has been a great deal of nostalgia for that time laced through British beer culture ever since.

> **The stronger beere is divided into two parts (viz.) mild and stale; the first may ease a man of drought, but the latter is like water cast into a Smith's forge, and breeds more heart-burnings, and as rust eates into Iron so overstale Beere gnawes aulet holes in the entrales, or else my skill failes, and what I have written of it is to be held as a Jest.**
>
> — John Taylor, *The Water Poet*, c. 1630

Ready for a Quiet Afternoon

Throughout the transition from an agricultural to an industrial economy, beer was an indispensable part of the good life for workers and gentlemen alike. *Still Life with Clay Pipes* by Pieter Claesz, 1636.

THEN CAME PORTER. Like industrialization, porter's story will be told elsewhere (see page 249), but for now it is enough to say that this was a phenomenon unlike anything the beer world had ever seen. Cheap, potent, flavorful, and largely wholesome, porter suited the mood of the moment and spawned the whole family of black beers — including stout — that lives on to this day.

An Exporting Nation

Exportation has played an important role in Britain's beer since the late fifteenth century. By that time British brewers had learned the art of hopped beer well enough to export it back to Holland, from whence it had originally come. As the empire grew, so did opportunities to sell all kinds of goods — including beer — around the world. And to the benefit of beer, cargo space on outbound ships was pretty much free, as heavy items were needed as ballast to stabilize the ship. So wherever there were Englishmen, there were casks and bottles of mellow old English beer. This was most famously the case in India, where there was a large contingent of soldiers, traders, and administrators. English beer was being shipped to them as early as the 1630s. At first it was just a trickle; then, as demand increased, a flood. Initially strong amber-colored or brownish ales were shipped, but when the porter phenomenon hit big, the stronger versions of it were sent as well.

Hogarth, *Gin Lane* (left), and *Beer Street* (right)
The English social critic's view of the disastrous impact of the unlicensed production and sale of spirits in the eighteenth century. Beer has long been viewed as a beverage of moderation.

East India Company Coat of Arms
This powerful group controlled the India trade
for over two centuries.

T HE MOST FAMOUS PART of the export story starts in the middle of the eighteenth century, with pale ale and eventually India Pale Ale. In the early 1780s, a London brewer named George Hodgson started exporting casks of an amber-colored, highly hopped October beer. This was a strong beer, designed for long keeping, and had been produced for a century or more. It suited the 6-month sea voyage and arrived in superb condition. There is no evidence that a special recipe for the India export market was developed at this time. After 40 years of booming success, his son, now running the brewery, got greedy and lost the good graces of the East India Company, the powerful monopoly that controlled trade in Britain's Asian exploits.

Meanwhile, the brewers up north in Burton-on-Trent had been renowned since the thirteenth century for strong, sweet, and relatively dark ales. Just a little before 1800, a canal project opened up a reliable route to the sea from Burton, and brewers of Burton vastly increased the amount of the Burton ale they were shipping up the Baltic Sea as far as Russia. The Russian connection collapsed because of the imposition of a high tariff in 1822, just as the kerfuffle over Hodgson left the Indian market wide open, and Burton's Allsopp brewery was quick to capitalize on this opportunity.

The paler, hoppy beer Hodgson had been selling was very different from the Burton beers

of the day, which were brownish in color and as little as 50 percent attenuated. Some work was needed to develop a paler, crisper beer that would convincingly replace the London beer. The gypsum-laden water of Burton was actually better suited than London's to a pale, hoppy beer. As the story goes, this beer required a paler malt than the brewery had been making, and the recipe supposedly was tested in a teacup.

Eventually, the beer became known as India Ale or India Pale Ale. These pale ales were highly hopped, following the general rule of increasing hops for "keeping" beers. Bass marketing literature tells a story of barrels of IPA being recovered from a foundered

The English beer is famous in the Netherlands and Lower Germany, which is made of barley and hops, for England yields plenty of hops, howsoever they also use Flemish hops. The cities of Lower Germany upon the seas forbid the public selling of English beer, to satisfy their own brewers, yet privately they swallow it like nectar. But in the Netherlands great and incredible quantity there is spent.
— Fynes Moryson, *Itinerary*, 1617

India-bound ship, the salvaged beer finding wild popularity with the English drinking public. There are many problems with this tale, but this pale, crisp beer was a big hit. Like porter before it, the new beer spread like wildfire and by the middle of the nineteenth century, pale and India Pale Ales had replaced porter as the fashionable beer in England.

BRITISH BEERS of the mid-nineteenth century were pretty strong by later standards. Consulting brewer George Amsinck's very detailed brewing notes give gravities in 1868 that range from 5 percent alcohol by volume for a single stout, mild, or running ale to a massive 13.8 percent London Ale, with many beers in the 5.5 to 7 percent range, far higher than today's English brews. Amsinck was a vocal critic of other British brewers and wrote in *Practical Brewings* (1868) that the brewers

OLD ENGLISH NAMES FOR STRONG BEER

Stingo

Huffcap

Nipitatum

Clamber-skull

Dragon's milk

Mad-dog

Lift-leg

Angel's food

Stride-wide

instituted "a system of low class brewing, shilling Ales and upwards at any price, allowing enormous discounts . . . these expenses must have been, in a vast number of instances, unproductive of any profit."

The Roots of Modern Styles

In 1880, the malt tax was abolished and replaced by a system that taxed beer based on the original gravity of the wort, which roughly corresponds to alcohol content. This graduated system — currently taxing alcohol percentage — stands to this day and had the effect of applying pressure to brew weaker and weaker beer, a trend that accelerated for the next half century.

Pale, bitter, and K-style beers. In late Victorian England, most styles of beer came in a number of different intensities. The strength of both pale and dark beers was indicated by one or more Xs, topping out at "XXXX." The term "bitter" as a beer style designation shows up midcentury as a consumer slang for the new pale ales and IPAs. In the south especially, the "K" designation was used to identify a range of pale, dry, and somewhat less bitter beers than proper pale ale. Like the X beers, these formed a range, starting at about 1.045 OG (11 degrees Plato) for single-K (also known as AK) beers, up to about 1.090 OG (24 degrees Plato) for "KKKK." Over time, the once-separate threads of pale ale, bitter, and K-style beers have become hopelessly entangled from a century and a half of common parlance, regional differences, overeager marketers, and the normal drift of any cultural product.

Dark beers. By late in the nineteenth century, porter was on its last legs. The really dark end of the beer spectrum was now occupied by its descendant, stout, proudly brewed with plenty of black patent malt, with no apologies for abandoning the old ways of brown malt and yearlong fermentations. Edging in to take porter's place was a beer called "mild," although light and dark varieties existed. The term is a very old one, referring to beer sold relatively fresh without long storage in wooden vessels. By the twentieth century, mild was often brewed from malt slightly darker than pale ale malt, with a dash of black malt for color, and thinned out with adjuncts. Londoners enjoyed their mild a ruby brown, but paler versions found favor elsewhere. All were lightly hopped compared to the pale ales of the day. Mild came

in a variety of strengths, but it topped out at about 1.070 OG (17 degrees Plato) in 1871 and dropped dramatically early in the next century.

The rise of low-gravity beers. The Great War was hard on English beer. All the usual shortages, rationing, and pressure for war production meant that beer gravity fell and pub hours shortened, while prices increased, ratcheting ever tighter as the war progressed. Taxes were hiked dramatically in preparation for war. By 1918, the government required that half of all beer be no stronger than 1.030, which meant an alcohol content of less than 3 percent. Breweries, beers, and tax levels never returned to their prewar conditions. On top of it all, beer was starting to be seen as an old-fashioned drink, lacking the modern sparkle of cocktails and the classiness of wine. All this stress just added to the pressures for consolidation, and as a result many breweries closed.

Late in the 1930s, there was an increase in beer consumption, but war was again on the horizon in Europe. The Second World War had similar effects to the first: thinner beer at higher prices, and this time it was personal. German bombs were destroying pubs and breweries. When the war was over, there was an immense amount of recovery to be done,

Pillar Ale Glass
These crystal glasses were popular, as they showed off the luminous optical effects of the new paler style of beer in the mid-nineteenth century.

limiting brewing progress for more than a decade. By 1950, there were one-third fewer breweries in England than there had been in the year 1940.

All of the classic styles were pretty much in place by 1900, and while they have ebbed and flowed for the past century, it's not likely that the twentieth century added much to any of them. Quite the opposite. English beers are weaker, less bitter, more adjunct filled, and less varied than they were in 1900. There's plenty of blame to go around, but these effects are a result of much larger social forces that have played out similarly in many other countries. And you can't argue that drinkers in Britain don't like their beers this way. Light-bodied, lower alcohol beers can be consumed in large amounts, allowing for convivial and even clear-headed drinking sessions, something we in the United States should keep in mind if we can pause our hoppy arms race long enough to think about it.

Real Ale, Rescued

Respect for beer and its long, colorful past had become so compromised that by the 1960s, England's traditional real ale was about to be replaced by inert keg beer delivered by tanker truck and squirted into large serving tanks in pub cellars. Real ale is discussed in detail in chapter 6, but this is living beer, still fermenting when it hits the pub. A small amount of continued fermentation in the cask carbonates the beer before the yeast settles out. Without pasteurization or filtration, real ale is more complex and subtle. Scientifically, the jury seems to be out on the benefits of natural carbonation per se,

Real Ale at the Covent Garden Beer Exhibition, London, 1975
While CAMRA focused solely on preserving English cask ale, it was the first modern consumer group dedicated to the craft of beer.

but because it comes along with a living, natural process, it's a very good thing.

It's easy to see why the forces of modern business are against real ale. It's fusty, complex, and inefficient. Casks are inconsistent and require a subtle skill in handling to get a great beer into the glass. Shelf life is limited, too. After a few days, the beer is too flat and lifeless — perhaps too sour as well — to sell. But it's also easy to see why it is so prized by those who take the time to open themselves to its charms. Subtle and silky, great real ale has a sense of life about it and a depth that makes for pint after fascinating pint. There's nothing else like it on Planet Beer.

An organization called the Campaign for Real Ale (CAMRA) formed in 1972 to lobby actively in support of cask ale tradition. They managed to halt the annihilation of real ale, but it's been a mixed success. Lager is big business in Britain, and still growing. There are plenty of lifeless, gassy keg beers out there these days. Real ale has been saved, but it is now a specialty beer no longer resembling anything mainstream, and perhaps never again will. As long as there is a viable marketplace of people who know the difference and are willing to make the effort to get it, there is money to be made, and real ale will survive. And recently a new generation of brewers is bringing fresh life and creative ideas to Britain's beer, while still honoring its traditions.

The Taste of Ale

All of these styles employ top-fermenting strains of yeast specific to English, Scottish, or Irish ales. Fermented between room and cellar temperatures, they are fruity and spicy compared to lagers. The strains vary widely but tend to be less ebullient than their Belgian cousins. A lot of the magic of British yeast lies in its ability to magnify and augment the flavors of the malt, hops, and other ingredients in the brew. Some accentuate a creamy maltiness, while others emphasize the woodiness of certain malts or the tangy, grassy flavors of hops.

Between about 1700 and 1847, British ale was by law an all-malt product. After that time, the use of sugar or other adjuncts was allowed, and British brewers have been using them ever since. Adjuncts may be good or bad. In small amounts, grains such as wheat or oats add luscious, creamy texture and improve head retention. Sugar or grits of corn or rice thin out the body and make for a lighter, less filling (i.e., more drinkable) beer. This may or may not be a good thing, but because most adjuncts are cheaper than barley malt, there is always the temptation on the part of the guys in finance to add more than the brewmaster thinks is necessary for a great beer. It's certainly something to pay attention to when you taste an English ale.

The malt itself leans toward the crisp and brisk with hints of toast, even in the pale beers. There is often a unique nutty flavor I always compare to walnuts and that is rarely reproduced when English-style beers are brewed elsewhere. The caramel character so often found in German amber and dark lagers is not a big player, either. An exception is the category of strong Scotch ales, in which those lush malt flavors are the star attraction.

All members of the pale ale family prominently feature hops. English hops have a family resemblance in the form of a rich, tangy grassiness. In addition to their own fine varieties, English brewers have long employed imported hops, but not in a way that would overstep the bounds of traditional aroma; in other words, no overtly American hop varieties in the aroma, although that's no longer true for the craft revival under way there. In the past, dark beers such as porter and stout were plenty hoppy, but not so much these days. Of all these dark beers, only Irish stouts retain anything like their original bitterness.

Ale must have these properties: it must be fresshe and cleare, it must not be ropy nor smoky, nor it must have no werte nor tayle.

— Andrew Borde, *A Compendious Regiment or a Dyetary of Helth*, 1542

> I've tasted hock and claret too, Madeira and Moselle,
> But not one of those boshy wines reveal this languid swell;
> Of all complaints from A to Z, the fact is very clear,
> There's no disease but what's been cured by glorious bitter beer.
>
> — MacLaghlan

In the United States, we seldom get English ales served properly. There are rare specialty casks that make it across the ocean, and a few survive the crossing with some life in them. The draft kegs of Bass and other big sellers are generally too gassy and served too cold. If you have control over it, 50 to 55°F (10 to 13°C) is about right. Take a fork and whip the beer in your glass briskly to release some of the gas and you'll at least be a little closer. Your best bet might be to search out an American craft brewery that brews them traditionally and serves on cask.

Pale Ale and Bitter

These constitute a tight-knit family of ales with confusing nomenclature. The "pale ale" name is more typically applied to bottled beer representing the strong end of the range, but there are plenty of draft versions. "Bitter" may encompass all strengths, and while the term usually refers to draft beer, packaged versions exist. The designations "Ordinary," "Best" or "Special," and "Extra Special Bitter" (ESB) are applied to beers of increasing strength, although this is by no means universal, and most breweries offer just two, not three.

This family of top-fermenting beers crystallized into its present form after World War I, and there has only been a little drift since then. In terms of flavor, these beers are built on a base of a lightly kilned malt called "pale ale" that brings a nutty quality and often just a hint of a toasty edge. For the most part, these are adjunct beers, which gives them a crisp, drinkable quality. Flaked barley or wheat are sometimes used to add a little creamy mouthfeel. It's not coincidence that the style name is "bitter." Hops are always a key player, sometimes dramatically so, although each brewery has a house character in this regard. English-style hops are mandatory, at least as far as aroma goes.

English Bitter

ORIGIN: Appeared 1850 as draft pale ale and grew lighter in gravity and body in the early twentieth century. It comes in a range of imprecise substyles, as noted earlier. Adjuncts are typically used to lighten the body and improve drinkability. It is best by far when served on cask as real ale. Despite their low gravity and adjunct recipes, the best of these beers can be seductively complex and appealing.

LOCATION: Britain, especially England; credible traditional versions also made by a few U.S. and Canadian craft brewers

AROMA: Hops first, plus nutty/woody malt; spice and fruit also evident

FLAVOR: Fresh hops plus nutty maltiness, crisp finish

BALANCE: Hop or malt balanced, bitter finish

SEASONALITY: Year-round

PAIR WITH: Wide range of food; roast chicken or pork; classic with curry

SUGGESTED BEERS TO TRY: This style really is a different beer served as a real ale. See if you can locate one at a specialty bar or local brewpub, and of course the English beers taste far better in their homeland. Anchor Small Beer, Coniston Bluebird Bitter, Fuller's Chiswick Bitter, Harviestoun Bitter & Twisted.

GRAVITY: Ordinary: 1.030–1.039 (7.6–9.8°P); Best/Special: 1.040–1.048 (10–11.9°P); Strong Bitter: 1.048–1.060 (11.9–14.7°P)
ALCOHOL: Ordinary: 2.4–3%; Best/Special: 3.8–4.6%; Strong Bitter: 4.6–6.2%
ATTENUATION/BODY: Very dry to medium
COLOR: 8–18 SRM, light-dark amber
BITTERNESS: 25–50 IBU, medium to high

Classic English Pale Ale

As noted, it's just about impossible to completely differentiate pale ale from the bitter family, and pale ale is pretty much synonymous with the top end of the bitter range. American brewers love this style and reinvented it as their own. Some American craft-brew examples could pass for English, but for the most part, American versions are stronger and almost always all malt, but the real difference hinges

on the hops. Proper English pale ales always display English hop character.

ORIGIN: Descended from amber-colored "October" beers brewed in English country estates, it was adopted in London well before 1800. A little later this style became strongly associated with the northern city Burton-on-Trent, and eventually all of England, being more or less the national beer. It experienced tremendous downward changes in gravities between 1870 and 1920.

LOCATION: England; credible versions made in the United States and elsewhere

AROMA: Clean malt plus a good dose of grassy/herbal English hops

FLAVOR: Crisp (it's the water), nutty malt, spicy hops

BALANCE: Even or dry/bitter; clean finish

SEASONALITY: Year-round

PAIR WITH: Wide range of food; meat pies, English cheese

SUGGESTED BEERS TO TRY: As with the bitter range, try to find this on cask, or properly bottle-conditioned. Firestone Walker Double Barrel Ale, Odell 5-Barrel Pale Ale

SPECIFICATIONS: See Strong Bitter specifications under English Bitter, beginning on page 239.

English India Pale Ale

While this style has become its own unique thing recently in the United States, historically it is very much a part of the broader pale ale family, overlapping considerably. However, in any brewer's portfolio, the IPA will be a little paler, stronger, and more bitter than their pale ale, which is in keeping with the history of the style. They can be tricky to recognize; one brewer's pale is another's IPA. As with pale ale, Americans brew lustier versions that call on the piney, grapefruit, and tropical fruit aromas of American and international hop varieties.

ORIGIN: True India Pale Ale evolved from October ales shipped to India, most famously by a London brewer, George Hodgson, around 1780. By 1830, Hodgson was out on his ear and Burton-on-Trent brewers had reinvented their beer into a crisper, drier version that became the standard for the style.

LOCATION: England; U.S. craft breweries

AROMA: Spicy English hops in the foreground, plus a nice backup of nutty malt

FLAVOR: Plenty of malt, but dominated by hops; should be some sense of balance even in the bitterest examples

BALANCE: Always hoppy but to varying degrees

SEASONALITY: Year-round

PAIR WITH: Strong, spicy food; bold, sweet desserts, such as carrot cake

SUGGESTED BEERS TO TRY: Brooklyn East India Pale Ale, Burton Bridge Empire IPA, Goose Island India Pale Ale, Meantime India Pale Ale, Summit India Pale Ale, Yards India Pale Ale

GRAVITY: 1.050–1.070 (12–17°P)
ALCOHOL: 5.0–7.5% by volume
ATTENUATION/BODY: Crisp, dry, but may have hints of malty richness
COLOR: 6–14 SRM, gold to amber
BITTERNESS: 40–60 IBU, high

Historical Style

Burton Ale

This darker cousin to IPA was what the Burton brewers were cooking up before the huge opportunity of India Pale Ale appeared. This rich, deep-amber, even brown-colored beer has plenty of residual sweetness and high original gravity. They were eagerly consumed all the way up the Baltic to Russia, which was Burton's original export market. Although this style is largely under the radar, a few versions are brewed commercially, and it deserves to be

better known. It appears that this beer was enjoyed in Scotland and may have actually morphed into Scotch ale when it was brewed there; a bit of a fad for it developed in the 1920s. Confusingly, "Burton Ale" was a trade term later applied to pale or India Pale Ales.

SUGGESTED BEERS TO TRY: Ballantine Burton Ale, Dogfish Head Burton Baton, August Schell's Burton Ale

English Golden Bitter or Summer Ale

It's great to see some new ideas coming out of British brewers after a long, dry century.

ORIGIN: A recent development from smaller UK breweries, this style is basically a lightened-up IPA designed to help fight the tide of lagers in the form of a crisp and quenching beer. Hopping, while generally light, tends to be a little less conventional than with bitter.

LOCATION: England; also U.S. craft breweries

AROMA: Clean malt plus light but characterful hop bouquet

FLAVOR: Bright, clean pale malt; firm hoppy finish

BALANCE: Even to reasonably hoppy

SEASONALITY: Summer

PAIR WITH: A wide range of food; chicken, seafood, spicy cuisine

SUGGESTED BEERS TO TRY: Hopback Summer Lightning, Wychwood Scarecrow Golden Pale Ale, Tomos Watkin's *Cwrw Hâf* ("Summer Ale" in Welsh)

GRAVITY: 1.038–1.053 (9.5–13.1°P)
ALCOHOL: 3.6–5% by volume
ATTENUATION/BODY: Dry, crisp
COLOR: 2–6 SRM, pale gold-amber
BITTERNESS: 20–45 IBU, medium

English Wheat Ale

This style pretty much tracks the history and specifications of golden bitter, although it is brewed with wheat and may have a somewhat lower hop profile.

Irish Ale

Ireland is most famous for stout, and that will be covered a little later with the rest of the stouts and porters. For a couple of centuries, stout was pretty much *the* beer of Ireland. Changing tastes, however, call for changing beers, so long-forgotten Irish red ale was born.

Irish Red Ale

In the Middle Ages, the Irish were famous for their red ale. Save for its color, little is known about it, but it likely followed the pattern of other medieval beers. Modern Irish red is quite a recent phenomenon that didn't exist much before the end of the twentieth century. It's probably a more important style in the United States than it is in Ireland itself, filling a need by Irish bars to have an amber beer to serve that is brewed in Ireland rather than England.

ORIGIN: While the term is ancient, there is no connection between modern Irish reds and medieval ones. The style was first promoted heavily by Coors, whose Killian's Irish Red was an early success for the mass-market brewer attempting to crack the craft sector.

LOCATION: U.S. craft breweries and sometimes even in Ireland

AROMA: Light sweet toffee, toasty notes; little in the way of hops

FLAVOR: Toffee and a little soft toast, dryish finish

BALANCE: A delicate beer, intermediate between classic Scottish ale and English bitter

SEASONALITY: Year-round

PAIR WITH: A wide range of food; salmon, roast pork, washed-rind cheese

SUGGESTED BEERS TO TRY: Caffrey's Irish Ale, Great Lakes Conway's Irish Ale, Harpoon Celtic Ale, O'Hara's Irish Red, Smithwick's Ale

GRAVITY: 1.036–1.046 (9–11.5°P)
ALCOHOL: 3.8–5.0% by volume
ATTENUATION/BODY: Dry, crisp
COLOR: 9–14 SRM, reddish amber to ruby
BITTERNESS: 20–28 IBU, medium

Scottish Ales

The beers of Scotland are closely related to their English cousins. Although there are some differences, they all come from the same broad tradition, and as industrialization progressed, the beers became even more similar.

Our standard picture of Scottish ale is of sweetish, lightly hopped, ruby-colored brews, and there are certainly examples that support this. But if you're over there looking for a classic dark, malty Scottish ale, you may have some difficulty laying your hands on one. Edinburgh has been famous for more than a century for its dry, minerally pale ales, built on water similar to Burton's. Scottish beers of today show a lot of variety, and don't differ in their essence from English ales.

Because the climate is cooler up north, Scottish beers are usually fermented at cooler temperatures than English ones. This means Scottish ales display less of the fruit and spice of English ales, which pushes the malt character more into the foreground. Hops were grown in Scotland, but it really is pretty far north for them, and there is currently no commercial production there. Whether it's a matter of the Scots not wanting to give the English their money or some less charming reason, some Scottish ales are lightly hopped, but at the same time, bitter beers also coexist.

As we're still in the British Isles, the nomenclature is going to be confusing. Scottish beer comes in several strengths historically designated in shillings (and sometimes written as 60/–, 70/–, and 80/–), which at some vague point in history was the actual price of a barrel of the stuff. This terminology has fallen into disuse, but the three price ranges correspond to the terms light, heavy, and export and correspond to the three strength levels of English bitter. At higher alcohol levels is a beer simply called Scotch ale, but this is also known as a "Wee Heavy," or by its shilling designation, 120/– ale. Sheesh.

Medieval Scottish ales must have reeked of smoke from the peat used as fuel to dry the malt. According to the old brewing books, brewers around 1700 clearly enjoyed the clean flavors of malt dried in the newer coal- or coke-fired indirect kilns. They viewed smoke-free beer as real progress, and it stayed that way for close to 300 years. But recently, as craft-oriented American brewers started reevaluating their roots, it seemed completely logical to reintroduce small amounts of peated malt back into Scottish beer, and they did just that. It should be noted that some of the water available to breweries runs through peat and picks up a certain phenolic tinge that may find its way into the beers.

Scottish Light Ale (60/–)

ORIGIN: Low end of Scottish draft beer range, similar history to English bitter

LOCATION: Scotland

AROMA: Clean maltiness, no evident hop aroma; hints of peat okay

FLAVOR: Dry maltiness, with hints of caramel and toast

BALANCE: Fat and malty, may be a little toasty

SEASONALITY: Year-round

PAIR WITH: Lighter food; simple cheeses, lighter preparations of salmon and chicken

NOTE: Generally unavailable in the United States. Check your local brewpub.

GRAVITY: 1.030–1.035 (7.6–8.8°P)
ALCOHOL: 2.5–3.2% by volume
ATTENUATION/BODY: Light and dry
COLOR: 17–22 SRM, amber to ruby brown
BITTERNESS: 10–20 IBU, low

Scottish Heavy (70/–)

ORIGIN: Middle of range of Scottish draft beers, similar history to English bitter

LOCATION: Scotland

AROMA: Clean maltiness, no evident hop aroma; hints of peat okay

FLAVOR: Soft maltiness, with hints of caramel and toast

BALANCE: Creamy maltiness balanced by barest hints of hops and a slight roastiness

SEASONALITY: Year-round

PAIR WITH: Lighter food; simple cheeses, lighter preparations of salmon and chicken

SUGGESTED BEERS TO TRY: Caledonian Amber Ale; other examples are rarely available in the United States. Check your local brewpub.

GRAVITY: 1.035–1.040 (8.8–10°P)

ALCOHOL: 3.2–3.9% by volume

ATTENUATION/BODY: Medium to very light

COLOR: 17–22 SRM, amber to brown

BITTERNESS: 10–20 IBU, low

Scottish Export
(80/–)

ORIGIN: Top of range of Scottish draft beers; similar history to English pale ale and bitter

LOCATION: Scotland

AROMA: Complex malt; nuances of cocoa; not a lot of evidence of hops

FLAVOR: Rich toffee/toasty malt flavors despite relatively light body; yeast character subdued; hints of peat rare but okay

BALANCE: Definitely malty but balanced by toasty elements and a kiss of hops

SEASONALITY: Year-round

PAIR WITH: Lighter food; moderately intense cheeses, lighter preparations of salmon and pork

SUGGESTED BEERS TO TRY: Belhaven Scottish Ale, McEwan's Export, Odell's 90 Shilling Ale, Three Floyds Robert the Bruce (pushing the strong end of the style)

GRAVITY: 1.040–1.052 (10.0–12.9°P)

ALCOHOL: 3.9–6.0% by volume

ATTENUATION/BODY: Moderately light to slightly full

COLOR: 13–22 SRM, amber to brown

BITTERNESS: 15–30 IBU, low

Scotch Ale/ Wee Heavy
(120/–)

ORIGIN: Evolved slowly as top of range of Scottish ale family, quite likely inspired by Burton Ale; a darkish barley wine, really

LOCATION: Scotland, U.S. craft breweries

AROMA: Huge complex malt, a mix of toffee and soft roastiness; little else, but sometimes a hint of peat

FLAVOR: Rich, toffeelike malt flavors go on and on; yeast character subdued; aged versions a little portlike

BALANCE: Fat and malty, may be a little toasty

SEASONALITY: Year-round

PAIR WITH: Sticky pudding and other substantial desserts

SUGGESTED BEERS TO TRY: AleSmith Wee Heavy, Brasserie de Silly Scotch Silly, Founders Dirty Bastard, Oskar Blues Old Chub, Thirsty Dog Wulver, Traquair House Ale

GRAVITY: 1.070–1.130 (17.1–30.1°P)

ALCOHOL: 6.5–10.0% by volume

ATTENUATION/BODY: Full and sweet

COLOR: 14–25 SRM, amber to ruby brown

BITTERNESS: 17–35 IBU, low

English Brown Ale

The beginnings of brown ale are lost in the mists of time. People have been brewing brown beers since the earliest days, but we pick up the story in about 1700, when the descendant of the old unhopped English ale, the amber or twopenny beer, was kicking around London. At the time there were other, more bitter brown beers on the scene, and these became porter. Despite the huge success of porter, lightly hopped dark beers managed to survive alongside their more popular cousins for quite some time. The terms "brown" and "nut brown" had been loosely applied to beer for centuries, but it appears that the word didn't become anything like a style description or a trade term until the end of the nineteenth century, and there's no evidence it has any connection to the twopenny of the earlier era.

Brown ale has never been the most popular beer, but there always seem to be customers for a beer that is a little toastier and less hoppy than pale ale. The style is split between the north and south of England. Northern browns are paler and a bit stronger than southern ones, and there is subtle variation from place to place. While some make a case for a southern form of brown ale, at this point it is pretty much indistinguishable from mild ale, and competitions such as the World Beer Cup consider them one and the same.

English Brown Ale

LOCATION: Northern England, especially Yorkshire and some U.S. craft breweries

AROMA: Complex and malty, may be hints of roast, no hop aroma

FLAVOR: Toasty, nutty, with some caramelly malt; light hopping

BALANCE: Delicate, crisp to very slightly sweet; clean finish

SEASONALITY: Year-round

PAIR WITH: Roasted meats and a wide range of hearty foods

SUGGESTED BEER TO TRY: Samuel Smith's Nut Brown Ale

GRAVITY: 1.040–1.052 (10.0–12.9°P)
ALCOHOL: 4.2–5.4% by volume
ATTENUATION/BODY: Dry to slightly sweet
COLOR: 12–22 SRM, medium to deep amber
BITTERNESS: 20–30 IBU, low to medium

Let misers turn their riches o'er,
And gaze on bags of gold;
With my wealth they must be poor
When all their treasure's told;
But I have more
True wealth in store,
And joys that never fail
Whilst friendship's shrine
My cot is mine,
And a glass of rich brown ale.
— John Hammond,
"A Glass of Rich Brown Ale"

Dark Mild Ale

The original meaning of this name designated a beer that was sold relatively fresh and hadn't undergone long wood aging (see English Old/Strong Ale, below). By 1880 or so, the everyday ales of London were starting to resemble modern English beers. Until about 1910, "mild" simply referred to any fresh, unaged beer and not to any particular color, strength, or style, and while they tended to be weaker than the aged beers, there was still a range of strengths. By the time World War I was over, *mild* certainly referred to a low-gravity session beer. Mild was immensely popular in the middle of the twentieth century; by 1960 it represented 61 percent of the English beer market. Although there are rare examples of pale mild, the most enduring form of mild is a dark, ruby-colored beer, and today a range of strengths is again available. By 1980, mild was just 14 percent of the English market.

LOCATION: Northern England, especially around Birmingham, and some U.S. craft breweries, whose interpretations generally tend to be bolder

AROMA: Complex and lightly roasty/malty, may be hints of roast, no hop aroma

FLAVOR: Slightly roasty with some caramelly malt; light hopping

BALANCE: Malty but with hints of roast and a crisp finish

SEASONALITY: Year-round

PAIR WITH: Roasted meats and a wide range of hearty foods

SUGGESTED BEERS TO TRY: Broughton Black Douglas, Moorhouse's Black Cat, Orkney Brewery Dark Island, Surly Mild, Wychwood

Hobgoblin Dark English Ale, Yards Brawler Pugilist Style Ale

GRAVITY: 1.030–1.038 (7.6–9.5°P), although considerably stronger versions exist
ALCOHOL: 3.0–3.8% by volume
ATTENUATION/BODY: Dry to slightly sweet in stronger versions
COLOR: 12–25 SRM, medium to deep amber
BITTERNESS: 10–25 IBU, low to medium

English Old/ Strong Ale/ Winter Warmer

This really encompasses two related styles. The "old" properly refers to a beer that has been aged in wooden vessels for a year or so, during which time it picks up a subtle acidity and a rich set of aromatics. Beers treated in this manner were called "stale" and were often blended with fresher beers when sold. There are few beers made this way in England these days, but this approach lives on in Flanders (see chapter 12).

Strong ale is just a catchall for anything strong in any shade of amber or brown. Other aspects of the beer, such as hopping, may vary widely, and many breweries' products along these lines don't bear the "strong" or "old" descriptor. The term is problematic in the United States, as federal rules prohibit brewers from making claims of strength (other than listing alcohol content).

Winter warmer is brewed in England as a winter beer and is usually dark, toasty, and sometimes modestly hoppy as well. Because the United States and England have widely differing views of what constitutes a strong beer, these may be as low as 5 percent alcohol in the UK. This is another prohibited term for labeling in the United States; the regulators consider "warmer" to indicate therapeutic properties.

ORIGIN: Ancient holdover from the days when all strong beers were aged in wood for up to a year

LOCATION: England, U.S. craft breweries

AROMA: Fruity, raisiny malt and possibly some toasty/roasty elements; may have some wild yeast character

FLAVOR: Fat and fruity caramel, a touch of hops; properly "stale" versions have a definite touch of acidity

BALANCE: Usually on the sweet side but may be evenly balanced

SEASONALITY: Year-round but really great in cold weather

PAIR WITH: Big, intense dishes such as roast beef and lamb; stands up to rich desserts

SUGGESTED BEERS TO TRY: Anderson Valley Winter Solstice Seasonal Ale, Deschutes Jubelale, North Coast Old Stock Ale, Fuller's Vintage Ale

GRAVITY: 1.055–1.088 (15–22°P)
ALCOHOL: 5.5–9.0% by volume
ATTENUATION/BODY: Medium to full in strong ales; old ales much more attenuated
COLOR: 10–25 SRM, amber to brown
BITTERNESS: 17–60 plus IBU, medium to high

English Barley Wine/Barleywine

ORIGIN: Another old one, it is descended from strong "October" ales brewed on country estates. The term was first used in 1903 by Bass for its No. 1 strong ale. There is a good deal of variety within the category. Of the handful of very strong English beers brewed, few are actually labeled with the term "barley wine."

LOCATION: England, U.S. craft breweries

AROMA: Rich, fruity malt and spicy hops

FLAVOR: Loads of complex malt backed up by hops

BALANCE: Malty or hoppy

SEASONALITY: Year-round; best in winter

PAIR WITH: Very intense food but better with dessert; try with Stilton cheese

SUGGESTED BEERS TO TRY: Anchor Old Foghorn, The Bruery Mash, J. W. Lees Harvest Ale, Midnight Sun Arctic Devil Barley Wine, Revolution Brewing Company Straight Jacket, Ridgeway Criminally Bad Elf

GRAVITY: 1.080–1.120 (19.3–28°P)
ALCOHOL: 8.0–12% by volume
ATTENUATION/BODY: Medium to full
COLOR: 8–22 SRM, amber to brown
BITTERNESS: 35–70 IBU, medium to high

Porter

Think you know what a porter is? Me neither.

Studying the history of porter is like staring into the multidimensional universe of theoretical cosmology, with multiple shifting parallel worlds constantly warping and shifting with the flow of time. The more you try to pin it

> **But all nations know that London is the place where porter was invented; and Jews, Turks, Germans, Negroes, Persians, Chinese, New Zealanders, Esquimaux, Copper Indians, Yankees and Spanish Americans are united in one feeling of respect for the native city of the most universally favourite liquor the world has ever known.**
>
> — Charles Knight, London, 1843

down, the more it wriggles free and becomes something unexpectedly different. Naturally, this can be a lot of fun.

Far from being invented (despite the tales about Ralph Harwood and the Bell Brewery in Shoreditch), porter emerged over a generation or more, transforming itself from an assemblage of brown ales into a pedigreed family of chestnut-colored brews that eventually came to be named for the transport workers who were its most visible enthusiasts. There never was a single thing called "porter." By the time the name came to be applied to it, there were many variations in both name and interpretation.

Porter has changed every generation during its nearly 3-century history. At first it was brewed mostly from a fairly heavily kilned (but not roasted) "brown" malt, adding a rich toastiness and full body. When brewers working with a hydrometer discovered how inefficient this was, they switched over to the more extract-rich pale malt after about 1790. This left them with the problem of how to achieve the former dark brown color. Various preparations of burnt sugar, though largely illegal, were employed, and this dramatically changed the taste of the beer.

Brewer and author William Tizard, in 1843, stated: "Scarcely does this our beer-sipping country contain any two brewers, particularly neighbors, whose productions are alike in flavor and quality, and especially in the article porter; even in London, a practiced connoisseur can truly discover, without hesitation and by mere taste, the characteristic flavor that distinguishes the management of each of the principal or neighbouring breweries. . . ."

In 1817 Daniel Wheeler's malt roaster allowed malt to be roasted to a deep black color, and this solved the coloring problem but changed porter once again. Throughout the nineteenth century, stout endured while porter languished as the gravity, bitterness, and color — and probably flavor, too — were largely stripped out of it. By World War I it was barely breathing in its homeland.

The World Beer Cup guidelines divide the universe of porter into "brown" and "robust." This distinction is a little arbitrary and was created at a time when porter hadn't been brewed in the British Isles for over twenty years. Charlie Papazian, founder of the American Homebrewers Association and Great American Beer Festival (among other things), admitted to me that he and famed beer writer Michael Jackson had felt there needed to be two kinds in the competitions, and so they cooked this up without much basis in historical reality. The 2015 BJCP guidelines lists these two subcategories as "English" and "American" versions, the latter being the more robust, which at least reflects current reality to some degree. As always, porter is a puzzle.

In reality, porters represent a fairly wide range of dark brown beers without any well-defined substyles. Some even encroach on stout territory. My personal take is that porter should have a sort of soft mocha or milk chocolate roastiness rather than a full-on espresso of a stout, and I think the history bears that out. Beyond that, almost anything goes.

ORIGIN: London, about 1700. Porter is considered the first industrialized beer; stronger versions are called "stout."

LOCATION: England, U.S. craft breweries

AROMA: Roasty maltiness; usually little or no hop aroma

FLAVOR: Creamy roasty-toasty malt, hoppy or not

BALANCE: Malt, hops, roast in various proportions

SEASONALITY: Year-round, great in cooler weather

PAIR WITH: Roasted and smoked food; barbecue, sausages, chocolate chip cookies

SUGGESTED BEERS TO TRY: Boulevard Bully! Porter, Fuller's London Porter, Great Lakes Edmund Fitzgerald Porter, Harviestoun Old Engine Oil, Meantime London Porter, Samuel Smith's Taddy Porter

GRAVITY: 1.040–1.052 (10–12.9°P)
ALCOHOL: 4.0–5.4% by volume
ATTENUATION/BODY: Medium
COLOR: 18–35 SRM, brown to near-black
BITTERNESS: 20–40 plus IBU, low to medium-high

Baltic Porter

ORIGIN: This type of porter is based on beers exported from England to Russia in the eighteenth century. In many ways, Baltic porter is the true inheritor of the porter mantle, as these have been continuously brewed for probably close to 2 centuries without interruption. Modern versions are lagers, rather than ales, but because they share history with the English versions, they are included here, and despite their lager fermentation, they're softly roasty, like a milky coffee; no one would mistake them for a stout.

LOCATION: Baltic region, including Poland, Lithuania, and Sweden; also U.S. craft breweries

AROMA: Soft, roasty maltiness; usually no hop aroma

FLAVOR: Creamy roasty-toasty malt, lightly hopped, fairly sweet on finish

BALANCE: Malt, hops, roast in various proportions

SEASONALITY: Year-round; great in cooler weather

PAIR WITH: Roasted and smoked food; barbecue, prime rib, chocolate cake

SUGGESTED BEERS TO TRY: Baltika #6 Porter, Carnegie Porter, Duck-Rabbit Baltic Porter, Jack's Abby Framinghammer, Okocim Porter, Smuttynose Baltic Porter

GRAVITY: 1.060–1.090 (14.7–21.6°P)
ALCOHOL: 6.5–9.5% by volume
ATTENUATION/BODY: Medium to full
COLOR: 17–30 SRM, brown to deep chestnut
BITTERNESS: 20–40 IBU, low to medium

Stout

The word "stout," meaning a strong black beer, goes back at least to 1630. The term was applied to the "stout butt beers" that would eventually go on to be named "porter." So all the history that applies to porter is also part of the stout story. Stout forms a widespread and varied family of beers whose members all share a deep, dark, roasty character.

ORIGIN: Stout is the son of porter and largely outstripped it, and it has various substyles from dry to sweet, weak to strong.

LOCATION: England, Ireland, United States, Caribbean, Africa — the world

AROMA: Roasty malt; with or without hop aroma

FLAVOR: Always roasty; may have caramel and hops, too

BALANCE: Very dry to very sweet

SEASONALITY: Year-round

PAIR WITH: Hearty, rich food; steak, meat pies; classic with oysters; stronger versions with chocolate

Irish Dry Stout

The Irish got into the brewing business in a big way around the same time as porter was being industrialized in England in the late eighteenth century. But because Ireland is a separate island, its beers evolved in a somewhat different direction. Exemplified by Guinness, which outcompeted all its rivals, Irish stout is characterized by the use of roasted barley rather than black roasted malt. This gives the beer a unique, sharp, coffeelike roastiness. Raw, unmalted barley is also used in the modern recipe, giving the beer a rich, creamy texture even in low-gravity incarnations.

ORIGIN: An Irish take on the stouts that originated in London

LOCATION: Ireland, plus craft brewers wherever they are found

AROMA: Sharp and coffeelike owing to the characteristic roast barley (as opposed to black malt); little or no hop aroma

FLAVOR: Sharply roasty and fairly bitter for its gravity. A hint of acidity and some creaminess from the use of flaked, unmalted barley

BALANCE: Very dry, crisp

SEASONALITY: Year-round

SUGGESTED BEERS TO TRY: Beamish Irish Stout, Guinness Draft, Murphy's Irish Stout, North Coast Old No. 38 Stout, O'Hara's Irish Stout

GRAVITY: 1.036–1.044 (9.0–11°P)
ALCOHOL: 4.0–4.5% by volume

ATTENUATION/BODY: Dry
COLOR: 25–40 SRM, black
BITTERNESS: 25–45 IBU, medium to high

Sweet (London) Stout/Milk Stout

Stout devolved to a rather feeble, soft, sweet, and roasty style in its birthplace. By the beginning of the twentieth century, it was positioned as a drink for invalids and was often sweetened with the addition of the unfermentable milk sugar lactose. Surprisingly, milk stouts are

experiencing a small wave of popularity in the United States, often served on nitro for a smooth, creamy texture.

SUGGESTED BEERS TO TRY: Left Hand Milk Stout (try it on nitro!), Mackeson XXX Stout, Samuel Adams Cream Stout, Three Floyds Moloko, Young's Double Chocolate Stout (contains no chocolate)

GRAVITY: 1.044-1.060 (11-14.7°P)
ALCOHOL: 4.0-6.0% by volume
ATTENUATION/BODY: Sweet, full
COLOR: 30-40 SRM, black
BITTERNESS: 20-40 IBU, low

Oatmeal Stout

The addition of raw or malted oats to stout seems to be a twentieth-century development. The oats add a very soft, rich creaminess and a hint of cookielike nuttiness.

SUGGESTED BEERS TO TRY: Anderson Valley Barney Flats Oatmeal Stout, Firestone Walker Velvet Merlin, McAuslan St-Ambroise Oatmeal Stout, New Holland The Poet Oatmeal Stout, Rogue Ale Shakespeare Oatmeal Stout

GRAVITY: 1.045-1.065 (11.2-15.9°P)
ALCOHOL: 4.2-5.9% by volume
ATTENUATION/BODY: Medium, rich, oaty
COLOR: 22-40 SRM, brown-black
BITTERNESS: 25-40 IBU, low to medium

Irish Extra and Foreign Extra Stout

These were the strong stouts sold at home as a luxury product but also exported to the ends of the British Empire. The style found its most ardent supporters in the tropics, and strong stouts are brewed everywhere from Jamaica to Nigeria to Singapore.

SUGGESTED BEERS TO TRY: D&G Dragon Stout, Bell's Special Double Cream Stout, Guinness Foreign Extra Stout, Lion Stout (Ceylon!), Pike Brewery XXXXX Stout, Schlafly Irish-Style Extra Stout

GRAVITY: 1.052-1.062 (12.8-15.3°P)/1.056-1.076 (13.8-18.5°P)
ALCOHOL: 5.5-6.5%/6.3-8.0% by volume
ATTENUATION/BODY: Medium to full
COLOR: 30-40 SRM, deep black
BITTERNESS: 35-50/50-70 IBU, medium to high

Imperial Stout

Stronger still, the "imperial" designation derives from this style's popularity with the Russian monarchy through most of the eighteenth century.

SUGGESTED BEERS TO TRY: Courage Imperial Russian Stout, Great Divide Yeti Imperial Stout, Harvey's Imperial Extra Double Stout, North Coast Old Rasputin Russian Imperial Stout, Stone Imperial Russian Stout, Three Floyds Dark Lord

GRAVITY: 1.075-1.115 plus (18.2-27°P)
ALCOHOL: 8.0-12.0% by volume
ATTENUATION/BODY: Medium to full
COLOR: 35 plus SRM, black
BITTERNESS: 50-90 IBU, high

CHAPTER 10

THE LAGER FAMILY

The history of lager is the tale of the beers that dominate the world, at least from a quantity point of view. When well brewed, lagers can be among the beer world's true delights. The lager family encompasses a variety of different styles — from ghost pale to deep chestnut, from weak to muscular — that all share the common characteristic of being fermented cool and stored, or "lagered," at cold temperatures for an extended period of time.

The locus of lager's origin is Bavaria and nearby regions. Lager stayed there until the middle to late nineteenth century, when an incredible fashion for it developed, and it spread to the rest of the world.

FOR SUCH A SUCCESSFUL FAMILY of beer, it's a little shocking how poorly its origins are documented. Like most beer styles, there is an oft-repeated, somewhat unsatisfying genesis tale: The story goes that brewers in Bavaria were fermenting beer either in natural caves or from cellars dug into the limestone hillsides. As time went on, their yeast became adapted to the cold, turning into a truly new strain sometime during the sixteenth century, give or take a century.

Northern German Roots

We do know that earlier, much of the brewing action was in the far north of Germany, in Bremen, Hamburg, and other cities of the Hansa trading league. Bavaria was then a rustic backwater, an image that is still cheerfully cultivated today, despite the fact that the area is home to BMW and other highly sophisticated enterprises.

Hansa towns were among the first in the world to produce hopped beer, which was shipped widely around the North Sea and Baltic regions. In those days, there were two distinct families of beer: red and white. They were so distinct that each had its own brewer's guild. White beers were hopped, while red beers were still brewed using the old gruit seasoning mix. Gruit was a mixture that included bog myrtle (*Myrica gale*), possibly yarrow, and sometimes wild rosemary, plus a host of unidentified spices pulled from the culinary kit of the day. Sold at a high price by the church or designated holder of the *Gruitrecht* (Gruit Right), gruit constituted an early form of beer tax.

By the late medieval era, Nuremberg, in northern Bavaria, was becoming known as a hop-trading center (500 years later it is still the center of the world hop trade). In southern Bavaria, unhopped red beers still dominated. Keep in mind that there was no German nation as we know it today. Instead, it was a collection of small principalities, each with its own laws, customs, weights, measures, and barrel sizes.

EINBECK WAS A TOWN famous for its beer as early as the thirteenth and fourteenth centuries. Einbeck was outside church control, which meant its brewers were not under obligation to use gruit. As a hop-trading center, it specialized in hopped beer, and large quantities of it were shipped to Bavaria, where it was all the rage. This new Einbecker beer was an inspiration to Bavarian brewers. Throughout history we see local brewers copying the imports over and over, especially with the adoption of hops. The brewing season in Einbeck was between the end of September and the beginning of May, which meant the beer was generally fermented at fairly cool temperatures; this may have contributed to the development of cold-adapted yeast, although this seasonal pattern of brewing was true for most of Europe as well.

The annals of the Munich town council in 1420 include a mention that can be interpreted as referring to lager beer. A Munich ordinance of 1487 (the forerunner of the *Reinheitsgebot*) limited brewers to hops, malt, and water — a sure sign that the old, unhopped gruit beers were gone for good. An edict in 1553 restricted brewing to between September 29 and April 23, and in 1612 Bavaria's Duke Maximilian I hired a northern brewmaster named Hans Pichler to bring the secrets of Einbeck brewing success south to Bavaria. The resulting cold-weather beers were known as *Braunbiers* (brown beers), and Munich has been famous for them ever since.

As elsewhere, brewing in Germany remained at a modest "craft" scale of production until the effects of the Industrial Revolution were felt there. An important force in the modernization of brewing in Bavaria was Gabriel Sedlmayr II and, in Austria-Hungary, Anton Dreher Sr. These two were the wunderkinder of Germanic brewing. Sedlmayr's family was in the brewing business already (Spaten), as was Dreher's (in Schwechat, near Vienna). They were fast friends, having been sent off to England in 1833 when they were just 22 to see what they could find out from the rapidly industrializing British breweries. They engaged in some industrial espionage, going so far as to make a hollow walking stick with a valve on the bottom that they could surreptitiously fill with fermenting beer when no one was looking, then take it back to their hotel to analyze. It must have been great fun, and they learned enough to come back and create empires of brewing whose legacies remain in Europe today.

It took several hundred years, but Bavarian-style lager eventually displaced most of the top-fermenting beers produced elsewhere in Germany and nearby countries. The final stroke was the incorporation of Bavaria into the German union in 1871, and the subsequent adoption of the *Reinheitsgebot* in 1906. By then there were a number of well-developed regional styles of lager that formed the basis for all of the present classic styles of lager. Pale types dominate the market, but there are many other fascinating and delicious lagers.

ALE OR LAGER?

A line is invariably drawn through the entire world of beer, slicing it into ale and lager kingdoms. Historically, culturally, and in terms of specific beer styles, this may be indisputable, but does it make as much sense from a flavor perspective? The difference hinges on fermentation, and for lager, a particular strain of yeast adapted to cool temperatures. This suppresses a lot of biochemical yeast activity, reducing fermentation-derived flavors: fruitiness and spiciness. As a result, lagers tend to showcase their raw materials rather than the exotic bouquet of yeast.

The difference between ales and lagers can be dramatic, especially comparing yeast-forward beers such as hefeweizen with the phenolic-to-ester spectrum of Belgian ale, but there is a huge gray area. Styles such as Altbier and Kölsch are top-fermented, but they are also lagered at fairly low temperatures. You can make a passable Pilsner with English yeast at the bottom end of its temperature range, and most people, unless highly trained, will never notice the hint of fruitiness. Most American mass-market beers proclaim their lager status but are in fact lagered far warmer (45 to 50°F [7 to 10°C], compared to just above freezing) and for much shorter durations than a classic historical lager. Budweiser, in fact, is famous for an apple character that may be part ester and part aldehyde, and Coors has a perceptable banana note. These fruity notes would probably be much less prominent if the beer were lagered at the cooler temperatures of classic lager.

Lager Comes to North America

Meanwhile in North America, lager beer had burst on the scene along with Germans immigrating here in the decades before the Civil War. America had been largely a spirits-drinking land up to this point. Consumption statistics are notoriously difficult to pin down, but 1810 government reports showed spirits consumption of just over 14 quarts of spirit alcohol per capita per year. Beer consumption at that time was estimated at just 5 quarts per capita per year, somewhere in the neighborhood of a 70:1 ratio in terms of servings of alcohol. States such as Pennsylvania, New York, and Massachusetts did a fair bit of brewing, but elsewhere either barley was difficult to grow or spirits were so cheap that it didn't make sense to brew.

Some of these German-American immigrant brewers had business visions big enough to match the opportunity. Men like Pabst, Busch, and the Uihleins of Schlitz had built vast beer distribution networks by the 1870s, bringing beer to the South and other places where there had been precious little before. They took advantage of every technological advancement: steam, railroads, refrigeration, pasteurization, and the telegraph. Driven by personalities of baronial proportions and equipped with great organizational skills, these ambitious German-American brewers created some of the first national brands in any product category. Even today, maintaining fresh beer in every market is no mean feat, but in the nineteenth century we're talking about beer in hand-corked bottles in wooden crates traveling thousands of miles in railcars, stopping every few hours to be reloaded with ice from a stash that had been cut from northern lakes and rivers and laid down at strategic locations the winter before.

Early on, the German-style beer in America was predominantly of the dark Munich type, but there were others. Brewers here took their inspiration from various German cities, so there were beers called Culmbachers, Erlangers, Duesseldorfers, and of course Pilsners and Budweisers. In the 1870s, Anton Schwartz, a brewing scientist working as editor of *American Brewer*, and others such as John Ewald Siebel of the Zymotechnic (later Siebel) Institute, began popularizing the adjunct

Stein from the Zymotechnic Institute, c. 1911
Now Siebel Institute, located in Chicago. Founded in 1868, it is America's oldest brewing school.

cooking methods needed to incorporate the body-lightening ingredients rice and corn. As a Bohemian, Schwarz was undoubtedly aware of the experimentation with adjuncts in Austria around that time — in contrast to *Reinheitsgebot*-bound Bavaria. At the same time, machine-made bottles and refrigeration allowed brewers to make and sell a beer that was pale, fizzy, and designed to be enjoyed ice cold. This was the birth of American adjunct beer. By Prohibition, it dominated the market.

The Flavor of Lager Beer

Lager beer is fermented cool and conditioned cold, which means the chemistry of yeast metabolism is slowed down. The fruity top notes of esters and other chemicals produced by ale fermentations are found in lagers at much lower levels. (In fact, in competitions, any evidence of fruitiness in a lager is cause for banishment from the judging table.) A long fermentation allows plenty of time for these chemicals to be reabsorbed and converted into less odoriferous compounds. This means the flavors in lagers are cleaner, less complex, and more focused on the malt and hops — to the exclusion of almost anything else. In lagers, brewers ask the raw materials to do the heavy lifting. It's the brewer's job to put them together correctly, and then stay out of the way.

There are hundreds of distinct strains of ale yeast but only two closely related groups of lager yeast, with some minor variations; this means that yeast-derived flavor and aroma aren't much of a consideration in lager, certainly not to the same extent as in ales.

Balance may be anything from overwhelmingly malty to bracingly hoppy. German- or

AMERICAN CRAFT EXAMPLES OF CLASSIC LAGER STYLES

Firestone Walker Pivo Pils
(Paso Robles, CA)

Victory Prima Pils (Downingtown, PA)

Great Lakes Dortmunder Gold
(Cleveland, OH)

Sierra Nevada Oktoberfest (Chico, CA)

New Glarus Uff-Da bock (New Glarus, WI)

Capital Dark (Middleton, WI)

Metropolitan Magnetron Schwarzbier
(Chicago, IL)

Boston Beer Company Samuel Adams
Double Bock

. . . AND A FEW ECCENTRIC AMERICAN LAGERS

Capital Autumnal Fire, an amber
doppelbock (Middleton, WI)

Dogfish Head Imperial Pilsner (Milton, DE)

Great Divide Hoss Rye Lager (Denver, CO)

Full Sail LTD, a rotating series of offbeat
lagers (Hood River, OR)

Czech-character hops are critical for most styles. Brewers of lagers, even craft brewers, tend to stick closely to the rule book, and there is little of the outrageous vamping that goes on in English- and Belgian-inspired ales. I love a well-made classic lager, but I'd like to see Americans loosen up a little and not be so reverential. A dash of creativity could help liven up this category in the marketplace.

Because most traditional Euro-lagers are all malt, it is always worth paying attention to the specific character of the malt. Is the malt bready, or does it have hints of honey or light caramel? Toffeelike, deeply caramelly, toasty, roasted? Generally, you won't find a lot of sharp toasted or roasted flavors; "smooth" is the watchword. Clean hop aromas and bitterness are the goal. They're not called "noble" hops for nothing. You may find herbal, almost minty aromas from German Hallertauers, and perhaps fruitier notes from Spalter, Tettnangers, and Saaz. Some of these aroma personalities are very style specific, so get to know your hops.

There should be little fermentation character. Any sign of fruitiness is a sign of a too-warm fermentation. A whiff of sulfur is acceptable, and maybe a dab of DMS (see page 87), but any discernible buttery aroma is a sign of trouble. However, make sure it's actually coming from the beer and not the tap line before you complain to the brewer. Harshness could be a number of things, but most likely it has to do with water chemistry. Some Canadian and third-world barleys may contribute a touch of husky, phenolic astringency that's an acceptable part of the style in those places.

Czech/Bohemian Pilsner

ORIGIN: This is the original source Pilsner, which has spawned thousands of imitators. It was invented in 1842, in the Czech town of Plzeň, in response to pale ale's popularity. The beer became widely known as Plzensky Prazdroj or Pilsner Urquell. *Urquell* means "original." The Bohemian Pilsner style is in flux, as newer management has taken away some of the funky complexity of Pilsner Urquell, and it's getting harder to find a

charmingly bold Czech Pilsner. Note that the beers of České Budějovice have for a long time represented a slightly lighter, drier, paler variation of the Czech pale lager.

The real deal, when you find it, will be a shimmering burnished gold, with a complex caramel bouquet just about overshadowed by a fresh, Saaz hop aroma. There are a lot of feeble imitations, so be picky.

Bohemian Pilsner is brewed at several strengths, but only the stronger version is exported. Inside the country, most people drink the lighter, less expensive version. There are also a number of amber and dark lagers, the most famous of which is the one brewed at U Fleků, the world's oldest brewpub, in Prague.

LOCATION: Czech Republic, also U.S. craft breweries

AROMA: Clean malt plus spicy perfume of Saaz hops

FLAVOR: Sweet malt, hints of caramel; Saaz hops

BALANCE: Somewhat or very much on the hoppy side; clean bitter finish despite sometimes-aggressive hop rates

SEASONALITY: Always appropriate

PAIR WITH: Wide range of lighter food, such as chicken, salads, salmon, bratwurst

SUGGESTED BEERS TO TRY: BrouCzech Lager, Czechvar (Budvar in Europe), Live Oak Pilz, Lagunitas Pils (although stronger than the classic style at 6 percent by volume), Pilsner Urquell, Staropramen Lager, Summit Pilsener

GRAVITY: 1.044–1.060 (11–14.7°P)
ALCOHOL: 4.2–5.8% by volume
ATTENUATION/BODY: Medium
COLOR: 3.5–6 SRM, pale to deep gold
BITTERNESS: 30–45 IBU, medium

German Pilsner

ORIGIN: Northern Germany, and it was based on the success of Czech Pilsner. Northerly versions are drier and more bitter.

LOCATION: Germany, elsewhere in Europe

AROMA: Clean malt plus a good dose of herbal/minty noble hops

FLAVOR: Crisp, smooth malt; herby Hallertau hops and solid bitterness

BALANCE: Even or dry/bitter; clean finish

SEASONALITY: Year-round but best enjoyed in warm weather

PAIR WITH: Wide range of lighter food, such as salads, seafood, bratwurst

SUGGESTED BEERS TO TRY: Firestone Walker Pivo Pils, Hill Farmstead Mary, Jever Pilsener, Mahr's Pilsner, Sierra Nevada Nooner Pilsner, Trumer Pils, Victory Prima Pils

GRAVITY: 1.044–1.050 (11–12.5°P)
ALCOHOL: 4.4–5.2% by volume
ATTENUATION/BODY: Crisp and dry
COLOR: 2–5 SRM, straw to pale gold
BITTERNESS: 22–40 IBU, medium

Münchener Helles

ORIGIN: Based on the success of Czech Pilsner, this came out of Munich, Germany. It took the Munich brewers until the 1870s to figure out how to treat the Isar River water to make a decent pale beer, but even so, it still reflects the local aversion to too much bitterness.

LOCATION: Munich, Germany; also U.S. craft breweries

AROMA: Clean malt plus good dose of herbal hops

FLAVOR: Rich, light caramelly malt, hint of hops

BALANCE: Even to malty; rich, soft finish

SEASONALITY: Year-round but best enjoyed in warm weather

PAIR WITH: Wide range of lighter food, such as salads and seafood; classic with Weisswurst

SUGGESTED BEERS TO TRY: Augustiner Lagerbier Hell, Spaten Münchner Hell (Premium Lager), Sly Fox Helles Lager, Stoudts Gold Lager, Surly Hell, Weihenstephaner Original

GRAVITY: 1.044–1.048 (11–11.9°P)
ALCOHOL: 4.7–5.4% by volume
ATTENUATION/BODY: Crisp, dry
COLOR: 3–5 SRM, pale gold
BITTERNESS: 16–22 IBU, low to medium

KELLERBIER

Many German breweries serve unfiltered versions of their house beers only in their rathskellers. With a slight milky haze, they are very fresh tasting and typically are a little more full-bodied than the same beer postfiltration. Kellerbier is the German equivalent of real ale. It makes you realize how much filtration takes away. Stylistically, they are just fresher and slightly richer-tasting versions of whatever Pilsner, helles, or other style of beer the brewery is making.

Dortmunder Export/Helles Exportbier

ORIGIN: Dortmunder, Germany's export beer, was the first famous pale lager in Germany. The city's brewers began to industrialize in about 1845, and by 1868 an observer noted that "Dortmunder is to Northwest Germany what Bavaria used to be for the whole country," as far as beer goes. With a shift away from local brewing traditions and raw ingredients, something different was definitely going on here. The "Bavarian process" of lager brewing was adopted in 1865, and the new pale beer was a huge hit. Sadly, after a hundred years of success, Dortmunder Export is now just about dead in its homeland.

Dortmunder was originally a slightly stronger beer designed for export. Fortunately, it is sometimes available in American craft-brewed versions. In terms of balance, it is intermediate between helles and Pilsner, but just a little stronger than either. The city of Dortmund has very unusual water chemistry, including carbonate, sulfate, and chloride, and this was well suited to the production of a moderately hopped pale beer.

LOCATION: Proper Dortmund-style lager is now easier to find from a few U.S. craft breweries. Munich brewers are offering this as a replacement for the classic Märzens for Oktoberfest attendees, so now this style is becoming the modern Oktoberfest beer.

AROMA: Clean malt plus soft hops

FLAVOR: Rich, light caramelly malt, hint of hops

BALANCE: Perfectly even, rich and round, but with a crisp, minerally finish

SEASONALITY: Year-round

PAIR WITH: Wide range of food: pork; spicy Asian, Cajun, Latin

SUGGESTED BEERS TO TRY: Ayinger Jahrhundert, DAB (Dortmunder Actien-Brauerei) Dortmunder Export, Great Lakes Dortmunder Gold, Three Floyds Jinx Proof, Two Brothers Dog Days Dortmunder Style Lager

GRAVITY: 1.048–1.056 (11.9–13.8°P)
ALCOHOL: 4.8–6.0% by volume
ATTENUATION/BODY: Medium
COLOR: 4–7 SRM, straw to pale gold
BITTERNESS: 20–30 IBU, low to medium

Historical Style

American Pre-Prohibition Pilsner

Before World War I, mainstream beers in America had considerably more character than they do today. Gravities were similar, or maybe a touch higher, and judging by the color of the beers in antique ads and photos, the beers were often darker in those days as well. Hop rates were several times what they are today. While all-malt examples did exist, most were adjunct beers, with typically around 20 to 25 percent of rice or corn grits in the recipe, similar to premium beers today. Another difference is that these were true lagers. Today's versions are fermented at higher temperatures for shorter time periods. As a result, hints of apple and banana esters are not uncommon among American mass-market "lagers."

SUGGESTED BEERS TO TRY: Brooklyn Lager, Narragansett Lager, Yuengling Traditional Lager. Also, keep your eyes open at your local

PALE LAGER AROUND THE WORLD

In addition to the classic styles, pale lager has become widespread and assumes a slightly different character in each of its adopted homelands. The following is by no means an exhaustive list.

China and India. These tend toward the rustic, and the local six-row barley usually adds a grassy or sometimes astringent character.

Japan. These form a whole range of products that as a whole are extremely clean and crisp. Rice, as you would expect, is the most common adjunct. All-malt examples exist, and premium products revolve around extreme freedom from harshness, an aesthetic borrowed from sake culture.

Australia. This country has a strong heritage of British-inflected brewing but has embraced lager as its own as well. The beers are in the international style, very much along the lines of the American adjunct Pilsners, but often with a somewhat higher hopping rate. Hops in Tasmania and New Zealand are quite different as well and account for the unique perfume of many beers brewed Down Under.

Poland. These are not far off from Czech beers, except they tend generally to be a little less bitter and maybe just slightly grainier tasting. They come in a wide range of strengths, starting at a conventional 4.5 to 5 percent by volume and moving up to more than 9 percent. I find the ones around 6.5 to 7 percent to be the most interesting. Poland has its own hop-growing region and a Saaz relative, Lublin, to go with it.

Canada. Canadian mainstream lagers are very similar to U.S. examples, but up to a half percent stronger in alcohol. The unique Canadian "blue" six-row malt, so named for its colored aleurone (skin) layer, may add a sharp, crisp graininess. Numerous fine craft beers exist, including authentic Pilsners, British-inspired ales from Toronto and points west, and a thrilling Belgian-inspired scene in Quebec.

Mexico and Latin America. Most of these products are of the standard industrial variety, with plenty of adjuncts to thin them down and make them highly thirst-quenching. Mass-market beers with heading agents, antioxidants, and much more than 50 percent adjunct are commonplace. Standouts do exist, including Bohemia and Negra Modelo from Mexico, and Guatemala's Moza, a bock-style lager. An exciting craft scene is thriving in many places in Latin America, but it faces many challenges.

Twenty-First Century Growler
People in Qingdao, Shandong Province, China, use plastic bags to carry take-away beer.

brewpub, as this style sometimes shows up as a summer seasonal.

GRAVITY: 1.044–1.060 (11–13°P)
ALCOHOL: 3.5–6.0% by volume
ATTENUATION/BODY: Medium
COLOR: 3–5 SRM, straw to pale gold
BITTERNESS: 25–40 IBU, medium

American Adjunct Lager

ORIGIN: Corn and rice adjunct beers date back to 1540 in America. This style as we know it developed in the late nineteenth century and then became ever more delicate as the twentieth century rolled on. This style of beer is the world's best-selling lager. The two main adjuncts used are corn and rice, usually not together. In mainstream brands, about 25 percent of the recipe is adjunct; the quantity rises as the price goes down, and sugar is sometimes used as a really cheap adjunct in bargain brands. In the United States, the upper limit by law for a "malt beverage," ironically a more restrictive category than "beer," is 75 percent adjunct, although most bargain brands of beer top out at about 50 percent adjunct.

LOCATION: United States; now international

AROMA: Hints of grainy malt, a hint of hops occasionally

FLAVOR: A light white-bread maltiness, with plenty of fizz. The barest tickle of bitterness, at least in mainstream U.S. versions; premium or European versions may have a modest bitterness. With corn as an adjunct there's a hint of palate-coating roundness, almost a little sweetness. Rice has a crisper finish, and if used in too large a quantity it can add a slightly harsh astringency.

BALANCE: Dry, with clean, crisp finish

SEASONALITY: Year-round but best enjoyed in warm weather

PAIR WITH: While these wash down millions of meals every day, the light, delicate nature of these beers means they will be overwhelmed by anything other than the lightest of dishes

SUGGESTED BEERS TO TRY: These beers are so ubiquitous I hardly need to make suggestions, but Budweiser, Coors Banquet, and Miller Genuine Draft are the category leaders. Pabst is marginally fuller in flavor.

GRAVITY: 1.040–1.050 (10.1–12.4°P)
ALCOHOL: 4.2–5.3% by volume
ATTENUATION/BODY: Crisp, dry, fizzy
COLOR: 2–4 SRM, straw to pale gold
BITTERNESS: 8–18 IBU, very low

American Light Lager

ORIGIN: Created in the 1940s as a diet beer for women, light beer was masculinized by Philip Morris, then the parent company of Miller, with their brand "Lite." Light lager now outsells regular lager. Fungally derived enzymes are used to reduce all starches present into fermentable sugars, ensuring that there will be no residual carbohydrates and that the maximum alcohol is produced with a minimum calorie count.

LOCATION: United States mostly, also international

AROMA: Slight hints of grainy malt, period

FLAVOR: Barest hints of malt, with a lot of fizz

BALANCE: Superdry, with clean, crisp finish

SEASONALITY: Year-round but best enjoyed in warm weather

PAIR WITH: Really not recommended as a companion to food

SUGGESTED BEERS TO TRY: Like American adjunct lagers, these beers are ubiquitous; Bud Light, Coors Light, and Miller Lite dominate the category.

GRAVITY: 1.028–1.040 (7.1–10.1°P)
ALCOHOL: 2.8–4.2% by volume
ATTENUATION/BODY: Superdry
COLOR: 2–3 SRM, pale straw to pale gold
BITTERNESS: 8–12 IBU, ultralow

SOME AMERICAN "HERITAGE" BREWERIES AND THEIR OLD-SCHOOL BRANDS

AMERICAN BREWERY	OLD-SCHOOL BRAND
August Schell	Schell's, Grain Belt
High Falls Brewing	Genesee
Minhas Craft Brewery	Huber, Rhinelander
Iron City	Iron City
Point Brewing	Point Special
The Lion Brewery	Stegmaier
Straub Brewery	Straub
Yuengling	Yuengling

American Malt Liquor

ORIGIN: Designed as a cheap intoxicant, malt liquor is brewed like other inexpensive industrial beers, with heaping helpings of adjuncts, often just sugar. Malt liquor is very lightly hopped and sometimes sweetened a little at packaging.

LOCATION: United States

AROMA: Slight hints of grainy malt, and perhaps a sweetish, alcohol aroma

FLAVOR: A dab of malt, with a sweetish finish, alcohol evident

BALANCE: Alcohol versus carbonation, and a little sweetness

SEASONALITY: Year-round

GRAVITY: 1.050–1.060 (12.4–14.7°P)
ALCOHOL: 5.2–8.1% by volume
ATTENUATION/BODY: Superdry
COLOR: 2–5 SRM, pale straw to pale gold
BITTERNESS: 12–23 IBU, low

Vienna, Märzen, and Oktoberfest

ORIGIN: Anton Dreher originally created this style in Vienna around 1840. Sometime after that, a similar beer was brewed in Munich by his pal Gabriel Sedlmayr II (then in charge of brewing at Spaten). *Märzen* means "March," and this term normally applies to a beer brewed in the late spring to use up the last of the previous fall's hops and malt before brewing ceased for the summer. So the general idea of March beer is probably quite old in Germany, as it is elsewhere. The first

Oktoberfest event happened in 1810, probably at least 50 years before the style that now bears its name existed. Early on, the revelers must have been drinking Munich's famous dunkel.

Originally, there may not have been all that great a distinction between these closely related beers, although Vienna brewers used malt that was slightly paler than the more highly kilned Munich malt. Vienna-style lager has been out of fashion in its birthplace for quite a while, but craft versions are appearing in some of Austria's small upstart breweries.

In Germany, the term *Oktoberfest* can be used only by brewers in Munich proper. It's more of an appellation than a style, with some versions getting paler and drier in recent years, while others stick to the old-fashioned Märzen; some brew both. Because of this bifurcation, it's useless to talk about it as a style, but the name still has meaning as a trade term in the United States and elsewhere outside of Europe. There are many great versions brewed by craft brewers as fall seasonals.

LOCATION: Germany, Austria, Mexico (thanks to an Austro-Hungarian colonial connection), U.S. and international craft breweries

AROMA: Malt, malt, malt, with an emphasis on a caramel and cookie character. Brewed primarily from either Munich or Vienna malt. Generally little or no hop aroma.

FLAVOR: Caramel malt, with hints of sweet toast, some bitterness

BALANCE: Malty, barely balanced by hops

SEASONALITY: September through October; also year-round, especially in the United States

PAIR WITH: Mexican cuisine and other spicy food; chicken, sausage, milder cheeses

SUGGESTED BEERS TO TRY: Ayinger Oktober Fest-Märzen, Firestone Walker Oaktoberfest, Paulaner Oktoberfest Märzen, Samuel Adams Octoberfest, Devil's Backbone Vienna, Figueroa Mountain Danish Red (Vienna)

MÄRZEN

GRAVITY: 1.054–1.060 (13.3–14.7°P)
ALCOHOL: 5.8–6.3% by volume
ATTENUATION/BODY: Medium
COLOR: 8–17 SRM, pale gold to dark amber
BITTERNESS: 18–24 IBU, low to medium

VIENNA

GRAVITY: 1.048–1.055 (11.9–13.6°P)
ALCOHOL: 4.7–5.5% by volume
ATTENUATION/BODY: Medium
COLOR: 9–15 SRM, pale gold to dark amber
BITTERNESS: 18–30 IBU, low to medium

Munich Dunkel

ORIGIN: Descended from ancient "red" beers in southern Germany, dunkel was the first lager style, probably developing as such in the sixteenth century. The carbonate-laden water was well suited for malty, brown beer, but brewers considered pale beer impossible until they figured out how to adjust the mineral content. Originally, the beers were brewed entirely from the amber-colored Munich malt, but more modern recipes are often a mix of Pilsner and Munich malts, with a little black malt added to replace the missing color.

LOCATION: Munich, Germany; also from U.S. craft breweries

AROMA: Rich, complex maltiness; no hop aroma

FLAVOR: Rich toasted cookie and caramel/toffee maltiness, gentle toasty overtones

BALANCE: Malty, barely balanced by hops and a softly bitter toastiness

SEASONALITY: Year-round; great in colder weather

PAIR WITH: Hearty, spicy food; barbecue, sausages, roast meat; bread pudding

SUGGESTED BEERS TO TRY: Ayinger Altbairisch Dunkel, Capital Munich Dark, Harpoon Dark, Hofbräuhaus Hofbräu Dunkel, Lakefront Eastside Dark

GRAVITY: 1.048–1.056 (11.9–13.8°P)
ALCOHOL: 4.5–5.6% by volume
ATTENUATION/BODY: Medium
COLOR: 14–28 SRM, ruby to deep brown
BITTERNESS: 18–28 IBU, medium

Historical Style

American Dark/ Bock

When German immigrant brewers came to the United States, they brought their rich, malty dunkel recipes with them. Over time, the beers lightened up in terms of weight and sweetness with the addition of corn or rice grits. Pilsner soon overtook darker beers, but they managed to hang on until the 1970s in greatly diminished form, especially as seasonal bock beers. Most of these have disappeared, but Yuengling and a few other regional heritage breweries still brew dark lagers. An especially light-bodied amber derivative, Shiner Bock, is the mainstay for Texas's Spoetzl brewery.

SUGGESTED BEERS TO TRY: Dixie Blackened Voodoo Lager, Shiner Bock, Yuengling Porter

German Schwarzbier

ORIGIN: Long brewed in certain parts of Germany, especially Augsburg, Bad Köstritz, and Kulmbach, they are Germany's darkest beers. *Schwarz* means "black," but in certain regions this term is casually used to denote any dark beer. There seems to have been some connection with the exploding popularity of English porter in the mid-nineteenth century, because the brewer and author Ladislaus von Wagner (1877) calls it *"Englischer Köstritzer."* In those days this beer was brewed with a peculiar mashing regimen called "satz" mashing, which features a long, cold soak of the mash in water and then a boiling of the hops in thinned mash, a step called "roasting" the hops.

LOCATION: Kulmbach, Bad Köstritz, Germany; also Japan (black beer); occasionally U.S. craft breweries

AROMA: Full roasty maltiness; little or no hop aroma

FLAVOR: Bittersweet, with a clean, cocoa roastiness

BALANCE: Roasty-malty, barely balanced by hops

SEASONALITY: Year-round, great in colder weather

PAIR WITH: Hearty, spicy food, such as barbecue, sausages, roast meat; bread pudding

SUGGESTED BEERS TO TRY: Sapporo Black Lager, Samuel Adams Black Lager, Sprecher Black Bavarian Lager, Köstritzer Schwarzbier, Kulmbacher Mönchshof Schwarzbier, Metropolitan Magnetron Schwarzbier

GRAVITY: 1.046–1.052 (11.4–12.9°P)
ALCOHOL: 4.4–5.4% by volume
ATTENUATION/BODY: Medium
COLOR: 17–30 SRM, ruby to deep brown
BITTERNESS: 20–30 IBU, medium

Historical Style

German Porter

This little-known style had its heyday in the mid- to late nineteenth century, in response to the unprecedented success of English porter. According to contemporary authors, there were two distinct styles: a sweet and malty one and a crisp, highly hopped version, both at 1.071 to 1.075 original gravity (17.3 to 18.2 degrees Plato). Both lager and top-fermented versions existed. Neuzeller Kloster Brau brews a porter that is imported into the United States.

Maibock/Heller Bock

ORIGIN: Einbeck, southern Germany, claims to be the origin point for bock beer. Even by 1613 it was described in *The Herbal Book of Johannes Theodorus* as "thin, subtle, clear, of bitter taste, with a pleasant acidity on the tongue, and many other good qualities." A Brunswick (near Einbeck) brewmaster brought to Bavaria by Maximilian I helped sort out the details of brewing this stronger style of beer there, or so the story goes. By the late eighteenth century, the style seems to have been widespread in southern Germany. Half a century later it was all over Europe, especially in France, where it was consumed with gusto.

LOCATION: Southern Germany, France, United States, Thailand

AROMA: Loads of light caramelly malt plus a hint of hops

FLAVOR: Rich, caramelly malt, soft bitter finish

BALANCE: Full, malty body; evenly balanced hops

SEASONALITY: Traditional in late spring (May), but now year-round

PAIR WITH: Rich or spicy food, such as Thai; cheesecake, apple strudel

SUGGESTED BEER TO TRY: Einbecker Mai-Ur-Bock

GRAVITY: 1.064–1.072 (15.7–17.5°P)
ALCOHOL: 6.3–7.4% by volume
ATTENUATION/BODY: Very full, rich
COLOR: 6–11 SRM, gold to amber
BITTERNESS: 23–35 IBU, low to medium

Dark (Dunkel) Bock

ORIGIN: Old paintings featuring bock beer rarely show anything darker than medium amber, so dark ones seem to have been very much the secondary form compared to the amber-colored ones. Dark bock is rather more important in the minds of American home and craft brewers than they were historically.

LOCATION: Southern Germany, U.S. craft breweries

AROMA: Loads of malt plus a hint of soft roast

FLAVOR: Rich toasted cookie and caramel malt notes; soft, bittersweet finish with hints of cocoa

BALANCE: Full, malty body, barely balanced by hops

SEASONALITY: Traditional in late spring (May) but now year-round

PAIR WITH: Rich or spicy food, washed-rind or high-fat bloomy-rind cheese

SUGGESTED BEERS TO TRY: Aass Bock, Einbecker Ur-Bock Dunkel, New Glarus Uff-Da bock, Schell's Bock, Weltenburger Kloster Asam Bock

GRAVITY: 1.064–1.072 (15.7–17.5°P)
ALCOHOL: 6.3–7.2% by volume
ATTENUATION/BODY: Very full, rich
COLOR: 14–22 SRM, amber to dark brown
BITTERNESS: 20–27 IBU, low

Doppelbock

ORIGIN: Created in 1629 as "Salvator" by the monastic Paulaner brewery in Munich. The Salvator name was used generically until the early twentieth century, when Paulaner, by then a secular operation, took steps to protect their name. The "-ator" suffix has stood since then, and most breweries everywhere end their doppelbock names with "-ator." This is still a rich beer, but it once was much heavier, with high gravities and very poor attenuation (the Wahl-Henius *American Handy Book of the Brewing, Malting and Auxiliary Trades* cites an 1897 Salvator at 4.61 percent alcohol but a starting gravity of 18.8°B/1.078!), but in response to changing tastes, its terminal gravity has decreased over the past 150 years, making the beer drier, less sweet, and more alcoholic.

LOCATION: Southern Germany, U.S. craft breweries

AROMA: Loads of complex malt; no hops evident

FLAVOR: Massive caramel malt; soft, roasty finish

BALANCE: Malt, barely balanced by hops and a soft roastiness

SEASONALITY: Year-round; great in colder weather

PAIR WITH: Rich, roasty foods (like duck!); perfect with chocolate cake and triple cream cheese

SUGGESTED BEERS TO TRY: Augustiner Bräu Maximator, Ayinger Celebrator, Ettaler Klosterbrauerei Curator, Metropolitan Generator, Tröegs Troegenator Doublebock, Weihenstephaner Korbinian

GRAVITY: 1.077–1.112 (18.7–26.3°P)
ALCOHOL: 7.0–10.0% by volume
ATTENUATION/BODY: Very full, rich
COLOR: 6–25 SRM, deep amber to dark brown
BITTERNESS: 16–26 IBU, low

Eisbock

This is simply a bock made even stronger by freezing it and removing some water in the form of ice, increasing the alcohol and everything else. Flavors are the same as regular bocks, but really concentrated.

GRAVITY: 1.078–1.120 (18.9–28°P)
ALCOHOL: 9.0–14.0% by volume, but beers up to 40% have been occasionally brewed
ATTENUATION/BODY: Very full, rich, liqueurlike
COLOR: 18–30 SRM, deep amber to dark brown
BITTERNESS: 25–35 IBU, low to medium

Rauchbier

Before the advent of direct-fired kilns, all malt was either smoky or air-dried. And while there is evidence in places such as Norway of some very primitive indirect kilns, it is clear that many European beers before 1700 had a certain smoky quality from the wood used to kiln the malt. The record shows that smoked beers were dropped from production in most places as soon as maltsters figured out how to dry the malt without smokiness, except in the Franconia region of northern Bavaria. Centered around Bamberg is a pocket of the old-style smoked beer, or rauchbier.

This specialty is in the lager category because most of these beers are lagered (the exception being a wheat beer), so they share a history and flavor profile with the rest of the Bavarian beer tradition. The only difference is the smoke. Wood, usually beech, is used in the kilns. The beers are brewed from various proportions of smoked and unsmoked malt to achieve the desired smoke level. A number of different beer styles are brewed, including bock and helles, but the most common smoked style is Märzen, whose rich maltiness stands up to the smoke, giving a unique balance to this beer.

Rauchbier can be startling on the first sip, but hang in there. The beer tastes better and better as your palate grows accustomed to it.

DESCRIPTION: See Märzen, helles, bock, and weizen, then add a layer of dry, hammy smoke. Mmmm, liquid bacon!

SUGGESTED BEERS TO TRY: Any of the Aecht Schlenkerla products: Braüerei Spezial Rauchbier, and occasionally a seasonal at your local brewpub

SPECIFICATIONS: These are brewed in a number of classic style versions, especially Märzen, but also helles, wheat, and bock.

Historical Style

Steinbier

In medieval days, brewers didn't always have access to metal brewing vessels and so had to make do with wood. This created some obvious problems in heating the mash and wort. The solution was to add heated rocks directly to the liquid, which gave up their heat quite efficiently. The last holdout of this ancient style was in late-nineteenth-century Carinthia, a mountainous southern region of Austria. There they brewed a very-low-gravity steinbier using oats and wheat malt. A Bamberg brewery called Allgauer reinterpreted the style, but production has ceased.

The rocks, a hard type of sandstone called "graywacke," were placed in a metal cage, heated to white hot, and then dunked into the wort. Rapid boiling ensued, and the rocks became encrusted with a thick layer of caramelized wort, which, when dissolved during fermentation, gave the beer a smoky, toffee flavor.

For obvious reasons, this is a challenging beer to brew, especially in commercial quantities, and only shows up as occasional special projects.

CHAPTER 11

CONTINENTAL ALES, WEISSBIERS, AND ALE-LAGER HYBRIDS

E ven in the great lager fatherland, there is ale. Of course, many hundreds of years ago, all beer was ale, or top-fermented beer, but most of these were swept into obscurity or extinction as the great flood of Bavarian and Bohemian lager gushed across Europe in the late nineteenth century.

ALL ALES USE YEAST that does its fermenting near the top of the wort. More importantly, ale yeast prefers warmer temperatures than lager yeast, most often between 65 and 73°F (18 and 23°C), although this varies by style. At these temperatures, yeast produces a great deal more of the fruity aroma molecules called esters, and other chemicals that add spicy, fruity complexity to beer. In most cases, the yeast strain is critical to the character of the beer. Yeasts for the Rhine Valley ales of Cologne and Düsseldorf are very neutral, with a delicate fruitiness, and because they are fermented at the cool end of the ale range and then cold-aged like lagers, their effect is subtle. The same is true for ale-lager hybrids, which are either fermented cool with ale yeast or,

WHAT'S IN A NAME?

Weis, Weiss, and Weisse all mean "white" in German and have long been used to describe the pale, hazy beers containing wheat that are found all along the northern tier of Europe.

Weizen means "wheat" in German and refers to the Bavarian or *süddeutsch* form of Weissbier.

Hefe means "yeast" and indicates a Weissbier with yeast, by far the most popular form.

Kristal indicates a crystal-clear weizen.

as in steam beer, at warmer temperatures but with lager yeast. The personality-laden yeast used for Bavarian weizen blasts the beer with a whole fruit basket of aroma: banana, bubble gum, and some spicy clovelike notes. There are no fruits or spices in the beer; the aromatic magic comes solely from the yeast.

Weissbier is the broad term that includes both the various shades and strengths of Bavarian hefeweizen and the tart and tingly Berliner Weisse. Compared to barley malt beers, wheat beers are lighter on the palate, with sharp aromas, creamy mouthfeel, and quenching finish, quite different from the blandness created by adjuncts such as corn or rice. Pale color and high carbonation levels enhance the refreshing qualities of this style.

Most of these beers are session beers, meant to be drunk in reasonably large quantities in the company of other beer lovers. Alt and Kölsch are delicious and are available in the United States, but to enjoy them to the fullest, you'll have to journey to their hometowns along the Rhine. In the bars and brewpubs there, the beers are served from small barrels perched right on the bar tops, and the beer is slipped into tall, paper-thin glasses. Refills are brought to your table automatically until you place a coaster over the top of your glass to tell them you've had enough.

The word *alt* means "old," in the sense of an old-time style. There are a few Altbiers outside of Düsseldorf. Pinkus Müller makes a pale Münster-style Alt. An amber Broyhan is still brewed by Lindener Gilde in Hanover — founded by Cord Broyhan in 1546. Dortmund was once famous as an Altbier town, gaining world renown for its strong Adambier a century ago. Due to the consolidation and Pilsnerization of the market, Dortmunder Alts are becoming harder to find.

Because the Bavarian lager tradition came late to the north of Germany, there are many unique local specialties that have almost been forgotten. Some, like gose, are enjoying a renaissance; others languish, ripe for rebirth.

Kölsch

The word *Kölsch* is an appellation. In Europe, only brewers in Köln (Cologne) may use the name, although that name protection does not extend to the United States. Kölsch is crisp but not sharp; balanced but not excessively bitter. There is a delightfully subtle fruitiness in the aroma, and a dryish palate with a hint of creaminess that may come from the addition of a small proportion of wheat (few classic brewers do this). Fresh, seductive, and never fatiguing, it is one of the world's great session beers. Some American craft breweries have recognized this and roll it into their lineup, usually as a summer seasonal.

ORIGIN: Köln (Cologne), Germany

LOCATION: Köln, Germany; also U.S. and international craft breweries

AROMA: Bready malt plus a touch of noble hops and a little fruit

FLAVOR: Clean, fresh malt; hops in the background

BALANCE: Evenly balanced; soft, bitterish finish

SEASONALITY: Year-round but best enjoyed in warm weather

PAIR WITH: Wide range of lighter food, such as chicken, salads, salmon, bratwurst

SUGGESTED BEERS TO TRY: Gaffel Kölsch, Goose Island Summertime, Reissdorf Kölsch, Saint Arnold Fancy Lawnmower Beer

GRAVITY: 1.044–1.050 (11–12.4°P)
ALCOHOL: 4.4–5.2% by volume
ATTENUATION/BODY: Low to medium
COLOR: 3.5–5 SRM, pale to medium gold
BITTERNESS: 18–30 IBU, low to medium

Düsseldorfer Altbier

There is a well-established tradition of brown, top-fermented beers along the Rhine in Lower Saxony. Düsseldorfer Alt seems to be descended from an older style called erntebier (harvest beer), which was much beloved in the nineteenth century.

The classic Alt is a copper-colored all-malt ale of everyday strength. Classic Alts may be bone dry or softly malty, but all are briskly bitter, with little hop aroma. Like Kölsch, Alt is tapped from barrels at the bar into small cylindrical glasses called "stanges."

Imports and American craft beer examples are rare, but when well executed it is a compelling session beer. Twice a year, in the fall and midwinter, German Altbier breweries make a slightly stronger version called *sticke* that is released without a lot of hubbub as a thank-you to their regular customers. One version is imported here, along with a Double Sticke that doesn't exist in its homeland. The Diebels brewery in Issum, up near the Dutch border, focuses on Alt and produces a credible Düsseldorf version that is widely available in the United States.

ORIGIN: Düsseldorf, Germany

LOCATION: Düsseldorf, Germany; U.S. craft breweries

AROMA: Clean toffee malt and possibly a hint of herbal hops

FLAVOR: Malty but crisp; a punch of noble hops

BALANCE: Toward the dry and bitter side; clean finish

SEASONALITY: Year-round

PAIR WITH: Wide range of medium-intensity food, such as roast pork, smoked sausage, or salmon

SUGGESTED BEERS TO TRY: August Schell Schmaltz's Alt, Metropolitan Brewing Iron Works Altbier, Zum Uerige Sticke Alt

GRAVITY: 1.044–1.052 (11–12.9°P)
ALCOHOL: 4.3–5.5% by volume
ATTENUATION/BODY: Crisp, dry
COLOR: 11–17 SRM, deep amber to ruby brown
BITTERNESS: 25–50 IBU, medium to high

American Cream Ale

I cut my teeth on this style while attending college in Cincinnati, Ohio, the western end of the cream ale belt. At that point, it was pretty similar to the adjunct lagers the surviving old regional breweries there were producing, but jacked up in alcohol ever so slightly. We loved it — but what did we know? The origin of the name "cream" is obscure, and the product was also known as "present use" ale. At first, cream ale may have been a way for brewers to offer an intermediate product between lager and strong stock ale by blending the two. After breweries began high-gravity brewing, it was simply a beer made slightly stronger by diluting the batch a little less and by sometimes adding sugar before pasteurization, and possibly a little hop oil for some aroma. In concept, it's not all that different from Kölsch, save for the corn or sugar adjuncts it normally contains.

ORIGIN: Late nineteenth century; a blend of lager and stock ale

LOCATION: Eastern/midwestern U.S. regionals and craft breweries

AROMA: Clean, grainy malt; perhaps a hint of hops

FLAVOR: Smooth, creamy malt; soft bitter finish

BALANCE: A touch of sweetness; clean, crisp finish

SEASONALITY: Year-round but best enjoyed in warm weather

PAIR WITH: Lighter foods and snacks; craft versions can stand up to somewhat more substantial food

SUGGESTED BEERS TO TRY: Hudepohl-Schoenling Little Kings Cream Ale, New Glarus Spotted Cow, Gennessee Cream Ale

GRAVITY: 1.042–1.055 (10.5–13.6°P)
ALCOHOL: 4.2–5.6% by volume
ATTENUATION/BODY: Dry to medium
COLOR: 2.5–5 SRM, pale straw to pale gold
BITTERNESS: 8–20 IBU, low to medium

Steam Beer

This term describes a beer style that was brewed around the time of the great influx of settlers into California, Washington, and other western states. Steam beer is said to get its name from the "steam" released when kegs were tapped, a consequence of very high carbonation levels. The unique feature of steam beer is that it was an attempt, in those early days, to brew a lager-type beer without access to ice or refrigeration. The high-temperature fermentation gives it a fruity, estery profile compared to a true lager.

It's a one-beer style. The only well-known steam beer in the United States is Anchor Steam, made by Anchor Brewing Company of San Francisco, which has tried to protect the term as an exclusive trademark. The BJCP and World Beer Cup both call the style "California common." Anchor left behind what little (if any) historic character remained in its Steam Beer when they completely reinvented it in 1971. The beer became a model for a multitude

of craft beers to follow: all-malt, including a healthy dose of crystal/caramel, plus a unique hop, in this case Northern Brewer.

ORIGIN: Western United States, especially California

LOCATION: San Francisco's Anchor Steam is the last surviving old-time steam beer brewery, but other craft breweries produce versions from time to time.

AROMA: Crisp malt with hints of caramel balanced by fresh herbal hops

FLAVOR: Malty but crisp, with a good helping of the dry-tasting Northern Brewer hops

BALANCE: Toward the dry and bitter side; clean finish

SEASONALITY: Year-round

PAIR WITH: Wide range of medium-intensity food, such as roast pork, smoked sausage, or salmon; fabulous with coconut-breaded shrimp

SUGGESTED BEERS TO TRY: Anchor Steam Beer, Flat Earth Element 115, Toppling Goliath Dorothy's New World Lager

GRAVITY: 1.048–1.056 (11.9–13.8°P)
ALCOHOL: 4.5–5.5% by volume
ATTENUATION/BODY: Slight richness but finishing crisp and dry
COLOR: 10–17 SRM, amber
BITTERNESS: 25–40 IBU, medium to high

Sparkling Ale

Let's start with Scottish versions. The 1902 *American Handy Book of the Brewing, Malting and Auxiliary Trades* lists a 1901 version at 18.03 degrees Balling (1.075), with an alcohol content of 8.6 percent by volume. A version of that era by McEwan's comes in at a beefy 21.6 degrees Balling (1.090), and 7.8 percent alcohol by weight (9.6 percent by volume), indicating a high terminal gravity and making it a very sweet beer. Both show moderate amounts of lactic acid, 0.15 and 0.38, respectively (contemporary lambics and Irish stouts both were about 1 percent, by comparison), which indicates some wood aging with its inevitable *Brettanomyces* activity. Hop rates are elusive, but an "X" Scottish ale of similar gravity from midcentury came in at 17 to 25 ounces (482 to 709 g) per barrel, which may have put it in the neighborhood of 40 to 60 IBUs.

In America, sparkling ale held a position between cream, or "present use" ale, and stock ale. Gravities were lower than in imported versions, about 1.057 (14 degrees Plato), roughly the same as cream ale. The difference was an extended lagering at 39°F (4°C). Three months is a typical aging time.

Sparkling ales survive in Australia more than anywhere else. Gravities are in the everyday drinking range of 1.038 to 1.050 (9.5 to 12.4 degrees Plato), 4.5 to 6.0 percent alcohol, with moderate hop bitterness.

SUGGESTED BEERS TO TRY: Coopers Sparkling Ale, Sam Adams Sparkling Ale

Bavarian Weissbier/ Hefeweizen

It is a golden summer afternoon, and you are whiling away what's left of the day in a lush and ancient beer garden. Hop shoots are curling up the trellis seeking a little sunshine. Only quiet conversation and the occasional clink of heavy glassware punctuates the tranquility. There is but one perfect beverage for this moment, and your lips form the word "Weissbier" as you place your order.

The ritual begins. A half-liter bottle shaped like a bullet appears, along with a very tall, vase-shaped glass. The glass is slipped over the top of the bottle, and the whole thing is inverted to a shallow angle. As the beer starts to flow, the bottle is withdrawn, keeping pace with the level of beer in the glass. Then, just before the bottle is completely drained, it is laid on the table and rolled back and forth several times to make sure the yeast on the bottom is well mixed with the remaining foam. This last remnant of meringuelike foam is heaped in a spiral on top of the considerable head already in the glass. This elegant creation is topped with a wedge of fresh lemon, and the ritual is complete, save for the drinking.

By the sixteenth century, wheat beer was solidly established as a regional specialty in Bavaria. The *Reinheitsgebot* has but one loophole, and this allows for the use of wheat in weizens. The Bavarian royal family held exclusive rights to brew wheat beers through a boom and bust cycle that lasted nearly 300 years, reaching its greatest popularity during the late seventeenth century. In 1872, the fad nearly spent, Georg Schneider negotiated the rights to brew this royal style, and the Schneider brewery still brews wheat beers in Munich. Wheat beers are now so popular in Bavaria that they account for nearly a quarter of all beers sold there.

Wheat beers should be served cool but not ice cold: 45°F (7°C) is about right. Weizen really should be served in its special vase-shaped glass, as it can hold the entire beer, including its frothy head. Erdinger, Bavaria's number one wheat-beer brewer, recommends that the glass be scrupulously clean and wetted first, to keep the head under some control. And the lemon should be cut with a grease-free knife, lest any oil interfere with the spectacular head.

Brewed with 50 to 60 percent malted wheat and the balance of malted barley, these beers are pale to deep gold with a definite yeasty haze. They are lightly hopped, with no apparent hop aroma. The aftertaste should be clean and smooth, with little lingering bitterness. The wheat contributes a firm, creamy texture and a bright, almost citric snap. Carbonation levels are very high, and because of the protein content of the wheat, the beer should have a dense, meringuelike head.

Weizens are top-fermented using a special ale yeast with a phenol off-flavor (POF) gene that allows it to make a chemical called 4-vinyl guaiacol, giving this style its characteristic clove/allspice aroma (see page 91). The fermentation character is always a balance between spice, banana, and bubble gum. The specific character varies from brewery to brewery. For some, these extreme fermentation characteristics are an acquired taste, but once you get acquainted with them, they're entirely lovable.

ORIGIN: Munich, Germany; originally a monopoly of the royal family; hugely popular in the eighteenth century

LOCATION: All over Bavaria; also U.S. and international craft breweries

AROMA: Fruity (bubble gum, bananas) plus spicy (cloves, allspice)

TO LEMON OR NOT TO LEMON?

There is no clear answer. The slice of lemon that often adorns the rim of the Weissbier "vase" goes in and out of fashion. I was told that weizen was once more sour, and when the recipes were changed, old-timers began squeezing lemons in their beer to add the missing acidity. Currently, you're likely to get it in the United States, so if you feel it is an abomination, by all means ask that it not be added when you order. On the other hand, it makes a nice presentation and adds to the spritzy character of the beer. I will say that if you're a beer geek seeking the respect of your equally geeky friends, you had best leave it off.

FLAVOR: Light graininess with milk-shake texture; not much in the way of hops, although "hopfen-weisse" versions are showing up; highly carbonated

BALANCE: Dry malty/grainy; some richness and creamy texture

Weizen in a nineteenth-century knobby glass

SEASONALITY: Year-round; traditionally enjoyed in the summer

PAIR WITH: Wide range of lighter foods; salads, seafood; classic with Weisswurst

SUGGESTED BEERS TO TRY: Erdinger Weissbier, Hacker-Pschorr Weisse, Schneider Weisse Weizen Hell; check your local brewpub in the summer

GRAVITY: 1.044–1.052 (11.0–12.9°P)
ALCOHOL: 4.9–5.6% by volume
ATTENUATION/BODY: Thick but dry
COLOR: 2–6 SRM, straw to pale amber
BITTERNESS: 8–15 IBU, low
NOTE: Kristal (filtered) versions have the same specs.

Bavarian Dunkelweizen

This is the same beer as Bavarian Hefeweizen but with added crystal or other dark malts. It's most often a deep amber color (*steinfarbenes* in German) rather than a true brown, and the emphasis is on caramel rather than toastiness. It may sometimes be a touch sweeter than the standard hefeweizens.

SUGGESTED BEERS TO TRY: Ayinger Urweisse, Schneider Weisse Unser Original, Franziskaner Weissbier Dunkel

GRAVITY: 1.044–1.056 (11.0–13.8°P)
ALCOHOL: 4.3–5.6% by volume
ATTENUATION/BODY: Thick but dry
COLOR: 14–23 SRM, pale to medium amber
BITTERNESS: 10–18 IBU, low

Roggenbier

This is a variant on Bavarian Dunkelweizen, substituting malted rye for the wheat. Rye gives the beer a mix of deep fruity/tobacco notes and some spiciness as well.

Weizenbock and Weizen Doppelbock

Bigger, stronger, and darker than dunkelweizen, this is the perfect winter wheat beer. All the same fruit-bowl aroma is there, but it also has some deep caramelized malt aromas, and maybe hints of toast as well. Despite the strength, these are very drinkable beers. Schneider also makes an eisbock version that is frozen to remove some water, which brings it up to 12 percent alcohol. It takes a cold day to stand up to that.

ORIGIN: Bavaria, Germany; a stronger, darker version brewed as a luxury product

LOCATION: Bavaria, Germany; also U.S. craft breweries

AROMA: Rich caramel malt plus fruity/spicy yeast

FLAVOR: Creamy, caramelly malt; hint of bitterness

BALANCE: Malty and sweet but highly carbonated

SEASONALITY: Year-round but best in cooler weather

PAIR WITH: Hearty food, such as roast pork, beef, smoked ham; big desserts; aged cheese

SUGGESTED BEERS TO TRY: Erdinger Pikantus, Schneider Mein Aventinus

GRAVITY: 1.064–1.090 (15.7–21.6°P)
ALCOHOL: 6.5–9.30% by volume
ATTENUATION/BODY: Medium
COLOR: 6–25 SRM, amber
BITTERNESS: 15–30 IBU, low to medium

Berliner Weisse

Berliner Weisse is a classic, but it has been losing ground in its homeland for almost 150 years. Only a single large brand remains in Berlin: Kindl. A second independent brewery, Berliner Bürgerbräu, closed recently but many local brewpubs continue the tradition.

It's a shame, because in many ways Weisse is right for the times. Low in alcohol with a sour, quenching finish, it's easy to drink in quantity as a summer refresher. Their yeasty sediment earned them the name "white beers." In Germany, they are served with a dash of raspberry syrup or essence of woodruff, but the latter has been banned in food and drinks in the United States and limited in Germany, so substitutes have been developed.

German brewers brought tart and spritzy Berliner-style wheat beers with them to America during the massive immigration that followed the Civil War. Once a prominent part of the product line of many lager breweries in the United States, Weisse beer was often brewed with corn grits (about 30 percent) rather than wheat and was between 1.040 and 1.048 (10 and 12°P), stronger than current Berliner versions. In the United States, it succumbed to the one-two punch of anti-German sentiment during WWI and then Prohibition and was forgotten for nearly a century.

Thanks to the growing popularity of kettle souring, which offers a safe and controllable method of lactic fermentation, Berliner Weisse is making a minor comeback, at least in the United States. Wort is run into the kettle, inoculated with lactic acid bacteria, and held between 112 and 120°F (44 and 49°C) for 12 to 48 hours. The wort is then boiled to kill any microbes before proceeding to fermentation.

ORIGIN: Berlin, Germany, part of a family of white beers developed in the late Middle Ages; related versions once popular in America's brewing heartland

LOCATION: Berlin, Germany, and U.S. craft breweries

AROMA: Bright yogurt tang; a little fruitiness

FLAVOR: Light graininess with sharp, yogurt acidity; highly carbonated

BALANCE: Superlight and dry, with tart, crisp finish

SEASONALITY: A traditional summer beer

PAIR WITH: The lightest salads and seafood, perhaps a mild cheese

SUGGESTED BEERS TO TRY: Bayerischer Bahnhof Berliner Style Weisse, The Bruery Hottenroth Berliner Weisse, Professor Fritz Briem's 1809 Berliner Style Weisse; also check your local brewpub for summer seasonal versions

GRAVITY: 1.028–1.032 (7–8°P)
ALCOHOL: 2.5–3.5% by volume
ATTENUATION/BODY: Tart and dry
COLOR: 2–4 SRM, pale straw to pale gold
BITTERNESS: 3–6 IBU, ultralow

Historical Style

Broyhan Alt

A brewer named Cord Broyhan in Hanover, Germany, invented this very famous white beer in 1526. Originally a wheat beer, by the late nineteenth century it had turned into a purely barley-malt beer. It was a modest-gravity beer and was said to have a vinous aroma and a salty-sour taste.

Historical Style

Grätzer/ Grodziskie

Grodziskie is a low-gravity ale brewed with oak-smoked wheat malt. It was once quite popular in West Prussia but died out for a while. Such variants on white beers were once very popular in northern Europe especially, and they represent the end of the spectrum that also includes Berliner Weisse and Belgian witbiers. Ranging from 1.028 to 1.032 in gravity, with correspondingly low alcohol at 2 to 2.8 percent by volume, this sourish, smoky, highly carbonated beer could have been enjoyed in quantity as an everyday thirst-quencher. Grodziskie would have been amber in color due to a proportion of well-kilned malt along the lines of "aromatic" or melanoidin types. Polish homebrewers have been working hard at reviving this fascinating style, going so far as presenting their beers to brewery workers who remember the beer, and even locating a special yeast strain hiding in a brewing culture library.

Historical Style

Gose

Gose is a white beer once very popular in northern Germany around Jena, Leipzig, and its namesake town, Goslar. Brewed from 40 percent barley malt and 60 percent wheat malt, gose is a very pale, top-fermenting beer seasoned with coriander and salt, which enhances body and mouthfeel in this very light beer. At some of the pubs, you could request your preferred level of salt.

I've always thought it was pretty interesting and even brewed it for Michael Jackson back in 1997. Gose is now being brewed by at least three brewers in Germany, and one example from Bayerischer Bahnhof is currently being imported into the United States. Here there is a real rebirth going on, as the tart, spicy, and slightly salty flavors have caught the attention of beer fans seeking something funky, unique, and fun. At last count several dozen breweries in the United States were brewing gose, including some very large craft breweries.

SUGGESTED BEERS TO TRY: Anderson Valley The Kimmie, the Yink, and the Holy Gose; Bayerischer Bahnhof Leipziger Gose; Döllnitzer Ritterguts Gose; Off Color Troublesome; Sixpoint Jammer

Lichtenhainer

This is a smoked, top-fermenting beer from northern Germany. Always a relatively low-gravity beer (1.045 [11°P] in 1886; 1.031 [7°P] in 1898), lichtenhainer featured a smoky palate from 100 percent barley malt, although up to a third wheat was used in later versions. Like many white beers, it was lightly hopped and had a good smack of acidity. It, too, is finding favor again, with a handful of versions being produced in the United States and Germany.

Lichtenhainer Mug
Sometimes beers are fun to present in a dedicated vessel.

CHAPTER 12

THE BEERS OF BELGIUM

Ahhh, Belgium! The great adventure theme park for the beer-curious, the wine lover's beer destination, the foodie's easy-pairing resource, a living museum of beer history — Belgium is many things to many people.

The beers of Belgium couldn't be more distinctive, even though brewing in Belgium has similar roots to those of other European countries. The current beer scene is a fascinating mix of ancient folkways and postmodern creativity.

BELGIUM IS A SMALL COUNTRY that never formed a great empire, but it was prosperous from an early age. In the late Middle Ages and Renaissance, Flanders (which forms an important portion of modern Belgium) was one of the economic powerhouses of northern Europe. Over the centuries, tiny Belgium has been dominated by all the nearby powers but was never completely absorbed into them.

Belgium comprises a number of smaller regions, each with its own language, culture, and, of course, beer specialties.

5,000 Years of Belgian Beer

We'll start the story with the same Iron Age Gauls we — and Caesar — encountered in England. One tribe, the Belgae, was reputedly a warlike mix of Celts and Germans who, it is said, loved beer. The widespread beverage-centered Beaker culture was present as early as 2800 BCE, so there is a very long tradition of drinking in Belgium. With the vacuum created by the collapse of the Roman Empire, power shifted to local lords and ecclesiastical authorities based in the abbeys.

BREWING MONKS

By the eighth or ninth century, monasteries dotted the countryside across northern Europe. Large amounts of beer were needed to ensure smooth functioning of the monasteries, so brewing was a necessary function. Because many of the religious orders specified that monks must work to support themselves, the brewing was not left to outsiders.

A famous medieval document shows the plan for the Monastery of St. Gallen, Switzerland, in about 830 CE. This was never built, but it served as an idealized example of the kind of organization and scale that were appropriate for such an institution. The plans show three distinct brewhouses, each dedicated to brewing a different grade of beer. Noble guests got a high-class beer brewed from barley and wheat, while the brothers and poor pilgrims had to make do with the lower-quality oat beers. It is estimated that such a brewery complex could have produced 350 to 400 liters (6 to 7 U.S. half-barrels) of beer per day, so there was definitely some drinking going on.

ONE OF THE EARLIEST WRITTEN references to the specifics of brewing comes from the abbess Hildegard of Bingen, who in 1067 noted that beer was mainly made from oats. She liked her nuns to drink beer because, she said, it gave them "rosy cheeks." Thirteenth-century documents mention beers made from barley, spelt, and something called siliginum, which scholars believe may have been rye. Other documents show that brewers in Liège and Namur paid their taxes in spelt, a brewing grain that is still traditional in those parts of Belgium almost a thousand years later.

In those early days, there was no hopped beer in Belgium. Bitterness was provided by a mixture called gruit, which contained a secret mix of herbs and spices disguised by its combination with crushed grain. The right to sell gruit, the *Gruitrecht*, was held by either a religious power or a political big shot. In the twelfth century, 5 pounds (2.3 kg) of gruit was required to brew a barrel of beer (2 kg/hL). It must have been big business back then, as the lavishness of the still-standing Gruithuis (gruit house) in Bruges can attest (see page 16).

BELGIAN BEER THROUGH TIME

1980s: Belgian beer in United States and other international markets for first time

1971: Duvel turns from dark to pale beer

1950s–60s: Period of expansion of specialty beers and high growth in exports

c. 1948–58: Jean DeClerck rebuilds Chimay brewery, writes amazing brewing book

1940–45: WWII reasonably devastating

1933–34: Westmalle trademarks "Trappistenbier" and creates pale tripel

1931: Orval starts brewing

1928: Alken Maes brews first Belgian Pilsner

1923: Duvel created as a dark clone of McEwan's Scotch Ale

1920s: Golden Age of Belgian beer

1919: Government bans on-premises sale of gin

WWI (1914–18): The Great War just about ruins Belgium. The beer fares pretty poorly, too

1908: Half of all beers in Wallonia: 5°P/1020 OG

1902–04: Professor Henri Van Laer's "Contest for the Improvement of Belgian Beer" leads to improved, "export quality" beers

1900: Imports from UK and Germany out-competed Belgian beers

1899: Rochefort establishes brewery

1890s: Brewing consultant George Maw Johnson: Belgian beer in sorry state

1871: Westvleteren starts brewing

1863: Chimay starts brewing

1856: Westmalle starts selling in local area

1851: Georges Lacambre writes *Traité Complet de la Fabrication des Bières*

1833: First monastery in Belgian territory opens after French Revolution

1822: Dutch take over, institute ridiculous tax law: brewers taxed on *volume* of mash tun

1797: All monasteries in Belgian territory closed because of French Revolution

1400–1750: Big gap in the beer history books

c. 1300: Hopped beer comes to Flanders

1254–98: King Gambrinus, a mythic personification of beer, may or may not have been Jan Primus, Duke of Brabant

Somewhat earlier: Romans describe Celtic Belgae tribe as warlike beer drinkers

A Brother at the Chimay Brewery
Although monasteries brewed in the Middle Ages, current abbey and Trappist beers are modern creations.

It is the Belgians who provided us with one of the mythic personifications of beer, King Gambrinus. He may have been an actual person named Jan Primus (Jean I), born around 1250, who ruled as Duke of Brabant, the part of Belgium that now includes Brussels. He was, by contemporary accounts, an all-around great guy: a warrior, a great lover, a bon vivant, and as politically skilled as he was ambitious. Or there are other candidates. It may have been the Burgundian John the Fearless (1371–1419), a cupbearer of Charlemagne who bore the name Gambrinus, or simply a corruption of a couple of different Latin phrases: *cambarus*, meaning "cellarer," or *ganae birrinus*, "tavern drinker." Since given his beer-king status by the Bavarian chronicler Johannes Turmair in 1519, Gambrinus has served as the jolly, fat-faced symbol of all that is good 'n' beery all across northern Europe. If you want to hoist a tankard in honor of his birthday, it is celebrated on April 11.

Hops first came into Flanders by way of beer imported from Hamburg and Amsterdam, certainly by the beginning of the fourteenth century. In 1364, the Bishop of Liège gave permission for local brewers to use hops and shortly thereafter levied a tax on hopped beer, a pattern we see whenever hops are introduced.

Throughout the centuries, we do get some observations about Belgian beer. The herbalist Johannes Theodorus (1588) states, "The beer of Flanders is a good beer. Above all, the double beer, such as is brewed in Ghent and Bruges, surpasses all the beer of the Netherlands." It is estimated that this double beer would have been in the neighborhood of 1.077 original gravity (19 degrees Plato) and possibly 6 to 7 percent alcohol. He also advises that wheat, spelt, rye, or oats could be used in two- or three-part combinations or singly if needed. Don Alonzo Vasquez, a Spanish sea captain

King Gambrinus on a German postcard, c. 1900

stationed in Belgium around 1616, reports, "Beer, which is brewed on a base of wheat, has a color as clear as linen and it froths forth when one pours it into the jug." These tantalizing tidbits are always far too brief, but they do give insight into the vibrancy of the Belgian beer scene back then.

BREWING MOVES INTO THE PUBLIC SPHERE

By the seventeenth century, brewing had moved well beyond the monasteries. Numerous public brewers existed, and the bourgeoisie in towns had established communal brewhouses similar to the Zoigl system in eastern Bavaria, where different individuals took turns brewing for their households. By 1718, there were 621 such breweries in Bruges alone.

About this time we start to see beers we can recognize. In 1698, the intendant of Flanders recorded, "The Flemish use for their beer a sort of barley named winter barley. After having germinated it in water, they add an eighth part short oats, milled without being germinated, and boil the lot for 24 hours. They then barrel the liquid in half-hogsheads where it ferments by means of a certain amount of yeast. Fifteen days later, the beer is fit to drink." It should be noted that this boiling of the mash might be an incorrect impression by a nonbrewing observer.

Monasteries saw their political influence wane over the centuries, but they were more influential centers of power in strongly Catholic Belgium than in most European countries. Even so, the monasteries closed in 1797 during the turmoil of the French Revolution and stayed shuttered during the Napoleonic struggles that followed. Most that reopened did so between 1830 and 1840. This created a 40-year gap, disrupting the traditions of monastic brewing. We don't know what was lost or forgotten during this period, but it is clear that today's Trappist beers have more to do with the twentieth century than the eighteenth.

In 1822, the Dutch administrators of Belgium instituted a tax system in which brewers were taxed, per batch, on the capacity of their mash tuns. As the English observer G. M. Johnson said in 1916, ". . . the reigning monarch was William I, of anything but blessed memory in brewing circles, for he was signatory to, if not otherwise responsible for, one of the most ridiculous and vexatious Excise laws that ever disgraced the annals of fiscal interference and fiscal stupidity. . . . For the space of some 60 years (1822–1885), the best minds in the Belgian brewing world seem to have concentrated on the problem of getting a quart into a pint pot." This strange system led to many peculiarities of Belgian beers, most importantly the turbid mash procedures that are still used, in modified form, to brew witbier and lambic. When the law was changed to an English-style excise system, consumers complained that the beers were thinner and not as fine as before. Eventually part of the old processes returned.

BELGIAN INDEPENDENCE

The Belgians finally gained their independence in 1830 after 13 changes of overlords. I'm sure there are other reasons for the uniqueness of Belgian beer culture, but I think one explanation is that as foreign princes came and went, people tried to hold on to things they felt were truly Belgian. Beer is as pure as it gets in that regard, and taxation aside, foreign potentates usually left it alone, as an adequate supply of beer helps to cool the embers of discontent.

A fairly complete description of the state of Belgian brewing in 1851 is given by Georges Lacambre in his *Traité Complet de la Fabrication des Bières*. "There is not a country," he says, "that brews so many specialties of different natures and varied tastes as Belgium and Holland." According to Lacambre, multigrain was the name of the game: ". . . although a few beers were brewed with barley malt exclusively, in most places they brew with barley, oats, wheat, and spelt concurrently." He points out that even the beers considered barley based, such as *bière d'orge* of Antwerp, contained "a little oats, or sometimes wheat." He notes the antiquity of many of these styles, which our earlier historical references confirm. There is much about Belgian beer that is very old indeed, especially the many adjunct beers broadly in the white-beer family. But despite the remarkable thoroughness of Lacambre's book, there's not a whisper about monastic beer or anything that sounds like farmhouse brewing in it.

FIFTY YEARS LATER, in 1895, G. M. Johnson reported the Belgian brewing scene to be in a very sorry state. Breweries were small and ill equipped, and the beers were largely weak and sourish and sold quickly to locals. In 1908, half the beers in Wallonia were 1.020 original gravity (5 degrees Plato) or lower, barely capable of producing 2 percent alcohol. Low import duties were part of the problem. Imported English and Scotch ales and German lagers were so cheap that Belgian brewers couldn't brew them at competitive prices, so imports dominated the premium beer segment.

Naturally the brewers weren't happy about this. Through the Belgian Brewers Guild, the prominent brewer Henri Van Laer organized a Contest for the Improvement of Belgian Beer in 1902. The object was to create some respectable beers in the 1.044 to 1.057 (11 to 14 degrees Plato) range, with an eye to exports. Since brewing details were to be made public,

 ## BELGIAN BEER ACCORDING TO G. LACAMBRE, 1851

Bière d'Orge d'Anvers (barley beer of Antwerp). Often brewed with a little wheat or oats, the best ones were all barley malt, around 5 to 6 percent alcohol by volume and aged for at least 6 months. Amber to brown in color; chalk sometimes added to kettle to darken wort. Lightly hopped, but with an emphasis on aroma. Well-aged batches often blended with fresher beer or sweetened with caramel syrup.

Bière d'Orge des Flandres (barley beer of Flanders, also called *uytzet*). Brewed around Ghent, mainly of amber-colored barley malt with a little wheat or oats. Two versions: an ordinary

at 3.2 percent alcohol by volume, and a double at 4.5 percent. Both were moderately hopped.

Bière Brune des Flandres (brown beer of Flanders). A lightly hopped 4 to 5 percent alcohol brown beer brewed from barley malt, sometimes with a little wheat or oats. Color entirely due to a 15- to 20-hour boil.

Bières de Maastricht, Masek, Bois-le-Duc. This was a family of very lightly hopped brown beers brewed in the Dutch parts of Belgium and popular in the interior of Holland, brewed from hard durum wheat, malted spelt, and low-protein wheat.

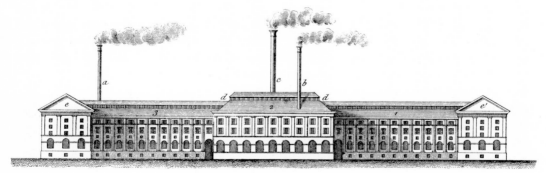

Grande Brasserie, Ghent, 1851
Lacambre's own brewery was a technological marvel, impressive even by today's standards.

few entered. When Van Laer held another contest in 1904, secrecy prevailed, and there was a flood of entries — a number of which, such as Palm Spéciale, Ginder Ale, and Op-Ale, still exist. Despite this encouraging development, it would be some time before things improved across the board.

THE GREAT WORLD WARS

World War I pushed the tailspin even faster. The Germans requisitioned all copper brewing equipment and instituted very strict rationing of materials and ingredients. Original gravities fell to 1.010 to 1.015 (3 to 4 degrees Plato), at that point not much more than weak barley tea. Brewers were so desperate for yeast-nourishing

---

***Bière d'Orge Wallones* (Verviers, Namur, Charleroi)** (Wallonian* barley beers). An unruly group, widely variable in taste and color; all between 4 and 5 percent alcohol by volume and aged 4 to 6 months before drinking. Versions from Liège and Mons employed hard (high protein) wheat, spelt, oats, and sometimes even buckwheat or broad beans.

Peetermann. A "strongly amber" variant of witbier, with gravities of 1.057 to 1.074 (14 to 18 degrees Plato). Chalk was usually added to darken the wort. The finished beer was poorly attenuated and described as "viscous."

Bières de Diest. Two types, including one called "*gulde bier*" or "*bière de cabaret*," which was 44 percent malt, 40 percent unmalted wheat, and 16 percent oats and was described as "unctuous and slightly sweet." The other, known properly as *diest*, was a dark, sweet beer, brewed from 55 percent malt, 30 percent unmalted wheat, and 15 percent oats and available in two strengths: a single at 1.047 to 1.049 (12 to 12.5 degrees Plato) and a double at 1.061 to 1.081 (15 to 19.5 degrees Plato). Diest had the reputation of being a nourishing beer, good for nursing mothers.

*Wallonia is the French-speaking portion of Belgium.

Bière Brune de Malines (brown beer of Mechelen). "Very dark," due to a 10- to 12-hour boil, usually with chalk added. One-quarter to one-third of a 180-month-old batch was blended into fresh beer for "a certain taste of old beer," very much along the lines of the Flanders sour beers, although Mechelen is no longer home to that style.

Bière de Hoegaerde. A pale wheat beer that he describes as "of little importance" but "very agreeable in the summertime," with "a certain acidity and refreshing mousy quality." Brewed from 63 percent malt, 21 percent unmalted wheat, and 16 percent oats.

Bières de Lierre, "Cavesse" (Lier). Brewed from 67 percent malt, 13 percent wheat, and 20 percent oats and available in two strengths. Lacambre describes this as a "*bière jaune*" (yellow beer) that had a lot in common with beers from Hoegaarden and Leuven.

Bières de Liège. Elsewhere called Liège saison, this style was brewed from barley and spelt malts plus oats and wheat. There were two strengths: a "*bière jeune*" (young beer) and a "*bière de saison*," by which was meant it was brewed in the proper brewing season of winter.

nitrogen that malt rootlets — normally used for animal feed — were added to the mash.

Once the war was over, matters took several years to improve. In 1919, the Belgian government banned the sale of gin in taverns and cafés. This opened up a market for stronger beers aimed at drinkers used to their fiery jenever (the local gin). By the 1920s, Belgian brewers had regained their footings, and the quality of their beer improved. Many of the old styles were dead, but others lived on. There was also a new hybrid class of beers that melded Belgian and English traditions. Duvel, for example, was first brewed in 1923 as a dark beer, using a strain of yeast from the Scottish brewery McEwan's. There was a lot of positive sentiment toward the British, who, after all, had come to the rescue with the rest of the Allies during the war.

The beer map of Belgium changed dramatically in the hundred years after Lacambre laid out its incredible variety. Some varieties, such as lambic and witbier, survived. Others, such as uytzet and the darker *bière brune de Flandres*, have new names but otherwise line up pretty well with current oak-aged, blended Flemish reds and brown ales. Many disappeared, and by the time Jean DeClerck was writing his epic brewing book midcentury, quite a few were just distant memories. In their place were new beers: Belgian pale ale, saison, and tripel.

Although Scourmont (Chimay) had been brewing since 1862, most of the modern Trappist beers showed up between the wars. Orval got its brewery going in 1931, and registered its image of a fish with a ring in its mouth in 1934. Westmalle registered the name Trappistenbier in 1933 and a year later created the first pale tripel, a beer that would become a widely copied icon for the style.

Postcards featuring ruined breweries were a macabre specialty after the Great War, bringing home the unimaginable scale of destruction.

The Bavarians had set up lager breweries in Belgium in the second half of the nineteenth century. The dark Munich style was known, but lager breweries in Belgium and France mainly focused on bière de mars (Märzen), bock, and later, blonde. In 1895 G. M. Johnson reported that only 25 of the 2,700 breweries in Belgium were dedicated to bottom fermentation, but many were sizable operations. One can see similarities between those dark Münchener and bock beers and some of the rich, luscious flavors that eventually found their way into dubbels. The first Pilsner brewed in Belgium was Cristal Alken in 1928. As everywhere else, Pilsner currently dominates the Belgian marketplace.

World War II was another disaster for Belgium, but this one was not as disruptive to brewing in the long run, probably because the brewing industry was in a pretty good state prior to the conflict. There were problems, to be sure, but after the war things picked up more or less where they left off. Pilsner kept growing at the expense of the local everyday beers such as Peetermann and white beer, until they disappeared. Belgian brewers eventually found a market for their luxurious beers, and today exports make up a growing 50 percent of their capacity.

The Uniqueness of Belgian Beer

Although there are specific styles (presented here at length), the Belgians favor an artisanal approach to brewing, meaning the brewer is considered an artist with no expectation of conforming to preexisting styles. More than half of all Belgian beers do not exactly fit into any style, and the styles they do claim tend to be interpreted rather casually. This makes it difficult to get a handle on things, but who doesn't like this kind of adventure?

There's a huge variety of strengths, colors, textures, and brewing methods; hundreds of distinctive yeasts and other microorganisms; fermentation in barrels; blended beers; sugar, honey, and caramel syrup in addition to malt; unmalted grains such as oats, wheat, spelt, and occasionally buckwheat; a whole basket of fruit; every conceivable kind of spice, including grains of paradise, chamomile, cumin, star anise, and a "medicinal lichen." The list is long, deep, wide, and exhilarating.

ONE THING THAT UNITES all this joyful chaos, with the exception of industrial Pilsners, is the use of highly distinctive yeast. Most Belgian beers do not use truly wild microorganisms; those are limited mostly to the lambic family and the sour *oud bruins* of Flanders. But the yeast in Belgium is very diverse, and the strain employed in a beer definitely puts its unique stamp on the finished product. Brewers encourage this by fermenting some styles at relatively high temperatures, which encourages fruity and spicy aromas. You can, in fact, take any kind of wort and ferment it with Belgian yeast, and the result will be a Belgian-tasting beer. There are some styles, however, such as saison, that absolutely depend on particular yeast strains, and if they're not used, the beer really becomes something else.

Because there are so many strains, it is sometimes difficult to understand their splendid variety. Leaving wild bugs out of the picture for now, I find it useful to think about Belgian yeast as a continuum ranging from fruity/estery on one end to sharp and phenolic on the other. An example of the first might be Brasserie d'Achouffe in the Ardennes; at the other end is saison, especially the dry and peppery yeast used by Brasserie Dupont. Of course, the aromatic balance is affected by temperature, pitching rate, and other factors, so brewers have plenty of control over this.

On the whole, there is much more emphasis on malt than on hops. The Belgian hop varieties have traditionally been of good aroma but very low in bittering ability. Hop aroma is so assertive that it can mask other, more delicate aromas, and the Belgians prefer a more layered, nuanced approach than what hop bombs offer. And some of the malty flavors actually come from dark-cooked caramel syrups and other types of sugar. Sugar can be a bad thing if used in excess, but it is mainly used in stronger Belgian beers to thin out the body and make them more drinkable.

Belgium was never much for purity laws, so the old traditions of herbs and spices other than hops still survive there. Lacambre makes an interesting comment about this, stating that coriander, orange peel, grains of paradise, and others are "English spices." And indeed, those do show up in English recipes until the mid-nineteenth century, especially in noncommercial estate breweries. Not all Belgian beers employ spices, and even in the ones that do, it's not always obvious. Generally, if you can pick out an individual spice, the brewer is doing it wrong. Bitter orange peel (or the small unripe form, curaçao) and coriander are the dynamic duo, essential in witbier and slipped into many others. The bright peppery zip of grains of paradise (an African relative of cardamom) is often encountered in saisons and other strong pale beers. Richer, deeper dark beers take

well to such spices as licorice, star anise, and even cumin.

There is an abundance of strong beer, and many of these are cork finished, a technique that makes a nice presentation and is being adopted for high-end beers in the United States and elsewhere. Carbonation varies widely, but most strong beers have a huge mousse from carbonation levels up to double what might be appropriate in "normal" beers. Bottle-conditioned beers are common as well. Yeast and a small dose of sugar are added at bottling, and the restarted fermentation creates carbonation, throwing a small deposit of yeast on the bottom of the bottle. To avoid muddying things up when serving, pour carefully or decant. While not unhealthful, the yeast mars the appearance and may add sludgy flavors to the beer.

BELGIUM IS THE ONLY COUNTRY to feature so many acid-tinged beers. The flavors of the ancient lambics really revolve around acidity, at times shockingly so. Sour Flanders red and brown ales live up to their names, and even in some witbiers and saisons, the tang of acidity adds life to these quenching styles.

The final thing to know about Belgian beer culture is that it's not just about the beer. Their highly evolved gastronomic tradition showcases beer as its most important element. You will find restaurants there focused on *cuisine à la bière*, a fantastic way to appreciate Belgian beers in the proper context. With a little research, you can create your own version of that experience just about anywhere. The variety, subtlety, and complexity of Belgian beer makes it a willing food partner.

Belgian Pale Ale

ORIGIN: The De Koninck brewery says its version was created by Johannes Vervliet in 1833; but Antwerp had long been known as a center of malt-based (as opposed to wheat) beers. Modern versions, Palm Spéciale in particular, were created in the early twentieth century to capture the part of the market dominated by imported British pale ales. These really do have a lot of similarities to British ale, including a crisp palate, a definite hop presence, and a nutty, slightly crisp malt character.

LOCATION: Antwerp, Belgium; U.S. craft breweries

AROMA: Clean malt plus spicy yeast notes; yeast character quite subtle compared to most other Belgian styles

FLAVOR: Light caramel malt, lightly hoppy

BALANCE: Evenly balanced; crisp, malty finish

SEASONALITY: Year-round

PAIR WITH: Wide range of foods, such as cheese, mussels, chicken, spicy dishes

SUGGESTED BEERS TO TRY: De Koninck, New Belgium Fat Tire Amber Ale, Palm Spéciale, Two Brothers Prairie Path Ale

GRAVITY: 1.048–1.054 (11.9–13.3°P)
ALCOHOL: 4.8–5.5% by volume
ATTENUATION/BODY: Medium
COLOR: 8–14 SRM, gold to deep amber
BITTERNESS: 20–30 IBU, medium

Belgian Blonde Ale

ORIGIN: Probably spurred by the growing popularity of Pilsners, these blonde ales started showing up in the 1920s.

LOCATION: Belgium

AROMA: Light, bready malt with characteristic fruity Belgian yeast, sometimes with some spicy esters as well

FLAVOR: Delicate malt, possibly with hints of very light caramel, barely balanced by clean bitterness

BALANCE: Evenly balanced; crisp, dry finish

SEASONALITY: Year-round

PAIR WITH: Wide range of foods, such as lighter cheese, mussels, and other seafood

SUGGESTED BEERS TO TRY: Affligem Blonde, Leffe Blonde, St-Feuillien Blonde

GRAVITY: 1.062–1.075 (15.2–18.2°P)
ALCOHOL: 4.8–5.5% by volume
ATTENUATION/BODY: Medium
COLOR: 4–7 SRM, gold to deep amber
BITTERNESS: 15–30 IBU, medium

Belgian Strong Golden Ale

ORIGIN: Moortgat's Duvel is the archetype of the style, but interestingly it was a dark beer until 1971. The first strong Belgian golden-colored ale was Westmalle Tripel, created in 1934. This brings up the question of what, if anything, is the difference between the tripel and strong golden styles. The latter is supposed to be the simpler, cleaner version, but there is a good deal of overlap and, as with many things Belgian, some degree of ambiguity. Complex, fruity yeast; grassy/herbal hop notes; and a crisp finish due to 20 percent corn sugar in the recipe are all-important characteristics of the style.

LOCATION: Belgium, U.S. craft breweries

AROMA: Spicy/fruity yeast plus malt plus hops

FLAVOR: Supercrisp malt, clean hoppy finish

BALANCE: Superdry but moderately bitter; highly carbonated

SEASONALITY: Year-round

PAIR WITH: Wide range of food; salmon, chicken, spicy cuisine such as Thai

SUGGESTED BEERS TO TRY: Brooklyn Brewery Brooklyn Local 1, Delirium Tremens, Duvel, North Coast PranQster Belgian Style Golden Ale

GRAVITY: 1.070–1.095 (17.1–22.7°P)
ALCOHOL: 7.5–10.5% by volume
ATTENUATION/BODY: Superdry
COLOR: 3.5–6.0 SRM, straw to gold
BITTERNESS: 22–35 IBU, medium to high

Belgian Strong Dark Ale

ORIGIN: This really is a catchall category rather than a style with a specific history. As Lacambre points out, there were a number of historic strong, darker beers, but there is no clear lineage from these older brews, with the possible exception of Gouden Carolus, a licorice-tinged

Brew Kettle, 1930s
This northern French or Belgian brew kettle reflects the rustic nature of many small breweries in the area at the time.

deep amber beer that claims descent from the old Mechelen style (see Lacambre, pages 286–87), although the taste and brewing process don't quite jibe with the old description. Modern versions include several Trappist beers (Rochefort and Westvleteren) and a number of more eccentric brews. Sugar, as a body thinner, is quite common.

LOCATION: Belgium, U.S. craft breweries

AROMA: Complex maltiness plus fruity/spicy yeast and maybe a hint of actual spices or licorice

FLAVOR: Fat, caramelly malt, barely balanced by hops

BALANCE: Malty to even; long, rich finish

SEASONALITY: Year-round, but holiday versions abound

PAIR WITH: Very hearty food; strong cheese; fabulous with chocolate

SUGGESTED BEERS TO TRY: Chimay Grande Réserve/Capsule Bleue, Dogfish Head Raison d'Etre, Het Anker Gouden Carolus, Goose Island Pere Jacques, Van Steenberge Gulden Draak

GRAVITY: 1.075–1.110 (18.2–25.9°P)
ALCOHOL: 8.0–12.0% by volume
ATTENUATION/BODY: Dry to moderately full
COLOR: 12–22 SRM, amber to brown
BITTERNESS: 20–35 IBU, medium

Abbey and Trappist Ales

The term "Trappiste" is an appellation, a legal designation with the enforceability of a trademark, allowing only brewers who meet certain requirements to use the name. Trappist beers must be brewed under the direct supervision of the monks at a brewery on the monastic property. Although the designation was in use by 1900, exclusive rights to the name Bière Trappiste or Trappistenbier were won for the group in 1962 as a result of a legal action spearheaded by Chimay. Abbey beers are of similar styles but are brewed by secular commercial breweries that may be under license to an active abbey, named for a defunct one, or with no specific monastic connection whatsoever.

Trappist ales are an unruly group, reflecting the beer traditions of the regions in which they're located. At present there are 11 Trappist breweries (see sidebar, pages 294–95): 6 in Belgium; 2 in the Netherlands; and 1 each in Austria, Italy, and the United States. Trappist

beers are highly individualistic, although Westmalle Tripel and Chimay Rouge (Dubbel) are archetypes of their specific styles. As a group, these are all superb beers. It's a rare beer fancier who doesn't have at least a couple of Trappist beers in his or her top 10. Singels are rare, often brewed just for the monks.

Abbey beers exist in greater numbers and tend to cleave to the convention of a brown dubbel and a blonde tripel, with the occasional blonde or strong dark tossed into the mix.

A FEW CLASSIC TRAPPIST BREWERIES AND THEIR ALES

Achel

(Brouwerij der Sint-Benedictusabdij de Achelse Kluis)

Founded in 1648, rebuilt in 1844. Some brewing was done in the late nineteenth century, but the brewery was dismantled by the Germans in World War I and not rebuilt and certified as a Trappist brewery until 1998. Beers include Blond 8, a tripel at 1.079 original gravity (19.1 degrees Plato); Bruin 8, at 1.079 original gravity (17.9 degrees Plato); Bruin Extra, at 1.090 original gravity (21.5 degrees Plato); plus the blond Achel 5 (at 5 percent alcohol), which is only available locally.

Chimay

(Abbaye de Notre Dame de Scourmont)

Brewing since 1863, the brewery was rebuilt in 1948 by the prominent Belgian brewing scientist Jean DeClerck, who had a lot to do with the current recipes. Chimay produces several beers, including Capsule Rouge, a classic dubbel at 1.063 original gravity (15.5 degrees Plato), 7 percent; Capsule Blanche (Cinq Cents), a briskly hopped tripel at 1.071 original gravity (17.3 degrees Plato), 8 percent; and Capsule Bleue (Grande Réserve), a big, chewy, strong dark at

1.081 original gravity (19.1 degrees Plato), 9 percent. Chimay also produces a 4.8 percent Dorée, intended for local consumption only.

Orval

Founded in 1132 but rebuilt in 1926 after a period of abandonment following the French Revolution, Orval produces one beer for public sale, an orangish, golden ale broadly in the saison style, at 1.054 to 1.055 original gravity (13.3 to 13.5 degrees Plato), crisply hoppy and very dry, spiked upon bottling with *Brettanomyces* yeast, which after some months starts to develop rich, barnyard aromas. Alcohol is 5.2 to 5.7 percent.

Belgian Abbey Dubbel

ORIGIN: Abbeys brewed these in ancient times, but modern abbey styles were created in the past 100 years.

LOCATION: Belgium, U.S. craft breweries

AROMA: Clean malt, soft hops, spicy/fruity yeast character; middle-color malts are crucial to this style and may manifest as soft hints of cocoa or deep, dried fruit character, such as raisins or prunes

La Trappe/Koningshoeven

(Onze Lieve Vrouw van Koningshoeven)
This brewery in the southern Netherlands has a somewhat complex history, having at times operated an on-site brewery and at other times brewing under license. The current products are fairly recent (dubbel, tripel, 1987; blonde, 1992). It brews a classic dark dubbel at 7 percent, a pale tripel at 8 percent, and a quadruple at 10 percent. The brewery also produces a 6.5 percent blonde, a seasonal bockbier at 7 percent, and a witbier. The brewery was decertified as a Trappist brewery between 1999 and 2005 but has now resolved its dispute with the International Trappist Association.

Rochefort

(Abbaye Notre-Dame de Saint-Remy in Rochefort)
Rochefort was founded in 1230, closed in 1794, then reoccupied by monks in 1889. The brewery was established a few years later, in 1899. They produce three beers designated 6, 8, and 10 but don't follow the degrees Belgian nomenclature. The 6 is actually 1.072 (17.5 degrees Plato), the 8 is 1.078 (19 degrees Plato), and the 10 is 1.096 (23.4 degrees Plato). They share a rich, bittersweet chocolaty character. Alcohol is 7.5 percent, 9.2 percent, and 11.3 percent, respectively.

Westmalle

(Abdij Onze-Lieve-Vrouw van het Heilig Hart van Jezus)
Founded in 1794, Westmalle began selling to the locals in 1856 and through commercial channels in 1921. The brewhouse was modernized in the 1930s, about when it launched its radical new pale tripel. Three beers are produced: an Extra that is enjoyed by the monks; the famous tripel at 1.080 original gravity (20 degrees Plato), 9.5 percent; and a rich dubbel, the recipe for which comes from the earliest times but was reworked in 1926, at 1.063 original gravity (15.7 degrees Plato), 7 percent.

Westvleteren

(The Abbey of Saint Sixtus of Westvleteren)
Established in 1831, the brewery started operations in 1871. It has never really expanded its operations, preferring to remain small. The brewery sells only to individuals, by appointment only, and with a strict limit. In fact, it recently has taken legal action to end gray market trading in its rare beers. The brewery produces a hoppy blonde at 1.051 (12.6 degrees Plato), 41 IBU, and two dark, raisiny beers: the 8, or Blue Cap, at 1.072 (17.5 degrees Plato), around 8 percent, and the 12, or Yellow Cap, at 1.090 (21.5 degrees Plato), 11 percent. Author Stan Hieronymus (*Brew Like a Monk*) reports considerable batch-to-batch variation.

FLAVOR: Soft, creamy malt; considerable spiciness

BALANCE: Malty, yet fairly dry on the palate due to the use of sugar (sometimes dark) as a body thinner

SEASONALITY: Year-round

PAIR WITH: Wide range of hearty food; perfect with barbecued ribs, abbey cheese, tiramisu, chocolate cake, medium-intensity desserts

SUGGESTED BEERS TO TRY: Affligem Dubbel, Chimay Première/Capsule Rouge, Ommegang Abbey Ale, Allagash Dubbel Reserve

GRAVITY: 1.062–1.075 (15.2–18.2°P)
ALCOHOL: 6.0–7.6% by volume
ATTENUATION/BODY: Medium dry
COLOR: 10–17 SRM, amber to brown
BITTERNESS: 15–25 IBU, low to medium

Belgian Abbey Tripel

ORIGIN: Westmalle Abbey in 1930s, in reaction to Pilsner and pale ale trends

LOCATION: Belgium, U.S. craft breweries

AROMA: Spicy/fruity with clean malt, a bit of hops

FLAVOR: Complex clean maltiness with lots of spicy depth; highly carbonated

BALANCE: Honeyed but dry, with clean, crisp finish

SEASONALITY: Year-round

PAIR WITH: Roast pork, rich seafood such as lobster, and creamy desserts such as crème brûlée

SUGGESTED BEERS TO TRY: Bosteels Tripel Karmeliet, Westmalle Tripel, New Belgium Trippel, Unibroue La Fin du Monde

GRAVITY: 1.075–1.085 (18.2–20.4°P)
ALCOHOL: 7.5–9.5% by volume
ATTENUATION/BODY: Rich, but dry
COLOR: 4.5–7 SRM, pale to deep gold
BITTERNESS: 20–40 IBU, medium

Saison

ORIGIN: Where to start? The history of saison as it is commonly told is quite problematic. Saison is said to have originated in farmhouse breweries, brewed for seasonal farm workers to sustain them in their labors. It's a compelling tale that fires the imagination of modern beer enthusiasts seeking rustic authenticity, but there's no real evidence for it.

Farmhouse brewing on a small and primitive scale undoubtedly existed in the foggy past, but by Lacambre's time it played no significant role in beer production. Yes, breweries in rural locations existed, but putting together a small brewery was a significant undertaking, even 150 years ago. Photos around 1900 typically show solid two-story brick buildings with a large central compound and around 20 people on staff, handling everything from manual mash stirring to cooperage to looking after the horses and tack. Beer was not something the farmer's wife was whipping up in her spare time.

Lacambre gives a sensible meaning for the name *saison*, the French word for "season." The term *en saison* meant brewed "in season," that is, between November and March, indicating a full-strength beer (by his numbers usually between 4.5 and 6.5 percent by volume) rather than the weak "single" beers brewed year-round and consumed so quickly that they didn't have time to go bad in the summer heat. It is highly unlikely that farm workers were

given strong beer as they toiled if their employers cared about cost — or productivity.

The other problem is that historically, the name saison was applied to the very eccentric beers from Liège way over in the east, near Germany. Liège saison was brewed with malt, wheat, oats, spelt, and even at times buckwheat or *fèves* (broad beans). The color was amber to brown, the same as all the beers farther west in the part of Wallonia now famous for saison. There are still a lot of dots that need connecting.

At some unknown point (I'm guessing the 1920s, as with many other styles), the modern blonde saison was born. In his 1977 *World Guide to Beer*, Michael Jackson gives only one terse sentence on the subject: "In the South of the country, top-fermented beers are sometimes called *saisons*." So it's clear that there wasn't a big important style revolving about this concept at that time. The boom, apparently, came later.

Today saison may or may not contain wheat, although at least one version (Saison d'Epeautre) contains spelt. Many saison brewers offer

Koelschip at DeDolle Brouwers, Belgium
Coolships were once the universal way to cool wort before fermenters. At lambic breweries they are used to encourage wild fermentations.

a range of strengths; some of the stronger ones are brewed with sugar to improve drinkability.

One of the defining things about the style is the yeast. The strains vary quite a bit, but Dupont's famously phenolic one is likely related to red-wine yeast. It is tolerant of very high fermentation temperatures — above 90°F (32°C), where it produces a lot of peppery phenols but not a lot of esters. Most yeasts at those elevated temperatures would create undrinkably estery beer, reeking of nail polish remover. It's a slow and cranky yeast to deal with, so many brewers start their saison with it and then switch over to a conventional yeast to finish the job. Spices are not required for the style, but grains of paradise, black pepper, and others are sometimes used to complement the character of the yeast.

TURBID MASHING AND SLIJM

Wheat beers go back centuries in Belgium, and in that dark past are all manner of extreme and extensive mashing procedures that make little sense to us today. In addition, the oddball regulation imposed on Belgian brewers between 1822 and 1885 that taxed the capacity of the mash tun influenced the way they brewed many types of beer. Belgian brewers produced lots of "single" or "ordinary" beers at very low gravities, and these have a richer, fuller taste if there are lots of unfermentables in the wort.

Brewing Belgian wheat beers demands special brewing procedures to extract fermentable and unfermentable materials. In lambic brewing, unfermentable dextrins are valuable as food for the *Pediococcus* bacteria; lacking that, the bracing sourness will be missing.

Historically, the game was to absolutely jam-pack the mash tun, which meant very little hot water was used. The normal false bottom wasted too much space, so to filter out the liquid, a stuik-mand, or brewer's basket (a tall wicker basket), was forced down into the mash, letting liquid dribble in through the woven sides. This was then scooped out with big ladles. The most important feature of turbid mashing is that this cloudy,

enzyme-rich wort, known as *slijm,* is run into a kettle fitted with a set of rotating chains that drag the bottom to keep the starch from sticking and scorching. As the slijm boils, the enzymes are destroyed. When this happens, the original mash is then reinfused with very hot water, and mashing proceeds. After a period of time, additional liquid is drawn off the mash and boiled. At this point the boiled slijm is reinfused into grain and mashed again, with more runoffs and boiling of wort. In actuality it's a lot more complicated than there is space here to discuss. The result of this Byzantine procedure is to impair the enzymes' ability to convert starch to fermentable sugar, so that the resulting wort is rich in dextrin.

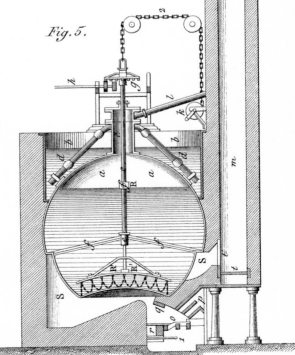

Fig. 5.

Chain Copper, Belgium, c. 1851
This boiling vessel was fitted with chains that were dragged across the bottom to keep fine particles from sticking and burning.

LOCATION: Hainault and Wallonia (Francophone), Belgium

AROMA: Complex, peppery spice; hints of bready malt and fresh hops; sometimes a whiff of citrus

FLAVOR: Creamy pale malt, clean hops; slight tang; may also use spices or *Brettanomyces* wild yeast; very crisp and dry on the palate, but soft and drinkable just the same

BALANCE: Superdry, with clean, hoppy finish

SEASONALITY: Traditional for summer and harvest but good year-round

PAIR WITH: Substantial salads, chicken, richer seafood dishes; very nice with bloomy-rind cheese; earthier versions great with ripened goat cheese

SUGGESTED BEERS TO TRY: Allagash Saison, Brasserie Dupont Saison Dupont, Brasserie des Géants Saison Voisin, Brasserie de la Senne Zinnebir; stronger interpretations include Bruery Terreux Saison Rue, North Coast Le Merle, Boulevard Tank 7

GRAVITY: 1.048–1.080 (11.9–19.3°P)
ALCOHOL: 3.5–9.5% by volume
ATTENUATION/BODY: Superdry
COLOR: 4–14 SRM, gold to amber (although dark versions exist)
BITTERNESS: 20–35 IBU, medium

Witbier/Bière Blanche/White Ale

Witbier is a difficult beer to brew well. The traditional recipe is 50 percent air-dried malt, 45 percent unmalted soft wheat, and 5 percent oats. Traditional wort production is similar to lambic, employing a turbid, or *slijm* ("silt" in English), mash that leaves a lot of starchy carbohydrates in the wort. When raw grains are used with more modern techniques, they need to be boiled briefly to gelatinize the starches, a procedure few small breweries are set up to do. For conventional mashes the best results seem to come from flaked wheat. Either way, the rich, creamy texture is an indispensable part of the style, a fact many brewers don't always realize.

Bitter orange peel and coriander are critical to witbier, but they need to be chosen carefully to avoid vegetal or unpleasantly bitter flavors, and they should always blend together into a harmonious whole rather than sticking out individually. Orange peel, if there is too much pith, can add a harsh, dry bitterness that's really unpleasant. Elderflower has some traditional history of use; chamomile or the peppery/piney grains of paradise are sometimes used as "secret spices."

Witbier is such a strong style that it can support a fair amount of vamping, so occasionally one sees stronger or darker variants that have a high chance of being delicious.

ORIGIN: This once widespread style showed up in medieval northern Europe in the eleventh century or so. White beers were the first hopped beers, although ironically today they are thought of as one of the few styles for which seasonings other than hops are essential. There were many variations, from *kvass* in Russia to Devon white ale in England; many died out by 1900. Berliner Weisse and the recently revived gose are survivors of this family.

The Flemish word *wit* means "white," describing the beer's straw color and hazy appearance. White beers invariably contain wheat and often other grains as well.

By the late nineteenth century, the style was centered around Leuven (Louvain), Belgium, and to a lesser extent the nearby town of Hoegaarden, where by 1955 the last traditional

A Very Young Pierre Celis (second from right), in the Tomsin Brewery, c. 1943
After the last witbier brewery closed in his hometown of Hoegaarden, Belgium, Celis saved the style by opening a brewery and producing Oud Hoegaarden Bier, now sold by InBev as Hoegaarden Witbier. Note that he is holding a *stuikmand*, the brewer's wicker basket used to separate wort from spent grains.

witbier brewery, Tomsin, had closed its doors. Ten years later, Pierre Celis, who had worked there as a youth, decided to revive the style. He founded the Brouwerij Celis (renamed de Kluis in 1978) in a hayloft and launched a beer called Hoegaarden. Eventually, the beer found success and was eventually sold to InBev, and witbier is now being brewed by many breweries worldwide. The industrial giant Molson Coors has had success with their quasi-craft version, Blue Moon.

LOCATION: Belgium, U.S. craft breweries, Japan

AROMA: Spicy yeast plus subtle notes of orange and coriander and possibly hints of other spices

FLAVOR: Dry creaminess; soft, acidic finish

BALANCE: Milk-shake texture but dry; a touch tart

SEASONALITY: Year-round but best enjoyed in warm weather

PAIR WITH: Lighter foods, such as mussels, salmon, chicken

SUGGESTED BEERS TO TRY: St. Bernardus Wit, Brasserie du Bocq Blanche de Namur, Allagash White, Bell's Winter White Ale, Unibroue Blanche de Chambly

GRAVITY: 1.044–1.052 (1.0–12.9°P)
ALCOHOL: 4.5–5.5% by volume
ATTENUATION/BODY: Dry to medium, very creamy
COLOR: 2–4 SRM, pale straw to gold, hazy
BITTERNESS: 8–20 IBU, low to medium

Lambic

ORIGIN: Lambic is an ancient beer brewed in the region surrounding Brussels. It's as weird as beer gets. Lambic has a high proportion (40 to 60 percent) of unmalted wheat and employs the turbid mash procedure discussed on page 298. The extremely diluted and protein-rich worts also require several hours of boiling (as opposed to an hour for most beers). Also, hops are aged for 2 or 3 years until there is very little bitterness or aroma left, as the lambic brewers are looking strictly for their antibacterial properties.

Lambic ferments spontaneously, or at least that's the idea. The classic method is to expose the cooling wort to the night air, upon which drifts an entire zoo of microscopic critters that perform various roles in fermenting and souring the beer. In the old days, the region was rich in fruit orchards that served as the natural ecosystem in which the microbes lived. These days the orchards are gone, and there is some feeling that the old ways are not as reliable as they once were. Part of the problem is that the whole process is so complicated; despite a lot of scrupulous research, there are great swaths of lambic science and practice that are still poorly understood. For instance, when the Lindemans brewery expanded some years ago, they sawed out a whole wall and bolted it in place in the new building, not wanting to take a chance that the necessary organisms wouldn't be there when they needed them.

Fortunately, many of the bugs are quite happily living in the barrels in which lambic is fermented. The stories about lambic brewers never cleaning the spiderwebs off the casks are true. Everybody's walking on pins and needles trying not to upset the delicate balance required for great lambic. No other beer depends so highly on voodoo.

The spontaneous fermentation of lambic begins with an attack by enterobacteria such as *E. coli*, which metabolize the small amount of glucose in the wort and then die off. Next, *Saccharomyces* does the bulk of the fermentation, converting maltose to alcohol and carbon dioxide. At this point things slow down a lot, the earthy and fruity aromas of *Brettanomyces* become apparent, and *Pediococcus* builds up a serious acidity. Long wood aging is required for these slow-acting bugs, and this allows the harsh acidity to mellow. Yeast species common in sherry production add another layer

 ## LAMBICS TO TRY

Straight lambic. Unblended sour beer, rarely available outside Brussels. This can be mellow or scorchingly sour, depending on the blender. It is usually served with little or no carbonation; the traditional method of serving was to provide the drinker with a bowl of sugar cubes and a "stomper" to crush the sugar in the bottom of the glass to add sweetness according to individual taste.
SUGGESTED BEERS TO TRY: Cantillon Bruocsella (1900) Grand Cru, Oud Beersel Lambic, Lambickx

Gueuze. Bottled blend of young and old lambic that was created sometime between 1850 and 1875, when machine-made bottles were available and the taxes on them were eliminated. Gueuze is bottle-conditioned and highly carbonated, although *sans acide carbonique* versions existed in the past. The word *gueuze* is probably related to our English word "geyser," with the obvious meaning that conveys.

SUGGESTED BEERS TO TRY: Cantillon Gueuze 100% Lambic, Lindemans Cuvée René, Drie Fonteinen Oude Gueuze

Faro. A diluted form of lambic, sweetened with caramel syrup and sometimes spiced up with seasonings, faro was by far the most popular form of lambic in the nineteenth century but is rare now.
SUGGESTED BEERS TO TRY: Lindemans Faro Lambic, Cantillan Faro

Fruit lambic. While it's reasonable to think that homemade versions of fruit lambic may have existed for centuries, fruit lambic as a commercial product was only created in the 1930s. Some examples include cherry (kriek), raspberry (framboise), peach, cassis, and many others.
SUGGESTED BEERS TO TRY: Cantillon Rosé de Gambrinus, Kriek Boon (nontraditional), Lindemans Kriek or Framboise

of flavor. Blending is essential to compensate for barrel-to-barrel variation. Even so, some barrels are just too sour, even when diluted and sweetened; in the old days, these were used to clean the brewery's copper kettles.

How sour should lambic be? This is a much-discussed question as a new group of enthusiasts rush to the style, often fixating on its unique acidity to the exclusion of everything else. While there is certainly a place for really sour lambic, it should be remembered that this is meant to be a balanced and incredibly complex beer — acidity is just one feature among many. It's also important to remember that for much of its history, most lambic was consumed in either the thinned and sweetened form, faro, or served with cubes of sugar at hand to cut down the acidity. It's not about low pH and rare "whales" to be hoarded but a pleasurable, refreshing, and profound beverage to be *enjoyed*.

LOCATION: Brussels, Belguim, and the immediate region to the south and west, although spontaneous fermentations are attempted with varying degrees of authenticity (and success) by U.S. and international craft brewers. The term "lambic" is an appellation, restricted to brewers in this Belgian region following approved recipes and procedures.

While they're not for everyone, wild-fermented beers are being developed by a number of American craft breweries and are occasionally available in limited quantities. Look for such products from Cambridge Brewing Company, Jolly Pumpkin, Lost Coast/Pizza Port, New Belgium, Russian River, and others.

AROMA: Yogurt, *Brettanomyces*, vinegar, fruitiness

FLAVOR: Sharp, acidic palate, amazing complexity

BALANCE: Very sharp and acidic, hints of sweetness

SEASONALITY: Year-round

PAIR WITH: Lighter food; cuts fat nicely; fruit versions perfect with desserts

SUGGESTED BEERS TO TRY: See page 301

Lambic Jug
This stoneware jug sums up the earthy sophistication of lambic.

Gueuze

LOCATION: Central Belgium, controlled by an appellation; a blend of young and old lambic, traditionally bottle-conditioned but sometimes packaged in other ways

AROMA: Hugely complex, with fruitiness (especially pineapple), barnyard/*Brettanomyces*, and sometimes hints of oak or vinegar

FLAVOR: From lightly to very acidic and quite dry, often with a woody tannic finish

BALANCE: Acidity against oak tannins; little hops or malt

SEASONALITY: Year-round

PAIR WITH: Nice with seafood and some cheeses but can be difficult to pair

 ## A FEW BELGIAN ECCENTRICS

A great number of Belgian beers make no attempt to conform to any particular style. If you are used to the clear delineation of German categories, this can be confusing at first. Just lighten up, strap in, and enjoy the ride.

Kwak. From Bosteels in Buggenhout, this beer is said to have been created by a brewer/innkeeper named Pauwel Kwak in 1791. It is a rich amber color and features a creamy, caramelly texture and a unique spice profile that is said to include licorice. It is nicely balanced and at 8 percent. It is served in a bulb-bottomed "stirrup cup" that announces its coaching heritage.

De Dolle Brouwers. Literally, "the Mad Brewers," this small brewery in Esen, outside Antwerp, was founded by a mother-and-sons team. They produce a wide range of beers, including a soft blonde Easter beer, a hoppy 8 percent amber, a strong (9 percent) sour, and a stout.

Wostyntje. This beer comes from Brouwerij Smisje. A mustardy-tinged (really!) blonde ale with an English hop profile, this is a seriously crisp and refreshing beer.

Poperings Hommelbier. From Van Eecke in Belgian hop country, this 7.5 percent blonde beer has a bright, fresh nose full of hops, softened by the subtlety of the Belgian approach.

Bush/Scaldis. This extremely strong (12 percent) golden ale from Dubuisson has a slight toffeelike maltiness balanced by a bright Goldings kind of hoppiness, all smoothed out by a long, cool-temperature conditioning. It is highly drinkable despite its strength.

D'Achouffe. This company in the Ardennes makes a range of character-filled brews, including a Scotch ale and an American-style IPA available only in the United States. All of the color in their beers comes from caramel brewer's syrups rather than specialty malts.

Brasserie de la Senne. This is a newer Brussels brewery with one eye on tradition and the other on the wider world of craft beer. Their flagship products Taras Boulba and Zinnebir are both supercrisp and dry blonde ales with a certain saison character, but the brewery makes delicious dark beers as well. The names and labels have entertainingly political content.

SUGGESTED BEERS TO TRY: See page 301

GRAVITY: 1.040–1.060 (10.0–14.7°P)
ALCOHOL: 5.0–8.0% by volume
ATTENUATION/BODY: Utterly dry
COLOR: 3–7 SRM, straw to gold
BITTERNESS: 0–10 IBU, very low

Sour Red and Sour Brown/Oud Bruin

ORIGIN: There are two regional focal points these days for sour brown ale in Belgium. One is in Roeselare, West Flanders, home of Rodenbach, and the other is centered around Oudenaarde, in East Flanders. The two types have many similarities but are not identical. Brown beer, oak aging, and blending of young and old beers were fairly common prior to 1800, but a very few beers of this type have survived to this day. The region and the style line up pretty well with the darker uytzet variation Lacambre describes in 1851, and blends of old and new — including a highly lactic sour brown style way east in Maastricht — seem to have been popular across the north of Belgium in that day.

West Flanders red is exemplified by Rodenbach. These reddish brown beers are brewed conventionally, then aged for close to 2 years in large wooden vats from which they pick up plenty of sourness from *Lactobacillus*, *Acetobacter* (vinegar bacteria), and the wild yeast *Brettanomyces*. This is not a spontaneous fermentation. Wood is a substrate that encourages the growth of these organisms, lending an earthy touch, plus vanilla and other nuances that smooth out the sharp, acidic flavors.

The Oudenaarde brown relies on yeast adulterated with *Lactobacillus* for its unique tart character. The Oudenaarde beers, typified by Liefmans Goudenband, have a complex earthiness about them and sometimes a touch of haze

as well. Liefmans, at least, is not aged in oak, but their Goudenband is a blend of young and old beers.

The reds, in particular, show a variety of blending strategies. They may have a good deal of the sour "old" beer, usually for the more premium products, or just a small amount for a sweet-sour flavor. Such "half-sour" beers as Jack-Op and Zottegem were once quite popular, and a few remain on the market.

Sour ales are fine bases for fruit beers, as the acidity gives the fruit what it needs to taste right. Cherry and raspberry versions of both styles can be found and are well worth seeking out.

LOCATION: Flanders, Belguim; sometimes attempted in the United States

AROMA: Deeply fruity/estery, with acidic notes (vinegar/pickle notes in red ales), hint of malt

FLAVOR: Mellow to sharp acidity with caramel malt or cooked sugar

BALANCE: Sweet and sour; almost no hops

SEASONALITY: Year-round

PAIR WITH: Tangy cheese, rich meat, fried dishes; try with a light fruit tart

SUGGESTED BEERS TO TRY: Jolly Pumpkin La Roja, Liefmans Goudenband, New Belgium La Folie, New Glarus Wisconsin Belgian Red (with cherries), Rodenbach Grand Cru, Verhaeghe Duchesse de Bourgogne

GRAVITY: 1.040–1.074 (10–18°P), most often in the middle of this range
ALCOHOL: 4–8% by volume
ATTENUATION/BODY: Medium to dry
COLOR: 10–22 SRM, deep amber to ruby, but pale versions exist
BITTERNESS: 10–25 IBU, low

French Bières de Garde

ORIGINS: France has always been on the fence about beer. There are passionate beer lovers there, but the wine culture is so strong that beer has trouble getting into the spotlight. Historically, two regions have been the fountains of beer culture in France. Germanic Alsace-Lorraine was France's lager powerhouse, shipping out a plentitude of blondes, bocks, and Märzens. In the Nord, near Belgium, the brews were rustic, top-fermenting brunes and blanches like those in neighboring Flanders and Hainault. The two regions come together in the present day biéres de garde style. The term, synonymous with the German word *lager*, means "beer to store" and originally had no connection to Bavarian beer or any particular style. It was simply a French language term for the "double" or stronger versions of their basic beers and was used in some parts of Belgium as well.

Then came trouble. In 1871, the Germans annexed Alsace-Lorraine after their victory in the Franco-Prussian war, so the greater part of French brewing capacity was no longer under French control. This forced the government to try to improve the brewing capabilities of the Nord breweries, which were not highly industrialized. It also meant a ready market for anything remotely resembling the bocks, blondes, and bières de mars (Märzens) they had been drinking, even if the words *Fermentation Haute* were on the label.

Despite all this, the brewers in the Nord were still pretty unsophisticated; contemporary reporters (R. E. Evans, *Journal of the Institute of Brewing*, 1905) found them in some disarray. As elsewhere, there were two terrible wars with a short, vigorous period between them. Breweries regained some strength in the gap and, perhaps spurred by the success of Belgian brewers across the border, began brewing export-quality luxury beers.

After the damage of the second war was repaired, luxury bottled beers became big business, and the northern French breweries, now in the hands of a more ambitious generation, started packaging up strong beers. Early on, these were mostly brown beers, eventually becoming a mix of brown or *ambrèe* and blonde brews. The blondes are much more popular these days. It's actually becoming fairly difficult to find the darker versions.

They're tasty but particularly profound beers, lacking the more characterful yeast of their Belgian cousins. But the good examples are delicious, and as one might expect from the French, they're very good with a wide range of foods.

LOCATION: Northern France, U.S. craft breweries

AROMA: Complex malt with earthy yeast character

FLAVOR: Caramel malt, hints of toast

BALANCE: Definitely malty, barely balanced by hops

SEASONALITY: Year-round, great in colder weather

PAIR WITH: Hearty, rich food; steak, roast pork, beef stew; simple desserts

SUGGESTED BEERS TO TRY: La Choulette Ambrée, Brasserie La Choulette Bière les Sans Culottes, Lost Abbey/Avant Garde, Russian River Perdition, Two Brothers Domaine DuPage

GRAVITY: 1.060–1.080 (14.7–19.3°P)
ALCOHOL: 6.0–8.5% by volume
ATTENUATION/BODY: Medium to full
COLOR: 6–19 SRM, pale to medium amber
BITTERNESS: 18–28 IBU, low to medium

CHAPTER 13

CRAFT BEER IN AMERICA AND BEYOND

Craft brews sprang from a passionate desire to save our palates from industrialized products that all tasted the same, to salvage the authentic flavors of the world's great beers, and to restore the artist's hand in the making of this beloved beverage. Like so many of the social movements brought on by changes in attitudes during the 1960s, it had audacious and maybe even naïve goals. Whether it has succeeded will have to be judged by history, but it sure is a lot of fun right now. The beer landscape is richer and deeper than ever, and just plain delicious.

Brewing with Purpose

The United States in 1975 was a pretty barren place for good beer. American breweries large and small had been battling it out over price in the decades since World War II, with the result that unbranded generic beer was being sold in supermarkets. The number of genuine specialty beers could be counted on one hand, with fingers to spare.

A number of factors came together to make craft beer a reality. First were the European experiences of military personnel and college students on backpacking adventures. In Britain they found beers with an intimate, personal sensibility; in Germany, beers with a sense of order and righteousness; and in Belgium, an unlimited fountain of beer ideas and ancient taproots. These were profoundly great places to start.

The blind optimism of the baby boomer generation gave us the certain knowledge that we could make whatever kind of future we could envision. So what if nobody had started a brewery in 50 years. How hard could it be?

Born in the Boneyard

In Boulder, Colorado, Charlie Papazian was leading a merry band of homebrewers that eventually coalesced into the American Homebrewers Association, which spread a fun, subversive message of beer self-reliance. Homebrewing was legalized in 1979, ushering in a real boom for hobbyist brewers, who started to dream of bigger things. Around the globe, homebrewing provides the reservoir of energy, ideas, and manpower from which commercial craft beer springs.

Many of these early craft breweries were built from castoffs salvaged from the dairy industry. If there is ever a Craft Beer Hall of Fame, one item on display should be a grundy tank, a seven-barrel cellar forced out of pubs by

Humble Beginnings
Sierra Nevada brewery and brewer/owner Ken Grossman in the early days, c. 1981

DEFINING CRAFT BEER AND CRAFT BREWER

"Craft" is one of those tricky terms that defies exact definition. When you drink craft beer anywhere in the world, you know it when you taste it, but the more precisely you try to define the term, the more challenging the definition becomes. Is craft beer simply about what is in the glass or does who brewed it make a difference? Must it be all malt? If so, then what about wheat beer? Is it about ownership? Can large industrial conglomerates make proper craft beer? Does calling a beer a "craft beer" make it so?

As it stands today, IRI and Nielsen, the two companies that collect supermarket scanner data, have two U.S. craft categories: Craft-Independent and Craft-Affiliated. The first follows the Brewers Association definition of craft beer and excludes those breweries with big-company or foreign connections. The second category covers all others, including craftlike beers such as Molson Coors's Blue Moon.

The Brewers Association (BA) recently updated their definition of a craft brewer as an entity producing less than six million barrels per year; having independence, defined as less than 25 percent ownership by another company that is not a craft brewer; and "traditional," defined as ". . . whose flavors derive from traditional or innovative brewing ingredients and their fermentation," and this specifically excludes flavored malt beverages.

As a former member of the BA board of directors involved in these discussions, I can say the process was long and wrenching, and in the end there was not unanimity. I personally view craft beer as art. This means that the ideas and recipes for the beers must come from the brewers, not from the marketing or accounting departments. It takes a passionate and often highly personal point of view to create something unique, memorable, and meaningful.

CAMRA, who derailed a plan by English brewers to use them for bulk delivery and serving of their beers. These cheap but functional tanks, now in surplus, were perfect for brewpubs, allowing pioneer brewers to hone their craft and build a relationship with their markets. Many of the craft breweries of that era started this way.

The first brewpub, Yakima Brewing and Malting, was opened in 1982 by a retired hop consultant named Bert Grant. While the restaurant business is a difficult one, brewpubs have managed to thrive. Over the years they have been a highly visible manifestation of craft beer, introducing millions to its charms. As of 2014, there were more than 1,400 brewpubs operating in the United States.

What is really significant about craft brewing is that a bunch of guys and gals who started in their basements with improvised breweries and family financing have managed to take over the conceptual helm of beer in this country. For well over a century, the biggest players determined the future of beer, be it pale, cold, fizzy, light, canned, cheap, dry, ice, or clear. The large public companies still wield an enormous amount of power and are by no means fading out of the picture, but the fact that they are now following the lead of the little guys and squirting out me-too, craftish brews shows where the creative energy lies. It's hard to point to another industry that has flip-flopped so dramatically.

An American Sense of Style

I place the beginning of modern craft beer in 1971, at San Francisco's Anchor Brewing Company. New owner Fritz Maytag was slowly working his way through Anchor's daunting list of problems, fixing them one by one. Eventually, the beer was in his sights. He and his crew rebuilt the beer pretty much from scratch: ditching the sugar adjunct and making it all malt, with crystal/caramel for color and flavor; hopping it with a new and unique variety, Northern Brewer; and settling on a yeast strain that gave solid, consistent results.

For the next several decades, the majority of craft beers have followed this pattern: pure American pale malt laced with crystal malt, topped off with a heaping helping of characterful North American hops — just an honest, handmade beer. For drinkers accustomed to the yellow fizzy industrial stuff, these assertive beers were a slap in the face. After an initial shock, people fell in love with the beers, and the rest is history. Old World tradition was the inspiration, but the result was uniquely American, showing respect for tradition even while creatively bending — and sometimes even breaking — it.

Lagers have always been a part of the craft-beer story, especially away from the coasts. But lagers pose a logistical problem: their extended lagering (storage) requires a lot of tank time, so a lager brewery needs perhaps twice the number of tanks as an ale brewery of the same capacity, an expensive requirement that has limited the number of craft lager breweries. In contrast to our freewheeling willingness to deconstruct ales, American craft lagers have stayed true to their original inspirations. Maybe it's an invisible *Reinheitsgebot* force field that resists efforts at deformation, but there are fewer distinctive craft reinventions of lager styles; however, that's beginning to change.

Belgian-style beer started to come into focus in the early 1990s. New Belgium Brewing in Fort Collins, Colorado, and the Celis Brewery in Austin, Texas, were the first American breweries to focus exclusively on Belgian-inspired beers. A second generation, including brewers such as Lost Abbey Brewing's Tomme Arthur and Russian River's Vinnie Cilurzo, is leading the charge, but many others are folding Belgian-inspired beers into their lineups.

Chicago's Goose Island (now a part of AB InBev) pioneered the use of bourbon barrels for aging beer, and barrel-aged beer has become a popular specialty item. Aging has extended into wine barrels, oak foudres, and even such exotic woods as the Paraguayan palo santo used by Dogfish Head.

Wild and sour beers, while still a small part of the market, have taken on a cultlike status as enthusiasts flock to these tangy, funky beers. While inspired by Belgian tradition, they are trying to push things into new directions. Tart, lactic specialties such as gose and lichtenhainer from northern Germany are being resurrected, and there is a minor craze in the Louisville, Kentucky, area for Kentucky Common, a nearly forgotten beer that had been dormant for a century or so.

Interesting ideas are all over the place. Recently, breweries have staked out their creative missions with such terms as "culinary" and "botanic" brewing and are trying to incorporate the full range of the world of foods and seasonings into their beers.

Dogfish Head's Impressive Tanks
These aging tanks, made of palo santo wood, are the largest wooden beer vats made since Prohibition.

CRAFT-BEER TRENDS IN BRIEF

Hops, hops, hops! The madness continues, as IPAs have become the dominant player in the category, spawning spin-offs such as white, black, Belgian, session, and lager versions. Hop growers are feeding the madness with a bounty of exciting new varieties, featuring aromas that range from tropical fruit to berry, melon, tangerine, and others. Brewers are frequently calling out specific varieties used in their products as consumers become aware of them.

Anything farmhouse. Although the history is fuzzy, this appealing idea with its hazy, rustic simplicity makes for compelling and satisfying beers. More extreme examples have some contact with oak or may be produced with the addition of *Brettanomyces* and other wild bugs.

Wild 'n' sour. While for some breweries these are small side projects, many new ones are being set up with the specific intent to focus on these complex styles and to find ways to make them reflect the terroir where they originate. Spontaneously created cultures can be risky, but they are an important tool, and when done right they can be delicious.

Resurrected history. The old brewing books are full of tantalizing descriptions of beers long vanished from the scene. Top-fermenting northern German styles such as gose are especially popular, but inspiration comes from many sources. Look for grodziskie, Kotbusser, lichtenhainer, Seef, Kentucky Common, sahti, Gotlandstricka, chicha, and many others.

Farm to brewery. It isn't always easy with beer, but when possible, breweries are looking at incorporating local ingredients into their beers. Hop production is coming back to the Great Lakes region, offering an opportunity for local

connections. Wet hopping using undried hops, often from the brewery's own garden, are another. Micromaltsters have access to unique heirloom varieties of malts, and they can process them in more flavorful ways than the large operations. On the flip side, having breweries actually located on farms is another trend.

Wood. While the creative possibilities of spirits barrels for beer have been mostly exhausted, people just love the rich, complex flavors they impart and are willing to stand in line for these beers. Many of the wild yeast, farmhouse, and other styles incorporate barrels or foudres into their process. Brewers in South America are using exotic hardwoods such as amburana and balsam wood in tanks.

Session and shandies. Customers and bar owners are both looking for beers that can be enjoyed in quantity, a task that a 7.5 percent IPA fails at miserably. Lighter "session" IPAs have been a pretty good hit, as have fruit- and wheat-based beers and blends incorporating lemonade or other sodas.

Nano. This term refers to tiny breweries, usually 5 barrel (6 hL) brewhouses or smaller. To survive, brewers must sell most of the beer directly to their customers. Many have unusual crowd-sourced or CSB (community-supported brewery) concepts.

Culinary, botanical, foraged, and "molecular" brewing. Dogfish Head Craft Brewery was an early pioneer, but recently there has been a new wave of breweries looking for ways to make artistic statements by utilizing all kinds of ingredients usually more associated with cooking than brewing. The use of wild, foraged ingredients is a small but fascinating development.

A Tempting Future

What does the future hold? Craft brewers in 2015 had 12.2 percent of the U.S. beer market in volume and 21 percent in dollars (that's about a fourfold increase from 3.5 percent in barrels and 5 percent in dollars in 2006). In Seattle, Washington, and in the entire state of Oregon, craft beer is pushing toward 50 percent of the market by dollars, so it's clear that, in some places at least, craft beer can get pretty big. The wine market might be a fair comparison: while there are some large players, no one company has anything close to a dominant share. As consumers move away from the mass-market brands, they seek a wide variety of continuously changing products, which has never been the big breweries' strong suit. The big industrial brewers have yet to demonstrate whether they can make money with a large number of low-volume brands.

In the last 5 years, a number of larger craft brewers have been acquired by international mass-market brewers as well as equity firms, as the founders of successful craft breweries reach retirement age and seek to cash out. That transfer of equity to the big players will continue, as the large brewers have shown themselves largely incapable of creating successful craftlike brands of their own. A big brewer can offer many advantages: technical and marketing assistance, access to raw materials, and especially a ride on the truck — distribution has always been a very challenging aspect of craft brewing.

Craft beer is becoming a worldwide phenomenon, with craft breweries popping up in Europe and everywhere else. Italy has an enthusiastic smattering of highly creative breweries, largely driven by a love of Belgian beers. North American hop aromas are showing up occasionally in beers in England. Even in tradition-bound Germany we're starting to see glimmerings of creativity. Australia and New Zealand have started cautiously, but their uniquely flavorful hops are providing a really exciting focus and voice for their beers. Scandinavia has a thriving scene in which bold American-style IPAs and other favorites coexist alongside reinterpretations of ancient farmhouse traditions. Japan recently relaxed its rule on the minimum size of a brewery, making small breweries possible, and craft beer in Korea is growing rapidly.

This book has now been published in simplified and traditional Chinese, so interest there is rising as well. Craft beer in Latin America is exploding from Mexico to the tip of Patagonia, and despite difficult business conditions, it is finding some success. There is interest in Africa and India as well. We're a small and interconnected world these days, and people are plugged into a global creative culture in which craft beer is a given. Just as beer enthusiasts in the United States, starting in the late 1970s, made their passion a business, beer lovers abroad will find a way to fill their glasses with beautiful, delicious craft beer.

Craft brewing adapts itself to the culture, market, and tastes of wherever it finds itself, but the basics are always the same: people passionate about the flavor of great beer brewing up fresh, character-filled beers of all strengths, shades, and sensibilities. Quality beer is part of a lifestyle that values the experience of living, of making every moment an adventure, every taste worth tasting. Craft beer is here to stay, but we need to reach out and turn people on to the world of choice, authenticity, and flavor it provides so well.

A Note on Craft Styles

While there are some specific styles called out on the following pages, be aware that no style or tradition escapes the reach of adventurous craft brewers, so consider these to be the ones that have developed clear definitions and strong positions in the market. And although the numbers here speak to very specific characteristics in the style paradigms, in reality there are a lot of brewers who disregard guidelines completely. This results in a landscape that can be a little confusing, but in the end it is much richer and filled with eccentric delights befitting a true artistic movement.

 ## SOME NEWER HOP VARIETIES BY LOCATION

Australia and New Zealand. Australian Galaxy is a big, bold hop with loads of tropical fruit and a dank earthiness. New Zealand has a huge range: Motueka with lemon-lime citrus; Nelson Sauvin with passion fruit and white grape, but a touch earthy; Pacifica combines orange citrus with grassy herbal notes; Pacific Gem brings black fruit with a woody edge; Pacific Jade offers complex fruity, peppery aromas; and Wakatu combines equal parts of pine and orange.

Czech Republic. New varieties are all based on the famous Saaz, but Kazbek brings along a lot of citrusy notes, and Bohemie is pleasantly fruity and very clean.

Germany. A trio of unique hops have gotten a lot of attention recently: Hallertau Blanc, with floral and tropical fruit notes; Mandarina Bavaria with clean and citrusy aromas; Hüll Melon, with notes of berry, pear, and melon. Saphir offers a bolder take on noble character, and Polaris shows wintergreen and eucalyptus notes.

France. Alsace has long been a hop-growing region, but exciting new varieties are coming now: Triskel, with fruity, citrus, and floral flavors, and Aramis, which is a little fruitier with spicy, citrusy notes.

Slovenia. Long a hop producer, this region has a very active breeding program and is starting to release some exciting varieties. Aurora has a nice tropical fruit aroma with dank undertones. Celeia is clean and neutral, just pleasant hoppiness with some fruity notes.

United States. Citra bounded onto the scene a few years ago and became immediately popular. At its best it's beautifully citrusy, but it can show toasted onion notes. Glacier is a pleasant and very clean super-Styrian type. Mosaic and Azacca offer citrus, mango/tropical, and a hint of pine. Jarrylo shows fruity banana and pear with hints of citrus and spice. El Dorado brings a lot of tropical fruit with a variety of other fruity notes.

American Blonde or Golden Ale

This is a basic, honest golden beer, usually all malt, but sometimes with wheat or other adjuncts added to increase creaminess and head retention.

ORIGIN: United States in the early 1980s, as brewpubs tried to create beers that would seem approachable for mass-market drinkers

LOCATION: U.S. craft breweries and everywhere else

AROMA: Pleasant bready or light cracker malt notes with hop aroma ranging from delicate to quite assertive

FLAVOR: Bready malt, perhaps with a hint of creamy caramel and some hop varietal flavor and bitterness

BALANCE: Medium body; crisp, mildly bitter finish

SEASONALITY: Year-round

PAIR WITH: Wide range of food; awesome with lighter dishes or anything fried

SUGGESTED BEERS TO TRY: Hill Farmstead Walden, Lawson's Finest Liquids Knockout Blonde, Real Ale Four Squared

GRAVITY: 1.038–1.054 (9.5–13.3°P)
ALCOHOL: 5.5–7.5% by volume
ATTENUATION/BODY: Crisp, dry
COLOR: 3–6 SRM, straw to pale gold
BITTERNESS: 15–28 IBU, medium, although some
    may be more bitter

American Pale Ale

More than any other, this style defines American craft beer. It is built on a base of pale ale malt, usually with the caramelly, raisiny flavors of crystal, counterbalanced by the fresh, pungent flavors of North American hops with their piney, citrus, and floral notes.

A substyle has developed called "session IPA." Technically, this style falls into this broader category but is perceived as a scaled-down and more drinkable version of the flavors found in full-strength IPAs. As a result, it tends to be at the pale and light-bodied end of the pale ale style, and hop aroma tends to be pretty pronounced as well.

ORIGIN: Late 1970s, as American brewers tried to satisfy their thirst for hops

LOCATION: U.S. craft breweries and elsewhere

AROMA: Malty, fruity, and classically with North American hops in the foreground

FLAVOR: Fresh hops plus a nutty maltiness, hints of raisins or caramel, crisp finish

BALANCE: Medium body; crisp, bitter finish

SEASONALITY: Year-round

PAIR WITH: Wide range of food; classic with a burger

SUGGESTED BEERS TO TRY: Deschutes Mirror Pond Pale Ale, Sierra Nevada Pale Ale, Three Floyds Alpha King Pale Ale, Maine Beer Co. MO, Ballast Point Grunion

GRAVITY: 1.045–1.060 (11.2–14.7°P)
ALCOHOL: 4.5–6.2% by volume
ATTENUATION/BODY: Medium
COLOR: 5–10 SRM, dark gold to pale amber
BITTERNESS: 30–50 IBU, medium to high

American IPA

IPA is just a paler, stronger, hoppier style of pale ale. And like pale ale, American versions showcase American hop varieties.

ORIGIN: Around 1985, as American brewers looked for other hop-delivery vehicles

LOCATION: U.S. craft breweries and elsewhere

AROMA: A blast of North American or other characterful hops in the foreground along with some malty, fruity aromas; newer versions tend to be paler and drier on the palate than the old-school versions

FLAVOR: Fresh hops plus a clean, bready maltiness, perhaps a hint of caramel, and a clean, crisp, bitter finish

BALANCE: Medium body; crisp, bitter finish

SEASONALITY: Year-round

PAIR WITH: Wide range of food; classic with a burger

SUGGESTED BEERS TO TRY: Anderson Valley Hop Ottin' IPA, Ballast Point Sculpin IPA, Bell's Two Hearted Ale, Firestone Walker Union Jack IPA, Harpoon IPA, Surly Furious, Victory HopDevil

 IPA VARIANTS

Black IPA/Cascadian dark ale. Oregon's Rogue Brewery generally gets the credit for the first one with their Skull Splitter, but the roots may go back further. The style is not a hoppy stout but starts with an IPA formulation that is colored black by the addition of a malt coloring syrup called Sinamar. The result is a beer that looks like a stout but has very little roasted flavor. Our eyes almost force us to find the dark malt, but if you taste one blind, you'll find very little roastiness. Aside from the color, the stats are the same as any IPA.

White IPA. At the other end of the style is this mashup of a witbier with IPA. The base includes a high proportion of wheat and possibly oats but at a higher strength and with the blast of hops you'd find in an IPA, although these can be a little subtler than regular IPAs. There should be a nice creaminess from the wheat along with a thin haze.

Belgian IPA. This is another mashup that brings hops and fruity/phenolic Belgian yeast together. These are tricky to brew, as there is a very narrow range of balance where both elements can coexist harmoniously. Bitterness and hop aroma tend to be less aggressive than full-on IPAs.

India pale lagers. Just as the name implies, these have hops often leaning toward Continental aroma profiles.

Session IPAs. These beers pose the question: Aren't they just pale ales? While technically true, in the market these are paler and less raisiny than typical pale ales and also may offer more hop aroma as well — essentially scaled down, more sessionable versions of modern American IPAs.

Rye and red IPAs. These typically feature a raisiny crystal malt character, sometimes with the spice and fruit of rye, with a ton of hops on top.

GRAVITY: 1.056–1.070 (13.8–17.1°P)

ALCOHOL: 5.5–7.5% by volume

ATTENUATION/BODY: Crisp, dry

COLOR: 6–14 SRM, gold to medium amber

BITTERNESS: 40–70 IBU, medium to high

Double/Imperial IPA

"Imperial" began as a term applied to beers shipped from Britain to the imperial court of the Russian Empire during the nineteenth century. Imperial came to be used as a designation for the top of a brewer's range, whatever the style. Of late, craft brewers have slapped the term on anything that moves: stout, porter, brown pale, blonde, Pilsner, and more.

Consumers have been enthusiastic about big bottles of strong imperial or double IPAs, and brewers have been happy to oblige them.

ORIGIN: Around 1995. More malt! More hops!

LOCATION: U.S. craft breweries and elsewhere

AROMA: A massive blast of hops along with some degree of maltiness

FLAVOR: Massive and distinctive hops in the nose, often with tongue-searing bitterness supported by a background of creamy maltiness; these big beers should have plenty of complexity and are best when superfresh

BALANCE: Medium to light body; long, bitter finish

SEASONALITY: Year-round but better away from the heat of summer

PAIR WITH: Very rich food, such as aged Gorgonzola or carrot cake

OTHER IMPERIALIZED BEERS

Pilsner
- Dogfish Head
- Odell
- Rogue Morimoto Imperial Pilsner
- Samuel Adams Hallertau Imperial Pilsner

Blonde Ale
- Ska Brewing True Blonde Dubbel

Red Ale
- Oscar Blues G'Night
- Tröess Nugget Nectar
- Lagunitas Lucky 13 Mando Large Red Ale

Brown Ale
- Dogfish Head Palo Santo Marron
- Lagunitas Brown Shugga'
- Tommyknocker Imperial Nut Brown Ale

Porter
- Flying Dog Gonzo Imperial Porter
- Full Sail Top Sail (bourbon barrel–aged) Imperial Porter
- Ska Brewing Nefarious Ten Pin Imperial Porter

SUGGESTED BEERS TO TRY: Dogfish Head 90 Minute IPA, Great Divide Hercules Double IPA, Stone Ruination Double IPA, Three Floyds Dreadnaught IPA

GRAVITY: 1.075–1.100 (18.2–24°P)

ALCOHOL: 7.9–10.5% by volume

ATTENUATION/BODY: Crisp, dry

COLOR: 6–14 SRM, gold to amber

BITTERNESS: 65–100 plus IBU, very high

Amber and Red Ale

In the early days, every large brewer with crafty aspirations was brewing up red ale and naming it after some furry woodland critter, hoping to make a fast buck in the craft-brewing business. Most of them went skulking back into the forest after the boom faded, and honestly, that's probably a good thing, because most of them were pretty insipid. In recent years, however, the style has evolved into a pretty assertive group of beers.

Amber ale is a session beer and needs to be very drinkable. Hops should be present but not too assertive. The emphasis should be on bitterness rather than aroma, although a little hop aroma can be a good thing. Amber ale that smells too hoppy crosses over into pale ale territory. Malt should have the upper hand — complex but not cloying.

Once pretty bland, red ale grows bitterer every year. Its malt character is usually dominated by medium to dark crystal/caramel malt that adds distinct burnt sugar and caramelized raisin aromas. Some versions incorporate rye into the recipe for a little spicy tang. Hopping varies but can be as assertive as IPAs.

ORIGIN: This was one of the first craft styles and was different without being too challenging. The term appeared in America in about 1990 for reddish, approachable beers not linked to specific historical traditions.

LOCATION: U.S. craft breweries

AROMA: Raisiny, burnt sugar caramel malt, with varying amounts or resiny, floral, or citrusy hops

FLAVOR: Plenty of caramel malt for raisin to burnt sugar flavors; hops variable, from delicate to very bold and bitter

BALANCE: Malty to assertively hoppy

SEASONALITY: Year-round

PAIR WITH: Wide range of food; chicken, seafood, burgers, spicy cuisine

SUGGESTED BEERS TO TRY: Alaskan Amber, Bell's Amber, Bear Republic Hop Rod Rye, Sierra Nevada Celebration Ale, Two Brothers Cane and Ebel, North Coast Ruedrich's Red Seal Ale

GRAVITY: 1.045–1.060 (11.2–14.7°P)
ALCOHOL: 4.5–6.2% by volume
ATTENUATION/BODY: Medium
COLOR: 10–17 SRM, pale to dark amber
BITTERNESS: 25–40 IBU, medium

Historical Style

Kentucky Common

This simple amber-colored beer was once widespread in the Ohio River Valley in and around Louisville, Kentucky. Dead for nearly a century, the first experimental batches were brewed back in the 1980s by my original homebrew partner, Ray Spangler, himself a Kentucky native. Grist was mainly six-row lager malt, with about one-third corn grits and a small amount of black malt for color. Hops were a mix of Cluster, possibly with some European noble type for aroma. Many brewers have recently experimented with sour mashing — which can give nice results — but it's highly unlikely that this was ever part of this beer's brewing routine. Gravity was in the 1.045 to 1.055 range (11.2 to 13.6°P), for 4.0 to 5.5 percent alcohol.

American Barley Wine

Like all the rest of the American craft versions of British beers, this style is differentiated by the enthusiastic use of hops, especially those that display all the piney, citrus qualities of American varieties. In England the term is applied to beers that by American standards are shockingly weak, but the American versions take no prisoners in the alcohol department. There is some overlap between stronger double IPAs and barley wines, but as a general rule barley wines are amber to brown.

LOCATION: U.S. craft breweries

AROMA: Richly malty, sometimes with loads of hops; often with leathery, sherrylike notes in aged examples

FLAVOR: Richly malty, sometimes a bit raisiny; may be fiercely bitter

BALANCE: Evenly to extremely hoppy

SEASONALITY: Very nice in the dark days of winter

PAIR WITH: Big food, especially aged cheese and intense desserts

SUGGESTED BEERS TO TRY: BridgePort Brewing Old Knucklehead, Hair of the Dog Fred, Middle Ages Brewing Company Druid Fluid, Rogue XS Old Crustacean, Sierra Nevada Bigfoot Barleywine Style Ale

GRAVITY: 1.080–1.120 (19.3–28.0°P)
ALCOHOL: 8.0–12.0% by volume
ATTENUATION/BODY: Medium to full
COLOR: 10–19 SRM, pale to dark amber
BITTERNESS: 50–100 IBU, high

American Brown Ale

Classic English styles have only a whisper of bitterness to offset their maltiness. American versions are more assertive, ranging from even-handed balance to downright hoppy; are bigger and browner than their English cousins; and typically have a strongly toasty palate and some sweetness.

LOCATION: U.S. craft breweries

AROMA: Toasted and toffee malt, possibly a hint of floral hops

FLAVOR: Plenty of caramel malt; delicate hop finish

BALANCE: Malty to somewhat hoppy, with toastiness as an additional balance element

SEASONALITY: Year-round

PAIR WITH: Wide range of food; chicken, seafood, burgers, spicy cuisine

SUGGESTED BEERS TO TRY: Bell's Best Brown Ale, Brooklyn Brown Ale, Lost Coast Downtown Brown Ale, Surly Bender

GRAVITY: 1.045–1.060 (11.2–14.7°P)
ALCOHOL: 4–6% by volume
ATTENUATION/BODY: Medium to full
COLOR: 18–35 SRM, deep amber to chestnut brown
BITTERNESS: 20–30 IBU, medium

Porter and Stout

Porter was the first beer in the world brewed and exported on an industrial scale. It is well known that George Washington was a fan and that after the Revolution, he regularly purchased bottled porter from Robert Hare's brewery in nearby Philadelphia, which was famous for its fine-quality beer. Eastern Pennsylvania has never completely lost its taste for porter. Yuengling still brews one in Pottsville, Pennsylvania.

For a recap of the particulars of porter and stout, see pages 249–53. American versions tend to be pretty close to these, although they often use American hop varieties and may color outside the lines a bit when it comes to style rules.

American Wheat Ale

This craft-brewed style first achieved popularity in the Pacific Northwest. This American take on wheat beer is fermented with standard ale yeast, without the exotic fermentation character of the German styles. Most contain between 30 and 50 percent wheat. American wheat beers gained popularity with young consumers looking for something truly different, and they brought a lot of people into the craft-beer fold. The style has gained new life as an aromatically hoppy style, pioneered by Three Floyds Gumballhead.

ORIGIN: U.S. brewpubs and craft breweries; originally a "starter" beer, but lately transformed into a hoppy summer refresher

LOCATION: U.S. craft breweries; British versions also popping up

AROMA: Soft fruitiness without the clove or banana of German weizens; ranging from a little to a lot of hop aroma

FLAVOR: Clean, creamy, and refreshing; hoppier than German weizens

BALANCE: Dry, with a little creamy texture from the wheat; sometimes a slight hint of tartness and mild to medium bitterness

SEASONALITY: Year-round but best in summer

PAIR WITH: Salads, lighter food such as chicken or sushi; simple cheeses

SUGGESTED BEERS TO TRY: Boulevard Unfiltered Wheat, Goose Island 312 Urban Wheat, Leinenkugel's Honey Weiss, Three Floyds Gumballhead Wheat Ale, Widmer Brothers Hefeweizen

GRAVITY: 1.040–1.055 (10–13.6°P)
ALCOHOL: 4.0–5.5% by volume
ATTENUATION/BODY: Light to medium
COLOR: 3–6 SRM, straw to gold
BITTERNESS: 15–30 IBU, low to medium

Fruit Beer

"Chick beers" are what some of the beer geeks call these. You know the brews: pink, fluffy little numbers; a bland wheat-beer base dolled up with a drop or two of raspberry essence. These uncomplicated fruit beers have their charms on a hot summer day, and while you still find them — especially at brewpubs — you may also encounter fruit beers that are a little more evolved. A current trend is to combine fruits with sour, lactic beers such as Berliner Weisse and the slighty salted gose. The fruits are moving beyond the Kool-Aid flavors as well, with mango, guava, watermelon, blood orange, and others, sometimes enhanced by subtle spicing.

There are a few breweries managing to get a good fruit buzz going with more-concentrated beers. Wisconsin's New Glarus brewery has put Door County cherries to good use in a big fruit bomb they call Wisconsin Belgian Red. They brew a raspberry offering as well. Not coincidentally, these two beers consistently medal at the Great American Beer Festival. Elsewhere, Bell's Brewing has long made a cherry stout that delivers the goods, and Delaware's Dogfish Head offers beers made from currants, apricots, and blueberries.

ORIGIN: U.S. brewpubs, as fun, summery beers aimed mainly at female customers

LOCATION: U.S. craft breweries

AROMA: Definite notes of whatever fruit is being used but usually not too much else

FLAVOR: Delicate fruitiness, featuring raspberries, apricots, cherries, blueberries, mango, passion fruit, watermelon; clean, tart flavors with some creaminess if brewed with a wheat or witbier base

BALANCE: Crisp and dry to a little sweet, although some amount of acidity is usually needed to give life to the fruit

SEASONALITY: Year-round

PAIR WITH: Salads and lighter food, lighter desserts

SUGGESTED BEERS TO TRY: Harpoon UFO R.A.Z., Leinenkugel's Berry Weiss, Pyramid Apricot Ale, Saranac Pomegranate Wheat; also try this popular summer seasonal at brewpubs

GRAVITY: 1.040–1.055 (10–13.6°P)
ALCOHOL: 4.0–5.5% by volume
ATTENUATION/BODY: Light to medium
COLOR: 3–12 SRM, straw to gold, but often tinted with the color of the fruit
BITTERNESS: 15–25 IBU, low

Shandies and Radlers

These will be discussed as cocktail mixes in chapter 14, but some are brewed and packaged ready to go. Generally, these are from larger breweries that have the ability to pasteurize, keeping the added sweeteners from fermenting in the package. Normally citrus is the star. Lemon is the classic, but grapefruit and lime are popular, and trendy flavors have been tried as well. Alcohol is usually quite low, in the 2.5 to 4.2 percent by volume range. These have become very popular as summer refreshers.

Pumpkin Ale

ORIGIN: U.S. craft breweries; as a harvest-themed fall seasonal, pumpkin beers can be a lot of fun and help to point out the agricultural roots of beer. The Elysian brewpub in Seattle holds a pumpkin beer festival featuring a couple of dozen pumpkin styles on tap, including a pumpkin barley wine and a beer conditioned in a giant pumpkin, which was tapped directly from the mighty vegetable.

LOCATION: U.S. craft breweries

AROMA: A nice spiciness, perhaps a little malt

FLAVOR: Delicate pumpkin sometimes overpowered by traditional pumpkin pie spice (cinnamon, clove, nutmeg, etc.) mix; subtle is better; some caramel malt adds interest

That's a Big Pumpkin Beer
The folks at Seattle's Elysian Brewing thought a pumpkin would make the perfect keg for one of their pumpkin beers.

BALANCE: Usually a little sweet

SEASONALITY: Autumn

PAIR WITH: Thanksgiving roast turkey and gingerbread

SUGGESTED BEERS TO TRY: Buffalo Bill's Pumpkin Ale, New Holland Ichabod Ale, Weyerbacher Brewing Imperial Pumpkin Ale; also check out Seattle's Elysian Brewing Company's Great Pumpkin Beer Festival in October

GRAVITY: 1.047–1.056 (11.7–13.8°P)
ALCOHOL: 4.9–5.5% by volume
ATTENUATION/BODY: Medium
COLOR: 6–12 SRM, gold to amber
BITTERNESS: 10–15 IBU, low

Up and Coming

Never-ending variety continues to be the mission for adventurous craft brewers, wherever they are. Here are some of the trends and ideas that brewers are pursuing these days.

Historical Re-Creations and Fantasies

The past is always present in brewing. Whether time-traveling back just a few decades or to the very beginnings of beer, history is a ready resource of ideas for the creative brewer. So often the necessary details of ancient beers are gone forever; consequently, most re-creations are just informed guesses. Sometimes there is some actual science, as when Anchor's Fritz Maytag collaborated with Sumerologist Solomon Katz to create a limited-edition beer

called Ninkasi, named for the Sumerian goddess of beer.

Other examples include a range of ancient Scottish beers, such as a Pictish heather beer called Fraoch, as well as pine and kelp brews; a coriander-tinged preindustrial "Jacobite" ale from Traquair House, also in Scotland; spruce-tip beer from Alaskan Brewing Co.; Kentucky Common beer now popular again in Louisville, Kentucky; and an Italian version of an ancient Egyptian beer called Nora, made from kamut (an ancient wheat), from Le Baladin.

In addition to the beer inspired by King Midas (see page 13), these resuscitated beers are always interesting, as they lend a kind of insight into the old traditions that you can't get from reading books. And as often as not, they are delicious as well.

Single-Hop Ales

The idea is to take a relatively straightforward recipe, such as an American pale ale, and spike it with just one kind of hop, which lets the varietal character shine through. This is a great way to learn about the unique character of individual hops. Aside from its educational aspect, it ties beer to the land and the seasons, creating a lot of excitement among consumers. A similar sense of excitement with single-hopped beers is percolating among British craft brewers.

Wet-Hopped Ale

Another technique gaining in popularity is "wet hopping." This is the use of fresh, undried hops right off the vine. Many California breweries are harvesting the cones off plants grown on their own property for this purpose. Brewers farther from hop country are shipping the hops via overnight courier, often at great expense. Beers hopped this way have fresh, green aromas and a certain just-picked briskness. California brewers hold a Wet Hop Beer Festival in San Diego every November. Sierra Nevada is using steam distillation to extract fresh hop oils for use in this type of beer year-round.

LOCATION: U.S. craft breweries

AROMA: Very much a matter of specific recipe and especially hop variety; spicy, flowery, piney, resiny, herbal, grapefruit, and other hop aromas

FLAVOR: Varies by base beer but should always have plenty of fresh bitterness

BALANCE: Definitely on the bitter side but should be counterbalanced by some nice malt

SEASONALITY: Harvest time

PAIR WITH: Bold foods such as steak, lamb, blue cheese

SUGGESTED BEERS TO TRY: Drake's Brewing Harvest Aroma Coma, Sierra Nevada Harvest Ale (Northern and Southern Hemisphere versions), Two Brothers Heavy Handed IPA

New Belgian–American Ales

A number of American brewers, inspired by Belgium, are using the ideas and techniques of that brewing culture to create uniquely American beers with some of the Belgian magic. Some have been reverential, re-creating the classics such as the Trappist beers, while others have taken a more free-wheeling approach. Several processes are involved: adding wild microorganisms such as *Brettanomyces*; barrel aging; blending, incorporating sugar, fruit, spices; and more. There is even some partnering with breweries in Belgium, in which batches from both sides of the Atlantic are melded into a single cuvée. The flavors of these Belgian-American beers are as varied and distinctive as Belgium itself.

SUGGESTED BEERS TO TRY: Goose Island Matilda; Russian River Salvation, Perdition, and others; Lost Abbey Cuvee de Tomme and others; seasonal specialties from New Belgium Brewing

Barrel-Aged Beers

The invention of the barrel is variously attributed to Bronze Age Celts, Vikings, or similar hairy, fur-cloaked tribes. By Roman times, barrels were in use across a wide area of northern Europe. Barrels served admirably in a preindustrial world, but the difficulty of cleaning and maintaining them caused them to be phased out by brewers around 1950. Stainless steel suits the squeaky-clean nature of international lager perfectly, but if you love the funky depths of a truly handmade beer, wood can offer that extra dimension.

Wood contains chemicals that dissolve in the beer over time, adding woody, oaky, and other flavors. Temperature swings cause the liquid to pump in and out of the wood, accelerating the process. Over a period of months, one of these substances, lignin, becomes transformed into vanillin, which is why vanilla notes are often found in whiskey and other barrel-aged spirits.

Wood is porous, which means that the barrel contents are exposed to air, creating the potential for oxidized flavors, both good and bad. Porosity offers lots of little nooks and crannies for microorganisms to hide, and this can be used to the brewer's advantage. Lambic and other sour beers depend on barrels to harbor their wild yeast and bacteria.

The bourbon industry uses the expensive charred-oak barrels only once for bourbon, so when emptied, they must move on and out. They are great for aging beer. The first bourbon-aged beer I ever heard of was from a group of suburban Chicago-area brewers who brewed five 10-gallon batches of imperial stout to fill a fresh bourbon barrel. Six months later they reconvened to bottle the beer. Shortly after that time, Goose Island Beer Company started experimenting with the style, one of the first commercial breweries to do so.

Barrel aging is not the best treatment for a Pilsner; strong and dark is the rule. Imperial stout is the classic, and barley wine may also benefit. A superstrong weizenbock, blonde barley wine, or triple bock might do with a dab of whiskey-barrel flavor as well.

LOCATION: U.S. craft breweries

AROMA: Malt and hops appropriate to the base beer, plus rich vanilla, toasted coconut, and perhaps hints of sherry- or port-type oxidized aromas

FLAVOR: The base beer plus rich, round vanilla, coconut, and caramelly flavors and perhaps a touch of woody tannins on the finish

BALANCE: Generally a bit on the sweet side

SEASONALITY: Best in cool weather

PAIR WITH: Huge, rich desserts and Stilton cheese

SUGGESTED BEERS TO TRY: Allagash Curieux, Firestone Walker Rufus, Goose Island Bourbon County Stout, Great Divide Oak Aged Yeti Imperial Stout, New Holland Dragon's Milk

Hyper-Beers

The trend for this type of beer began on the East Coast in about 1994, most famously championed by Boston Beer Company's Jim Koch; but Dogfish Head's Sam Calagione was there early on. These supergravity beers contain as much as 25 percent alcohol, and retail for up to $200 a bottle for beers such as Samuel Adams Utopias. Even at that price, company representatives say they are barely breaking even!

Beer yeast often runs into trouble above 10 percent alcohol, so alcohol-tolerant strains are needed. After an initial fermentation is dosed with sugar little by little, the alcohol content gradually rises. Often wood aging is employed as well. The flavors of these beers have more in common with spirits and liqueurs. Utopias has won numerous blind taste-offs against competitors such as port and Calvados.

LOCATION: U.S. and international craft breweries

AROMA: Immense maltiness, along with barrel character of vanilla and coconut; plenty of fruity esters, alcohol

FLAVOR: Massive taste, sweetish, creamy, dried fruit, spice, alcohol; in darker examples, roast malt character; hops are generally pretty subdued

BALANCE: Usually a little sweet

SEASONALITY: A slow, contemplative tipple by the fire

PAIR WITH: Stilton, walnuts; a dessert in itself

SUGGESTED BEERS TO TRY: Dogfish Head 120 Minute IPA, Dogfish Head World Wide Stout, Hair of the Dog Dave, Samuel Adams Utopias, Baladin Xyauyù

GRAVITY: 1.12 plus (28°P plus)
ALCOHOL: 14–26% by volume
ATTENUATION/BODY: Medium to full
COLOR: 18–55 SRM, deep amber to fully opaque black
BITTERNESS: 50–100 plus IBU, medium to very high

CHAPTER 14

A SIP BEYOND

Reading a book will not make you a beer expert. Beer exists in the sensory realm, and no amount of prose can take the place of coming nose to nose with as many different beers as possible and tasting, evaluating, contemplating, and *experiencing*. You can go solo if you have to, but really, this task is best and most enjoyable when pursued in the company of others. Everyone sees things differently. We bring our own personal histories to the table, and the interchange of insights leads to a richer, fuller understanding of beer, as well as a stronger community. The two are inseparable, as far as I'm concerned.

The Joys of Beer Clubs

I used to cleave to the old Groucho Marx adage of refusing to join any club that would have me as a member. But that was before I found out about beer and homebrewing clubs, which are some of the most welcoming organizations on earth.

Some of you may already enjoy their benefits: easy camaraderie among a willing pool of drinking pals; an exchange of information about beer, brewing, and life in general; organized activities; and an opportunity to achieve something bigger than one could manage alone. For those of you not yet hooked up, I urge you to connect with an existing club or, if need be, start your own.

Charlie Papazian started teaching homebrewing classes back in the late 1970s, and that led to the founding of a local club. With his fearless vision of a brighter, beerier tomorrow in mind, Charlie turned his club into the American Homebrewers Association, which eventually spawned the Association of Brewers, now the Brewers Association. This organization represents America's commercial craft brewers as well as its homebrewers. Big things start small.

Good beer in this country depends on the vital and dynamic culture that supports it. Individuals working as a greater community brought about the exciting beer culture we enjoy today. Those interpersonal connections will sustain and build it in the future.

Organizations exist at every level: local, national, international, and virtual. It may be worthwhile to participate on all of these levels. Right now, most local groups are homebrew-focused, but most craft brewers know that homebrewers are their most ardent and vocal supporters. There is a lot we can do together, and the benefits flow to everyone.

Many homebrewing groups run commercial events in addition to their homebrewing activities. The well-respected beer festivals in Madison, Wisconsin, and Portland, Oregon, are organized in large part by homebrewers. Depending on the size and experience of the club, there is a range of possible events, from beer and food–pairing workshops, style classes, and tasting dinners to festivals large — multiday extravaganzas such as the Spirit of Belgium, put on every few years by BURP, a renowned homebrewing club in the Washington, D.C., area — and small. Homebrew clubs are your key to getting involved with the Beer Judge Certification Program and your single best way to build your tasting skills and vocabulary through experience as a beer judge. A list of clubs can be found at www.homebrewers association.org.

Increasingly, women have become part of the beer scene, a welcome change from the beards 'n' bellies of the early days. Tasting groups such as Girls Pint Out hold meetings and take field trips to beer destinations. Brewer Teri Fahrendorf founded a professional organization called the Pink Boots Society. Membership is open to any woman "who earns at least part of your income from beer." The group organizes meetings across the country and has a scholarship program.

Here are some of the larger beer enthusiast and brewing organizations.

The Brewers Association (www .brewersassociation.org). This craft-brewing trade association, publishing company, and homebrewers organization was formed in 2005 with the merger of the Association of Brewers and the Brewers Association of

America. It represents America's small, independent producers of craft beer. Much of its activities are aimed at promoting and protecting craft breweries, but the BA also produces the Great American Beer Festival, the huge annual beer expo held in Denver, usually around the end of September. In 2015, 3,800 beers from 750 breweries were served to more than 60,000 attendees. It is a professional organization, and membership is open to breweries and others in the beer trade.

The American Homebrewers Association (www.homebrewersassociation .org). This organization is part of the Brewers Association and is America's national homebrew club. It is a membership organization that publishes a bimonthly magazine on beer and brewing (*Zymurgy*); runs the National Homebrew Competition, the largest brewing competition the world has ever known; and organizes the National Homebrewers Conference, a yearly chance for homebrewers from all over to get together to share their knowledge, enthusiasm, and, of course, beer. The AHA also runs a growing forum, a collegial environment where homebrewers help each other with questions about beer, brewing, and beer-travel recommendations.

Support Your Local Brewery (www .craftbeer.com). This program of the Brewers Association is designed to create a ready force of volunteers willing to speak up to their government when their access to good beer is threatened. As legislatures react to recent Supreme Court decisions regarding distribution, there are politics afoot in many states that could seriously impede your access to good beer. In many states, beer enthusiasts have helped repeal or change unreasonable state laws, such as North Carolina's limit on alcohol content in beer, and they have helped defeat legislation that would negatively impact small brewers in Wisconsin, California, and elsewhere. In these cases, beer enthusiasts do make a difference. Membership is free and open to all.

Beer Judge Certification Program (www.bjcp.org). Formed in 1985, the BJCP is responsible for procedures and judge certification for homebrewing competitions. It is a nonprofit association, run entirely by volunteers. Although it is dedicated primarily to homebrewing, there is a great deal of useful material on its site, including study guidelines for the judge certification exam, thoughtful and detailed style guidelines, and judging score sheets. To become a member, a prospective judge pays a one-time fee to take the exam, and then is a life member whose judging level and experience are tracked at no charge by the BJCP. A discussion group can be accessed from the BJCP website. This is increasingly an international organization, as communities develop and material is translated into the local languages.

Cicerone Certification Program (www.cicerone.org). This program was created by industry insider Ray Daniels to be the beer equivalent of a wine sommelier, something that's been needed in the beer world for some time. The Cicerone program serves as a testing and certification authority for beer servers, consultants, and others in the beer trade. Participants take a test and demonstrate industry experience to rise to four different levels of certification. The organization is expanding its programs into Europe, Asia, Australia, and Latin America.

Beer forums (www.beeradvocate.com and www.ratebeer.com). These threaded forums have developed into sizable communities, and BeerAdvocate spun off a magazine as well. Both offer plenty of space to exchange views on the relative merits of favorite (and most despised) beers, although RateBeer is a little more narrowly focused in this direction.

Untappd (www.untappd.com). This social media app serves as a tool for people to connect, as well as rate beers and bars.

Craft foods movement. Beer is part of the broader craft foods movement, so it makes sense to pursue it in this context. In organizations such as Slow Food (www.slowfoodusa .org), you'll find people who are already excited about high-quality, locally produced food and drink. Producers and retailers of artisanal foods are always looking for ways to get their products in front of willing customers, and they know that good beer is a powerful draw. As you probably already know, enjoying beer in the context of great, fresh, authentic food adds a delightful dimension to our favorite beverage.

Brew It Yourself

If you're of a creative bent, and especially if you like to cook, you might enjoy brewing some of your own beer. In its basic form, it is neither complicated nor expensive, and the results can be profoundly rewarding. Homebrewing is the only way to really get your hands on the process behind the beer, which I think gives you insights unavailable to the nonbrewer.

Everything one needs to brew great beer is at your fingertips these days. Malt in a rainbow of colors and flavors awaits your recipe. Hops may be had in dozens of spicy, herbal, citrusy,

Homebrewing Gear
Homebrewing is a relatively inexpensive hobby to get started in, and the rewards are great brews and a much better knowledge of beer.

resiny, and tropical varieties. Yeast, once by far the weakest link in the homebrew chain, is available in dozens of pedigreed strains, freshness dated for your brewing pleasure. Many of the thorny technical issues have been wrestled to the mat. Information flows in beery electronic rivers. Clubs abound.

Getting started doesn't have to be a big deal. A brewing kit at your local homebrew shop will run you between $100 and $300, depending on how luxe you want to get. Those truly dedicated to the hobby can eventually spend a lot more, but it is usually an incremental process, one stainless steel gizmo at a time. For now, the basics will do just fine.

But why go to the trouble of brewing your own? Great beer is all about the process and the choices already made. Going through the actual process tunes your senses to the many flavor, aroma, and texture elements that make up a beer.

And once you start brewing, you become part of the community of homebrewers — a surprisingly passionate, collegial, and mystical society.

When you have a batch of beer under your belt (literally), you will have few answers and a lot more questions. Read, taste, listen, and grow. You will be rewarded with mightily good beer and an amazing feeling of accomplishment.

Breweriana

Beer has a whole material culture associated with it in the form of packaging, marketing, branding, glassware, brewery buildings, and much more. This area of interest is every bit as fascinating for many people as the sensory aspects of beer.

Collecting breweriana has a powerful allure, but it can also be a valuable tool to understand the attitudes, products, and role of beer in any given time and place. Breweriana can add another layer of understanding about beer itself, through the words, images, and methods used to advertise it. Although not a serious collector of the garage-filling type, I have gained several insights by keeping my eyes on breweriana as it flows through transaction paths such as eBay. The JPEGs are free for the taking and frequently reveal tidbits about beer styles not found in books.

People collect everything associated with beer, from bottle caps to delivery trucks. At its simplest, breweriana collecting can be a nice way of remembering your beer journey by saving coasters or bottles from beers you've enjoyed. These inexpensive trinkets, if framed or displayed properly, make evocative and eye-pleasing displays for your home pub. At

the highest levels, collectors become experts on the history of a brewery or a region, shelling out tens of thousands of dollars for items that may complete certain areas of their collections. Collectors are generous about sharing information, and they may make presentations, lead bus tours of defunct breweries or living bars, or write articles or books on their favorite subjects. Most beer-producing regions now have a book describing the local brewing history, and these are well worth getting if you're interested in the beer history of your region.

Glassware is especially fun to collect, because you can actually use it. Prices range from just pennies for modern or vintage glasses to thousands of dollars for rare Georgian twist-stem engraved examples. My own taste runs to handblown nineteenth-century glassware, which can be found without shelling out big bucks just often enough to keep me engaged in the hunt. It's fun to drink beers in period glassware. As you admire the glassware's charm, it's transporting to wonder what stories it could tell.

Beer on the Page

Old beer and brewing books are of obvious value to the student of beer. Period brewing texts can help decipher the confusing stories of historic beers. There are collections of lore, historical reviews, serious archaeology and history, and a wide array of brewery-published books, usually issued to celebrate some milestone. While they are generally scarce, copies of meaningful books do turn up in used book stores, sometimes for very reasonable prices. The most reliable sources are the online bookseller networks such as www.alibris.com and www.abebooks.com that have listings from all over the world.

Fortunately, many of the most rare and valuable beer books exist in reprint versions, now ever more commonly available as free downloads. Large numbers of the charmingly evocative 1889 *Curiosities of Ale and Beer* are easy to find, as it was printed in an inexpensive edition in 1965. Beerbooks.com and beerinnprint.co.uk are two other good sources for hard-to-find beer books.

You may also find cookbooks published by breweries, most typically in the 1940s and '50s, which are designed to showcase their beers

---

Labeled Beer Bottles, c. 1910
Old beer bottles are everywhere, but labeled examples are much harder to find.

with the casseroles and other dishes of the era. I've had a great deal of fun collecting photos of anonymous people drinking beer in earlier times, and these add one more dimension to our understanding of people's relationship to the world's best drink.

Beer Cocktails and Other Beer Drinks

Why beer cocktails? First and foremost, they taste good. In addition, they expand the range of beer's possibilities and can be especially useful in those places that have limited beer variety. They're fun and fresh and bring creativity right into the barroom, customized for the mood, the moment, and the customer. Beer cocktails go back centuries; they are warming, cooling, refreshing, and satisfying and offer tons of fun and endless variety.

Spirits cocktails are hot these days because of their creativity, house-made authenticity, and fascinating combinations of flavors, and beer cocktails can bring all that to the party. They turn bartenders from handle pullers into active participants and even stars, with the kind of theater that really lights up a room.

The very first beers may have been a cocktail mix of sorts. Chemical evidence from the tomb of the legendary King Midas has shown

---

**The days are short,
the weather's cold,
By tavern fires tales are told.
Some ask for dram*
when first come in,
Others with flip
and bounce begin.**

— *New England Almanac, 1704*

*A small measure of spirits

---

barley, grapes, and honey all in the same pot, a mix that anthropologist Patrick McGovern has dubbed "Neolithic grog." It's likely it also contained infusions of herbs and spices. Since the very beginning it's been human nature to want to mix things up and try out all the possibilities in the search for interesting flavors — especially in our drinks.

Beer cocktails may be simple blends of two or more different beers or straightforward mixes with soda or lemonade designed to do little more than quench one's thirst. At the more elaborate end, they may incorporate artisanal spirits, handmade bitters and syrups, and surprising garnishes.

As a cocktail ingredient, beer can bring many things. Its carbonation can liven things up and make the drink more aromatic, adding volume that can reduce the booziness of a drink. Beer's bitterness can offset sweetness and improve balance just as bitters or amaro liqueurs do. Its great range of color can add visual appeal or set a mood. Specialty beers can add fruit, spices, oaky aged flavors, and more.

Radlers, Shandies, and Sparkling Wine Mixes

These are simple drinks: just fresh beer mixed with a nonalcoholic soda or fruit drink. "Shandy" is an English term for any mix of beer and nonalcoholic soda or juice, and in German, *Biermischgetränke* indicates the same idea. Shandy traditionally was lemonade blended with bitter but now may be made with lager,

often with carbonated lemonade or citrus soda. The French know it by the name *panaché*.

Legend has it that *radler* — the German name for "cyclist" — was invented at a Munich tavern in 1922 that ran short on beer when the cycling club stopped by. It certainly answers that need, but the mix, usually about 50/50, probably existed earlier.

There are endless variations of beer and juice or soda: hefeweizen and orange juice is *frühstuck Weisse*; Düsseldorfer Altbier and cola is a "diesel," although similar drinks with different beers are known by that name and others (*krefelder, colaweizen, brummbru, greifswalder, mazout*, and fir tree) elsewhere in Europe; a shandygaff is a nineteenth-century mixture of beer and ginger beer.

These classics are not high culinary art, but they serve their refreshing purpose well. There's no reason not to branch off and try your own. Many of the beers and juices listed in the brunch cocktails on page 336 work splendidly together in other combinations. They are just a few to get your juices flowing.

Berliner Weisse is today served with either a raspberry *Himbeersaft* or the screaming-green woodruff-based Waldmeister syrup, although the latter herb contains the banned substance safrole, so substitutes have been concocted. A century ago, Berliner Weisse was more commonly mixed with liqueur — either caraway-based kümmel or the cherry-pit flavored eau-de-vie kirsch. Either gave this light beer a little more kick.

While not strictly shandies, drinks composed of beer blended with wine or cider are also easy and popular. A snakebite is equal parts of lager and hard cider. The black velvet was created in 1861 during a period of mourning for England's Prince Albert. It is a mix of champagne and stout, with the champagne floated on top of the stout and served in a champagne flute.

Spiked beers called *chelada* and *michelada* are widespread in much of Mexico, although the terminology changes confusingly. Classically, a chelada always contains lager, lime, and salt, sometimes with a little chile; a michelada adds flavorings such as chile sauce, Maggi (an umami-rich vegetable sauce), and Worcestershire sauce, but the terms vary quite a bit. A version with clam juice is also popular, and all have a reputation as a hangover cure. Chile-and-lime-flavored salt, perfect for spicing things up or rimming the glass, is sold in supermercados; a popular brand is Tajín. Cheladas work best with lighter-bodied Mexican lagers, so if you're using craft beers, make sure they're not too heavy or strongly flavored. Witbier can work nicely but is obviously not traditional. Recipes from my partner from Monterrey, Champi Garza, follow, along with his beer recommendations.

Chelada

    Pinch of salt, plus more for rimming glass
    Pinch of Tajín (optional)
1–1½ large Persian limes or 2–3 key limes (*limon agrio*), juiced
  1 12-oz beer (such as Dos Equis Dark Lager or Victoria)
    Ice cubes

Rim a large glass with salt or Tajín chile mix. Juice the limes into the glass. Add the salt and Tajín, if using, and mix well. Add the beer and ice, mix, and enjoy.

Michelada

    Pinch of salt, plus more for rimming glass
    Pinch of Tajín (optional)
1–1½ large Persian limes or 2–3 key limes (*limon agrio*), juiced
  2 short shakes of Maggi sauce
  4 long shakes of Worcestershire sauce
  1 short shake of Tabasco (or more)
  1 12-oz beer (such as Dos Equis Dark Lager or Victoria)
    Ice cubes

Rim a large glass with salt or Tajín chile mix. Juice the limes into the glass. Add the Maggi sauce, Worcestershire sauce, Tabasco, salt, and Tajín, if using, and mix well. Add the beer and ice, mix, and enjoy.

Ojo Rojo (Red Eye), Clamato con Cerveza (Favorite Beer: Indio)

    Pinch of salt, plus more for rimming glass
    Pinch of Tajín (optional)
1–1½ large Persian limes or 2–3 key limes (*limon agrio*), juiced
  7 oz Clamato juice
  2 short shakes of Maggi sauce
  4 long shakes of Worcestershire sauce
  1 short shake of Tabasco (or more)
  1 12-oz beer (such as XX Lager or Victoria)
    Ice cubes
  1 celery stick
  1 skewer of seafood, such as cooked clams, shrimp, or raw oysters (optional)

Rim a large glass with salt or Tajín chile mix. Juice the limes into the glass. Add the Clamato juice, Maggi sauce, Worcestershire sauce, Tabasco, salt, and Tajín, if using, and mix well. Add the beer and ice, and mix. Garnish with a celery stick and a skewer of seafood, if using.

Creative Radlers/ Shandies

Passion fruit juice + blonde weizenbock

Guanabana + Belgian witbier

Mango nectar + saison

Pear juice + Belgian tripel

Tamarindo soda + IPA

Cherry juice + oatmeal stout

Pomegranate juice + red rye ale

Brunch Beer Cocktails

This early meal is a delightful occasion for a lighter, fruitier kind of beer, and there are just about unlimited variations. The flavors of certain beer types and fruits go together wonderfully, and honestly, this is very hard to screw up. If you're doing it at home, I recommend choosing a dozen items off the list on page 336 and letting everyone have at it, including the kids (minus the alcohol, of course). In my experience, all the lighter-colored beers go well with a wide range of fruits, but the darker beers really do seem to work best with red fruits.

Speaking of brunch, a Bloody Mary can be lightened and brightened by the addition of beer. Regular ol' lager works, but with the exception of the fruit beers, most of the ones in the Mix 'n' Match Breakfast Cocktails List (page 336) work nicely in various ways. Note that a splash of passion fruit juice will really bring back the fresh, fruity flavor tomatoes seem to lose when they're processed.

Beer Blends and Other Classic Beer Drinks

The inhabitants of eighteenth-century London were calling for beer blends like "three threads" and "five threads," each thread representing one of the beer types that were mixed together into the final drink. Whether porter really was created to simplify the bartender's job is an open matter, but at any rate the tradition is very old, and a great way to add variety when only a limited number of different beers is available. Now we have so much choice in the United States that these are somewhat rarer than they used to be, but they still can be useful and fun.

Black and Tan. Equal parts Guinness draft stout plus pale ale, with the stout floated on top

Boilermaker (UK only). Equal parts bottled brown ale and draft mild ale

Dirty Ho. Two or three parts Belgian witbier (classically Hoegaarden), plus one part Lindemans Framboise

Foggy Night in the Sierras. Two parts Sierra Nevada Pale Ale plus one part Anchor Old Foghorn Barleywine

Chocolate Truffle. Three parts chocolate or imperial stout plus one part Framboise (raspberry) Lambic

Hot Beer Drinks

Central heating wasn't once what it is now, and people relied on warming drinks made from ale, spirits, and seasonings to take the chill off their bones. The line between liquid and bread wasn't so finely drawn either, and people tended to load up their brews with toast, oatmeal, eggs, cream, fruit, and more. The old line about beer and breakfast would fit right in here.

Ale-brue. A few recipes for this have survived from Renaissance times. A thick drink called "ale-brue" or "ale-berry" was ale boiled with spices, sugar, and sops of bread, often with the addition of oatmeal. One ditty goes: "Ale brue thus make thou shall / With grotes [oats], safroun and good ale." Such porridge-like drinks later came to be known as "caudle" and were popular in the American colonies.

CONSTRUCTING A BEER COCKTAIL

While some beer cocktails are very basic and require no real thinking to prepare, more complex recipes require a little more planning.

Use the right glass. A shaker pint is okay for a radler/shandy, Bloody Mary, or chelada, but spirits-based cocktails with beer demand smaller glasses — usually 10 to 12 ounces (300 to 350 mL). Rocks glasses are general purpose, but taller ones shine with citrus-focused drinks or layered concoctions. Brunch cocktails often shine in champagne flutes.

Be conscious about the alcohol total. A typical cocktail such as a Manhattan or martini hovers around 2.5 to 3 ounces (74 to 89 mL) of proof spirit, but some drinks use as little as a single ounce. In beer cocktails, it probably makes sense to use 1 to 2 ounces (30 to 60 mL) of spirits, to keep things under control.

Balance sweet, sour, and bitter. Cocktails usually balance sweet, sour, and often bitter tastes. Getting this right is a foundation for all the aromatic complexity you might want to add. The right beer can contribute any of these, along with a range of aromas. If you're making a fruity cocktail, remember, fruit needs acidity to make it pop.

Carefully layer aromatics. You want to create an overall effect, which usually means some dominant flavor note. Other harmonious flavors can be blended to add depth. Vanilla notes from oak-aged spirits can draw flavors together and add richness. Peppery notes can sharpen and focus flavors. As you're adding layers, think about a hierarchy: what's most and least important?

Let the beer shine through; don't overwhelm it. Consider the intensity of the beer when deciding how much to add, as you don't want it to get lost. Malt brings caramel, dried fruit, toast, and roasted notes that work with sweet, oak, and spicy flavors. Hops have a range of herbal, pine, and citrus aromatics that blend nicely with fruit and gin/juniper flavors while off-setting sweetness.

Pay attention to texture. This is a big part of what beer brings to a cocktail. While the frothy bubbles and lively prickle of carbonation are almost always welcome, wheat, rye, and oats add a pleasant, creamy mouthfeel to a cocktail.

Don't be afraid to steal. That's a long-standing tradition in the world of art. There are plenty of cocktail recipes out there that can easily be adapted to work with beer as a central element. Depending on the character of the beer, you may think of it as a replacement or augmentation for bitters, amaro liqueurs, fruit juice, soda, or even some of the spirits themselves.

Garnishes set the mood. Not only are they a visual punctuation, a well-chosen garnish can add the final aromatic note in a fun and celebratory way. Creative glass-rimming mixes can include anything from coriander to smoked sea salt to Oaxacan worm and chile salt or crushed Tasmanian pepperberries. Don't forget there are beer-specific ingredients as well. Ground and sieved crystal malt (I prefer crystal wheat, as it has no husk) or even black malt can be used in rimming mixes, as can broken-up hop pellets, which can also be used to impart their aroma into salt. If you can get your hands on them during harvest time, fresh hop cones are beautiful, aromatic, and a poignant reminder of the briefness of the season.

Have fun! Don't forget we're in the happiness business. Take good notes so you can do it all again.

Sack posset. No less a figure than Sir Walter Raleigh had a personal recipe for "sack posset," which actually sounds a lot like eggnog: "Boil a quart of cream with *quantum sufficit* of sugar, mace and nutmeg, take half a pint of sack [sweet sherry] and the same quantity of ale, and boil them together." He suggests letting it all mull together in a covered pewter bowl by the fire for a couple of hours. I would estimate between half and a whole cup of sugar and ⅛ teaspoon each of nutmeg and mace as "sufficit."

Buttered ale. Seventeenth-century England saw a craze for "buttered ale," which comprised unhopped ale (by then just about extinct) mixed with sugar and cinnamon, heated, and topped off with a dollop of butter. Samuel Pepys mentions it in his famous diaries as a morning pick-me-up.

Flip. This famous hot beer drink is also known as "yard of flannel," which is a reference to the long, smooth stream formed by the creamy liquid as it was poured back and forth between two vessels to froth it up. Flip had a good long run in England, the American

MIX 'N' MATCH BREAKFAST COCKTAILS LIST

These ingredients are pretty friendly to each other. Just pick one from each of the first three columns, mix, add a garnish, and serve. Honestly, it's hard to go wrong.

Beer	Fruit	Additions	Garnish/Rim
Hefeweizen	Orange Juice	Prosecco or Cava	Grated Lime
Berliner Weisse	Lemonade	Hard Cider	Lemon/Lime Twist
Dunkelweizen	Peach/Apricot Nectar	Champagne	Citrus Wedge
Witbier	Cherry Juice	Hard Lemonade	Black Pepper
Belgian Blonde	Mango Nectar	Cherry Syrup	Ground Coriander
Belgian Dubbel	Raspberry Juice	Grenadine	Pineapple Slice
Porter	Litchi Juice	Raspberry Syrup	Grapes
Oatmeal Stout	Pear Nectar	Lemon or Lime Juice	Lemongrass
IPA	Black Currant Soda	Black Currant Syrup	Fresh Basil
Peach Lambic	Passion Fruit Nectar	Sparkling Moscato	Rosemary
Raspberry Lambic	Pineapple Juice	Brachetto d'Aqui	Powdered Chiles
Cherry Lambic	White Grape Juice	Tonic Water	Slivered Jalapeños
Belgian Sour Brown	Apple Juice	Ginger Ale	Mint Sprigs

 + + +

colonies, and elsewhere, and it was beloved for several unique qualities, not the least of which was having a red-hot poker thrust into it.

To make flip at home, place 1 quart of strong ale, a couple of ounces of good aged rum, 4 tablespoons of brown or muscovado sugar, a small piece of cinnamon, a couple of cloves, and a piece of lemon zest in a medium saucepan. Heat just to a simmer, but do not boil. After the sugar has dissolved, turn off the heat, and remove the cinnamon and other solid ingredients. Beat 4 eggs in a small bowl. Gradually add some of the hot ale mixture to the eggs, stirring steadily. Then slowly add the egg mixture to the ale in the pan, and beat furiously until foamy.

Caramelizing Flip
A red-hot "loggerhead" is used to caramelize this ale, sugar, and egg drink.

Next comes the most dramatic — and some would say essential — step in the flip-making process: the insertion of a glowing-hot fireplace poker in the warm beverage. This causes the mixture to boil violently and creates a smoky, caramelized flavor much prized by flipophiles. Needless to say, this is an operation that should take place outdoors and with all reasonable safety precautions. It is good for a holiday spectacle. Garnish with whipped cream, if you like, and a little freshly grated nutmeg.

Flip is associated with a unique drinking glass. It is a wide, tapered glass, often decorated with molded or engraved designs, ranging in size from less than 1 pint to a wastebasket-sized behemoth holding 6 quarts or more. These were passed around the party and must have been a test of coordination and strength, and possibly sobriety as well. One that I own, circa 1800 and decorated with stylized palm trees, weighs more than 10 pounds when filled.

Crambambull (beernog). It's just a short hop from flip to eggnog, which, when made with ale, is called crambambull. At a holiday party last year, our host whipped up a batch of homemade eggnog sans alcohol, thinking that celebrants could enjoy it unadulterated, or spike it with bourbon or rum as desired. As the host had also laid in a store of tasty beers, I seized on the opportunity to re-create history by using the ale to spike the nog. Gasps ensued, but after a few nervous sips, the nog got very beery. While the idea of adding beer to eggnog may seem strange to us, strong ale would have been pretty much essential in all such early drinks.

George Washington was kind enough to leave us a formula for eggnog, considerably more appetizing than his famous small beer recipe (see page 27): "1 pint brandy, ½ pint rye whiskey, ½ pint Jamaica rum, ¼ pint sherry, [unspecified number of] eggs, 12 tablespoons sugar, 1½ quarts milk, 1 quart cream." The eggs are separated and the sugar is creamed into the yolks, then the milk and cream are added, and then beaten egg whites. He counsels, "Let set in a cool place for several days, taste frequently." Yeah, I bet he did.

A typical modern eggnog recipe has us separate 4 eggs, beat the yolks with ½ cup of sugar until smooth, then mix in 1½ cups of milk and 1 cup of cream. Season with a little nutmeg or mace and sometimes a dash of vanilla, then beat the egg whites and fold them into the mixture. Many recipes call for the cream to be whipped before adding it, and I think this does improve the texture. I should mention that the prepared eggnog sold in milk cartons is beneath consideration. Make it fresh or don't bother.

The recipe above makes an ideal base for experimenting with beernog. A reasonable approach is to fill a 12-ounce glass one-third full of hearty ale; add ½ ounce of bourbon, rye, or dark rum; and top it off with the prepared nog mixture, leaving room for a dollop of whipped froth on top. This is a concoction that really puts you in the holiday spirit.

But what kind of beer is best? In our little taste test, we had success with Anchor Christmas Ale, and I expect any similar dark, wassail-type holiday ale would fit right in. Barley wine, imperial stout, doppelbock, and Scotch ale all work well, and we found that the sweet mixture made for a palatable drink even when mixed with a strong, hoppy pale ale, although the bitterness was not to everyone's taste.

On Christmas Eve, did you ever think that Santa might be sick of milk and cookies? What he would really like is beernog! That'll get the stockings filled to overflowing.

Note: These eggnog recipes call for raw eggs. While this is traditional and done every day with no harm, some health experts recommend against this. If you are dubious, specially processed eggs made for raw consumption may be available in a health food store in your area.

Ponche. This is a Mexican favorite around the holidays, served hot and traditionally containing beer — or not. *Ponche* simply means "punch," and it's subject to a lot of variation. Place three 12-ounce bottles (or equivalent) of strong brown ale or doppelbock into a 3-quart saucepan, and gently heat. Add 4 ounces or more of piloncillo (unrefined Mexican cane sugar), 6 ounces of apple juice concentrate, 6 ounces of guava purée, a few sticks of cinnamon, a healthy handful of raisins, a whole orange (sliced), and a few whole cloves or allspice. Heat to a simmer, and stir the lump sugar to dissolve. Add 6 to 8 ounces of tejocote, small yellow fruits available frozen, or sometimes fresh, around the holidays. When it's not quite to boiling, remove from the heat, and add 4 ounces of aged rum or brandy — or añejo tequila if you dare. Serve with cinnamon sticks and orange slices in the mugs.

Bishop. Heat 4 cups of ale and 1 tablespoon of brown sugar in a saucepan. Stud 2 large oranges with 4 whole cloves each, and bake at 250°F until very soft, about 25 minutes. Slice each orange into quarters, removing the seeds, and add the oranges to the beer mixture. Remove from the heat, and let stand for 30 minutes. Reheat to a warm serving temperature, but do not boil. Serve hot in a stoneware mug with a piece of the orange.

Buttered beer. Start with 1 quart of strong brown or Scotch ale in a medium saucepan. Add a couple of pats of unsalted butter, ¼ cup of brown sugar, and a pinch each of powdered ginger and powdered licorice (if you can find it — try an Indian grocery store). Heat to just below the boiling point while stirring gently to dissolve the sugar, then serve.

Crab ale. The authentic recipe calls for roasting a wild apple (you can use a few crabapples) until it's hissing hot, then adding it to a soup bowl of ale that has been sweetened with 1 tablespoon of sugar. Top with a slice of toast and a garnish of ground cinnamon and nutmeg.

Crabapple lambswool (wassail). Heat 1 quart of ale with 1 pint of sherry and a healthy dash of freshly grated nutmeg nearly to boiling. Add 1 tablespoon of brown sugar and ½ teaspoon of ground ginger. Pour into a heated punch bowl, and float 6 freshly roasted and cored crabapples, or any small, tart roasted apples, on top.

Cool Beer Classics

Two hundred years ago, a wild profusion of drinks called "beer cups" were the rage. The particulars of many are lost now, but tantalizing names such as "Humpty Dumpty," "clamber-down," "hugmatee," "knock-me-down," and "cuddle-me buff" offer clues to the nature — or at least the effect — of these drinks, and remind one of the slightly racy names of cocktails today. Here are a few related old recipes to consider.

Ale punch. Add 2 ounces of turbinado or muscovado sugar and the zest of 1 lemon to a punch bowl. Squeeze the juice from the lemon into the sugar, straining out the seeds and pulp. Let stand for 30 minutes, then remove the lemon zest. Add 2 quarts of pale or amber ale, ½ pint of sherry, and a handful of ice cubes. Stir to make sure the sugar is dissolved and garnish with lemon wedges or slices.

Black velvet. Originally created during the mourning period for Queen Victoria's husband, Prince Albert, it consists of equal parts chilled champagne and stout layered in a large flute glass.

Brown Betty. This drink is named after a famous bread maker in Oxford, England. Combine 1 cup of cognac, 3 whole cloves, 1 quart of brown or amber beer, and ½ cup of brown sugar; stir gently to dissolve the sugar. Chill for 2 hours before serving.

Capillare. An antique and aromatic refresher, it is generally served in summer. Combine 1 quart of pale ale or IPA, 6 ounces of sweet white wine, 2 ounces of brandy, the juice and zest of half a lemon, a dash of freshly grated nutmeg, and a few sprigs of mint (the original recipe calls for borage). Add the mixture to 1 pint of hot simple syrup (1 cup of sugar dissolved in 1 pint of boiling water) plus 1 ounce of orange-flower water (if you want to be really authentic, the orange-flower water should be poured over the fronds of a maidenhair fern). Add 6 ounces of orange curaçao and serve iced or chilled in a large pitcher.

Beer 'n' Shots

The simplest true beer cocktails are the addition of a shot of something to a shot of beer. The ratios are usually anywhere from 1:4 to 1:8 of spirit to beer. These are pretty basic and are mostly used to get wherever your head is headed quickly. A historical brewhouse pick-me-up is a scotchie, which is a shot of Scotch whiskey dumped into a glass of hot first wort from the brew.

Boilermaker/Depth Charge. Beer plus shot of whiskey, with the shot dropped glass and all into the beer.

Irish Car Bomb. Politically incorrect (at least in the UK) name for stout with half a shot of Irish whiskey and half a shot of Irish cream liqueur mixed together, then the whole shot dropped into the beer, glass and all. The original recipe had Kahlúa as well. Drink up; the cream liqueur will curdle when mixed with beer.

Caribbean Night. Foreign export stout with a shot of coffee liqueur, mixed.

Liverpool Kiss (Black & Black). Stout with a shot of crème de cassis, mixed.

Teacher's Creature. To a pint of Scottish ale, add 1 shot each of scotch and Drambuie, then mix.

Modern Beer Cocktails

Despite the fabulousness that great craft beer brings, cocktails are equally hot right now, probably because they offer endless variety and an opportunity for bartenders to show off their creativity and match the drinks to the vibe. There's no reason beer should stay away from this. It's a useful ingredient for bringing rich, balanced flavors as well as a bit of fizz, and it makes a short drink into a tall one without adding reckless amounts of alcohol.

The usual approach is to mix one or two spirits together, add acidic or sweet elements or both, something like bitters for a touch of extra aroma, and then mix in a beer immediately before garnishing and serving. What kind of beer? Well, that depends on what's being mixed, but it's unlikely that there are any beers that are off-limits. Think about the flavors beer can bring: caramel, dried fruit, and roasted

elements; bitterness, an important element in many old- and new-school cocktails; herbal, floral, and citrus aromas from the hops; and fruity and spicy fermentation characters; plus the zip of carbonation, which helps lighten a drink and releases aroma. And, of course, specialty beers, fruit, spices, funky acidity, coffee, chocolate, oak character, and more are available.

The bitterness in beer that can be a real bother when cooking can actually be helpful here. It balances the sweetness from syrup or liqueurs and vanilla wood notes if brown spirits are used, giving the cocktail a bit of a bitter backbone other elements can play off.

Here are a number of creative beer cocktails from contemporary restaurants, bars, lounges, and beer enthusiasts:

Hopping in the Rye: IPA, grapefruit juice, gin infused with Cascade hops, lemon, and caramelized honey (Library Bar, Los Angeles)

Summer Shandy: Hefeweizen, Hum Botanical Spirit, lemon juice, grapefruit juice, and lemon/lime soda (Terzo Piano, Chicago)

Bitches Brew: Mescal and Bloody Mary mix, topped off with a few ounces of Tecate (The Breslin, New York City)

---

pH: Vodka, lychee syrup, lemon juice, raspberry purée, rose water, and Framboise Lambic (WD-50, New York City)

Perfect Storm: Lager, Gosling's Black Seal Rum, Domaine de Canton, and ginger (The Gage, Chicago)

Green Devil: Duvel Belgian strong golden ale, gin, and absinthe (Stephen Beaumont, Toronto, Canada)

Dutch Devil: Duvel, Bols Genever, Angostura bitters, and a sugar cube, topped with a sprig of crystallized ginger (Jacob Grier, author, *Cocktails on Tap*)

Trippel Dubbel: Saxo Belgian blonde ale, tangerine or orange-kumquat syrup, lemon juice, rye whiskey, and Gran Classico orange-rhubarb liqueur (Rogue 24, Washington, D.C.)

Black & Yellow: Dark ale on top, bottom a mix of kumquat-infused gin, yuzu juice, and St-Germain elderflower liqueur (WD-50, New York City)

Robert Frost: Magic Hat No. 9, apple juice, amaretto, and lemon juice (Spare Room, Los Angeles)

Orange Hop-sicle: 3 oz IPA, 2 oz Cointreau, 2 dashes Peychaud's Bitters, ½ oz simple syrup (Donnelly Group, Vancouver, Canada)

Cascadian Revolution: 3 oz Cascadian Dark Ale, ½ oz Grand Marnier, 1 teaspoon Clear Creek Eau de Vie flavored with Douglas fir, stirred with ice, and strained into a martini glass, topped with drop of hop oil (www.NewSchoolBeer.com)

Vim and Vigor: Flemish Red Ale, Leopold Brothers Apple Whiskey, and GranGala, served with a cinnamon stick and a sprig of thyme (Leopold, Chicago)

Baverniess: 3 oz Guinness, 1 oz bourbon, 1 oz Amaro Averna, 3 dashes Angostura bitters, ½ oz maple syrup, and squeeze of orange juice, rimmed with crushed walnuts (Donnelly Group, Vancouver, Canada)

YOU NAME IT

It's helpful to have a good name, preferably one that's a bit naughty, or some ironic and obscure cultural reference. Mix 'n' match from each column, and you get the idea:

Naughty	Penguin
Wicked	Poolboy
Screaming	Housewife
Runaway	Bishop/Nun
Sloppy	Tipple/Nipple
Klingon	Angel/Devil
Shameless	Debutante
Lucky	Trucker
Wayward	Poodle
Hairy	Elvis

Beggar's Banquet: Beer, bourbon, lemon juice, and maple syrup (The Breslin, New York City)

Chocolate Martini: Reduction of Green Flash Double Stout, dark rum, chocolate bitters, and Spanish orange-and-vanilla-scented Licor 43 (Todd Thrasher, Eat Food Group, Washington, D.C.)

Ursus Rodeo: 1 oz imperial stout, 1 oz Canadian whiskey, ½ oz Drambuie, ¼ oz Grand Marnier, dash orange bitters, served with an orange twist (Acadia, Portland, OR)

A Final Word

Three ingredients — grain, water, and hops — are transformed by yeast. Beer is shockingly simple, yet dazzling in the range of rich sensations it can offer. Its amber depths contain more ideas, sensations, and stories than can fit into a lifetime. It is my sincere hope that this book has given you some notion of this, and I can assure you that there is far more out there that will amply reward your attention. Your trip with me is at an end, but your journey continues.

We are fortunate to live in an age when all things are possible in the world of beer. This did not happen by accident. It took the efforts, imagination, and just plain contrariness of brewers, entrepreneurs, and informed beer lovers to make it happen. Beer, like any other art, is an interactive experience. Great beer depends on a community to sustain it and give it meaning. Without this, it becomes just another industrial commodity. Beer is only as good as the people who seek it out, support it, keep it honest, and, most important of all, enjoy the genuine pleasures of it. Never take it for granted.

This book began with a beer, so perhaps it should conclude with one, too. Uncap something special, and pour it into a treasured glass. Give it the time it needs to settle into perfection. Ahh, beer! Raise the glass, as have countless others before you, and toast someone special. Pause for a sniff, and then drink deep. Grain, water, hops, and yeast — and yet so much more. Use your head, your heart, and your soul, and you can taste the whole world in it.

While some in epic strains delight.
Whilst others pastorals invite
As taste or whim prevail;
Assist me, all ye tuneful nine,
Support me in the great design.
To sing of nappy ale.
Some folks of cider made a rout,
And cider's well enough, no doubt,
When better liquors fail;
But wine, that's richer, better still (deny't who will)
Must yield to nappy ale.
Oh! whether thee I closely hug
Is honest can or nut-brown jug,
Or in the tankard hail;
In barrel or in bottle pent,
I give the generous spirit vent,
Still may I feast on ale.
But chief when to the cheerful glass,
From vessel pure, thy streamlets pass,
Then most thy charms prevail;
Then I'll bet, and take the odds,
That nectar, drink of heathen gods,
Was poor compared to ale.
Give me a bumper, fill it up:
See how it sparkles in the cup;
Oh, how shall I regale!
Can any taste this drink divine,
And then compare rum, brandy, wine,
Or aught with nappy ale?

O blest potation! still by thee,
And thy companion Liberty,
Do health and mirth prevail;
Then let us crown the can, the glass,
And sportive bid the minutes pass
In quaffing nappy ale.
Ev'n while these stanzas I indite,
The bar-bell's grateful sounds invite
Where joy can never fail.
Adieu, my muse! adieu, I haste
To gratify my longing taste
With copious drafts of ale.

— John Gay (1686–1732), "Ballad on Ale"

A
GLOSSARY
OF BEER AND
BREWING TERMS

NOTE: For beer styles, refer to the index to find definitions and detailed information.

A

acetaldehyde. Chemical present in beer with an aroma that is variously described as green apple, latex paint, wet grass, pumpkin guts, and avocado. Usually indicative of incomplete conditioning.

acetic. Aroma descriptor for vinegar aroma from *Acetobacteria*. Common in sour, wood-aged beers.

acrospire. The shoot of the barley grain, which develops during malting.

adjunct. Any fermentable added to barley malt for brewing — especially rice, corn, and roasted unmalted wheat, roast barley, and sugar.

adsorption. Physical process involving the adherence of particles to one another at the microscopic level. Important in fining and other processes.

aftertaste. Lingering flavor after liquid has left the mouth.

albumen. Older term for class of proteins found in malt. Much of it coagulates or breaks down during brewing.

alcohol. A type of simple organic compound containing one or more hydroxyl groups (OH) per molecule. Ethanol is the type found in fermented beverages. Other types also occur in beer and other fermented products, but in much smaller quantities.

aldehydes. Group of important flavor chemicals found in beer and other foodstuffs. Most commonly associated with stale flavors in beer.

ale. Any beer produced with top-fermenting yeast. In the old days, a strong unhopped beer.

alkalinity. A measure of water's buffering capacity, expressed as ppm of calcium carbonate.

alpha acid. Complex of substances that compose the bitter component of hop flavor.

Alt or Altbier. German type of beer made from top-fermenting yeast. Includes Kölsch and used as a proper name for Düsseldorfer Alt.

amino acids. A group of complex organic chemicals that form the building blocks of protein. Important in yeast nutrition.

amylase (alpha and beta). Primary starch-converting enzymes present in barley and malt. They both break the long chains of starch molecules into shorter, fermentable sugars.

ASBC. American Society of Brewing Chemists. Standards-setting organization for beer analysis in North America.

attenuation. The degree to which residual sugars have been fermented out of a finished beer.

autolysis. Self-digestion and disintegration of yeast cells. This can give rise to soapy off-flavors if beer is not racked off dead yeast after primary fermentation.

B

°Balling. European measurement of specific gravity based on the percentage of pure sugar in the wort. Expressed in degrees. This measurement system is still employed in the Czech Republic.

barley. Cereal grains, members of the genus *Hordeum*. When malted, the primary ingredient in beer.

barrel. Standard unit in commercial brewing. A U.S. beer barrel is 31 gallons; a British barrel is 43.2 U.S. gallons.

Baumé. Hydrometer scale used to estimate alcohol content by subtracting postfermentation reading from prefermentation reading.

beer. Broad term that describes any fermented, nondistilled beverage made from barley malt or other cereal grains. Originally denoted products containing hops instead of other herbs.

beta glucans. A group of gummy carbohydrates in malt. Some grains and malts have high levels, causing problems with runoff and fermentation.

body. A quality of beer, largely determined by the presence of colloidal protein complexes and unfermentable sugars (dextrins) in the finished beer.

Brettanomyces. Genus of yeast sometimes used in brewing, capable of producing barnyard (horsey), pineapple, and other aromas.

bung. Wooden plug for barrel or cask.

Burtonize. To treat water so that it approximates the well water of Burton-on-Trent, England, famous for pale ales and IPAs.

buttery, butterscotch. Flavor descriptor for diacetyl in moderate to high concentrations.

C

calcium. Mineral ion important in brewing-water chemistry.

CAMRA. Campaign for Real Ale, Britain's traditional beer preservation movement.

caramel malt. *See* crystal malt.

Cara-Pils. Trade name for a specially processed malt used to add body to pale beers. Similar to crystal but not roasted. Also called dextrin malt.

carbohydrates. The class of chemicals including sugars and their polymers: starch and dextrins.

carbonate. 1. To add carbon dioxide gas to the beer. 2. Alkaline water mineral ion associated with limestone.

carbonation. Fizz due to carbon dioxide (CO_2) dissolved in beer.

cask. British term for a barrel-shaped vessel used to serve beer.

cereal. Broad term for a group of grass plant species cultivated as food grains.

cheesy. Flavor descriptor for isovaleric acid, mostly found in old hops.

chill haze. Cloudy residue of protein that precipitates when beer is chilled.

chocolate (malt). Dark brown roasted malt.

cold break. Rapid precipitation of proteins occurring when wort is rapidly chilled.

colloid. A state of matter involving minute particles suspended in a liquid and increasing its viscosity. Beer is a colloid, as is gelatin. Especially related to body, haze, and stability.

conditioning. The process of maturation of beer, whether in bottles or in kegs. During this phase, complex sugars are slowly fermented, carbon dioxide is dissolved, and yeast settles out.

cone. The part of the hop plant used in brewing; properly called strobiles (catkins), not flowers.

conversion. Occurs in the mash, of starch to sugar.

copper. The brewing kettle, named for its traditional material of construction.

corn sugar. Dextrose, sometimes added as an adjunct.

crystal malt. A specially processed type of malt that is used to add body and caramel color and flavor to amber and dark beers. Comes in several shades of color.

D

decoction. Continental European mashing technique that involves removing a portion of the mash, boiling it, then returning it to the mash to raise its temperature.

dextrin. A family of long-chain sugars not normally fermentable by yeast. Contributes to body in beer.

diacetyl. A powerful flavor chemical with the aroma of butter or butterscotch.

diastase. An enzyme complex present in barley and malt that is responsible for the conversion of starch into sugars.

diastatic activity. An analytical measure expressed in degrees Lintner of the power of malt or other grains to convert starches to sugars in the mash.

diatomaceous earth (DE). Microscopic skeletons of single-cell creatures made of almost pure silica, used in the filtering of beer.

disaccharide. Sugars formed by the combination of two simple sugar units. Maltose is an example.

DMS. Dimethyl sulfide, a powerful flavor chemical with an aroma of cooked corn, sometimes found in beer.

dough-in. The process of mixing crushed malt with water in the beginning of the mash operation.

draft, draught. Beer from a cask or a keg, as opposed to bottled beer. Generally unpasteurized.

dry hopping. A method of adding hops directly to a tank or cask at the end of fermentation, increasing hop aroma without adding bitterness.

dunkel. German word for "dark," as in dark beer. Usually refers to Munich dark style.

E

endosperm. The starchy middle of a cereal grain that serves as the food reserve for the young plant, and the source of fermentable material for brewing.

entire. Old term meaning to combine the first, middle, and last runnings into one batch of beer. This began in the large mechanized porter breweries in London during the 1700s and is standard practice today.

enzymes. Proteins that act as catalysts for reactions crucial to brewing, including starch conversion, proteolysis, and yeast metabolism. Highly dependent upon conditions such as temperature, time, and pH.

ester. Large class of compounds formed from the combination of an organic acid and an alcohol and responsible for most fruity aromas in beer, especially top-fermented ones.

ethanol. The (ethyl) alcohol found in beer; its intoxicating component.

ethyl acetate. A common ester in beer; fruity in small amounts, solventlike at high concentrations.

ethyl alcohol. *See* ethanol.

European Brewing Convention (EBC). Continental standards organization for brewing. Most commonly encountered as a term applied to malt color: degrees EBC (about double degrees Lovibond/SRM).

export. Trade term usually for a higher-gravity or better grade of product.

extract. 1. Alternative word for gravity; 2. Term used to refer to concentrated wort in dry or syrup form.

F

FAN (free amino nitrogen). Type of protein breakdown products in the wort. Amino acids and smaller molecules are included. Indicates yeast nutrition potential.

fermentation. Biochemical process of yeast involving the metabolism of sugars and the release of carbon dioxide and alcohol, along with many important by-products.

fining(s). Clarifying agents that are added postfermentation, which help pull yeast and other particulates out of the beer.

firkin. British cask containing 10.8 U.S. or 9 Imperial gallons (40.9 L).

first runnings. The sugar-rich wort that drains off at the beginning of runoff. Used in former times to make a strong beer; nowadays blended in with the rest of the batch.

fusel alcohol. Higher (more complex) alcohols, found in all fermented beverages.

G

gelatin. Used in brewing as a fining agent.

gelatinization. An irreversible phase change of starch resulting in liquefaction of the starch, making it accessible for enzymatic conversion into sugars.

germination. The sprouting of barley, the most important step of malting.

glucose. Corn sugar or dextrose. A simple sugar sometimes used in brewing.

gravity. *See* original gravity.

grist. Ground grain ready for brewing.

grits. Ground, degermed corn or rice used in brewing.

gruit. Medieval herb mixture used in beer.

gyle. A single batch of beer.

gypsum. Calcium sulfate ($CaSO_4$), a water mineral ion, especially welcome in the production of pale ales.

H

hardness. A term indicating the presence of water mineral levels, especially calcium. Various scales are used.

heterocyclics. Important, ring-shaped aroma molecules responsible for the full range of malty aromas in beer. Produced by the Maillard reaction.

hop. A climbing vine of the *Cannabaceae* family, whose cones give beer its bitterness and characteristic aroma.

hop back. A strainer tank used in commercial brewing to filter hops and trub from boiled wort before it is chilled.

horsey, horse-blanket. Terms used to describe the barnyard aromas contributed by *Brettanomyces* wild yeast.

hot break. The rapid coagulation of proteins and resins, assisted by the hops, during boiling.

humulene. One of the most plentiful of the many chemicals that give hops their characteristic aroma.

husk. The outer covering of barley or other grains. May impart a rough, bitter taste to beer if sparging is carried out incorrectly.

hydrolysis. The enzyme-driven breakdown of proteins and carbohydrates.

hydrometer. Glass instrument used in brewing to measure the specific gravity of beer and wort.

I

IBU (international bitterness unit). The standardized measure of hop bitterness in beer, stated as ppm of dissolved iso-alpha acids present in beer. *See also* discussion of international bitterness units on pages 112–114.

infusion. Mash technique of the simplest type, used to make all kinds of English ales and stouts. Features a single temperature rest, rather than the series of gradually increasing steps common in other mashing styles.

ion. Water minerals in the form of an electrically charged half molecule.

Irish moss. A marine algae used during wort boiling to enhance the hot break. Also called carrageenan.

isinglass. A type of gelatin obtained from the swim bladder of certain types of fish (usually sturgeon), used as a fining agent in ales.

iso-alpha acid. Bitter hop resins chemically changed by the boil, and present in beer. Also processed hop extract, sometimes used to add bitterness after fermentation.

isomerization. The chemical change during wort boiling that causes hop alpha acids to become more bitter and soluble in wort.

K

kettle. Boiling vessel, also known as a "copper."

krausen. The thick foamy head on fermenting beer and also the fermenting beer itself.

krausening. The practice of adding vigorously fermenting young beer to conditioning beer in order to speed maturation.

L

lactic acid. An organic acid that is a by-product of *Lactobacillus*, responsible for the tart flavor of Berliner Weisse and some Belgian ales.

Lactobacillus. Large genus of bacteria. May be either a spoilage organism or purposely added to such products as gose or Berliner Weisse.

lactose. Milk sugar. Unfermentable by yeast, it is used as a sweetener in milk stout.

lager. Beers made with bottom-fermenting yeast and aged at near-freezing temperatures.

lauter tun. A sparging vessel.

lightstruck. An off-flavor in beer that develops from exposure to blue/UV light. Even a short exposure to sunlight can cause this skunky odor to develop. Often occurs to beer in green bottles sold from lighted cooler cases. Brown bottles are excellent protection.

°Lovibond. Beer color measurement (in degrees), now superseded by the newer SRM and EBC methods. Still commonly used in reference to grain color.

lupulin. The resiny substance in hops containing all the resins and aromatic oil.

M

Maillard browning. The browning reaction between carbohydrates and nitrogenous material, also known as nonenzymatic browning. Responsible for most of the color and malt flavor in beer.

malt. Barley or other grain that has been allowed to sprout, then dried or roasted.

malt extract. Concentrated commercial preparations of wort. Available as syrup or powder, in a wide range of colors, hopped or unhopped.

maltose. A simple sugar that is by far the predominant fermentable material in wort.

maltotetraose. Type of sugar molecule consisting of four units of glucose hooked together.

maltotriose. Type of sugar molecule consisting of three units of glucose hooked together.

mash. The cooking procedure central to brewing, during which starch is converted into sugars. Various enzyme reactions occur between 110 and 166°F (43 and 74°C).

mash tun. Vessel in which mashing is carried out.

melanoidin. Group of complex color compounds formed by heating sugars and starches in the presence of proteins. Created in brewing during grain roasting and wort boiling.

milling. Term for grain grinding or crushing.

mouthfeel. Sensory qualities of a beverage such as body and carbonation, supplied by the trigeminal nerves.

N

nitrogen. Element used as a measure of protein level in malt and important as a yeast nutrient. As a gas (N_2) it is used to pressurize "nitro" beers.

O

original gravity (OG). Measure of wort strength expressed as specific gravity; the weight of the wort relative to the weight of water.

oxidation. Chemical reactions that occur between oxygen and various components in beer, resulting in leather, honey, and other cardboard off-flavors.

oxygen. Element important in yeast metabolism, especially during startup, but may cause problems for long-term storage. *See also* oxidation.

P

parti-gyle. Antiquated brewhouse practice in which first runnings become strong ale, second runnings become ordinary beer, and the last and weakest runnings become small beer.

pasteurization. The process of sterilizing by heat. Used in almost all mass-market canned or bottled beer.

peptide. Short fragment of a protein. Also the bond holding amino acids into chains of protein.

pH (potential of hydrogen). Logarithmic scale used to express the level of acidity and alkalinity in a solution; 7 = neutral; 1 = most acid; 14 = most alkaline. Each step on the scale represents a tenfold change from the previous one.

phenol. Chemical family responsible for spicy, smoky, and other aromas in beer.

phenolic. Flavor term referring to phenol flavors and aromas.

°Plato. European and American scale of gravity based on percentage of pure sugar in the wort. A newer, more accurate version of the Balling scale.

polishing. Final filtration prior to bottling in commercial brewing. Renders beer sparkling clear.

polyphenol. Tannins, important in beer in connection with protein coagulation and chill haze.

polysaccharide. Polymers of simple sugars. Includes a range from complex sugars through dextrins up to starches.

ppb. Parts per billion; 1 microgram per liter.

ppm. Parts per million; 1 milligram per liter.

precipitation. A chemical process involving a material coming out of solution.

primary fermentation. Initial rapid stage of yeast activity when maltose and other simple sugars are metabolized; lasts about a week.

priming. The process of adding sugar to beer before bottling or racking to kegs. Restarts fermentation, pressurizes with carbon dioxide gas.

protein. Complex nitrogenous organic molecules important in all living matter. In beer, involved in enzyme activity, yeast nutrition, head retention, and colloidal stability. During mashing, boiling, and cooling, they may be broken apart and precipitated.

proteinase. Enzyme that breaks proteins apart into smaller, more soluble units. Most active at 122°F (50°C).

protein rest. During mashing, a 120 to 125°F (49 to 52°C) temperature rest for 20 minutes or more to eliminate proteins that cause chill haze.

proteolysis. The breaking up or digestion of proteins by enzymes that occurs in the mash around 122°F (50°C).

proteolytic enzymes. Enzymes naturally present in barley and malt that have the power to break up proteins in the mash.

Q

quarter. An English measure of malt equal to 336 pounds (152.4 kg); of barley, 448 pounds (203.2 kg).

R

racking. Transferring the fermenting beer from one vessel to another to avoid tainting by off-flavors that result from autolysis.

rauchbier. A lager beer made in Germany from smoked malts.

Régie. Belgian/French gravity scale still applied to some Belgian beers (e.g., 1.050 OG = 5.0 degrees Régie).

Reinheitsgebot. Bavarian beer purity law, enacted in 1516.

runnings. Wort that is drained from the mash during sparging.

runoff. The draining of wort from the mash during sparging.

S

saccharification. The conversion of starch to sugars in the mash through enzyme activity.

Saccharomyces. Scientific genus name of brewer's yeast. *Saccharomyces cerevesiae* is top-fermenting (ale); *S. pastorianus* is bottom-fermenting (lager) yeast.

salt. 1. Minerals present in water that have various effects on the brewing process. 2. sodium chloride.

secondary fermentation. Slow phase of yeast activity during which complex sugars are metabolized and "green beer" flavors are reabsorbed; may take weeks or months.

session beer. Lighter in gravity and alcohol, it is designed to be consumed without overtaxing the drinker in either flavor or intensity. It is typically less than 4.5 percent alcohol; examples include British bitter, witbier, and American mass-market lager.

set mash. Condition that sometimes develops during sparging that makes runoff difficult.

six-row. A type of barley most often grown in hot climates. High diastatic activity makes it ideal for the mashing of corn or rice adjuncts, which have no starch-converting power of their own.

skunky. Faint rubbery aroma caused by overexposure of beer to light. *See also* lightstruck.

sparge. Process of rinsing mashed grains with hot water to recover available wort sugars.

specific gravity. A measurement of density, expressed relative to the density of water. Used in brewing to follow the course of fermentation.

spelt. A grain intermediate between barley and wheat that has been used in brewing since ancient times.

SRM (Standard Reference Method). Measurement of beer color, expressed as 10 times the optical density (absorbance) of beer, as measured at a blue (430 nanometer) wavelength in a spectrophotometer. Nearly the same as the older Lovibond color series, measured with a set of specially colored glass samples.

starch. Complex carbohydrates, long polymers of sugars, converted into simple sugars during mashing.

starch haze. Cloudiness in beer from suspended starch particles. Usually caused by (1) incorrect mash temperature, resulting in incomplete saccharification; or (2) sparging temperatures over 180°F (82°C), which can dissolve residual starch from the mash.

steep. The process of soaking grain in water to begin malting.

step mash. Mashing technique using controlled temperature steps.

strike. The addition of hot water to the crushed malt to raise the temperature and begin mashing.

T

tannin. Polyphenols, complex organic materials with a characteristic astringent flavor, extracted from hops and the husks of barley.

terpenes. Group of flavor chemicals forming the main component of hop oils.

top fermentation. Ale fermentation. At warmer temperatures yeast stays on top of the beer as it ferments.

torrefaction. Process of rapidly heating grain so it puffs up like popcorn. Commonly applied to barley and wheat. Often used in British pale ales.

trisaccharide. Sugar molecule consisting of three simple sugars linked together.

trub. Coagulated protein and hop resin sludge that precipitates out of wort during boiling and again at chilling.

two-row. The most common type of barley for brewing everywhere in the world; has a lower protein content and a finer flavor than six-row.

U

ullage. Empty space at the top of a wooden barrel.

underlet. The addition of water to a mash in progress from below so the grains float a bit. Encourages quicker and more thorough mixing.

undermodified. A term applied to malt that has not been allowed to germinate to an advanced stage.

W

Weiss. Term applied to German wheat ales of the Bavarian, or süd-deutsch, style.

Weisse. German word meaning "white"; applied to the tart wheat beers of the Berliner style.

weizen. German word for "wheat." Synonymous with Weiss.

whirlpool. Device used to separate hops and trub from wort after boiling. Wort is stirred in a circular motion and trub collects in the center of the whirlpool. Clear wort is drained from the edge.

wind malt. A type of very pale malt dried in the sun or by exposure to the air, without kilning. Once used in the production of witbier.

wort. Unfermented beer, the sugar-laden liquid obtained from the mash.

wort chiller. Heat exchanger used to rapidly cool wort from near boiling to pitching temperature.

X-Y-Z

yeast. Large class of microscopic fungi, several species of which are used in brewing.

zymurgy. The science of fermentation, also used as the name of the magazine of the American Homebrew Association.

ATLAS OF BEER FLAVORS AND ORIGINS

Fruity aromas are most often associated with yeast and the esters they produce as by-products of fermentation. Dried fruit flavors are more commonly associated with caramel malts, most particularly in the middle of the color range.

FRUITY			Malt/Adjuncts	Hops/Seasonings	Fermentation	Aging/Wood	Wild/Contaminated
	Dried	Golden raisins	○				
		Fig	○				
		Black raisin	○				
		Prune	○				
		Cherry			◐		○
	Berry	Strawberry			◐		
		Grape		○	◐		
		Cherry			◐		
		Raspberry		○	◐		
		Black currant, Ribena				●	
	Stonefruit	Green apple (acetaldehyde[1])			◐		
		Apple (ripe; ethyl hexanoate)	○	◐	◐		
		Pear	○		◐		
		Apricot	○		◐		
		Peach	○				
		Melon	○				
	Tropical	Papaya	○				
		Bubble gum			◐		
		Banana (isoamyl acetate)			◐		
		Pineapple (isoamyl acetate)				○	
		Mango (ethyl butyrate)	○				
		Passion fruit	○				
	Citrus	Grapefruit	○				
		Lemon	○				
		Lime	○				
		Orange (sweet)	○				
		Marmalade	○				
		Tangerine/mandarin	○				

[1]Note that this is a common descriptor for acetaldehyde, but the chemical presents itself in many other ways.

Floral aromas are most commonly associated with hops and other seasonings used in beer.

FLORAL			Malt/Adjuncts	Hops/Seasonings	Fermentation	Aging/Wood	Wild/Contaminated
	Perfumy	Rose (geraniol)		◐			
		Orange blossom		◐			
		Tuberose (sweet floral)		◐			
	Pungent	Geranium (geraniol)		◐			
		Marigold		◐			
	Herbal	Lavender		◐			
		Jasmine		◐			
	Fruity	Chamomile		◐			
		Elderflower		◐			

Key: ○ = positive attribute in most or all cases; ◐ = may be positive or negative depending on intensity and context; ● = negative attribute in most or all cases

(chart continues on next page)

Spicy and phenolic aromas have a wide range of sources and may or may not be appropriate, often depending on the style.

		Malt/Adjuncts	Hops/Seasonings	Fermentation	Aging/Wood	Wild/Contaminated
SPICY/PHENOLIC	**Harsh** — Burnt match/sulfite (sulfur dioxide[2])			○		
	Husky	○				
	Tannic	○			◐	
	Smoky	◐				○
	Peppery — White pepper		◐	◐		
	Black pepper		◐	◐		
	Grains of paradise		◐			
	Hot/capsicum/spicy			◐		
	Hot alcohol			◐	◐	
	Anise — Licorice	◐	◐		◐	
	Fennel		◐			
	Aniseed (ethyl hexanoate[3])		◐	◐		
	Star anise		◐			
	Sweet — Clove		◐	○		
	Allspice		◐			
	Cassia		◐			
	Vanilla		◐		◐	
	Ginger		◐			

[2] Not a phenolic flavor, but fits here in terms of flavor affinities.

[3] This chemical also is known for a ripe apple character.

Vegetal and herbal aromas can have a wide range of origins, but many of these terms are most commonly used to describe the aromas of hops.

		Malt/Adjuncts	Hops/Seasonings	Fermentation	Aging/Wood	Wild/Contaminated
VEGETAL/HERBAL	**Resiny** — Rosewood/tropical				○	
	Oak				○	
	Pine		○			
	Sagebrush		○			
	Marijuana		○			
	Dried — Coriander (linalool, others)	○				
	Straw/hay	◐	◐			
	Dried/toasted onion		◐			
	Dried/toasted garlic		◐			
	Tobacco					◐
	Thyme	◐				
	Fresh — Minty		◐			
	Oregano		◐			
	Grassy		◐			
	Celery		◐			
	Cilantro		◐			
	Dill/fresh oak			◐		
	Lemongrass		◐			
	Raw pumpkin/squash (acetaldehyde[4])			●		●
	Nuts — Walnut	◐				
	Coconut				○	
	Cooked — Cabbage					●
	Creamed corn (dimethyl sulfide/DMS)	●				●
	Soy sauce				◐	

[4] Note that this is a common descriptor for acetaldehyde, but the chemical presents itself in many different ways. See page 96.

Key: ○ = positive attribute in most or all cases; ◐ = may be positive or negative depending on intensity and context; ● = negative attribute in most or all cases

The sugary category covers sugary aromas rather than sweetness on the tongue, although for some tasters, they may be hard to tell apart.

SUGARY			Malt/Adjuncts	Hops/Seasonings	Fermentation	Aging/Wood	Wild/Contaminated
	Raw	Sugary	◐				
		Worty	◐				
		Turbinado, etc.	◐				
		Treacle	◐				
		Molasses	◐				
	Cooked	Light caramel	◐				
		Medium caramel	◐				
		Toffee	◐				
		Dark caramel	◐				
		Caramelized fruit	◐				

Malt aromas are almost all derived from Maillard browning and caramelization during kilning. Because these processes are widespread in the culinary arts, the vocabulary tends to reflect familiar cooked foods.

MALTY & MAILLARD			Malt/Adjuncts	Hops/Seasonings	Fermentation	Aging/Wood	Wild/Contaminated
	Grainy	Grainy	◐				
		White bread	◐				
		Corn grits	◐				
	Toasty (dry)	Cracker	◐				
		Biscuit	◐				
		Bread crust	◐				
		Toasted bread	◐				
	Toasty (sweet)	Cookie	◐				
		Cake	◐				
		Overbaked cookie	◐				
	Caramel	Caramel	◐				
		Toffee	◐				
	Roasty	Roast	◐				
		Cappuccino	◐				
		Coffee	◐				
		Chocolate	◐				
		Espresso	◐				
		Ashtray/campfire	◐				

Aged or stale aromas from oxidation that don't fit in elsewhere are listed here. Some oxidized flavors may be found in the Fruity and Earthy/Animal categories.

AGED/STALE			Malt/Adjuncts	Hops/Seasonings	Fermentation	Aging/Wood	Wild/Contaminated
	Papery	Wet newspaper (trans-2-nonenal)					●
		Cardboard (trans-2-nonenal)					●
		Ballpoint pen[5]			●		●
	Meaty	Leathery (isobutyl quinolone)					●
		Soy sauce (umami taste)					●
		Brothy					●
	Vinous	Sherry, port, maderized				◐	
		Vinous (furfural ethyl ether)				◐	
		Solventy oxidized					●

[5] Hard-to-categorize aroma, usually from stale malt extract

Key: ○ = positive attribute in most or all cases; ◐ = may be positive or negative depending on intensity and context; ● = negative attribute in most or all cases

(chart continues on next page)

Minerals can add tastes, aromas, and mouthfeel. There are a few situations where they are appropriate, but often they (especially metals) are negative in their flavor impact.

The acidic category includes acidic aromas rather than acidity on the palate, and these are almost always a result of fermentation and/or bacterial activity.

Chemical aromas are usually unwanted evidence of wild yeast, bacterial activity gone wrong, or contamination by chlorine or bromine sanitizers.

			Malt/Adjuncts	Hops/Seasonings	Fermentation	Aging/Wood	Wild/Contaminated	Water
MINERAL	Metallic	Metallic (generic)			●	●		
		Iron				●		
		Copper				●		
	Mineral[6]	Gypsum/plaster (calcium sulfate)						◐
		Chalky (calcium carbonate)					◐	◐
		Salty (sodium chloride)						◐

[6] All are water minerals.

			Malt/Adjuncts	Hops/Seasonings	Fermentation	Aging/Wood	Wild/Contaminated	Water
ACIDIC	Soft	Lactic/yogurty (lactic acid)	◐			◐		
		Vinous		◐	◯	◐		
		Tangy			◯			
	Pungent	Cidery				◯		
		Citric/sharp				◐		
		Acetic/pickle/vinegar (acetic acid)				◐		

			Malt/Adjuncts	Hops/Seasonings	Fermentation	Aging/Wood	Wild/Contaminated	Water
CHEMICAL	Solvent	Solvent/nail polish (ethyl acetate[7])			●	●		
		Petroleum			●			
		Mineral spirits			●			
	Alcohol	Alcohol/ethanol			●	●		
		Rubbing alcohol (propanol[8])			●	●		
	Plastic	Styrene (fusels[9])			●	●		
		Plastic			●	●		
	Phenol	Band-Aid (chlorophenol[10])				●		
		Medicinal (chlorophenol[10])				●		
		Bakelite				●		
		Electrical fire				●		

[7] Acetaldehyde in large quantities can be solvently.
[8] And other fusels
[9] Some fusels can present as a plastic/phenolic aroma
[10] Also bromophenol

Key: ◯ = positive attribute in most or all cases; ◐ = may be positive or negative depending on intensity and context; ● = negative attribute in most or all cases

Earthy and animal aromas are usually signs of something gone wrong, most often a wild or contaminated fermentation. Musty odors are usually from contamination of malt, hops, cork, or beer in a wet location.

EARTHY/ANIMAL

		Malt/Adjuncts	Hops/Seasonings	Fermentation	Aging/Wood	Wild/Contaminated	Light Exposure
Fatty	Buttery (diacetyl[11])			○			
	Cheesy (isovaleric acid)	○			●		
	Rancid butter, vomit (butyric acid)				●		
	Stale oil			●			
	Soapy			●			
Animal/Fetid	Goaty (caprylic acid[12])				●		
	Horse blanket (4-ethyl phenol)				◐		
	Enteric/outhouse				●		
	Garbage/bad breath (mercaptan)			●	●		
	Rotten eggs (hydrogen sulfide)			●			
	Fresh yeasty			○			
Musky	Honey/beeswax (ethyl phenylacetate)				○		
	Rubbery/latex				●		
	Catty/cat pee/ribes	●					
	Skunky (lightstruck; methyl mercaptan[13])						●
Musty	Earthy (geosmin)				●		
	Corked (trichloroanisole)				●		
	Musty/moldy (2-ethyl fenchol)				●		

[11]Vicinyl diketones, including 2,3-pentanedione
[12]Also caprolic, capric, capranoic acids
[13]Specifically light damage

Key: ○ = positive attribute in most or all cases; ◐ = may be positive or negative depending on intensity and context; ● = negative attribute in most or all cases

FURTHER READING ON BEER STYLES, FLAVORS, HISTORY, AND MORE

Cornell, Martyn. *Beer: The Story of the Pint*. London: Headline Book Publishing, 2003.

———. *Amber, Black and Gold*. Gloucestershire: The History Press, 2010.

Hieronymous, Stan. *Brew Like a Monk*. Boulder: Brewers Publications, 2005.

———. *Brewing with Wheat*. Boulder: Brewers Publications, 2010.

———. *For the Love of Hops*. Boulder: Brewers Publications, 2012.

Hennessey, Jonathan, and Mike Smith, Art from Aaron McConnell. *The Comic Book Story of Beer*. Berkeley: Ten Speed Press, 2015.

Herz, Julia, and Gwen Conley. *Beer Pairing: The Essential Guide from the Pairing Pros*. Minneapolis: Voyageur Press, 2015.

Hornsey, Ian. *A History of Beer and Brewing*. London: The Royal Society of Chemistry, 2004.

Jackson, Michael. *Michael Jackson's Great Beer Guide*. New York: DK Publishing, 2000.

———. *Ultimate Beer*. New York: DK Publishing, 1998.

———. *Michael Jackson's Great Beers of Belgium, 5th Edition*. Boulder: Brewers Publications, 2008.

McQuaid, John. *Tasty: The Art and Science of What We Eat*. New York: Scribner, 2015.

Mosher, Randy. *Radical Brewing*. Boulder: Brewers Publications, 2004.

Ogle, Maureen. *Ambitious Brew*. Orlando: Harcourt, 2006.

Oliver, Garrett. *The Brewmaster's Table*. New York: HarperCollins, 2003.

———. *The Oxford Companion to Beer*. Oxford: Oxford University Press, 2009.

Pattinson, Ron. *The Home Brewer's Guide to Vintage Beer: Rediscovered Recipes for Classic Brews Dating from 1800 to 1965*. Beverly, MA: Quarry Books, 2014.

Perrier-Robert, Annie, and Charles Fontaine. *Beer by Belgium, Belgium by Beer*. Esch/Alzette, Luxembourg: Schortgen, 1996.

Saunders, Lucy. *The Best of American Beer and Food: Pairing & Cooking with Craft Beer*. Boulder: Brewers Publications, 2007.

Shepherd, Gordon M. *Neurogastronomy: How the Brain Creates Flavor and Why it Matters*. New York: Columbia University Press, 2011.

Steele, Mitch. *IPA: Brewing Techniques, Recipes and the Evolution of India Pale Ale*. Boulder: Brewers Publications, 2012.

ORGANIZATIONS AND WEBSITES

The American Homebrewers Association
www.homebrewersassociation.org

BeerAdvocate
www.beeradvocate.com

Beer Judge Certification Program (BJCP)
www.bjcp.org

The Brewers Association
www.brewersassociation.org

Cicerone Certification Program
www.cicerone.org

Randy Mosher
http://randymosher.com

RateBeer
www.ratebeer.com

Slow Food USA
www.slowfoodusa.org

Untappd (app)
www.untappd.com

White Labs
www.whitelabs.com

Wyeast Lab
https://wyeastlab.com

PHOTOGRAPHY CREDITS

INDEX

Page numbers in *italic* indicate photographs or illustrations; page numbers in **bold** indicate charts or graphs.

Belgian, 289
Czech/Bohemian, 259
German, 260
glass, tapered, 169, 171, *171*,
174, *174*
invention of, 23, 212
malt for, 74, 77, 89, 219
market domination and, 31
Pilsnerization, 26, 271
Pilsner Urquell, 23, *23*, 259
Plato, degrees, 104, **104**
Plzen, Czechoslovakia, 23, 69
pokal (glassware), 175, *175*
polyphenols, 55, 87
ponche (beer drink), 338
porter, *218*, 232, 233, 249–250,
318–19
Baltic, 250–51
black malt for, 218–19, *219*
German, 267
IPA and, 235
rise of, 18–19, *19*
postfiltration process, 85
"potentiation," 53
pours, 148–49, *148*, *149*
bar pour, 117
draft beer, 160–61
foam and, 117, *117*, 160, 172
tasting and, 60
Weissbier, 175
Practical Brewings (Amsinck), 235
presentation of beer, 141–179. *See
also* glassware; pours
checklist for, 142
draft beer, 147–161
judging and, 134
packaged, 144–47
quantity and, 143
serving temperature, 134, 142–
43, **143**
Prohibition, 28–29, *29*, 31, 33, 35,
106, 231. *See also* Repeal (of
Prohibition law)
protein structure of beer, 116
pumpkin ale, 5, 320–21
pumpkin beers, 320, *320*
punch, ale, 339
pycnometer, 105

Q

qualities of beer, 103–19

R

radlers, 320, 331–33, *333*
Raleigh, Sir Walter, 336
rancid butter aroma, 92
RateBeer, 58
rathskellers, 260
rauchbier, *218*, 268–69, *269*
real (cask) ale, 4, 161–68, *167*. *See
also* Campaign for Real Ale
(CAMRA)
carbonation and, 94, 119
casks for, 95
events and, 138
hand pumps for, 165, *165*
pour, 149, *149*
rescue of, 237–38, *237*
serving temperature, 143
shelf life, 164, 166
"real attenuation," 108
reception-style tasting, 136
recipe, art of the, 76–77
"red" beers, 265
refractometer, 105
refrigeration, 21, 220–21
Reinheitsgebot, 23, 80–81, 255, 256,
258, 275, 309
Repeal (of Prohibition law), 34, 35
retronasal taste, 61, *61*, 130
Richardson, John, 21, 105
roastiness, 52, 57, 113, 183, 188,
206, 250
roggenbier, 278
runoff process, 78–79

S

Saaz hops, 64, 77, 79, 83, 89, 259
Saccaromyces spp., 88, 301
sack posset (drink), 336
saison ("season") beers, *205*,
296–99
sake, 8, 47, 55, 262
salt, in water, 69
sanitation, 8, 98, 102, 168–69
"satz" mashing, 266

Saunders, Lucy, 205
schenkbier, 27, 222, 230
Schlitz, 31, 257
Schneider, Georg, 275
Schwartz, Anton, 257–58
score sheets, 57
Scotland, 15, 221, 225, 227, 242,
321
Scottish ales, 243–45
Scotch ale/wee heavy, 245
Scottish export, 245
Scottish heavy, 244–45
Scottish light ale, 244
seasonings, 14, *14*, 24, *24*, 290
seasons. *See* saison ("season") beers
Sedelmayr, Gabriel II, 256, 264
sensory enhancement practices, 51
sensory evaluation. *See also*
mouthfeel; olfaction
cognitive factors, 58–59
multisensory perception, 52–53
senses and, 39–40
taste, sense of, 40–42
tastes, basic, 42–47
visual/multimodal perception,
56–58
sensory vocabulary
acetaldehyde, 96
autolysed, 101
barnyard, brett, 92
buttery, 90
cheesy, 81
chlorophenol, 102
clove, allspice, 91
dimethyl sulfide (DMS), 87
esters, other, 94
estery/banana, 93
estery/solvent, 91
ethanol/ethyl alcohol, 94–95
goaty, 92
higher alcohols/fusels, 95
honey, 99
hop aroma, 84
hop bitterness, 83
hydrogen sulfide, 93
leathery, oxidized, 99
mercaptan, 96
metallic, 70
musty/mold, 101–2
oxidation, 88

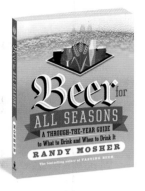

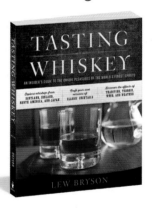